Methodos Series

Methodological Prospects in the Social Sciences

Volume 12

Editors
Daniel Courgeau, Institut National d'Études Démographiques
Robert Franck, Université Catholique de Louvain

Editorial Advisory Board
Peter Abell, London School of Economics
Patrick Doreian, University of Pittsburgh
Sander Greenland, UCLA School of Public Health
Ray Pawson, Leeds University
Cees van der Eijk, University of Amsterdam
Bernard Walliser, Ecole Nationale des Ponts et Chaussées, Paris
Björn Wittrock, Uppsala University
Guillaume Wunsch, Université Catholique de Louvain

This Book Series is devoted to examining and solving the major methodological problems social sciences are facing. Take for example the gap between empirical and theoretical research, the explanatory power of models, the relevance of multilevel analysis, the weakness of cumulative knowledge, the role of ordinary knowledge in the research process, or the place which should be reserved to "time, change and history" when explaining social facts. These problems are well known and yet they are seldom treated in depth in scientific literature because of their general nature.

So that these problems may be examined and solutions found, the series prompts and fosters the settingup of international multidisciplinary research teams, and it is work by these teams that appears in the Book Series. The series can also host books produced by a single author which follow the same objectives. Proposals for manuscripts and plans for collective books will be carefully examined.

The epistemological scope of these methodological problems is obvious and resorting to Philosophy of Science becomes a necessity. The main objective of the Series remains however the methodological solutions that can be applied to the problems in hand. Therefore the books of the Series are closely connected to the research practices.

More information about this series at http://www.springer.com/series/6279

Emmanuel Lazega • Tom A.B. Snijders
Editors

Multilevel Network Analysis for the Social Sciences

Theory, Methods and Applications

Editors
Emmanuel Lazega
Institut d'Etudes Politiques de Paris, SPC
CSO-CNRS, Paris, France

Tom A.B. Snijders
Department of Sociology
University of Groningen
Groningen, The Netherlands

Nuffield College
University of Oxford
Oxford, UK

Methodos Series
ISBN 978-3-319-24518-8   ISBN 978-3-319-24520-1   (eBook)
DOI 10.1007/978-3-319-24520-1

Library of Congress Control Number: 2015957593

Springer Cham Heidelberg New York Dordrecht London
© Springer International Publishing Switzerland 2016
This work is subject to copyright. All rights are reserved by the Publisher, whether the whole or part of the material is concerned, specifically the rights of translation, reprinting, reuse of illustrations, recitation, broadcasting, reproduction on microfilms or in any other physical way, and transmission or information storage and retrieval, electronic adaptation, computer software, or by similar or dissimilar methodology now known or hereafter developed.
The use of general descriptive names, registered names, trademarks, service marks, etc. in this publication does not imply, even in the absence of a specific statement, that such names are exempt from the relevant protective laws and regulations and therefore free for general use.
The publisher, the authors and the editors are safe to assume that the advice and information in this book are believed to be true and accurate at the date of publication. Neither the publisher nor the authors or the editors give a warranty, express or implied, with respect to the material contained herein or for any errors or omissions that may have been made.

Printed on acid-free paper

Springer International Publishing AG Switzerland is part of Springer Science+Business Media (www.springer.com)

Acknowledgments

The authors and editors of this volume thank Daniel Courgeau and Robert Franck, editors of the *Methodos* series, for their encouragement, advice, and patience. We are grateful to Julien Brailly, Guillaume Favre, Anuška Ferligoj, and Malka Older for advice in the preparation of this volume. The book benefitted from intellectual developments for which Mark Tranmer's Leverhulme group was very important. Finally, we thank the European Sciences Foundation, ECRP Program, as well as the Program 'Dynamique des réseaux multiniveaux' (DYREM) of Sorbonne Paris-Cité, for financial support for the meetings that led to this publication. Many thanks to Bernadette Deelen-Mans, Stéphanie Dubois, Edith Martine, and Céline Ottenwelter for providing administrative support for these meetings.

Contents

1 Introduction 1
Emmanuel Lazega and Tom A.B. Snijders

Part I Theory

2 The Multiple Flavours of Multilevel Issues for Networks 15
Tom A.B. Snijders

3 Synchronization Costs in the Organizational Society:
Intermediary Relational Infrastructures in the Dynamics
of Multilevel Networks 47
Emmanuel Lazega

Part II Methods

4 Modeling Individual Outcomes Using a *Multilevel Social
Influence* (MSI) Model: Individual Versus Team Effects
of Trust on Job Satisfaction in an Organisational Context 81
Filip Agneessens and Johan Koskinen

5 Multilevel Models for Multilevel Network Dependencies 107
Mark Tranmer and Emmanuel Lazega

6 Multilevel Network Analysis Using ERGM and Its Extension 125
Peng Wang, Garry Robins, and Petr Matous

7 Correspondence Analysis of Multirelational Multilevel Networks.... 145
Mengxiao Zhu, Valentina Kuskova, Stanley Wasserman,
and Noshir Contractor

8 Role Sets and Division of Work at Two Levels of Collective
Agency: The Case of Blockmodeling a Multilevel
(Inter-individual and Inter-organizational) Network 173
Aleš Žiberna and Emmanuel Lazega

Part III Applications

9 Comparing Fields of Sciences: Multilevel Networks of Research Collaborations in Italian Academia 213
Elisa Bellotti, Luigi Guadalupi, and Guido Conaldi

10 Market as a Multilevel System 245
Julien Brailly, Guillaume Favre, Josiane Chatellet, and Emmanuel Lazega

11 Knowledge Networks in High-Tech Clusters: A Multilevel Perspective on Interpersonal and Inter-organizational Collaboration 273
Julia Brennecke and Olaf N. Rank

12 Inter-organizational Network Influence on Long-Term and Short-Term Inter-individual Relationships: The Case of a Trade Fair for TV Programs Distribution in Sub-Saharan Africa 295
Guillaume Favre, Julien Brailly, Josiane Chatellet, and Emmanuel Lazega

13 Multilevel Bilateralism and Multilateralism: States' Bilateral and Multilateral Fisheries Treaties and Their Secretariats 315
James Hollway and Johan Koskinen

14 Knowledge Sharing in Organizations: A Multilevel Network Analysis 333
Paola Zappa and Alessandro Lomi

15 General Conclusion 355
Emmanuel Lazega and Tom A.B. Snijders

Author Index 363

Subject Index 371

Chapter 1
Introduction

Emmanuel Lazega and Tom A.B. Snijders

Theoretical developments and the emergence of new epistemological insights are based on interactions between old problems and new methodologies (Courgeau 2003). At least two methodologies have helped social scientists of the past two generations in overcoming the traditional divide between individualistic and holistic approaches in the social sciences: multilevel analysis and social network analysis. The purpose of this book is to provide an exploration of the diverse ways in which these two methodologies can be brought together in statistical approaches to multilevel network analysis, specifically their combination in the development of three areas: theory, techniques, and empirical applications in the social sciences. The combination of approaches opens up new avenues of research and improves the necessary management of so-called 'ecological fallacies' (Robinson 1950; Courgeau 1999, 2002, 2004, 2007) in complex systems of inequalities: for example, when looking at problems as different as school performance of pupils or career development in labor markets.

With respect to theory, this book describes the development of multilevel network reasoning by showing how it can explain behavior by insisting on two different ways of contextualizing it. The first method consists of identifying levels of influence on behavior and identifying in sophisticated ways different aggregations of actors and behaviors as well as complex interactions between levels and therefore between context and behavior. The levels in multilevel analysis refer to the different units of

E. Lazega (✉)
Institut d'Etudes Politiques de Paris, SPC, CSO-CNRS, 19 rue Amélie, 75007 Paris, France
e-mail: emmanuel.lazega@sciencespo.fr

T.A.B. Snijders
Department of Sociology, University of Groningen, Grote Rozenstraat 31, 9712 TG Groningen, The Netherlands

Nuffield College, University of Oxford, Oxford, UK
e-mail: tom.snijders@nuffield.ox.ac.uk

analysis. Each level of analysis corresponds to a population, so multilevel studies will refer to several populations (Bryk and Raudenbush 1992; Goldstein 1995; Bressoux et al. 1997; Snijders and Bosker 2012). For example, Kenny and LaVoie (1985) developed a Social Relations Model for dyadic dependent variables in which groups, individuals, and dyads are the relevant units of analysis. They propose a model in which level 1 is the individual, level 2 the dyad, and level 3 the group. Similarly, for the p_2 models which were proposed for binary dyadic dependent variables, "the multilevel p_2 model can be regarded as a three-level random effects model where Level 1 is formed by the tie observations, cross-nested in the actors (Level 2), who are nested in the networks (Level 3)" (Zijlstra et al. 2006, p. 3). In the same spirit, but with a dynamic perspective, Snijders and Baerveldt (2003) developed a multilevel model for friendship networks between pupils in several classes within the same school in order to understand the respective influence of each level on deviant behavior. In these network data structures the traditional approach of multilevel analysis based on hierarchical nesting cannot be followed exactly, because the levels of dyads and actors are not nested; but non-nested structures are also accommodated in multilevel analysis more generally (Courgeau 2003; Snijders and Bosker 2012).

A second, more recent method of contextualization, consists of identifying different systems of collective agency as distinct levels of analysis, differentiating for example among levels of collective action with different goals; specific resource interdependencies between members; and specific social processes that help members manage dilemmas of collective action at each level. Individuals today are members of an organizational society (Coleman 1990; Perrow 1991) because they act in organized, if not highly regulated and bureaucratized, social and economic contexts (companies, associations, families, etc.) that influence their behavior and that they in turn can try to shape. Individuals interact with each other, but are also embedded in (or construct) groups and organizations that interact with each other. Such superposed levels of agency can be examined separately as well as jointly, since they are linked by the affiliation of members of one level to collective actors at the higher level. Affiliations can be considered as indicators of deeper processes characterizing the "duality" of individuals and groups (Breiger 1974; Brass et al. 2004; Rousseau 1985), and thus the co-constitution of these levels as the expression of their vertical interdependencies and complexity. Their superposition is not static (Courgeau and Baccaïni 1997; Lazega 2012): through actors' efforts to endogenize context at each level, they influence each other's evolution. This raises issues of synchronization in these complex dynamics, and brings up the question of how the hidden social costs of this synchronization are shared, spread, or dumped (Lazega, this volume).

Another purpose of this book is to offer new case studies and datasets that explore new avenues of theorizing and modeling, as well as new applications of this methodology. As also shown in Rozenblat and Melançon (2013), an increasing number of datasets is being made available to test the value of theoretical ideas and the efficiency of methods. Although heterogeneous with respect to units of analysis and methods, models of multilevel network analysis presented in this volume tend to take into account a variety of structural dependencies, both within and between levels. The conclusion extends theoretical, methodological and empirical results of this new epistemology by speculating on the insights provided for our knowledge of societies that have become "organizational" societies, i.e. rationalized, managerialized, and marketized.

This book thus identifies a plurality of levels, assumes that actors operate across more than one of them, and provides a bouquet of models for multilevel network datasets to account for vertical and horizontal interdependencies in social life. It shows how concepts applied to analyze single-level networks can be extended to a multilevel perspective, and in turn be extended by it. In this way, it opens and explores new avenues of research for the emerging stream of multilevel network analyses. The volume ends with a general conclusion outlining the importance, limits and perspectives of these current methodologies.

The following outline summarizes the content of the book in terms of theory, methods and applications by suggesting the way in which each chapter contributes to the exploration of structure in multilevel network analysis, from descriptive and inductive techniques to stochastic models (from network autocorrelation models to p_2 models to ERGMs), accounting for both horizontal and vertical interdependencies.

Theory

Part I of the book provides the theoretical foundation for this combined approach. In Chap. 2, Tom Snijders describes the complementarity between these approaches from a methodological perspective. By providing a sketch of multilevel models, statistical models for social network analysis, multilevel network models, and models for multilevel networks, this chapter offers a background to the methods of analysis used in this book. Multilevel analysis, in which individuals' actions, beliefs and performances within groups are analyzed taking into account their nested collective memberships (Snijders and Bosker 2012; Multilevel Network Modeling Group 2012) does not take into account the dyadic interdependencies between individuals based on their relationships or links between groups. It is not plausible that such groups lack an internal structure, nor that they lack links among each other. Network analyses help in introducing more realistic approximations of the internal structure of these groups and of their interdependencies into the modeling of human and social action. This chapter summarizes the 'multilevel' perspective in network analysis. The basis for this is the presence in networks of units of various different, interconnected kinds: individuals, ties, subgroup structures, groups, and perhaps more. These kinds of units represent populations, which can be modeled as having random variability. The fundamental idea of multilevel analysis, to explain dependent variables by models containing multiple sources of random variation and including explanatory variables defined as aggregates over higher-order units, is fruitfully applied here to network models. This approach opens room for the simultaneous study of the contributions of several levels of social phenomena through the 'multilevel analysis of networks'. The second method of contextualization mentioned above is expressed by the 'analysis of multilevel networks', which considers several interconnected system of agency. Following Wasserman and Iacobucci (1991), for cross-sectional data this can be expressed by the multilevel exponential random graph modeling (ERGM) approach of Wang et al. (2013). Each 'level' here is a set of actors, or agents, and the levels are interdependent with respect to the conditions for action and/or outcomes. A hierarchical nesting relation between the levels, which is the traditional basis of statistical multilevel analysis, is not required for the data structure of multilevel networks.

Multilevel network analysis means analyzing separately, then jointly, several levels of collective agency. In Chap. 3, Emmanuel Lazega argues that finding structure in society is a complex task if one is to take the meso-level of society seriously. His chapter explores the sociological meaning of introducing dynamics into the study of different and superposed systems of interdependencies and collective agency. In particular, he looks at the issue of "synchronization costs" between the temporalities that characterize the different levels. These specific social costs are related to carrying out collective action in the organizational society, i.e., a society in which multilevel structures, defined as superposed levels of collective agency, make cross-level social processes increasingly visible. These processes are modeled using network analysis. Synchronization costs are associated with building and maintaining specific social forms, in particular, social status and social niches, as intermediary relational infrastructure that helps individuals and groups manage their complex multilevel interdependencies and the dilemmas of their multilevel collective action. This helps them create new corporate entities that they can try to use as "tools with a life of their own" (Selznick 1949). It is suggested that the energy for creating and managing this relational infrastructure comes from catching-up dynamics between levels, where collective actors operate in different temporalities while under pressure to coordinate and stabilize this synchronization. Catching-up dynamics are associated with organized mobility of actors and relational turnover (OMRT) in their respective networks, a perspective combining White's (1970), Snijders' (1996), and Snijders et al. (2013) approaches. In this context, specific dimensions of social inequalities also become visible since actors who manage these social forms are in a position to benefit from their investments in synchronization costs as they become productive –in particular in terms of reshaping their meso-level opportunity structure – whereas others are likely to see their own investments in synchronization be lost, providing no return.

Methods

This new domain of interest brings together very different innovative methods, new theorizing, and applications to a wide diversity of problems. Part II of the book presents a series of different statistical frameworks and methods articulating social network analysis and multilevel analysis.

In Chap. 4 Filip Agneessens and Johan Koskinen use multilevel network analysis to look at the impact of network position and team structure on individual outcomes. They model individual outcomes using what they call a *Multilevel Social Influence (MSI)* model. This model explains individual differences in behavior and attitudes by considering the (individual level) *network position*, while simultaneously looking at the influence of the (group level) *network structure*. Such an approach requires a multilevel method, where both levels are explicitly modeled. However, while the network nature of the data offers the possibility of simultaneous investigation of the impact of the network level and the individual level position, the complex network interdependence within a single network make classical multilevel modeling unsuitable. The complex interdependence of social networks makes the models more complicated, as there is a need to control for both levels as well as for social contagion and autocorrelation. Their application considers an organizational setting focusing on the importance of trust relations for employee job satisfaction. They simultaneously consider how individual differences in being trusted by colleagues (within a team) impact a person's satisfaction, while at the same time also examining how the structure of the group (density and centralization) might impact the job satisfaction of all members of the group. The multilevel network nature of the data offers the possibility of simultaneous investigation of graph-level, positional and dyadic explanations. This introduces non-standard dependencies as the networks among level 1 units imply both contextual effects different from standard multilevel effects (such as team-level means) as well as direct network dependencies, the latter called level 1½.

In Chap. 5 Mark Tranmer and Emmanuel Lazega consider models for multilevel network dependencies, where one or more attributes of the level 1 network nodes varies across the levels of the multilevel network in which they are embedded. They apply Tranmer's multilevel model called Multiple Membership Multiple Classification (MMMC) model and explains how it can be used to estimate the relative share of variation in the different components of a multilevel network. They outline the ways in which this modeling approach differs from other models that are currently used for network dependencies. They also explain how the MMMC model can be used with statistical software. The approach is illustrated with an analysis of Lazega et al. (2008)'s multilevel network data on French cancer researchers, focusing on variations in research impact scores for the workers as the motivating and illustrative example. This approach can also be applied in the context of more traditional groups such as schools (Tranmer et al. 2014).

In Chap. 6, Peng Wang, Garry Robins and Petr Matous provide a summary presentation of Multilevel Network Analysis using ERGMs and their extensions. Through the integration of vertical dependencies, exponential random graph models (ERGMs) represent network structure as endogenous based on the assumption that network ties are conditionally dependent, that is, that the existence of a network tie depends on the existence of other network ties conditioning the rest of the network (Frank and Strauss 1986; Lusher et al. 2013; Snijders et al. 2006; Robins et al. 2007). In multilevel network contexts, ERGMs offer a statistical framework that captures complicated multilevel structure through some simple structural signatures or network configurations based on these tie dependence assumptions. But for multilevel network models, network ties are interdependent not only within levels but also across levels. The interpretation of ERGM parameters makes hypothesis testing about multilevel network structure possible.

Wang et al. (2013) pioneered ERGM specifications for multilevel networks, and demonstrated the features of multilevel ERGMs with simulation studies and modeling examples. Combining multilevel network structure and nodal attributes, Wang et al. (2015) proposed Social Selection Models (SSMs) where the existence of multilevel network ties are conditionally dependent on not only the existence of other network ties but also on nodal attributes. They demonstrated that nodal attributes may affect network structures both within and across levels. After reviewing the multilevel network data structure, multilevel ERGM and SSM specifications as proposed in Wang et al. (2013, 2015), the authors apply these models to a dataset collected among 265 farmers and their communication network in a rural community in Ethiopia. The resulting model provides an informative description of this farming community. There are similarities as well as clear distinctions between the entrepreneurial farmers and the rest. Without considering the meso- and cross-level effects, we might argue that the two types of farmers have similar network behavior, i.e., both are active within their religion and region; both have flat degree distribution, and both tend to form network closures. The meso- and cross-level effects, however, show that the network is segmented by the farmer types, where popular meso-level nodes tend not to communicate within levels, but popular within-level nodes tend to communicate across levels through the meso-level network. The example highlights the features of these models and their theoretical importance, i.e. within-level network structures are interdependent with network structures of other levels; and within level nodal attributes can affect multilevel network structures.

In Chap. 7, Mengxiao Zhu, Valentina Kuskova, Stanley Wasserman, and Noshir Contractor propose a correspondence analysis of multilevel networks. The past decade has seen considerable progress in the development of $p*$ (also known as exponential random graph) models. Ideally, social science theory should guide the identification of parameters that map on to specific hypotheses. However, in the preponderance of cases, extant theories are not sufficiently nuanced to narrow down the selection of specific parameters. Hence there is a need for some exploratory techniques to help guide the specification of theoretically sound hypotheses. They take the example of individuals being members of work teams. Modern technologies enable individuals to self-assemble and participate in more than one team. Teams often share one or more members with other teams and hence, are not independent of each other. In addition, the assemblage of these teams is embedded in prior communication and collaboration networks. The case becomes more complicated when considering relations at both the individual level and at a combination of individual and team levels.

In order to address these issues, they propose the use of correspondence analysis, incorporating multiple relations and attributes at both individual and team levels. The descriptive analysis preempts concerns about independence assumptions. Correspondence analysis can be used as an exploratory tool to examine the features of the dataset and the relationships among variables of interest, and the results can be presented visually using a graph that shows those relationships as well as observed raw data. They present the theory for this approach, and illustrate with an example focusing on combat teams from a fantasy-based online game. The results offer important multilevel insights and show how this approach serves as a stepping stone for more focused analysis using techniques such as multilevel p*/ERGMs.

In Chap. 8, Aleš Žiberna and Emmanuel Lazega present an application of Žiberna's (2014) method of blockmodeling multilevel network data and an application of this method. The chapter presents a blockmodeling analysis of multilevel (inter-individual and inter-organizational) networks. Several approaches are presented, and used to blockmodel such networks. Each blockmodel represents a system of roles (White et al. 1976) and therefore a form of division of work that is likely to change over time in fields of organized collective action. Using a case study, they show that while the systems of roles are quite similar at both levels (structures divided into core and periphery with bridging cores interpreted in terms of division of work between actors' and organizations' specialties, location, status, etc.), the roles are performed at different levels by units with different characteristics. The added value of this true multilevel analysis is to show how groups at different levels are connected. In the empirical case analyzed in the chapter, the division of work at the level of individuals and the division of work at the level of laboratories can complement and strengthen each other in the case of some segments of the population, while this reinforcement does not occur for other segments. For the same roles, the mix of specialties at one level is different from the mix of specialties at the other level, notably because the two levels do not manage the same resources. Thus, this analysis tracks the meeting of top down and bottom up pressures towards structural alignment between levels.

Applications

Although the differentiation between the 'methods' and 'applications' sections is not clear-cut, the following chapters contain examples of applications of the different methods described in the previous part. Several social areas are covered in these rich and original analyses: multilevel networks are analyzed in scientific fields and in various industries, markets and organizations. While several authors use traditional multilevel models applied to social networks, others use the neo-structural framework with separate levels of agency expressed by analysis of multilevel networks, depending on the kind of data that are available to them.

In Chap. 9, Bellotti et al. use a multilevel approach to compare scientific fields. They model the multilevel structure of scientific work, looking at social networks of collaborations between scientists, and how these networks are embedded in disciplinary and organizational levels. The dependent variable is the success of individual scholars in Italian academia. They adopt the structural approach of

Lazega et al. (2008) and analyze the local system of public funding to academic disciplines in Italy using bipartite networks. They observe the variability of structural effects across disciplinary areas that they expect to be organized in different but comparable ways. They find an overarching importance of academic rank and of brokerage roles in obtaining research funding, together with some other interesting results, like the less impactful but still significant importance of working with an established group of long-term colleagues, and differences between sub-disciplines. The importance of adopting a multilevel perspective is indicated by the relevance of the meso-categories, which combine individual network data with organizational properties. Despite the lack of impact of macro categories (university and sub-disciplinary affiliations), results show the necessity of controlling for these various nested levels, which the analysis of individual characteristics would not be able to account for. They show that in order to be successfully funded what counts more than being a big fish (a scientist with a lot of connections) working in a big pond (a large university) is being in a brokerage position interacting over the years with different research groups.

In Chap. 10, Julien Brailly, Guillaume Favre, Josiane Chatellet and Emmanuel Lazega revisit the notion of embeddedness by looking at networks of contracts as inter-organizational networks modelled jointly with social, interpersonal networks. Economic sociology has established the interdependencies between economic and social structures using the notion of the embeddedness of the economic in the social. Since Granovetter's (1985) and White's (1981, 1988) work about the interactions between economics and social relations, economic sociologists have shown that it is important to know the social structure of a specific milieu to understand its economic structure. For example, globalized markets require long distance partnerships between companies, "global pipelines" as Bathelt and Schuldt (2008) call them. But what kind of relationships do these partnerships represent? Behind each partnership between firms there are always inter-individual ties (Gulati 1995), with their own particular history. The authors use a multilevel framework to jointly analyze the economic networks between firms and the informal networks between their members in order to reframe the embeddedness hypothesis. Based on a network study of a trade fair for television programs in Eastern Europe they show that while each level has its own specific processes they are also partly nested. Beyond this result, they observe that these levels of agency emerge in different contexts and that they are diachronically related. They show that in order to understand performance in a market one needs to look at this dual positioning of individuals and organizations.

In order to explore the complex interactions between these embedded spheres, they provide a multilevel (individual and organizational) reading of an economic market by modeling its underlying social 'meta-system'. To illustrate, they reconstruct a multilevel network in the given market. They consider two levels of action: the first approximated by an advice network between individual actors; the second measured by the contract network between the organizations to which the individuals belong. The issue is to model the global structure generated by these two levels of agency that are in part nested. To investigate this meta-system, the formalization used is that of Wang et al. (2013) developed for multilevel ERGMs.

The multilevel ERGM represents the feedback between the inter-individual social relations and the inter-organizational economic relations (structural vertical dependence hypothesis between the levels). A traditional ERGM at each level shows differences in structuration and temporality between the levels. To manage these different temporalities, organizations develop specific mechanisms of learning and knowledge transmission (represented here by affiliation links). At the same time, recent contracts and current inter-organizational negotiations constitute a specific context for the inter-individual relations (inter-organizational links). The authors show that the cross-level effects and especially the multilevel tetradic substructure (Lazega et al. 2013; Brailly and Lazega 2012) are helpful in investigating the articulation of this meta-system.

In Chap. 11, Julia Brennecke and Olaf Rank examine the relationship between organizations' embeddedness in networks of research and development (R&D) collaborations, and their managers' and researchers' interpersonal knowledge networks in the context of high-tech clusters. Complex cross-level processes are assumed to characterize the networking activities of individuals at the micro-level and their organizations at the macro-level, leading to systematic interdependencies between knowledge networks at the two levels. They apply exponential random graph models (ERGMs) for multilevel networks to data collected in two German high-tech clusters and find that micro- and macro-level knowledge networks are highly interdependent. Specifically, organizations' tendency to maintain formal R&D collaborations interacts positively with their managers' popularity as providers of knowledge but negatively with their activity of seeking knowledge from colleagues. Moreover, managers and researchers exchange knowledge at the micro level if their organizations formally collaborate and vice versa. Their findings contribute to research on the determinants of formal and informal knowledge sharing in the context of institutionalized high-tech clusters.

In Chap. 12, Guillaume Favre, Julien Brailly, Josiane Chatellet and Emmanuel Lazega look at the same process of multilevel embeddedness as that in the chapter by Brailly et al. While a social exchange may involve two persons in the two firms, a transaction involves the two companies as entities at a different level. They therefore propose to use a multilevel framework to look at these networks at different levels of agency. In particular, they study the influence of inter-organizational relationships on the formation of inter-individual relationships in a context of a trade fair. Through a multilevel analysis of a trade fair for TV programs distribution in sub-Saharan Africa they study the influence of a deal network between companies on informal information exchanges among their members. While the inter-individual relationships which exist prior to the event are strongly influenced by the organizational structure, the relationships which are created during the event do not follow that logic. A process of synchronization is observed between levels, but not in the direct context of the trade fair. They argue that trade fairs could be conceived as temporary intermediary organizations in which individuals can break free from the influence of the organization to which they are affiliated and create ties without taking into account the organizational structure. Exponential random graph models are used at each level to measure and model this mutual influence between levels.

In Chap. 13 James Hollway and Johan Koskinen provide an application to international relations. They look at why and when some states establish multilateral treaties instead of bilateral treaties. This is a consequential question for vital issues such as international fisheries management. While multilateral treaties tend to represent attempts at establishing collective fisheries management and conservation policies, bilateral treaties tend to be more geared towards gaining access to coastal fisheries resources. The nature of the ties differs, which is in line with the concept of multilevel networks, and the authors argue that there are essential dependencies between the several networks. The first, meso-level network consists of a cross-level affiliation network of state ratifications to multilateral fisheries treaties. The second, micro-level network consists of states' dyadic bilateral treaty commitments with each other. Finally, these treaties succeed each other and deal with partially overlapping issues and regions, and such treaty references express additional higher-level dependencies and give a third one-mode, macro-level network. To adequately interrogate the resulting complex, interdependent multilevel system, they argue that it is necessary to address the multiple active levels simultaneously. For this, they draw on the conceptual tool of multilevel networks (Lazega et al., 2008; see also Breiger 1974). They apply recent advances in analyzing multilevel networks using exponential random graph models (Wang et al. 2013; see also Chap. 6 by Wang et al. in this volume). They find that a relatively parsimonious model that takes the multilevel dependencies into account explains the overall structure better than one that ignores these dependencies, combining parameters estimated for each network independently. Furthermore, the structural dependencies best describing 'big fish' (high bilateral or multilateral degree states) differ from those for the 'small fish' in both 'big ponds' (multilateral treaties) and 'small ponds' (bilateral treaties). While there is a geography effect, small fish sharing a bilateral treaty has little effect on whether they also share multilateral treaties. This shows that the interaction between bilateralism and multilateralism can be fruitfully analyzed using the multilevel network paradigm. Finally, they seek to explain what drives state choice of multilateral and bilateral treaties by incorporating and modeling the relational dynamics around several nodal attributes.

In Chap. 14, Paola Zappa and Alessandro Lomi provide an application of multilevel network analysis to the process of knowledge sharing in organizations. Their research question is about the effect of mandated hierarchical relations between organizational subunits on the presence of informal network ties connecting organizational members across those subunits. They argue that the failure of prior studies to address this multilevel question leaves uncertainty about the actual role that social networks play in organizations, and, more specifically, that informal network ties connecting organizational members across the formal boundaries of organizational subunits may not be independent from the relationship of hierarchical coordination linking the subunits. They focus on boundary-crossing ties because extant research has demonstrated their direct association with a wide variety of desirable organizational outcomes. They adopt the multilevel exponential random graph models of Wang et al. (2013) to examine how formal relations among organizational subunits affect the presence of interpersonal communication and exchange of advice among members of the top management team in a multiunit organization. They show that informal interpersonal ties are sustained and shaped by the hierarchical relations linking subunits in which organizational participants are located. In particular, ties across subunits are more likely to be observed between managers working in units that are themselves connected by mandated hierarchical relations. They also show that the dependence of interpersonal relations on formal hierarchical relations is partly moderated by the tendency of interpersonal interaction to weaken or reverse the direction of hierarchical relations. Finally, they suggest that the effect of formal structure is contingent on the specific relationship that under consideration.

Acknowledgements We are grateful to Sorbonne Paris-Cite (Dyrem Programme, 2013–2016) and to the European Science Foundation for supporting the preparation of this volume.

References

Bathelt, H., & Schuldt, N. (2008). Temporary face-to-face contact and the ecologies of global and virtual buzz. *SPACES Online, 6*, 1–23.
Brailly, J., & Lazega, E. (2012). Diversité des approches de la modélisation multiniveaux en analyses de réseaux sociaux et organisationnels. *Mathématiques et Sciences Sociales, 198*, 5–32.
Brass, D. J., Galaskiewicz, J., Greve, H. R., & Tsui, W. (2004). Taking stock of networks and organizations: A multilevel perspective. *Academy of Management Journal, 47*, 795–819.
Breiger, R. L. (1974). The duality of persons and groups. *Social Forces, 53*, 181–190.
Bressoux, P., Coustère, P., & Leroy-Audouin, C. (1997). Les modèles multiniveau dans l'analyse écologique: le cas de la recherche en éducation. *Revue Française de Sociologie, 38*, 67–96.
Bryk, A. S., & Raudenbush, S. W. (1992). *Hierarchical linear models*. Newbury Park: Sage.
Coleman, J. S. (1990). *Foundations of social theory*. Cambridge: Harvard University Press.
Courgeau, D. (1999). De l'intérêt des analyses multi-niveaux pour l'explication en démographie. *Population, 54*, 93–116.
Courgeau, D. (2002). Evolutions ou révolutions dans la pensée démographique ? *Mathématiques et Sciences Humaines, 160*, 49–76.
Courgeau, D. (Ed.). (2003). *Methodology and epistemology of multilevel analysis* (Collection Methodos). Dordrecht: Kluwer Academic Publishers.
Courgeau, D. (2004). *Du groupe à l'Individu: Synthèse multiniveau*. Paris: Éditions de l'INED.
Courgeau, D. (2007). *Multilevel synthesis: From the group to the individual*. Dordrecht: Springer.
Courgeau, D., & Baccaïni, B. (1997). L'Analyse multiniveaux en sciences sociales. *Population, 4*, 831–864.
Frank, O., & Strauss, D. (1986). Markov graphs. *Journal of the American Statistical Association, 81*, 832–842.
Goldstein, H. (1995). *Multilevel statistical models*. London: Edward Arnold.
Granovetter, M. S. (1985). Economic action and social structure: The problem of embeddedness. *American Sociological Review, 91*, 481–510.
Gulati, R. (1995). Does familiarity breed trust? The implications of repeated ties for contractual choices in alliances. *Academy of Management Journal, 38*(1), 85–112.
Kenny, D. A., & La Voie, L. (1985). Separating individual and group effects. *Journal of Personality and Social Psychology, 48*, 339–348.
Lazega, E. (2012). Sociologie néo-structurale. In R. Keucheyan & G. Bronner (Eds.), *Introduction à la théorie sociale contemporaine*. Paris: Presses Universitaires de France.

Lazega, E., Jourda, M.-T., Mounier, L., & Stofer, R. (2008). Catching up with big fish in the big pond? Multi-level network analysis through linked design. *Social Networks, 30*, 157–176.

Lazega, E., Jourda, M.-T., & Mounier, L. (2013). Network lift from dual alters: Extended opportunity structures from a multilevel and structural perspective. *European Sociological Review, 29*, 1226–1238.

Lusher, D., Koskinen, J., & Robins, G. (Eds.). (2013). *Exponential random graph models for social networks: Theory, methods, and applications* (Structural analysis in the social sciences series). New York: Cambridge University Press.

Multilevel Network Modeling Group. (2012). What are multilevel networks. University of Manchester. Available at: http://mnmg.co.uk/Multilevel%20Networks.pdf

Perrow, C. (1991). A society of organizations. *Theory and Society, 20*, 725–762.

Robins, G. L., Snijders, T. A. B., Wang, P., Handcock, M., & Pattison, P. E. (2007). Recent developments in exponential random graph (p*) models for social networks. *Social Networks, 29*, 192–215.

Robinson, W. S. (1950). Ecological correlations and the behaviour of individuals. *American Sociological Review, 15*, 351–357.

Rousseau, D. M. (1985). Issues of level in organizational research: Multi-level and cross-level perspectives. *Research in Organizational Behavior, 7*(1), 1–37.

Rozenblat, C., & Melançon, G. (Eds.). (2013). *Methods for multilevel analysis and visualisation of geographical networks* (D. Courgeau, & R. Franck, Methodos series, Vol. 11). Dordrecht: Springer.

Selznick, P. (1949). *Leadership in administration*. Evanston: Row, Peterson & Co.

Snijders, T. A. B. (1996). Stochastic actor-oriented models for network change. *Journal of Mathematical Sociology, 21*, 149–172.

Snijders, T. A. B., & Baerveldt, C. (2003). A multilevel network study of the effects of delinquent behavior on friendship evolution. *Journal of Mathematical Sociology, 27*, 123–151.

Snijders, T. A. B., & Bosker, R. J. (2012). *Multilevel analysis: An introduction to basic and advanced multilevel modeling* (2nd ed.). London: Sage.

Snijders, T. A. B., Pattison, P. E., Robins, G. L., & Handcock, M. (2006). New specifications for exponential random graph models. *Sociological Methodology, 36*, 99–153.

Snijders, T. A. B., Lomi, A., & Torló, V. (2013). A model for the multiplex dynamics of two-mode and one-mode networks, with an application to employment preference, friendship, and advice. *Social Networks, 35*, 265–276.

Tranmer, M., Steel, D., & Browne, W. J. (2014). Multiple-membership multiple-classification models for social network and group dependences. *Journal of the Royal Statistical Society: Series A (Statistics in Society), 177*(Part 2), 439–455.

Wang, P., Robins, G. L., Pattison, P. E., & Lazega, E. (2013). Exponential random graph models for multilevel networks. *Social Networks, 35*, 96–115.

Wang, P., Robins, G., Pattison, P., & Lazega, E. (2015). Social selection models for multilevel networks, *Social Networks*, http://dx.doi.org/10.1016/j.socnet.2014.12.003

Wasserman, S., & Iacobucci, D. (1991). Statistical modeling of one-mode and two-mode networks: Simultaneous analysis of graphs and bipartite graphs. *British Journal of Mathematical and Statistical Psychology, 44*, 13–44.

White, H. C. (1970). *Chains of opportunity: System models of mobility in organizations*. Cambridge: Harvard University Press.

White, H. (1981). Where do markets come from? *American Journal of Sociology, 87*, 517–547.

White, H. (1988). Varieties of markets. In B. Wellman & S. D. Berkowitz (Eds.), *Social structures: A network approach*. Cambridge: Cambridge University Press.

White, H. C., Boorman, S. A., & Breiger, R. L. (1976). Social structure from multiple networks. I. Blockmodels of roles and positions. *American Journal of Sociology, 81*, 730–780.

Žiberna, A. (2014). Blockmodeling of multilevel networks. *Social Networks, 39*, 46–61.

Zijlstra, B., Van Duijn, M., & Snijders, T. A. B. (2006). The multilevel p2 model a random effects model for the analysis of multiple social networks. *Methodology, 2*, 42–47.

Part I
Theory

Chapter 2
The Multiple Flavours of Multilevel Issues for Networks

Tom A.B. Snijders

Away from Atomistic Approaches

It is strange that the assumption that data obtained from human respondents represent independent replications has been so pervasive in statistical models used in sociological research. Sociology, after all, is about the interdependence among individuals, and about the ways in which individuals make up larger wholes such as families, tribes, organizations, and societies. Of course we know some of the reasons for this: statistical models founded on independence assumptions are convenient and have properties that can be mathematically ascertained; surveys are a major means of getting social information and ideally are obtained from probability samples containing a lot of independent operations in obtaining respondents; and, indeed, independence assumptions may yield good first-order approximations for statistical modeling. However, as early as 1959 Coleman (1959, p. 36) made an eloquent plea for taking social structure into account in methods of data collection and analysis. Coleman writes: "Survey methods have often led to the neglect of social structure and of the relations among individuals. (...) But (...) one fact remained, a very disturbing one to the student of social organization. The *individual* remained the unit of analysis. (...) Now, very recently, this focus on the individual has shown signs of changing, with a shift to groups as the units of analysis, or to networks of relations among individuals". He goes on to discuss methods for survey data collection and for data analysis that reflect this change in perspective, away from the focus on atomistic individuals. The analysis methods he discusses

---

T.A.B. Snijders (✉)
Department of Sociology, University of Groningen, Grote Rozenstraat 31, 9712 TG Groningen, The Netherlands

Nuffield College, University of Oxford, Oxford, UK
e-mail: tom.snijders@nuffield.ox.ac.uk

include contextual analysis, the precursor of present-day multilevel analysis, and the study of subgroups and cliques, still now of crucial importance in social network analysis. He concludes by saying that these methods "will probably represent only the initial halting steps in the development of a kind of structural research which will represent a truly sociological methodology", and mentions the promise of electronic computers.

In the past half century, since Coleman wrote these words, great advances have been made in methodologies for analyzing groups, or collectives, along with individuals; or, more generally, for simultaneously analyzing variables defined on different domains. The name 'multilevel analysis' has replaced[1] 'contextual analysis'. Great strides also have been taken in the study of relations among individuals, known now as social network analysis. Network analysis likewise treats variables defined in various different domains, such as sets of nodes and sets of node pairs, and it is concerned with groups, but by and large multilevel analysis and social network analysis have developed separately, meeting each other only incidentally. Recently, however, developments in social network analysis have led to combinations of these two strands of methodology. We are still in an early phase of the junction of multilevel analysis and social network analysis, and we may echo Coleman in saying that this book presents some 'initial halting steps' of this junction. This chapter gives an overview of some concepts and techniques that now can be seen as playing important roles in the combination of multilevel and network analysis.

Multilevel Analysis

To be able to discuss multilevel network analysis, we need to present a sketch about 'regular' multilevel analysis.

Origins

Multilevel analysis, as a collection of methods, was born from the confluence of two streams. On the one hand, sociological methodologists had been developing quite some conceptual precision for inference relating individuals to collectives, for which variables need to be combined that are defined in several different domains. On the other hand, statisticians had already extended analysis of variance and regression analysis, the general linear model, to linear models combining fixed with randomly varying coefficients.

Let me first sketch some highlights on the sociological methodology side. Lazarsfeld and Menzel (1961), in their paper *On the relation between individual*

---

[1] Albeit with a shift of meaning.

and collective properties—written in 1956, reprinted as Lazarsfeld and Menzel (1993)—distinguish variables according to the set of units to which scientific propositions are meant to apply. For propositions about individual and collective properties, they state that there need to be sets of units both at the individual and at the collective level. Here 'individual' may refer to individual humans, but also, e.g., individual organizations or other groupings; 'collective' refers to sets of 'individuals'. Lazarsfeld and Menzel go on to define three types of properties defined for collectives. Analytical properties are obtained by a mathematical operation performed on each member, for example the mean of an individual variable, or the correlation between two variables. Structural properties are obtained by a mathematical operation performed on the relations of each member to some or all of the other members, for example the 'cliquishness' of a network. Global properties, finally, are properties of collectives that cannot be directly deduced from properties of individual members, e.g., the type of government of a city.

As for properties of individuals, Lazarsfeld and Menzel discuss that the correlation between individual variables may be considered as a correlation between the individuals but also between the collectives, pointing to the *ecological fallacy* presented in Robinson (1950): the mistake of regarding associations between variables at one level of aggregation as evidence for associations at a different aggregation level; an extensive review was given by Alker (1969). Researchers became aware of the importance of the different levels, or sets of units, in which variables are defined, and as suggested here the focus was on nested levels, representing individuals and collectives.

During the 1970s, methods for contextual analysis were developed taking into account these levels of analysis, and trying to avoid ecological fallacies. This was called 'contextual analysis' mainly by sociologists (Blalock 1984), and 'multilevel analysis' by educational researchers (Burstein 1980).

Statisticians had a few decades earlier developed models that waited to be discovered by these social scientists. In the analysis of variance, precursor and paradigmatic example of the general linear model, models had been developed where coefficients could themselves be random variables, allowing for the investigation of multiple sources of random variation in, e.g., agricultural and industrial production. Models with only fixed, fixed as well as random, or only random coefficients were called fixed, mixed, and random models, respectively (Wilk and Kempthorne 1955; Scheffé 1959).

In the early 1980s contextual analysis and linear mixed (or generalized linear mixed) models were brought together by several statisticians and methodologists: Mason et al. (1983), Goldstein (1986), Aitkin and Longford (1986), and Raudenbush and Bryk (1986). These researchers also developed estimation algorithms and implemented them in multilevel software packages, making use of the nested structure of the random coefficients to achieve efficiency in the numerical algorithms. The scientific gains from the combination of contextual analysis and random coefficient models are also discussed by Courgeau (2003). A more extensive history of these developments is given in Kreft and de Leeuw (1998).

Hierarchical Linear Model

The prototypical statistical model used in multilevel analysis is the *Hierarchical Linear Model*, which is a mixed effects linear model for nested designs (Raudenbush and Bryk 2002; Goldstein 2011; Snijders and Bosker 2012). This generalizes the well-known linear regression model. It is meant for data structures that are hierarchically nested, such as individuals in collectives, where each individual belongs to exactly one collective. The most detailed level (individuals) is called the lowest level, or level one. The Hierarchical Linear Model is for the analysis of dependent variables at the lowest level. The basic idea is that studying the simultaneous effects of variables defined at the individual level, as well as of other variables defined at the level of collectives, on an individual-level dependent variable requires the use of regression-type models that include error terms for each of those levels separately; the Hierarchical Linear Model is a linear mixed model that has this property.

In the two-level situation—let us say, individuals in groups—it can be expressed as follows. Highlighting the distinction with regular regression models, the terminology speaks of *units* rather than cases, and there are specific types of unit at each level. We denote the level-1 units, individuals, by i and the level-2 units, groups, by j. Level-1 units are nested in level-2 units (each individual is a member of exactly one group) and the data structure is allowed to be unbalanced, such that j runs from 1 to N while i runs, for a given j, from 1 to n_j. The basic two-level hierarchical linear model can be expressed as

$$Y_{ij} = \beta_0 + \sum_{h=1}^{r} \beta_h x_{hij} + U_{0j} + \sum_{h=1}^{p} U_{hj} z_{hij} + R_{ij} . \tag{2.1}$$

Here Y_{ij} is the dependent variable, defined for level-1 unit i within level-2 unit j; the variables x_{hij} and z_{hij} are the explanatory variables. Some or all of them may be defined at the group level, rendering superfluous the index i for such variables. Variables R_{ij} are residual terms, or error terms, at level 1, while U_{hj} for $h = 0, \ldots, p$ are residual terms, or error terms, at level 2. In the case $p = 0$ this is called a *random intercept model*, for $p \geq 1$ it is called a *random slope model*. The usual assumption is that all R_{ij} and all vectors $U_j = (U_{0j}, \ldots, U_{pj})$ are independent, R_{ij} having a normal $\mathcal{N}(0, \sigma^2)$ and U_j having a multivariate normal $\mathcal{N}_{p+1}(\mathbf{0}, \mathbf{T})$ distribution. Parameters β_h are regression coefficients (fixed effects), while the U_{hj} are random effects. The presence of both of these makes (2.1) into a linear mixed model. Similar models can be defined for nesting structures with more than two levels, e.g., employees in departments in firms.

In most practical cases, the variables with random effects are a subset of the variables with fixed effects ($x_{hij} = z_{hij}$ for $h \leq p$; $p \leq r$). The Hierarchical Linear Model can then be expressed in the appealing form

$$Y_{ij} = (\beta_0 + U_{0j}) + \sum_{h=1}^{p} (\beta_h + U_{hj}) x_{hij} + \sum_{h=p+1}^{r} \beta_h x_{hij} + R_{ij} , \tag{2.2a}$$

which shows that it can be regarded as a regression model defined for the groups separately, with group-specific intercept

$$(\beta_0 + U_{0j}) \tag{2.2b}$$

and group-specific regression coefficients

$$(\beta_h + U_{hj}) \tag{2.2c}$$

for $h = 1, \ldots, p$; variables X_h for $p + 1 \leq h \leq r$ have regression coefficients that are constant across groups. This pictures the Hierarchical Linear Model as a linear regression model defined by the same model for all groups, but with regression coefficients that differ randomly between groups.

Going back to the teachings of Lazarsfeld and Menzel, it can be concluded that multilevel analysis elaborates the inference about individual and collective properties as a system of nested samples drawn from nested populations: a population of individuals nested in a population of groups (or collectives). The fact that, in practice, groups will be finite, whereas the populations are mathematically considered as if they were infinite, is usually glossed over in research aiming to generalize to social mechanisms or processes (as distinct from descriptive survey research about concrete groups, without the aim of generalization to other groups) (see Cox 1990; Sterba 2009).

Non-nested Data Structures

It soon transpired that the relevant data structures are not always nested, because social structures often are not. A basic example in studies of school effectiveness is that neighborhoods may also be an important factor for student achievement, but schools will have students coming from diverse neighborhoods while neighborhoods will have students attending different schools. This leads to a data set where students are nested in schools and also nested in neighborhoods, but schools and neighborhoods are not nested in each other; the term used for non-nested category systems is 'crossed', so that this would be called a cross-nested data structure. To present an extension of model (2.1) for such a cross-nested data structure, consider again a data structure with individuals i nested in groups j but now also nested in aggregates k of a different kind (in the example of the previous sentence, neighbourhoods). Denote by $k(i,j)$ the aggregate k to which individual i in group j belongs. In the simplest extension there is only a random intercept V_k associated with k, leading to the equation

$$Y_{ij} = \beta_0 + \sum_{h=1}^{r} \beta_h x_{hij} + U_{0j} + \sum_{h=1}^{p} U_{hj} z_{hij} + V_{k(i,j)} + R_{ij}. \tag{2.3}$$

The default assumption for the V_k is that again they are independent and normally distributed with mean 0 and constant variance, and independent of the U and R variables. A further extension is to mixed-membership models (Browne et al. 2001), in which individuals may be partial members of more than one group.

Frequentist and Bayesian Estimation

Multilevel models such as (2.2), in which parameters vary randomly between groups, provide a natural bridge between the frequentist paradigm in statistics, which treats parameters as fixed quantities which are unknown, 'out there', and the Bayesian paradigm, which treats parameters as random variables; in both paradigms, of course, the observations are the material that helps us get a grip on the values of the parameters. In the multilevel case, the random variation of parameters can be linked to a frequency distribution of parameters in the population of groups, which may be estimated from empirical data. Accordingly, this bridging ground is often called *empirical Bayes* (see, e.g., Raudenbush and Bryk 2002, and Chapter 5 of Gelman et al. 2014). Bayesian estimators[2] for the parameters such as (2.2a) and (2.2b), using the sample of groups to get information about the corresponding population, are called *empirical Bayes estimators*. For the parameters β, σ^2, and $\mathbf{T}$ in (2.1), frequentist as well as Bayesian estimators have been developed.

Especially for non-nested data structures, Bayesian estimators may have algorithmic advantages, and Bayesian Markov chain Monte Carlo ('MCMC') algorithms are often employed (Draper 2008; Rasbash and Browne 2008) for such more complex models. These are algorithms which use computer simulations, very flexible but also much more time-consuming than traditional algorithms. Today, Bayesian methods for multilevel analysis are often proposed and used without much attention paid to the distinct philosophical underpinnings. This lack of attention does not, however, take away the differences. The Bayesian approach can be a useful way to account for prior knowledge; this is discussed for the special case of multilevel analysis by Greenland (2000), and elaborated more practically in Chapter 5 of Gelman et al. (2014). Using this approach requires, however, that one pays attention to the sensitivity of the results to the choice of the prior distribution. In addition there are interpretational differences, but these may be less important because of the convergence between frequentist and Bayesian approaches discussed in Gelman et al. (2014, Chapter 4).

---

[2]In frequentist terminology these are not called estimators but predictors, because they refer to statistics that have the purpose to approximate random variables.

What Is a Level?

The various extensions of the basic multilevel model have made even more pressing the question '*What is a level?*' which has harrowed quite a few researchers even in the case of the more basic nested models. The mathematical answer is that, for applications of linear mixed or generalized linear mixed models, a level is a system of categories for which it is reasonable to assume random effects. More elaborately, this means that we assume that the categories j on which the variables U_j are defined (which are latent variables in model (2.1)) may be regarded has having been sampled randomly from some universe or population $\mathscr{G}$, making the U_j into independent and identically distributed random variables, and our aim is to say something about the properties of the population $\mathscr{G}$ rather than about the individual values U_j of the units in our sample. In the case that the U_j are one-dimensional quantities, the property of interest concerning population $\mathscr{G}$ could be, e.g., the variance of U_j. In practical statistical modeling, the assumption that the units in the data were randomly sampled from the population is usually taken with a grain of salt (again cf. Cox 1990; Sterba 2009). The essential assumption is *residual exchangeability*, which can be described as follows. The random effects, R_{ij} and U_j in (2.1) and also V_k in (2.3), are residuals given that the explanatory variables x_{hij} are accounted for; these residuals are assumed to be exchangeable across i and j (or k) in the sense that they are random and as far as we know we have no *a priori* information to distinguish them for different units in the data. Any R_{ij} could be high or low just as well as any $R_{i'j}$ in the same group j or any $R_{i'j'}$ in a different group j'; any U_{0j} could be high or low just as well as any other $U_{0j'}$; etc.

In this sense, multilevel analysis is a methodology for research questions and data structures that involve several sources of unexplained variation, contrasting with regression analysis which considers only one source of unexplained variation. Employing the Hierarchical Linear Model, as in (2.1) or its variants with additional levels, gives the possibility of studying contextual effects on the individual units. But also in more complex structures where nesting is incomplete, random effects will reflect multiple sources of unexplained variation. In social science applications this can be fruitfully applied to research questions in which different types of *actor* and *context* are involved; e.g., patients, doctors, hospitals, and insurance companies in health-related research; or students, teachers, schools, and neighborhoods in educational research. The word 'level' then is used for a type of unit, or a category system, for which a random effect is assumed. The basic phenomenon we are studying will be at the most detailed level (patients or students, respectively), and the other levels may contribute to the variation in this phenomenon, e.g., as contexts or other actors.

Lazarsfeld and Menzel (1961, first page) mentioned that, to be specific about the intended meaning of variables, we should 'examine (them) in the context of the propositions in which they are used'. This focus on propositions also sheds light on the question about what can be meaningfully considered as a '*level*' in multilevel analysis. We have to distinguish between the individual level, which is the level of the phenomena we wish to explain, the population of units for which the dependent variable is defined; and higher, collective levels, which do not need to be mutually nested, but in which the individuals are nested. To be a level requires, in the first place, that the category system is a population—a meaningfully delimited set of units with a basic similarity and for which several properties may be considered, such as a well-defined set of schools, of companies, of meetings. A category system then is a meaningful higher level if it is a population that we wish to use to explain[3] some of the variability in our phenomenon and also, potentially or actually, we may be interested in finding out which properties of the categories/units explain the variability associated with this category system.

To illustrate this, suppose we are interested in the phenomenon of juvenile delinquency as our dependent variable, and we consider neighborhoods as collectives. The individual level is, e.g., a set of adolescents living in a certain area at a certain time point; the dependent variable is their delinquency as measured by some instrument. We may observe that neighborhoods differ in average juvenile delinquency, and we then may wonder about the properties of neighborhoods—perhaps neighborhood disorder, of which a measurement may be available—that are relevant in this respect. This step, entertaining the possibility that there might be specific properties of neighborhoods associated with their influence on juvenile delinquency, and analyzing this statistically, is the step that makes the neighborhood a meaningful 'level' in the sense of multilevel analysis. In the paradigm of multilevel analysis we will then further assume that in addition to the effect of disorder there may be other neighborhood effects, but conditional on the extent of disorder and perhaps other neighborhood properties that we take into account, the neighborhoods are exchangeable (as far as we know) in their further, residual, effects.

The fact that we are interested in statistically analyzing the effect of the categories on the dependent variable also implies that for a level to be meaningful in a practical investigation, the total number of its units in the data set should be sufficiently large: a statistical analysis based on a sample of, say, less than 10 units usually makes no sense.

Dependent Variables at Any Level

The Hierarchical Linear Model is considered a model for dependent variables at the lowest level of the nesting hierarchy. However, it is so amazingly flexible that it can just as well be used for complex configurations of multiple dependent variables defined for several different levels. This was proposed, quite casually, already by

---

[3] 'Explaining' is meant here in the simple statistical sense, without considering deeper questions of causality.

Goldstein (1989a,b). It is also explained in Goldstein (2011, Section 5.3). The basic idea can be made clear by showing, for a two-level structure, the model for interdependent dependent variables $Y^{(1)}$ at level 1 and $Y^{(2)}$ at level 2. Denoting by x_h and z_h any explanatory variables and by w_h explanatory variables at level 2, the model reads

$$Y^{(1)}_{ij} = \beta_0 + \sum_{h=1}^{r} \beta_h x_{hij} + U_{0j} + \sum_{h=1}^{p} U_{hj} z_{hij} + R_{ij} \tag{2.4a}$$

$$Y^{(2)}_{j} = \gamma_0 + \sum_{h=1}^{q} \delta_h w_{hj} + V_j, \tag{2.4b}$$

where $(U_{0j}, \ldots, U_{pj}, V_j)$ is a $(p+2)$-dimensional random residual at level 2, with a multivariate normal distribution. By using products with dummy variables this can be written as a single Hierarchical Linear Model, see Goldstein (2011, p. 150). Not all multilevel modeling software will allow for this complexity, but Goldstein's program MLwiN (Rasbash et al. 2014) handles such models straightforwardly.

This model for a two-level nested hierarchy allows studying a dependent variable $Y^{(2)}$ at the higher level, and the idea can be extended to other multilevel structures, not necessarily nested.

An equivalent model was proposed independently by Croon and van Veldhoven (2007) and further elaborated by Lüdtke et al. (2008). These authors proposed models where the regression of level-1 variables is on latent level-2 variables, thus allowing analysis methods that correct for unreliability of measurement of level-2 variables. They developed and investigated estimators using structural equation modeling. Recently, similar models were elaborated for latent classes, i.e., discrete rather than normally distributed latent variables (Bennink et al. 2013).

Models for Social Networks

This section gives an overview of some statistical models for explaining social networks, as represented by directed graphs; we will focus on models and issues that are related to the treatment of multilevel networks in the next section. A wider overview of statistical models for networks is given in Snijders (2011).

The nodes $1, \ldots, n$ of the digraph refer to social actors, and ties are represented by tie variables Y_{ij} with the value 1 if a tie $i \to j$ exists, and 0 otherwise. The digraph then can be represented by its adjacency matrix $\left(Y_{ij}\right)_{[1 \leq i,j \leq n]}$. Y denotes the random digraph and y one outcome, or realization of it; henceforth we shall usually denote outcomes, or deterministic variables, by small letters and random variables by capitals.

The Basic Multilevel Nature of Social Network Analysis

Social network analysis (Wasserman and Faust 1994; Carrington et al. 2005) is fundamentally a multilevel affair with a focus on relations rather than attributes, thereby combining the actor level and the dyadic level. A basic issue for social network analysis is the study of how relations—the dyadic level—and individual characteristics—the monadic level—impinge on one another. This has led to models studying how a given, fixed network influences individual actor attributes, with a variety of network autocorrelation models (e.g. Doreian 1980; Leenders 2002) and models for social influence (Friedkin 1998). Network autocorrelation models use correlation structures to represent dependencies between the values of linked actors. In this volume, they are used in the contributions by Agneessens and Koskinen (2015) and Bellotti et al. (2015). Another way to model this was proposed by Tranmer et al. (2014), who used the multiple membership models of Browne et al. (2001) to represent network effects on individual outcomes. This has the limitation that the network effects are represented only by additive random effects of the affiliations of the individual, and the advantages of flexibility in choosing these affiliations (which can include, e.g., clique or other subgroup memberships) and the possibility to combine this with other random effects, representing other types of context. This method is used in this volume in Tranmer and Lazega (2015).

In the literature about social support and social capital, multilevel models have been used for studying characteristics of ties in egocentric networks, taking into account the hierarchical structure of ties nested in egocentric networks (van Duijn et al. 1999). In this field, Wellman and Frank (2001) specifically paid attention to the importance of including in the model not only attributes calculated for the actor and the dyadic level, but also for the network level more generally.

This chapter focuses, however, on models for networks where the collection of ties itself is the dependent variable. While in traditional models for social networks the focus was on the relations, and individual attributes were considered quite circumspectly or as an afterthought, modern statistical methods representing network data are in the realm of generalized linear models and incorporate dyadic as well as actor attributes in a very straightforward way; we see this, e.g., in MRQAP modeling (Dekker et al. 2007), the p_2 model (van Duijn et al. 2004), latent space models (Hoff et al. 2002), exponential random graph models (Lusher et al. 2013), and stochastic actor-oriented models (Snijders 2001). The presence of variables defined at different levels does not by itself bring these models close to the Hierarchical Linear Model, however—the exception being the p_2 model.

As discussed in Snijders (2011), there are several quite different approaches for representing network dependencies in probability models that can be used as a basis for statistical inference. Leaving aside conditionally uniform models (which cannot incorporate general attributes) and MRQAP (which controls for network structure but does not represent it), we can distinguish latent variable models, of which the p_2 model, latent space models, and stochastic block models (Nowicki and Snijders 2001) are major representatives; exponential random graph models; and stochastic actor-oriented models as the main approaches.

p_2 Model

Let us begin with the p_2 model. For a network represented by a digraph on n nodes, it postulates the existence of random sender effects $U = (U_1, \ldots, U_n)$ and random receiver effects $V = (V_1, \ldots, V_n)$. As proposed in van Duijn et al. (2004), conditionally on (U, V) and given dyadic covariates $x_h = (x_{hij})_{[1 \leq i,j \leq n]}$ (some or all if which may depend only on i or only on j, making them actor covariates), in the p_2 model the probability distribution for each dyad (Y_{ij}, Y_{ji}) is given by

$$P\{(Y_{ij}, Y_{ji}) = (a, b) \mid U, V\} = c_{ij} \exp\left(a\left(\sum_h \beta_h x_{hij} + U_i + V_j\right)\right.$$
$$\left. + b\left(\sum_h \beta_h x_{hji} + U_j + V_i\right) + ab\rho\right) \quad (2.5)$$

where $a, b \in \{0, 1\}$ and c_{ij} is a norming constant independent of (a, b). One of the covariates will be constant, representing the intercept. ρ is a reciprocity parameter. Variables U_i and V_i are, respectively, the latent sender and receiver effects at the actor level, and can be correlated for the same actor i, but are independent across different i. Conditional on (U, V), the dyads (Y_{ij}, Y_{ji}) are assumed to be independent but there is dependence between Y_{ij} and Y_{ji} with a strength depending on parameter ρ. In this way, random effects are used to represent those dependencies between network ties that follow from actor differences, while the model also represents tendencies toward reciprocity. In the bestiary of statistical models, this qualifies as a generalized linear mixed model, and therefore is akin to the Hierarchical Linear Model.

It should be noted that the p_2 model is a close relative of the so-called Social Relations Model (Kenny and La Voie 1985; Kenny et al. 2006), a random effects model with a similar structure for continuous relational variables Y_{ij} assumed to have normal distributions. The relation between the Social Relations Model and the Hierarchical Linear Model was discussed in Snijders and Kenny (1999).

Latent Space Models

Another latent variable model for networks is the latent metric space model, proposed by Hoff et al. (2002). Here the nodes in the network are assumed to have locations in a metric space, and the probability of a tie depends on the distance between the nodes. Denoting the location of node i by α_i, and the distance between α_i and α_j by $d(\alpha_i, \alpha_j)$, the probability of a tie in this model is given by

$$\text{logit}(P\{Y_{ij} = 1 \mid \alpha\}) = -d(\alpha_i, \alpha_j) + \sum_h \beta_h x_{hij} \quad (2.6)$$

where again x_{hij} are values of covariates with logistic regression coefficient β_h. This expresses that actors who are closer to each other, controlling for covariates, have a larger probability of being tied. Although the model was formulated for arbitrary metric spaces, it is being applied mainly for 2- or 3-dimensional Euclidean spaces.

This model was extended by Handcock et al. (2007) to a random effects model for the locations according to a mixture model, with the purpose to represent clusters of actors. Krivitsky et al. (2009) further extended this to a model where also the actors have main effects for activity U_i and popularity V_j,

$$\text{logit}(P\{Y_{ij} = 1 \mid \alpha, U, V\}) = -d(\alpha_i, \alpha_j) + \sum_h \beta_h x_{hij} + U_i + V_j \qquad (2.7)$$

where the U_i and V_i are (unfortunately!) assumed to be independent.

One of the attractive features of the latent Euclidean space models is their visual interpretation: an estimated 2-dimensional model corresponds directly to a graphical layout of the network, where ties will correspond to relatively short distances.

Exponential Random Graph Models

The Exponential Random Graph Model, fondly abbreviated to ERGM, is a generalized linear model for graphs and digraphs, representing the dependence between the ties in a direct way. It was proposed by Frank (1991) and Wasserman and Pattison (1996), and is treated in the extensive recent textbook by Lusher et al. (2013).

This model is defined by the probability function

$$P_\theta\{Y = y\} = \exp\left(\sum_h \theta_h u_h(y) - \psi(\theta)\right), \qquad (2.8)$$

where y is the digraph, the $u_h(y)$ ($h = 1, \ldots, p$) are statistics of the graph, and θ is a p-dimensional parameter. The function $\psi(\theta)$ takes care of the normalization requirement that the probabilities sum to 1. There may be covariates defined on the nodes, and on the dyads, on which the $u_h(y)$ may depend. This is still an extremely general model, and Snijders et al. (2006) discussed how to specify it in practically feasible and fruitful ways, avoiding the so-called 'near-degeneracy'. Lusher et al. (2013, Chapter 6) contains an extensive presentation of statistics $u_h(y)$ that may be included in the specification of an ERGM.

The dependence on actor and dyadic covariates can be implemented by defining some of the $u_h(y)$ as sums of ties weighted by covariates, such as

$$u_h(y) = \sum_{i,j} v_i y_{ij}$$

for the sender effect of an actor covariate V, or

$$u_h(y) = \sum_{i,j} v_{ij} y_{ij}$$

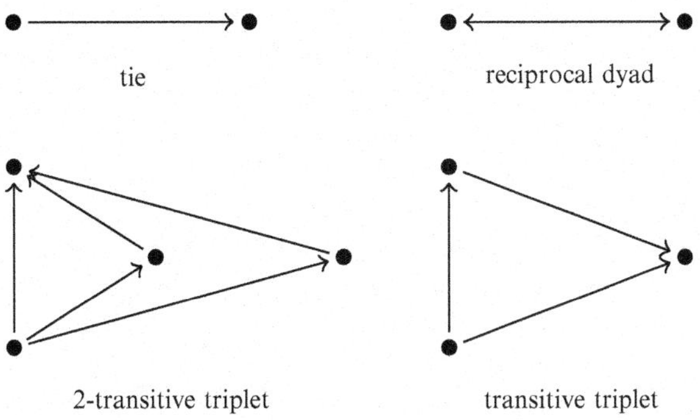

Fig. 2.1 Examples of subgraphs, counts of which are used in ERG models

tie

reciprocal dyad

2-transitive triplet

transitive triplet

for a dyadic covariate V. Dependence between tie variables, such as reciprocity and transitivity, is expressed by defining some of the $u_h(y)$ to be counts of subgraphs like those in Fig. 2.1. The literature mentioned explains this more fully, e.g., Lusher et al. (2013, Chapter 7).

Stochastic Actor-Oriented Models

Longitudinal network data potentially give much more information about the antecedents as well as consequences of network configurations than cross-sectional data. They also require more effort to collect, but there already are a large number of longitudinal network data sets, and their number is growing.

The Stochastic Actor-oriented Model ('SAOM'; Snijders 2001) is a statistical model for network dynamics that has been developed for the interdependent dynamics of networks and (monadic) actor variables (Steglich et al. 2010) and various other network structures. We sketch it here for the case of interdependent networks and actor variables, calling the latter 'behavior' just as a general term, and denoting the 'behavior' of actor i by Z_i. The network is Y, the vector of behaviors for all actors is $Z = (Z_1, \ldots, Z_n)$. The method assumes that data are available for a number of discrete observation moments, the panel waves, and that the process of change in network and behavior runs on in between the observation moments. The probabilities of changes in network ties depend on the network configurations in which the actor is involved who sends the ties; this can be formulated in a model where the changes in network and in behavior result from choices by the actors. The interpretation is that actors control their outgoing ties and their behavior, subject to constraints determined by network context, attributes, and path dependence (inertia).

In the basic model, the network is a directed graph and the behavior is a discrete variable with a finite number (say, 2–10) of ordered categories, integer coded (1, 2, etc). The time parameter is continuous, meaning that at any moment between the observations, a change in tie or behavior is possible. The model is a Markov chain, which means that the probabilities of change at any moment depend only on the current state (y, z) of the network and behavior, together with the available covariates. The dynamic process is defined as follows. At random moments, the frequency of which is determined by 'rate functions', a randomly selected actor i gets the opportunity to change either one outgoing network tie Y_{ij} or the behavior Z_i. The behavior can change only by unit steps, $+1$ or -1. The actor can also let the network and behavior stay as it is. The network tie to be changed, or the change in the behavior, is determined probabilistically by the so-called *evaluation functions* and the current state of the network and behavior (y, z). There are separate evaluation functions for the network and the behavior, and the probability of a particular change is greater when it would lead to a higher change in the evaluation function.

Specifically, the model has two components, a waiting model for timing of changes and a choice model for outcome of changes. The timing component is relatively simple. It must satisfy the consequence of the Markov assumption that waiting times between changes have an exponential distribution; to this are added considerations of interdependence between actors, and interdependence between networks and behavior. The assumption is that each actor has a rate function $\lambda_i^Y(y, z)$ for the network and a rate function $\lambda_i^Z(y, z)$ for the behavior. The waiting time for the next opportunity for a change in an outgoing tie of actor i is exponentially distributed with parameter $\lambda_i^Y(y, z)$, and for the next opportunity for a change in behavior of actor i it is exponentially distributed with parameter $\lambda_i^Z(y, z)$. At any given moment, the briefest of these waiting times across all actors is selected, the choice model is activated, which usually will lead to a change in state, and then the model starts again with the new state.

To define the choice model, suppose that the current state of the network and behavior combination is $(y^{(0)}, z)$, and actor i gets the opportunity for a network change. Then the set $\mathscr{C}$ of possible networks that could result from this change opportunity is composed of all networks y' for which in comparison with network $y^{(0)}$ exactly one outgoing tie $i \to j$, for some $j \neq i$, is either added or dropped; and, in addition, the network $y^{(0)}$ itself, representing no change. Denote the evaluation[4] function for the network for actor i by $f_i^Y(y, z)$, defined for all possible network-behavior configurations (y, z). The probability that the resulting network is y' is given by

$$P\{\text{next } Y = y'\} = \frac{\exp\left(f_i^Y(y', z)\right)}{\sum_{y \in \mathscr{C}} \exp\left(f_i^Y(y, z)\right)} \quad (y' \in \mathscr{C}). \tag{2.9}$$

For behavior changes the set of possible changes has only 3 elements: up, stay, down; and the evaluation function for behavior is used. For the rest, all is analogous. The dynamic process then consists of a repetition of these steps, where the result of the previous step is always he starting point of the next.

---

[4]We restrict the discussion to specifications with only an evaluation function; see Ripley et al. (2015) for more general models.

The heart of the model is the specification of the evaluation functions. These are defined as linear combinations of theoretically argued and/or empirically necessary characteristics of the network and the behavior,

$$f_i^Y(y,z) = \sum_h \beta_h^Y s_{ik}^Y(y,z) \text{ and } f_i^Z(y,z) = \sum_h \beta_h^Z s_{ik}^Z(y,z). \quad (2.10)$$

These characteristics $s_{ik}^Y(y,z)$ and $s_{ik}^Z(y,z)$ are called 'effects.' On the network side, these can be dependent on the network position of actor i. For example, tendencies toward reciprocity and transitivity, respectively, can be represented by positive parameters for the reciprocity and transitive triplets effects,

$$s_{ik}^Y(y) = \sum_j y_{ij} y_{ji}, \qquad s_{ik}^Y(y) = \sum_{j,h} y_{ij} y_{jh} y_{ih}$$

as in Fig. 2.1; but, contrasting with ERG modeling, the role of actor i is now special, as it is used to denote the focal actor of whom the evaluation function is being considered.

The network and behavior dynamics become interdependent when some of the effects for network change of actor i, $s_{ik}^Y(y,z)$, depend on behavior z, not only on the behavior of the actor i but also of the other actors. E.g., the cross-product 'ego × alter behavior' interaction term

$$s_{ik}^Y(y,z) = \sum_j y_{ij} z_i z_j$$

will reflect (if it has a positive coefficient) that actors who have themselves a higher value of z_i will have a larger probability to create and maintain ties with other actors j accordingly as these in their turn have a higher z_j value. On the other side, some of the effects for behavior change of actor i, $s_{ik}^Z(y,z)$, can depend on the network y. An example is the 'average behavior alter' effect

$$s_{ik}^Z(y,z) = \frac{z_i \sum_j y_{ij} z_j}{\sum_j y_{ij}},$$

defining $0/0 = 0$. If its coefficient is positive, this effect will imply that actors whose connections have on average a higher z_j value, will themselves tend to increase more, or decrease less, in their own z_i value. In models including such effects, the changes in the network lead to changes in the change probabilities for behavior and vice versa: the actors are each others' changing environment.

These dynamic models can be studied by computer simulation which is also how parameters are estimated: see the mentioned literature. Further information is at http://www.stats.ox.ac.uk/~snijders/siena/.

Choice of Model

The range of statistical network models is starting to be bewildering and it may be helpful to point out some differences in their properties. All these models can incorporate fixed effects of quite arbitrary covariates, so the difference is only in how they represent structural network features.

The p_2 model represents only three aspects of networks: differences between actors in popularity (indegrees) and activity (outdegrees), and reciprocity. Further structural features such as transitivity are not modeled.

The latent Euclidean space models represent networks by embedding the actors, as nodes, in a 2- or 3-dimensional Euclidean space. (More dimensions are possible but unusual.) This is visually very attractive. Network dependencies such as reciprocity, transitivity, and higher-order dependencies are represented only as consequences of this embedding. On the one hand the model is inflexible in the representation of network dependencies, as there are no free parameters for this purpose: the tendencies towards reciprocity and transitivity follow jointly from the spatial arrangement of the nodes, and cannot further be tuned. On the other hand the model is very flexible in choosing the locations of the nodes. This has a downside: the likelihood surface for the location of the nodes is often quite multimodal, a problem that is not really resolved by giving the locations a probability distribution as in a random effects model. I think it is doubtful that the intricacies of social space can be well represented by Euclidean space.

The Exponential Random Graph Model represents network dependence directly by using subgraph count statistics as statistics $u_h(y)$ in (2.8), as discussed in Lusher et al. (2013, Chapters 6, 7). A large number of triadic and higher-order structures can be considered, and are indeed used in practical network research, as is illustrated by the same book. The Stochastic Actor-oriented Model represents network dependencies, somewhat similarly, by the effects $s_k(y)$ in (2.10), and here also a large array of structural effects can be considered (Ripley et al. 2015).

An illuminating difference between ERGM and SAOM models on the one hand, and latent variable models (spatial or otherwise) on the other hand, is the consequence of restriction to a smaller set of nodes and the importance of network delineation. The former models do not allow restriction to a random subset of nodes; for the ERGM this was elaborated in Snijders (2010). The reason is that ERGMs and SAOMs represent dependencies, and cutting off arbitrary nodes would be an amputation. For the latent variable models, on the other hand, it is conceptually unproblematic to consider only a subset of nodes: if a random subset of nodes with their incoming and outgoing ties is dropped, the information available in the data is reduced but the model formulation of the rest remains intact. In practice, however, it appears that working with a somewhat restricted node set in ERGMs and SAOMs usually does not strongly change results except for the fact that the data set is less informative, so this difference may be more important theoretically than practically.

This issue may be regarded as a practical advantage of latent variable models, but it also highlights that these represent networks in a descriptive way but not in their essential dependence structure.

In some research the focus is on the structural dependencies directly, and then the ERGM and SAOM will be preferable. In other research the estimates of the random effect variances (sources of variability) and the posterior predictions of the random effects and spatial locations may be important, leading to preference for a latent variable model.

Whether the latent variable approach or the directly structural approach of the ERGM and the SAOM yield a better representation of empirical social networks is still an open question. In a sense this question is ill-posed because both models have flexible opportunities for model specification, so a poor fit may always be remedied by a more appropriate specification. Other open questions include: how important a good fit for such models is in practice; and how robust conclusions can be for a model that fits poorly on characteristics that has a poor fit on characteristics that are secondary to the main research questions.

Multilevel Network Analysis

The combination of the terms 'multilevel' and 'social networks' leads to a multiplicity of directions. Above it was mentioned that social networks combine different types of units—social actors and social ties—and variables can and will be defined on both of these sets. Varieties of the ERGM (Daraganova and Robins 2013) and of the SAOM (Steglich et al. 2010) combine dependent network variables with dependent actor variables. But this volume is about other combinations. The current section is about *multilevel network analysis*: the combined network analysis for several independent groups. Section "Analysis of Multilevel Networks" is about *analysis of multilevel networks*: the analysis of structures with nodes of several types, connected by ties of several types.

Why Combine Several 'Parallel' Networks?

Multilevel network analysis, where the term 'multilevel' is used in the sense of hierarchical nesting, is a combined network analysis for several groups, applying the same model to each group. We then have several networks, with different actor sets and assumed to be mutually independent, that may be combined in a single analysis with a common model but allowing parameter values to be different. Why should we do this?

In general, multilevel analysis may have several main purposes. I formulate them for the case where individuals are the lower-level units and groups the higher-level units. These purposes are entwined, and the salience of each of them will differ depending on the application considered.

⇒ Obtain results from the combination of data sets about multiple groups, taking into account the 'random' variability between individuals within groups as well as the 'random' variation between groups, with standard errors (or other measures of uncertainty of the results) that account for these two sources of variation.
⇒ Increase the amount of information (sample size) compared to analyzing a single group.
⇒ Generalize to the population of groups.
⇒ Test effects of group-level variables.
⇒ Analyze the groups jointly in a way that allows more detail and precision than would be possible when analyzing the groups separately. This sometimes is formulated by saying that the analysis of each group 'borrows strength' (Morris 1983) from the other groups, which is possible because of the assumption that this group is a member of the same population as the other groups. This is related to the idea of 'empirical Bayes' estimates mentioned in section "Frequentist and Bayesian Estimation".

All except the last purpose are also, potentially, goals of meta-analysis (e.g., Hedges and Olkin 1985). The main difference between multilevel analysis and meta-analysis is that, usually, meta-analysis is a two-step procedure, using finished analyses of the single groups and combining these in overall conclusions, whereas multilevel analysis usually unites these two parts of the analysis. Meta-analysis also can be more liberal with respect to the model assumptions concerning the group level. The correspondence between meta-analysis and multilevel analysis is discussed in Raudenbush and Bryk (2002), Chapter 7, and Snijders and Bosker (2012), Section 3.7. A two-step approach can also be used in multilevel analysis provided that the groups individually are large enough, cf. Achen (2005).

While we assume that the same model applies to all groups, they will have different parameter values. In addition, groups will usually have different sizes and different distributions of explanatory variables; in consequence, the standard errors resulting from analyses per single group will also differ across groups. To be used in a valid way, meta-analytic and two-step approaches should take these differences into account—which is automatic in multilevel analysis via the Hierarchical Linear Model.

For multilevel network analysis, any or all of these purposes may apply. One major purpose is to generalize to a population of networks. It was noted by Snijders and Baerveldt (2003) and Entwisle et al. (2007) that traditional social network analysis focused on the analysis of single networks, while nevertheless usually implying that the mechanisms and processes uncovered have a larger validity than only for the particular group under study. But these authors also noted that more and more studies are being done where data is collected for multiple networks considered to be similar. On the level of networks, traditional social network research mostly was based on $N = 1$ studies. To have a statistical basis for generalizing to a wider population, however, one needs to analyze data for several networks that may be regarded, in some sense, as replications of each other. The target population then will be a population of networks, and almost always will be somewhat vaguely described and perhaps have a somewhat hypothetical nature. This is often the case for the populations at higher levels in multilevel analysis. Above, Cox (1990) and Sterba (2009) were already mentioned as references about this topic; some further philosophical considerations about the use of probability models for multilevel and network data are presented in Sections 1.1.1 and 14.1.1 of Snijders and Bosker (2012) and on pages 135–137 of Snijders (2011). The practical question is whether a particular collection of networks is homogeneous enough with respect to the social processes taking place to justify pursuing a common conclusion by using all of them together; as well as to justify applying a common statistical model, with parameters that are allowed to vary from group to group according to a joint probability distribution in the population of groups.

The 'replications' may be network studies in several similar schools, several similar companies, etc. The *Adolescent Society* study of Coleman (1961) was based on detailed investigations of friendship networks in 10 schools, juxtaposed as 10 interconnected case studies. More recent examples such as the *PROSPER* study (Moody et al. 2011), the *ASSIST* study (Campbell et al. 2008; Steglich et al. 2012), and the *School Social Environments* study (Light et al. 2013) have provided network data to be analyzed by multilevel or meta-analytic means.

Two-Step Meta-for-Multilevel Network Analysis

In the following model for two-step meta-analysis, the population at the higher level is made explicit. It is assumed that independent groups—in the meta-analysis case these may be individual studies or publications—are combined, being regarded as a sample from a population of groups. The focus often is on one parameter at a time, so that the parameter is one-dimensional and denoted by θ. The dependent variable at the group level is the parameter estimate from group k, denoted by $\hat{\theta}_k$. The assumption of the random effects model for meta-analysis (cf. p. 210 in Raudenbush and Bryk 2002; Snijders and Bosker 2012, p. 37) is

$$\hat{\theta}_k = \theta_k + R_k = \mu_\theta + E_k + R_k. \qquad (2.11)$$

Here θ_k is the true parameter in group k; R_k is the estimation error within this study; μ_θ is the mean of parameter θ in the population of groups; and E_k is the deviation of this group from the population mean. R_k reflects within-group variability and E_k reflects between-group variability. From the point of view of estimating θ_k, R_k is regarded as error variation and E_k as true variation.

These are independent residuals both with expected value 0. The secret of this analysis method is that the within-group analysis provides us with an estimate of the standard error $\sigma_k = \text{s.e.}(\hat{\theta}_k)$ which is the standard deviation of R_k, and we act (almost always) as if we know this standard error exactly. Armed with this extra information we can estimate not only μ_θ but also $\text{var}(E_k) = \text{var}(\theta_k)$ without the 'hat' on top of θ, the 'true between-group variance' of θ_k; as opposed to

$$\text{var}(\hat{\theta}_k) = \text{var}(R_k) + \text{var}(E_k),$$

which is the 'observed between-group variance'.

If the number of groups is large enough, such a study also permits the assessment of effects of variables X_h at the group level, by entering them in the model as predictor variables:

$$\hat{\theta}_k = \mu_\theta + \sum_h \beta_h x_{hj} + E_k + R_k, \quad (2.12)$$

where x_{hj} is the value of X_h for group k. In most practical cases the number of networks in a data set for a multilevel network analysis will be not very large, so the number of variables X_h of which the effect can be studied will be low.

For model (2.11) an explicit estimator in a network context was suggested by Snijders and Baerveldt (2003), using a method derived by Cochran (1954). The maximum likelihood (ML) or restricted maximum likelihood (REML) estimators under the assumption that R_k and E_k have normal distributions will usually be more efficient. This can be calculated by multilevel software such as HLM (Raudenbush et al. 2011) and MLwiN (Rasbash et al. 2014), and by R packages such as metafor (Viechtbauer 2010). This two-step approach was used for multilevel network analysis, e.g., by Lubbers (2003) and Schaefer et al. (2011) who combined ERGM analyses for several groups; and by Mercken et al. (2012) and Huitsing et al. (2014) who combined Stochastic Actor-oriented Models for several groups.

Integrated Multilevel Network Analysis

The other possibility is to integrate the within-network and between-network models in one joint model and analyze this in one simultaneous analysis. The generic way to do this is by postulating a between-network probability model, where the parameters of the within-network model are supposed to be drawn independently from a common across-network distribution: in other words, a random effects model. This is more complicated than the two-step approach, and for every type of within-network model a multilevel model has to be specifically elaborated. The integrated approach is sketched in Sweet et al. (2013, Section 2), who call this the *Hierarchical Network Model*.

The great potential advantage to this is the possibility of 'borrowing strength' as was mentioned above. In many settings where network data are collected, the groups are rather small—e.g., school classes with sizes between 20 and 40—and for each group separately an analysis might be possible only with a quite meagre model specification. The consequence then is that various effects of focal interest may have to be left out because the data for each individual group does not support parameter estimation for a truly interesting model, or the possibilities of controlling for additional or competing mechanisms are reduced. In such a case, a random effects multilevel model can be very helpful; sometimes the analysis may even be impossible without it. In addition, an integrated random effects multilevel model will often be more efficient, and an integrated analysis may be in itself more attractive than a two-step analysis.

The first multilevel network analysis model of this kind was presented by Zijlstra et al. (2006), a multilevel version of the p_2 model. To define this extension, indicate the groups by k and the tie variable from actor i to actor j in group k by Y_{kij}. The simplest multilevel version of the p_2 model (2.5), containing random intercepts W_k for the groups, then is given by

$$P\{(Y_{kij}, Y_{kji}) = (a, b) \mid U, V, W\}$$
$$= c_{kij} \exp\left(a \left(\sum_h \beta_h x_{hij} + W_k + U_i + V_j\right)\right.$$
$$\left. + b \left(\sum_h \beta_h x_{hji} + W_k + U_j + V_i\right) + a b \rho\right), \quad (2.13)$$

again for $a, b \in \{0, 1\}$, where c_{kij} does not depend on a or b. This means that (on the logistic scale) there is a random main effect for the groups, but further they are similar. More elaborate models can be obtained by adding random slopes for some of the X_h, and the reciprocity coefficient ρ may also get a random effect.

Several applications of this model were published, e.g., by Vermeij et al. (2009) and Rivellini et al. (2012).

There is a lot of recent and current activity in extending other network models to multilevel versions. Sweet et al. (2013) elaborated their 'Hierarchical Network Model' for the case of the latent Euclidean space model, and presented an application with a random intercept and an (unfortunately, uncorrelated) random slope. In another publication (Sweet et al. 2014) these authors elaborated a multilevel version of the hierarchical mixed membership latent block model of Airoldi et al. (2008). Koskinen and Snijders (2016) are working on a multilevel extension of the Stochastic Actor-oriented Model, and a brief documentation of this is given in Ripley et al. (2015).

Hierarchical Structures

Much like the situation of multilevel analysis with the Hierarchical Linear Model and its variants, multilevel network analysis is also a hierarchical type of model for a hierarchical data structure. Estimation for this hierarchical data structure again may be regarded as empirical Bayes estimation, where the group-level parameters θ_k have a frequency distribution about which we get information thanks to the observed sample of groups. The analysis of each group borrows strength from the data of the other groups. Therefore, multilevel network analysis is particularly appropriate for combining the data of many small networks, each of which would be too small to permit analysis by a suitably specified ERGM or SAOM.

For single-level as well as multilevel network analysis, frequentist as well as Bayesian estimation methods have been proposed. Bayesian methods are potentially more compatible with the hierarchical nature of multilevel network analysis, and may be helpful for incorporating prior knowledge in cases where the number of groups is rather small. More research is needed to make meaningful comparisons between estimation methods, be they Bayesian or frequentist, for these complicated models.

Analysis of Multilevel Networks

Brass et al. (2004) proposed that for network studies in organizational research, it is important to consider both intra-organization and inter-organization networks. Lazega et al. (2008) pioneered a study with a linked intra- and inter-organizational design. Models and methods for the complex network structures that are necessary for the analysis of such designs are now in an early stage of development, and this volume aims to contribute to this domain.

A multilevel network (Wang et al. 2013) can be defined as a network with nodes of several types, where a distinction is made between types of ties according to the types of nodes that they connect. Thus, if types of nodes are A, B, C, etc., there is a distinction between $A - A$, $B - B$, $C - C$ ties, etc., and also between $A - B$, $A - C$, etc., ties. The first are intra-type, the second inter-type ties. Some of the networks may be the networks of interest, others may be fixed constraints, still others may be non-existent or otherwise outside of consideration. The intra- and inter-organization network of Brass et al. (2004) and Lazega et al. (2008) is composed of organizations (type A) and their members (type B), where $A - A$ ties can be organizational cooperation, competition, etc., while $B - B$ ties can be interpersonal collaboration, acquaintance, etc. The primary two-mode $A \times B$ network then will be the membership or affiliation network, where the simplest situation is one of complete nesting, and each individual is a member of exactly one organization; the $B \times A$ network may be superfluous, and then could be defined formally as an empty network. The design will be especially interesting if $B - B$ ties between members of different organizations are also recorded, so that interpersonal ties within as well as between organizations can be included in the analysis. Another example is the co-evolution of a one-mode and a two-mode network as studied by Snijders et al. (2013), where A is a set of individual students, B a set of companies, the $A \times A$ network represents friendship or advice ties, while the two-mode $A \times B$ network represents that the student is potentially interested to work for this company; $B \times B$ and $B \times A$ networks were not used.

Fig. 2.2 Adjacency matrix for combined node set

$$\begin{array}{c} & A & B \\ A & \text{one-mode } A \times A & \text{two-mode } A \times B \\ B & \text{two-mode } B \times A & \text{one-mode } B \times B \end{array}$$

This kind of multilevel network can potentially be studied by extensions of the models mentioned above. This is sketched in the following sections for the Exponential Random Graph Model and the Stochastic Actor-oriented Model.

A representation that is quite generally useful for handling multilevel relational structures was proposed by Wasserman and Iacobucci (1991). This defines a combined node set as the union or disjoint union of the A, B, etc., node sets. The combined node set allows treating the various one-mode and two-mode networks as subgraphs of an overall graph, with its associated adjacency matrix as in Fig. 2.2.

If some of the within-type or between-type networks are undefined, meaningless, or not studied for other reasons, the corresponding sub-matrices can be defined as structurally null blocks, i.e., having all entries equal to 0.

Exponential Random Graph Models for Multilevel Networks

Mathematically, model (2.8) can be used straightforwardly for multilevel networks, because it defines a general exponential family of graphs (directed or non-directed), and the node set can be taken as the union or disjoint union of the A, B, etc., node sets, as mentioned above. The outcome space of graphs can be restricted so that certain blocks in the adjacency matrix are fixed; e.g., a two-mode network of affiliations of individuals to organizations might be considered an exogenously fixed datum of the analysis.

Of course, turning the general ERG model into a model for multilevel networks in this way is not as easy as it might seem from the previous sentences. The model must be specified in a way that corresponds to the differences between the node sets; and the existing algorithms must be tuned for the estimation of parameters in the model. This was accomplished by Wang et al. (2013). The following is a very brief sketch.

To express the ERGM for a multilevel network with two node sets A and B, let us refer to the one-mode $A \times A$ and $B \times B$ networks by A and B (a manageable misuse of notation) and to the two-mode $A \times B$ cross-level network by X. Then the multilevel network can be denoted by (y_A, y_B, y_X), and the vector of statistics $s(y)$ in (2.8) can be split into parts depending on each of y_A, y_B, and y_X separately, and each of their combinations; leading to the formulation of the multilevel ERGM as

$$\begin{aligned} P_\theta\{(Y_A, Y_B, Y_X) = (y_A, y_B, y_X)\} = \exp\big(&\theta_A s_A(y_A) + \theta_B s_B(y_B) \\ &+ \theta_X s_X(y_X) + \theta_{AX} s_{AX}(y_A, y_X) \\ &+ \theta_{BX} s_{BX}(y_B, y_X) + \theta_{ABX} s_{ABX}(y_A, y_B, y_X) - \psi(\theta)\big)\,, \end{aligned} \quad (2.14)$$

where $\theta = (\theta_A, \theta_B, \theta_X, \theta_{AB}, \theta_{AX}, \theta_{BX}, \theta_{ABX})$. The θ and s symbols all denote vectors. This decomposes the model in parts with the following statistics:

$s_A(y_A)$ internal dependence of the one-mode network A, specified as in Lusher et al. (2013, Chapter 6).

$s_B(y_B)$ internal dependence of the one-mode network B, analogous.

$s_X(y_X)$ internal dependence of the two-mode network X, specified as in Lusher et al. (2013, Section 10.2).

$s_{AX}(y_A, y_X)$ bivariate interdependence between the A and X networks; interdependence between a one-mode and a two-mode network is not treated specifically in the ERGM literature (as far as I know), but since two-mode networks have less structural features than one-mode networks, the directions for specifying bivariate networks given in Lusher et al. (2013, Section 10.1) can be followed.

$s_{BX}(y_B, y_X)$ bivariate interdependence between the B and X networks, analogous.

$s_{ABX}(y_A, y_B, y_X)$ three-way interdependence between the A, B, and X networks, to which Wang et al. (2013) is specifically devoted. For example, a basic three-way effect expressing the multilevel structure is the effect that ties between individuals will tend to go together with ties between the organizations they are members of. This is the *C4AXB* effect discussed in their Section 6.5.

In practice, all cross-level dependencies will be crucial in giving a meaningful representation of the multilevel network, and the three-way interdependence represented by $s_{ABX}(y_A, y_B, y_X)$ will often be the main point of scientific interest. The other parameters are also interesting in their own right. Wang et al. (2013) find that including three-way and other between-level dependencies may simplify the intra-network models compared to modeling the A, B, and X networks independently, which reflects the theoretical notion that internal structure will be shaped depending on external or contextual demands, pressures, and possibilities, and 'controlling for' the between-level dependencies gives a purified view of the intra-network mechanisms.

As is mentioned in the discussion of Wang et al. (2013), the determination of the levels in a multilevel network can be done in several ways, depending on the aims of the research. One possibility is to define node sets based on their different nature and way of connecting to other nodes, such as individuals and organizations. Another possibility is to distinguish nodes of the same basic kind by attributes, thus permitting a model with arbitrary differences between the ways in which the nodes relate to other nodes, depending on these attributes. The discussion above focuses on the first method, but the multilevel ERG model can be applied also to the other way of determining node sets.

In this volume, this model is applied in several varieties. Two chapters in this volume provide examples of the nested case. Both are about managers in companies. The study by Brennecke and Rank (2015) is concerned with the interdependence of the knowledge sharing network between managers (B) and the R&D collaboration network between the companies (A). Zappa and Lomi (2015) study advice and communication relations between managers (B) in subsidiaries

(A) of an international multi-unit industrial group. The cross-level relation (X) is membership affiliation, the within-A relation is the hierarchical reporting relation between the subsidiaries.

Hollway and Koskinen (2015) apply the multilevel ERGM to a study about multilateral fisheries treaties, where the node sets are the countries (A) and the multilateral treaties (B). This is a crossed rather than nested design because countries can be members of several treaties. The chapter by Brailly et al. (2015) considers one node set of buyers and another of sellers, where moreover the buyers as well as the sellers are nested in their respective organizations. This is analyzed as two separate bipartite buyer × seller networks, one for the organizations and one for the individuals, where some of the variables of the other level of aggregation (individuals and organizations, respectively) are obtained by projection (aggregation or disaggregation).

The second way of determining the levels is represented by Wang et al. (2015), who present an application of the multilevel ERG model where the two node sets are entrepreneurial and non-entrepreneurial farmers, who differ so strongly in their network structures that a multilevel ERGM is able to give a much better representation than a regular one-mode network analysis. An exploratory method for derivation and specification of hypotheses in multilevel ERG models is proposed by Zhu et al. (2015).

Stochastic Actor-Oriented Models for Multilevel Networks

For the Stochastic Actor-oriented Model likewise, the basic mathematical model explained in section "Stochastic Actor-Oriented Models" can be used,[5] if it is specified in accordance with the multilevel structure. The actor-oriented nature of this model requires specifying something about agency: which sets of actors will be specified as those making the choices? In the standard actor-oriented model for two-mode networks (Koskinen and Edling 2012; Snijders et al. 2013) with node sets A and B, there is agency in only one node set, so ties are regarded as being directed from A to B and determined by the actors of type A.

Again, we consider a multilevel network with two node sets, A and B. In this discussion we leave out the dependent behavioral variable, but it could be added in a rather direct way. In the general situation there could possibly be ties from A to B as well as ties from B to A; for the current exposition the second kind of tie will be ignored, so that again we consider two one-mode networks internal, respectively, to the actor sets A and B; and one two-mode network X supposed to be directed from A to B, with agency in the A nodes.

The specification of the model for the RSiena package (Ripley et al. 2015) is possible by employing the representation with a combined node set $A \cup B$ as above

---

[5]I thank James Hollway for pointing out this possibility.

$$\begin{array}{c} \begin{array}{cc} A & B \end{array} \\ \begin{array}{c} A \\ B \end{array} \begin{pmatrix} \text{internal } A & 0 \\ 0 & \text{internal } B \end{pmatrix} \\ \text{networks } A, B \end{array} \quad \begin{array}{c} \begin{array}{cc} A & B \end{array} \\ \begin{pmatrix} 0 & \text{two-mode } A \times B \\ [\text{two-mode } B \times A] & 0 \end{pmatrix} \\ \text{network } X \end{array}$$

Fig. 2.3 Two dependent networks for combined node set

but now with two dependent networks, as displayed in the block structure for the adjacency matrices shown in Fig. 2.3. The reason why the data must be separated and treated as two dependent networks instead of one as in the ERGM (Fig. 2.2) will be explained further below.

To avoid confusion, in the rest of this section we shall refer to the original networks as the one-mode and two-mode networks, and to the two constructed networks used for the analysis in RSiena as the multi-networks. Both multi-networks have node set $A \cup B$. The multilevel network is specified as a multivariate network of two multi-networks, consisting of

(1) a one-mode multi-network containing the two one-mode networks as diagonal blocks, and off-diagonal blocks that are structurally 0;
(2) another one-mode multi-network containing the $A \times B$ network as an off-diagonal block; all the rest are structurally zero blocks. If the data structure would also include a $B \times A$ two-mode network with agency in the B nodes, this could be included as the $B \times A$ off-diagonal block in the second multi-network. If the $A \times B$ network would be a fixed context and not a dependent variable (e.g., if it denotes an externally given membership structure), then the second multi-network would be replaced by a dyadic covariate.

The rate functions and evaluation functions have to be differentiated according to the node sets. For the evaluation functions, this differentiation leads to the following structure, where $f_i^A(y_A; y_B, y_X)$ is the evaluation function for actors in A for their ties with other A actors, relevant for Y_A as the dependent variable; $f_i^B(y_B; y_A, y_X)$ the evaluation function for actors in B for their ties with other B actors, for dependent variable Y_B; and $f_i^X(y_X; y_A, y_B)$ the evaluation function for actors in A for their ties to B actors, relevant for dependent variable Y_X:

$$f_i^A(y_A; y_B, y_X) = \theta^A s_A(y_A) + \theta^{AX} s_{AX}(y_A; y_X) + \theta^{ABX} s_{ABX}(y_A; y_B, y_X)$$

$$f_i^B(y_B; y_A, y_X) = \theta^B s_B(y_B) + \theta^{BX} s_{BX}(y_B; y_X) + \theta^{BAX} s_{BAX}(y_B; y_A, y_X)$$

$$f_i^X(y_X; y_A, y_B) = \theta^X s_X(y_X) + \theta^{XA} s_{XA}(y_X; y_A)$$
$$+ \theta^{XB} s_{XB}(y_X; y_B) + \theta^{XAB} s_{XAB}(y_X; y_A, y_B) \, . \quad (2.15)$$

The functional dependence of these evaluation functions on the other one-or two-mode networks reflects inter-network dependence. The arguments before the semicolon have the role of dependent variable, those after the semicolon are the explanatory variables. Because of the endogeneity according to the Markov model, the state of the Markov process being (y_A, y_B, y_X), the dependent variables also are used as explanations for their own further changes. This model contains more terms compared to the decomposition (2.14) of the ERG model for multilevel networks, because the multivariate associations between two networks are represented in the SAOM—with its 'co-evolution' aspect—as two interdependent one-sided influences.

The separation into two multi-networks (or more, for structures with more than two actor sets) is necessary to separate the choice models. In the SAOM for one network the changes in all the outgoing ties of an actor are considered together, as options in one choice process. Putting the ties of A actors to other A actors in a different network than their ties to B actors means that the ties are chosen in separate, interdependent choice processes; if these ties were put into one multi-network the choices of ties to A would be weighed against ties to B and vice versa, and this would be less natural, given that node sets A and B are of a different nature and $A - A$ ties are conceptually different from $A - B$ ties. The construction of two multi-networks represents that for the A actors there are two distinct but interrelated choice processes, corresponding to the two dependent variables Y_A and Y_X in (2.15), for both of which the agency is with the A actors.

This implies that the multilevel SAOM, contrasting with the multilevel ERGM, is aimed firstly at representing network structures where the several node sets, and especially the ties between several different node sets, are of a different nature. It is less suitable for representing node sets of the same basic kind, differentiated only by an attribute. The different kinds of ties in the multilevel SAOM are distinguished also by having their own timing models, which play no role in the multilevel ERGM. The notion that compensation between different outgoing ties of one actor (e.g., a collaboration tie from i to j_1 may serve the same purpose for i as a collaboration tie from i to j_2) is meaningful for ties of the same kind, but less so between the different sets of ties $A - A$ versus $A - B$, is built into the choice model and also in the model specification for the SAOM—the choice of the effects in (2.15)—, whereas for the ERGM it is only built into the choice of the effects (2.14).

A Forward Look

Multilevel analysis of networks (section "Multilevel Network Analysis") is a natural and important development as more and more data sets are collected that contain similar 'parallel' networks in multiple groups—disconnected groups, or at least, sets of groups for which the inter-group connections are being ignored in the analysis. One of its great advantages is that it allows the study of contextual effects at the network level, i.e., the effects of network-level variables. The analysis of multilevel networks (section "Analysis of Multilevel Networks"), on the other hand, is a different and greater conceptual step. It permits studying in one model the structure of ties between several different node sets, which has some similarity to developments in multilevel analysis that permit studying dependent variables at any level, as discussed in section "Dependent Variables at Any Level". Thereby it enables the representation of social systems with multiple agency and of the structural effects of combined agency patterns. Applications of multilevel ERGMs have started to appear and are contained in this volume; applications of multilevel SAOMs will be coming. These new techniques may well have interesting repercussions on theory development.

The research program heralded by Coleman (1959) has flourished in the past half century with the development of multilevel analysis and social network analysis. Their combination is a young branch on this tree, or rather two branches, one being multilevel analysis of networks and the other the analysis of multilevel networks. This book reflects some of its recent developments and hopefully contributes to further blossoming.

References

Achen, C. H. (2005). Two-step hierarchical estimation: Beyond regression analysis. *Political Analysis, 13*, 447–456.

Agneessens, F., & Koskinen, J. (2015). Modelling individual outcomes using a Multilevel Social Influence (MSI) model: Individual versus team effects of trust on job satisfaction in an organisational context. In E. Lazega & T. A. B. Snijders (Eds.), *Multi-level network analysis for the social sciences: Theory, methods and applications* (pp. 81–106). Cham: Springer.

Airoldi, E. M., Blei, D. M., Fienberg, S. E., & Xing, E. P. (2008). Mixed membership stochastic blockmodels. *The Journal of Machine Learning Research, 9*, 1981–2014.

Aitkin, M., & Longford, N. (1986). Statistical modelling issues in school effectiveness studies. *Journal of the Royal Statistical Society, Series A, 149*, 1–43, with discussion.

Alker, H. R. (1969). A typology of ecological fallacies. In M. Dogan & S. Rokkan (Eds.), *Quantitative ecological analysis in the social sciences* (pp. 69–86). Cambridge, MA: MIT Press.

Bellotti, E., Guadalupi, L. & Conaldi, G. (2015). Comparing fields of sciences: Multilevel networks of research collaborations in Italian academia. In E. Lazega & T. A. B. Snijders (Eds.), *Multi-level network analysis for the social sciences: Theory, methods and applications* (pp. 213–244). Cham: Springer.

Bennink, M., Croon, M. A., & Vermunt, J. K. (2013). 'Micro–Macro multilevel analysis for discrete data: A latent variable approach and an application on personal network data. *Sociological Methods & Research, 42*, 431–457.

Blalock, H. M. (1984). Contextual effects models: Theoretical and methodological issues. *Annual Review of Sociology, 10*, 353–372.

Brailly, J., Favre, G., Chatellet, J., & Lazega, E. (2015). Embeddedness as a multilevel problem: A case study in economic sociology. In E. Lazega & T. A. B. Snijders (Eds.), *Multi-level network analysis for the social sciences: Theory, methods and applications* (pp. 245–272). Cham: Springer.

Brass, D. J., Galaskiewicz, J., Greve, H., & Tsai, W. (2004). Taking stock of networks and organizations: A multilevel perspective. *Academy of Management Journal, 47*, 795–817.

Brennecke, J., & Rank, O. N. (2015). Knowledge networks in high-tech clusters: A multilevel perspective on interpersonal and inter-organizational collaboration. In E. Lazega & T. A. B. Snijders (Eds.), *Multi-level network analysis for the social sciences: Theory, methods and applications* (pp. 273–294). Cham: Springer.

Browne, W. J., Goldstein, H., & Rasbash, J. (2001). Multiple membership multiple classification (MMMC) models. *Statistical Modelling, 1*, 103–124.

Burstein, L. (1980). The analysis of multilevel data in educational research and evaluation. *Review of Research in Education, 8*, 158–233.

Campbell, R., Starkey, F., Holliday, J., Audrey, S., Bloor, M., Parry-Langdon, N., Hughes, R., & Moore, L. (2008). An informal school-based peer-led intervention for smoking prevention in adolescence (ASSIST): A cluster randomised trial. *The Lancet, 371*, 1595–1602.

Carrington, P. J., Scott, J., & Wasserman, S. (2005). *Models and methods in social network analysis*. New York: Cambridge University Press.

Cochran, W. G. (1954). The combination of estimates from different experiments. *Biometrics, 10*, 101–129.

Coleman, J. S. (1959). Relational analysis: The study of social organizations with survey methods. *Human Organization, 17*, 28–36.

Coleman, J. S. (1961). *The adolescent society*. New York: The Free Press of Glencoe.

Courgeau, D. (2003). From the macro-micro opposition to multilevel analysis in demography. In: D. Courgeau (Ed.), *Methodology and epistemology of multilevel analysis; Approaches from different social sciences* (pp. 43–91). Springer.

Cox, D. R. (1990). Role of models in statistical analysis. *Statistical Science, 5*, 169–174.

Croon, M. A., & van Veldhoven, M. J. P. M. (2007). Predicting group-level outcome variables from variables measured at the individual level: a latent variable multilevel model. *Psychological Methods, 12* 45–57.

Daraganova, G., & Robins, G. (2013). Autologistic attribute models. In D. Lusher, J. Koskinen, & G. Robins (Eds.), *Exponential random graph models* (pp. 102–114). Cambridge: Cambridge University Press.

Dekker, D., Krackhardt, D., & Snijders, T. A. B. (2007). Sensitivity of MRQAP tests to collinearity and autocorrelation conditions. *Psychometrika, 72*, 563–581.

Doreian, P. (1980). Linear models with spatially distributed data: Spatial disturbances or spatial effects? *Sociological Methods & Research, 9*, 29–60.

Draper, D. (2008). Bayesian multilevel analysis and MCMC. In J. de Leeuw & E. Meijer (Eds.), *Handbook of multilevel analysis* (pp. 77–139). New York: Springer.

Entwisle, B., Faust, K., Rindfuss, R. R., & Kaneda, T. (2007). Networks and contexts: Variation in the structure of social ties. *American Journal of Sociology, 112*, 1495–1533.

Frank, O. (1991). Statistical analysis of change in networks. *Statistica Neerlandica, 45*, 283–293.

Friedkin, N. E. (1998). *A structural theory of social influence*. Cambridge: Cambridge University Press.

Gelman, A., Carlin, J. B., Stern, H. S., Dunson, D. B., Vehtari, A., & Rubin, D. B. (2014). *Bayesian data analysis* (3rd ed.). Boca Raton, FL: Chapman & Hall/CRC.

Goldstein, H. (1986). Multilevel mixed linear model analysis using iterative generalized least squares. *Biometrika, 73*, 43–56.

Goldstein, H. (1989a). Efficient prediction models for adult height. In J. M. Tanner (Ed.), *Auxology 1988: Perspectives in the science of growth and development* (pp. 41–48). London: Smith-Gordon.

Goldstein, H. (1989b). Models for multilevel response variables with an application to growth curves. In R. Darrell Bock (Ed.), *Multilevel analysis of educational data* (pp. 107–125). San Diego, CA: Academic.

Goldstein, H. (2011). *Multilevel statistical models* (4th ed.). London: Edward Arnold.

Greenland, S. (2000). Principles of multilevel modelling. *International Journal of Epidemiology, 29*, 158–167.

Handcock, M. S., Raftery, A. E., & Tantrum, J. M. (2007). Model-based clustering for social networks (with discussion). *Journal of the Royal Statistical Society, Series A, 170*, 301–354.

Hedges, L. V., & Olkin, I. (1985). *Statistical methods for meta-analysis*. New York: Academic.

Hoff, P. D., Raftery, A. E., & Handcock, M. S. (2002). Latent space approaches to social network analysis. *Journal of the American Statistical Association, 97*, 1090–1098.

Hollway, J., & Koskinen, J. H. (2015). Multilevel bilateralism and multilateralism; States' bilateral and multilateral fisheries treaties and their secretariats. In E. Lazega & T. A. B. Snijders (Eds.), *Multi-level network analysis for the social sciences: Theory, methods and applications* (pp. 315–332). Cham: Springer.

Huitsing, G., Snijders, T. A. B., Van Duijn, M. A. J., & Veenstra, R. (2014). Victims, bullies, and their defenders: A longitudinal study of the coevolution of positive and negative networks. *Development and Psychopathology, 26*, 645–659.

Kenny, D. A., Kashy, D.A., & Cook, W.L. (2006). *Dyadic data analysis*. New York: Guilford Press.

Kenny, D. A., & La Voie, L. (1985). Separating individual and group effects. *Journal of Personality and Social Psychology, 48*, 339–348.

Koskinen, J. H., & Edling, C. (2012). Modelling the evolution of a bipartite network – Peer referral in interlocking directorates. *Social Networks, 34*, 309–322.

Koskinen, J. H., & Snijders, T. A. B. (2016). Multilevel longitudinal analysis of social networks. In preparation.

Kreft, I. G. G., & de Leeuw, J. (1998). *Introducing multilevel modeling*. London: SAGE.

Krivitsky, P. N., Handcock, M. S., Raftery, A. E. & Hoff, P. D. (2009). Representing degree distributions, clustering, and homophily in social networks with latent cluster random effects models. *Social Networks, 31*, 204–213.

Lazarsfeld, P. F., & Menzel, H. (1961). On the relation between individual and collective properties. In A. Etzioni (Ed.), *Complex organizations: A sociological reader* (pp. 422–440). New York: Holt, Rinehart and Winston.

Lazarsfeld, P. F., & Menzel, H. (1993). On the relation between individual and collective properties. In R. Boudon (Ed.), *Paul Lazarsfeld: On social research and its language* (pp. 172–189). Chicago: The University of Chicago Press.

Lazega, E., Jourda, M.-T., Mounier, L. & Stofer, R. (2008). Catching up with big fish in the big pond? Multi-level network analysis through linked design. *Social Networks, 30*, 159–176.

Leenders, R. Th. A. J. (2002). Modeling social influence through network autocorrelation: Constructing the weight matrix. *Social Networks, 24*, 21–47.

Light, J. M., Greenan, C. C., Rusby, J. C., Nies, K. M., & Snijders, T. A. B. (2013). Onset to First alcohol use in early adolescence: A network diffusion model. *Journal of Research on Adolescence, 23*, 487–499.

Lubbers, M. J. (2003). Group composition and network structure in school classes: A multilevel application of the p^* model. *Social Networks, 25*, 309–332.

Lüdtke, O., Marsh, H. W., Robitzsch, A., Trautwein, U., Asparouhov, T., & Muthén, B. (2008). The multilevel latent covariate model: A new, more reliable approach to group-level effects in contextual studies. *Psychological Methods, 13*, 203–229.

Lusher, D., Koskinen, J., & Robins, G. (2013). *Exponential random graph models*. Cambridge: Cambridge University Press.

Mason, W. M., Wong, G. Y., & Entwisle, B. (1983). Contextual analysis through the multilevel linear model. *Sociological Methodology, 14*, 72–103.

Mercken, L., Steglich, C. E. G., Sinclair, P., Holliday, J., & Moore, L. (2012). A longitudinal social network analysis of peer influence, peer selection, and smoking behavior among adolescents in British schools. *Health Psychology, 31*, 450–459.

Moody, J., Brynildsen, W. D., Osgood, D. W., Feinberg, M. E., & Gest, S. (2011). Popularity trajectories and substance use in early adolescence. *Social Networks, 33*, 101–112.

Morris, C. N. (1983). Parametric empirical bayes inference: Theory and applications. *Journal of the American Statistical Association, 78*, 47–55.

Nowicki, K., & Snijders, T. A. B. (2001). Estimation and prediction for stochastic blockstructures. *Journal of the American Statistical Association, 96*, 1077–1087.

Rasbash, J., & Browne, W. J. (2008). Non-hierarchical multilevel models. In J. de Leeuw & E. Meijer (Eds.), *Handbook of multilevel analysis* (pp. 301–334). New York: Springer.

Rasbash, J., Steele, F., Browne, W. J., & Goldstein, H. (2014). *A users' guide to MLwiN*. Centre for Multilevel Modelling, University of Bristol, Bristol.

Raudenbush, S. W., & Bryk, A. S. (1986). A hierarchical model for studying school effects. *Sociology of Education, 59*, 1–17.
Raudenbush, S. W., & Bryk, A. S. (2002). *Hierarchical linear models. Applications and data analysis methods* (2nd ed.). Newbury Park, CA: SAGE.
Raudenbush, S. W., Bryk, A. S., Cheong Y. F., Congdon, R. T., & du Toit, M. (2011). *HLM 7: Hierarchical linear and nonlinear modeling*. Lincolnwood, IL: Scientific Software International.
Ripley, R. M., Snijders, T. A. B., Bóda, Z., Vörös, A., & Preciado, P. (2015). Manual for Siena version 4.0. Technical report, Oxford: University of Oxford, Department of Statistics; Nuffield College.
Rivellini, G., Terzara, L., & Amati, V. (2012). Individual, dyadic and network effects in friendship relationships among Italian and foreign schoolmates. *Genus, 67*, 1–27.
Robinson, W. S. (1950). Ecological correlations and the behavior of individuals. *Sociological Review, 15*, 351–357.
Schaefer, D. R., Simpkins, S. D., Vest, A. E., & Price, C. D. (2011). The contribution of extracurricular activities to adolescent friendships: New insights through social network analysis. *Developmental Psychology, 47*, 1141–1152.
Scheffé, H. (1959). *The analysis of variance*. New York: Wiley.
Snijders, T. A. B., & Kenny, D. A. (1999). The social relations model for family data: A multilevel approach. *Personal Relationships, 6*, 471–486.
Snijders, T. A. B. (2001). The statistical evaluation of social network dynamics. In M. E. Sobel & M. P. Becker (Eds.), *Sociological Methodology – 2001* (Vol. 31, pp. 361–395). Boston/London: Basil Blackwell.
Snijders, T. A. B. (2010). Conditional marginalization for exponential random graph models. *Journal of Mathematical Sociology, 34*, 239–252.
Snijders, T. A. B. (2011). Statistical models for social networks. *Annual Review of Sociology, 37*, 131–153.
Snijders, T. A. B., & Baerveldt, C. (2003). A multilevel network study of the effects of delinquent behavior on friendship evolution. *Journal of Mathematical Sociology, 27*, 123–151.
Snijders, T. A. B., & Bosker, R. J. (2012). *Multilevel analysis: An introduction to basic and advanced multilevel modeling* (2nd ed.). London: SAGE.
Snijders, T. A. B., Lomi, A., & Torlò, V. (2013). A model for the multiplex dynamics of two-mode and one-mode networks, with an application to employment preference, friendship, and advice. *Social Networks, 35*, 265–276.
Snijders, T. A. B., Pattison, P. E., Robins, G. L., & Handcock, M. S. (2006). New Specifications for Exponential Random Graph Models. *Sociological Methodology, 36*, 99–153.
Steglich, C. E. G., Sinclair, P., Holliday, J., & Moore, L. (2012). Actor-based analysis of peer influence in A Stop Smoking In Schools Trial (ASSIST). *Social Networks, 34*, 359–369.
Steglich, C. E. G., Snijders, T. A. B., & Pearson, M. A. (2010). Dynamic networks and behavior: Separating selection from influence. *Sociological Methodology, 40*, 329–393.
Sterba, S. K. (2009). Alternative model-based and design-based frameworks for inference from samples to populations: From polarization to integration. *Multivariate Behavioral Research, 44*, 711–740.
Sweet, T. M., Thomas, A. C., & Junker, B. W. (2013). Hierarchical network models for education research: Hierarchical latent space models. *Journal of Educational and Behavioral Statistics, 38*, 295–318.
Sweet, T. M., Thomas, A. C. & Junker, B. W. (2014). Hierarchical mixed membership stochastic blockmodels for multiple networks and experimental interventions. In E. M. Airoldi, D. Blei, E. A. Erosheva, & S. E. Fienberg (Eds.), *Handbook of Mixed Membership Models and Their Applications*. Boca Raton: Chapman & Hall/CRC Press.
Tranmer, M., & Lazega, E. (2015). Multilevel models for multilevel network dependencies. In E. Lazega & T. A. B. Snijders (Eds.), *Multi-level network analysis for the social sciences: Theory, methods and applications* (pp. 107–124). Cham: Springer.

Tranmer, M., Steel, D., & Browne, W. J. (2014). Multiple-membership multiple-classification models for social network and group dependences. *Journal of the Royal Statistical Society: Series A (Statistics in Society), 177*, 439–455.

van Duijn, M. A. J., Snijders, T.A. B., & Zijlstra, B. H. (2004). p_2: A random effects model with covariates for directed graphs. *Statistica Neerlandica, 58*, 234–254.

van Duijn, M. A. J., van Busschbach, J. T., & Snijders, T. A. B. (1999). Multilevel analysis of personal networks as dependent variables. *Social Networks, 21*, 187–210.

Vermeij, L., Van Duijn, M. A. J., & Baerveldt, C. (2009). Ethnic segregation in context: Social discrimination among native Dutch pupils and their ethnic minority classmates. *Social Networks, 31*, 230–239.

Viechtbauer, W. (2010). Conducting meta-analyses in R with the metafor package. *Journal of Statistical Software, 36*, 1–48.

Wang, P., Robins, G., Pattison, P., & Lazega, E. (2013). Exponential random graph models for multilevel networks. *Social Networks, 35*, 96–115.

Wang, P., Robins, G. L., & Matous, P. (2015). Multilevel network analysis using ERGM and its extensions. In E. Lazega & T. A. B. Snijders (Eds.), *Multi-level network analysis for the social sciences: Theory, methods and applications* (pp. 125–144). Cham: Springer.

Wasserman, S., & Faust, K. (1994). *Social network analysis: Methods and applications.* New York/Cambridge: Cambridge University Press.

Wasserman, S., & Iacobucci, D. (1991). Statistical modelling of one-mode and two-mode networks: Simultaneous analysis of graphs and bipartite graphs. *British Journal of Mathematical and Statistical Psychology, 44*, 13–43.

Wasserman, S., & Pattison, P. (1996). Logit models and logistic regression for social networks: I. An introduction to Markov graphs and p^*. *Psychometrika, 61*, 401–425.

Wellman, B., & Frank, K. A. (2001). Network capital in a multi-level world: Getting support from personal communities. In N. Lin, K. Cook, & R. S. Burt (Eds.), *Social capital: Theory and research* (pp. 233–273). Chicago: Aldine De Gruyter.

Wilk, M. B., & Kempthorne, O. (1955). Fixed, mixed, and random models. *Journal of the American Statistical Association, 50*, 1144–1167.

Zappa, P., & Lomi, A. (2015). Knowledge sharing in organizations: A multilevel network analysis. In E. Lazega & T. A. B. Snijders (Eds.), *Multi-level network analysis for the social sciences: Theory, methods and applications* (pp. 333–354). Cham: Springer.

Zhu, M., Kuskova, V., Wasserman, S., & Contractor, N. (2015). Correspondence analysis of multirelational multilevel network affiliations: Analysis and examples. In E. Lazega & T. A. B. Snijders (Eds.), *Multi-level network analysis for the social sciences: Theory, methods and applications* (pp. 145–172). Cham: Springer.

Zijlstra, B. J. H., Van Duijn, M. A. J. & Snijders, T. A. B. (2006). The multilevel p_2 model. *Methodology: European Journal of Research Methods for the Behavioral and Social Sciences, 2*, 42–47.

Chapter 3
Synchronization Costs in the Organizational Society: Intermediary Relational Infrastructures in the Dynamics of Multilevel Networks

Emmanuel Lazega

The Meso Level in Organizational Societies, Relational Infrastructure and Synchronization Costs

Sociologically, the organizational society is a class society in which the distribution of resources has to be specified at the meso level, where individual destinies depend in part on their capacities to use organizations as "tools with a life of their own" (Selznick 1949). This specification is necessary because, especially after two centuries of bureaucratization, i.e. "rationalization" of social and economic life associated with modernity, variations in (and coevolution of) individual and collective behavior cannot be understood exclusively in macro terms. They also depend on the distribution of control, efficiency, opportunities and constraints that are organizationally and institutionally shaped, with large variations in such shapes. For social scientists, finding position and structure in society is therefore still a complex task if it has to be carried out in a meaningful way, i.e. in a way that makes conflicts more intelligible.

Over two centuries, Weberian bureaucratization has begun to construct societies that Charles Perrow (1991) calls "organizational" and Ronald Breiger (1974) "dual".

Support for this project is provided by the *Dynamique des réseaux multiniveaux* (DYREM) project, funded by Sorbonne Paris-Cité. I thank Tom Snijders for help and advice, as well as Avner Bar-Hen, Julien Brailly, Ulrik Brandes, David Chavalarias, Patrice Duran, Guillaume Favre, Johannes Glückler, Lise Mounier, Marie Jourda, Martin Mader and Christophe Prieur for stimulating discussions related to this project. I am grateful to Daniel Courgeau who initiated the publication of this volume after reading the paper by Brailly and Lazega (2012).

E. Lazega (✉)
Institut d'Etudes Politiques de Paris, SPC, CSO-CNRS, 19 rue Amélie, 75007 Paris, France
e-mail: emmanuel.lazega@sciencespo.fr

© Springer International Publishing Switzerland 2016
E. Lazega, T.A.B. Snijders (eds.), *Multilevel Network Analysis for the Social Sciences*, Methodos Series 12, DOI 10.1007/978-3-319-24520-1_3

Duality points to at least two levels of collective agency that co-constitute each other: an inter-individual level and an inter-organizational level (between collective entities of all kinds including families, companies, non-profit organizations, or public administrations). In this context, the rationalization of agency in terms of control and efficiency imposes strong multilevel interdependencies and simultaneously requires unprecedented amounts of coordination among actors, within and between levels. Actors think in multilevel terms ("this person is a big fish in a big pond") and are required to manage these exceptionally complex interdependencies (functional, epistemic, normative, emotional, etc.) in increasingly sophisticated ways at different levels simultaneously, thus facing multiple dilemmas of collective action. Identifying some of the social realities at stake in multilevel networks leads to the notions of overlap and complementarity between levels (Lazega et al. 2008, 2013) and shows that they co-constitute each other through vertical differentiations between members and relational strategies that are important for their achievements. Without this multilevel coordination, both between individuals, between organizations, and cross-level between individuals and organizations, neither individuals nor organizations can access or mobilize on their own all the resources that are needed to produce, compete and survive (Brailly et al. Chap. 10, in this volume; Brennecke and Rank 2015, Chap. 11, in this volume; Favre et al. 2015, Chap. 12, in this volume; Hollway and Koskinen 2015, Chap. 13, in this volume).

Here the term multilevel refers to the fact that in a stratified society, there are many superimposed levels of agency, each of them characterized by horizontal interdependencies that sociologists can examine as sets of 'local' social systems. Individuals acting on their own behalf in a highly personalized inter-individual system of interdependencies constitute a specific level of agency, with its own resources, commitments and rules. Interpersonal interdependencies consist of individuals tied together within or across organizations through cowork, advice, and friendship relationships (among others), as well as the rules that organize their social exchanges. The content of these relationships varies. This level of agency is different from that of the organizations to which these same individuals are affiliated. Interorganizational interdependencies are created most often by contractual agreements between organizations specifying the contributions, rights, and responsibilities of each organization in the pursuit of a particular objective; but they also depend on the existence of institutions that guarantee the credibility of these contractual agreements. Organizations, in which hierarchy reflects wider societal stratification,[1] are represented by their managers, who interact with other

---

[1] The term 'organizational society' has several dimensions. As Perrow (1991) puts it, it means that large-scale public or private organizations "absorb" societal functions that were/could be fulfilled by communities. It also means that a system of interdependent organizations, that are interlinked at the meso-level in a multi-level network, shapes the opportunity structure of citizens by coordinating various forms of "opportunity hoarding" (Tilly 1998). Finally it is also a metaphor to express that all individuals today play at both – individual and organizational – levels simultaneously and that domination in the Weberian sense is linked to the control of organizations as "tools with a life of their own".

managers from different organizations at this inter-organizational level of agency. At that level, interdependencies are much less personalized. Resources, commitments and rules are different in nature from those characterizing the inter-individual level of agency. This approach to the multilevel dimension of society is called the 'linked design' (Lazega et al. 2008), where the link between distinct but interdependent levels of collective agency is created by affiliation of members of one level in members of another level (typically individuals in organizations).

The boundaries of interorganizational and interpersonal networks are defined by the relevance of each kind of relationship in facilitating access to resources and coordinate collective action in the pursuit of particular objectives; but also by the social space in which the specific social processes driven by these relationships take place in a meaningful way (Lazega and Pattison 1999, 2001). Generic social processes (solidarities and discriminations, collective learning and socializations, social controls and conflict resolution, regulation and institutionalization, etc.) are, in part, the product of the regularities and relational infrastructures constructed in the management of interdependencies between actors in conflict or in cooperation. These processes facilitate the management of the dilemmas of collective action at each level of agency (Lazega 2001).

Multilevel Networks of Collective Action and Intermediary-Level Relational Infrastructure

It is useful to further elaborate the connection between the management of dilemmas of collective action and its multi-level dimension. At each level of collective agency (inter-individual or inter-organizational), individual or organizational actors have both convergent and divergent interests. Within organizations, interests are divergent between stakeholders, whether employees, owners or representatives of the owners (managers). The extent to which individuals sharing a common organizational interest nevertheless find it in their interest to free ride instead of bearing their share of the organizational effort, is a crucial issue for the success of collective action (Olson 1965). All try to promote their respective interests by using the organization as a "tool with a life of its own" (Selznick 1949). Divergent interests between stakeholders mean that collective action requires interest alignments to take place in negotiation. As political and strategic actors trying to promote their special interests and define priorities for the collective (Merton 1957; Crozier 1963; Krackhardt, 1990), members identify other members with common interests, build ties with each other (sharing resources and commitments in a reference group), and select representatives to promote their interests in negotiations. Alignment of interests between stakeholders in this negotiation can be relatively temporary and frequently renegotiated.

At each level of collective agency, relative success requires both social and political organization for each kind of stakeholder. With hierarchy derived from property rights, expertise, and control of resources in "the environment" (including outside networks), owners and management usually have disproportionately more means than employees to coordinate their efforts and to shape collective action. With asymmetrical power distribution coming from "exogenous," higher-level sources in the social stratification, they can force their subordinates to bear relatively higher costs of organizing with less gains per capita from successful collective action. Competition and collaboration take place both within and between organizations. Within and between levels of collective action, work for powerful stakeholders/principals is what triggers the negotiations for control of an actor's own sphere of work and protection of his or her own interests in individual/organizational competition. This is where the construction and/or maintenance of "social forms", i.e. relational infrastructure, becomes a step towards coordination within and between levels.

The same is true at the interorganizational level, where organizations as agents face similar dilemmas. Willingness and capacity to coordinate and align are crucial at that level too (Granovetter 1994; Lazega 1996). As theorized by Lazega and Mounier (2002) and shown by Brailly et al. (Chap. 10, in this volume), Comet (2007), Delarre (2005), Eloire (2010), Favre et al. (2015, Chap. 12, in this volume), Montes (2014), Oubenal (2013), Penalva (2010), Pina-Stranger and Lazega (2011), Varanda (2005), social processes also facilitate the management of the dilemmas of collective action at the inter-organizational level, especially by lowering the costs of coordination and cooperation among competitors in industries and markets (Lazega 2009).

Since control of "the environment" is crucial in the use of the organization as a "tool with a life of its own" to serve a stakeholder's view of collective interests, any kind of alignment of interests has both an intra-level dimension and a cross-level dimension. Controlling outcomes at one level increases the capacity to control outcomes at another level, usually downwards. From this perspective, a social phenomenon must be observed at several different levels of collective action, separately and jointly. Superposed levels of agency are diachronically related, although they do not often evolve in sync. For example, in a global market, inter-organizational ties can be arms-length long-distance relationships and deals between two companies dependent on (or are embedded in) inter-individual social relationships (Brailly et al. Chap. 10, in this volume; Favre et al. 2015, Chap. 12, in this volume).

Dynamics of such multilevel systems of collective agency assume, as also suggested by Berends et al. (2011) or Grossetti (2011), that the evolution of networks at one level of collective action is influenced by that of another level of collective action, and the other way around in recursive ways. Such dynamics can be considered to be the outcome of a meta-process bringing together both individuals and organizations, in which the evolution of one level explains in part (in causal terms) the evolution of the other. Level 1 relationships can emerge as a result of the emergence of level 2 relationships. Actors of level 1 may be able under certain circumstances to change the structure of level 2, especially by bringing an intermediary level into the picture, a substructure such as workgroups between which individuals move. Such substructures include individuals and are capable of collective action. They are included in the organization, and therefore in the inter-orgnizational level of collective action. This kind of intermediary level substructure – including social forms such as status and niches – represent a lever and the locus of co-constitution between levels.

To take into account this vertical complexity of the social world, it is necessary to differentiate and articulate these levels, and their respective dynamics, in measurements and models. This not only makes the analysis of individual goals, relations and conflicts inseparable, but distinct, from that of organizational goals, relations and conflicts. It also adds a problem that we will call a problem of "synchronization" between levels (Lazega and Penalva 2011). Synchronization is a task of scheduling and coordinating individual and collective efforts over time. Social sciences are currently struggling to combine multilevel and dynamic approaches to social phenomena at the meso-level. A first step in the study of the systems dynamics of multi-layered interdependencies was to propose a structural form for articulating these levels that examines separately the oppositions and interdependences at each level; and that articulates them based on the systematic information on the affiliation of each individual at the first level (inter-individual) to one of the organizations of the second level (inter-organizational).

Synchronization of Temporalities Within and Across Different Levels of Collective Agency

From the perspective of a theory of collective action that takes time into account in a systematic way, synchronization takes place when individuals who perform their tasks need to reorganize their activities in order to coordinate and keep in pace with each other, while at the same time coordinating across levels with the ongoing demands of the various organizations in which they are respectively affiliated. Synchronization refers to coordination of different temporalities (short term and long term for example) and rhythms characterizing collective activities at each level separately and at both levels jointly.[2] It is carried out through investments in resources (of all kinds, including time and energy, for example) in activities, relationships and affiliations when trying to stabilize these rhythms.

These investments are made by actors who try to keep or reshape their opportunity structure. Indeed synchronization as stabilization or as inducement of change at one's own level or across levels, below or above, depends on the capacity of individuals to maintain/build a relational infrastructure made of social forms at an intermediary level. Relational infrastructure refers to regularities in relationships that make sense from the perspective of both the individual and from the perspective

---

[2] Each level in multilevel systems of collective agency has its own temporalities: rhythms of self-maintenance and rhythms of actions. In fact one could argue that a level of collective agency exists because it has its own temporality. I thank David Chavalarias for this insight.

of the group: it includes in particular vertical and horizontal social differentiations such as social status and social niches. Relationships are defined as both channels in which resources flow between exchange partners (economic dimension), and commitments between these exchange partners (moral and symbolic dimension). Relational definition of social status refers, for example, to kinds of centrality in the networks of these actors. Relational definition of social niches refers to close relationships with actors similar in terms of relational profiles, i.e. (approximately) structurally equivalent actors. A social niche makes sense in a system of niches reflecting a role system, i.e. a form of division of work at the collective level (White et al. 1976) in which individuals think that they know their place. As defined here, such social forms represent the intermediary level between collective agency at the inter-individual level and collective agency at the inter-organizational level.

Saying that synchronization depends on a relational infrastructure at an intermediary level is equivalent to saying that actors coordinate across levels by creating and maintaining a structure that helps them filter and transform opportunities into locally available and appropriate resources. The presence and use of the right horizontal differentiations (a system of social niches) and vertical differentiations (heterogeneous forms of status) improves actors' chances of stabilizing this synchronization between levels and thus diminish its costs, for individuals and for collectives. Their absence increases the costs of synchronization at both levels. Members of niches share resources that are needed to keep pace and manage the intensity of change. Status helps in defining the rhythm at both levels. Social forms are attempts to structure the context in one's interactions, gaining power, shaping structure, organizing serendipity in a Mertonian sense. Relational infrastructure is made, among other ingredients, of relationships and can be identified using network analyses.

Multilevel forms of agency thus depend on synchronizations at the meso level, and stabilization of synchronization is made easier when actors invest in relationships as resources and commitments needed to build or maintain this relational infrastructure of social forms. The latter can help combine different temporalities, such as long term and short term. Many unsuccessful investments in relationships are "sunk" costs of synchronization. For others they are boosting or lifting in the sense that they help create or use these relational infrastructures; the latter become intermediary level entities providing leverage: they can later become full-fledged formal organizations combining short and long term decisions so as to harness the benefits of both opportunism and staying capacity for actors who control them as tools. Dynamics of multilevel networks help track these efforts and their outcomes. For example in trade fairs such as that examined by Brailly et al. (Chap. 10, in this volume) or by Favre et al. (2015, Chap. 12, in this volume), sales representatives in a trade fair need to create social ties to each other in order to transform the opportunities that come attached into contracts that will be signed by their respective companies. The temporalities of creation or maintenance of steady social ties with sales representatives from other companies and that of signing contracts between companies are not the same. Synchronizing the temporalities of creation of new personal professional contacts (short term in the trade fair, long term over many trade fairs the same year) with the temporality of signature and enforcement of contracts (longer term depending on organizational procedures that are triggered in trade fairs but become independent of them) is an issue of synchronization between levels of collective agency. Status and niches are key relational infrastructures helping competing sales representatives selecting each other for cooperation in finding exchange partners and sign contracts (Brailly et al. 2015). Over time, interpersonal relations in such niches can become stronger and more durable than affiliations, leading for example to mobility of members from one firm to another (Lazega 1996).

When society depends on short-sighted markets that are built and dominated by gigantic and well-coordinated organizations (private and public), social ties that are needed to stabilize synchronization (and reduce transaction costs) can only be built by individuals already strongly endowed with relational capital that is well managed in such relational infrastructures; while individuals without much relational capital and infrastructure are kept out of contracting until/unless they make successful efforts to integrate socially in the organized system supporting the market. Either way, companies usually have the power to dump these social costs of stabilizing synchronization on their individual members and on society at large – that is expected to take care of the victims of the system. From the individual perspective, incurring the social costs of stabilizing synchronization (without a strong relational infrastructure providing leverage) is equivalent to making huge efforts that will end up being sunk costs. Thus abandoning social organization to short-sighted markets raises the issue of inequalities in the face of dumping such costs of synchronization on individuals. This constitutes an important and not so visible societal problem that can only be further understood by designing and mobilizing methods able to account for the dynamics of multilevel networks and to measure hidden social costs of stabilization of synchronization between stratified levels of collective agency. This chapter is a very initial and exploratory framing of the study of these dynamics of co-evolving levels and synchronization with intermediary level relational infrastructures.[3]

There are many levels in actors' contexts, beyond the organizational one. However for the purpose of this chapter it is sufficient to consider two plus the intermediary level of relational infrastructures. The intermediary level is created by actors who establish new relationships and social forms, new groups and new hierarchies within or beyond the boundaries of an organization in which they are affiliated, thus trying to reshape and expand their opportunity structure beyond the limitation imposed upon them by pre-existing structures of collective action. In an illustration below, half of the observed population of highly competitive scientists deploy "independentist" strategies, i.e. all their new personal ties are beyond the constraining perimeter predefined by their organization's inter-organizational network, with no overlap between the two levels. If/when successful, the kind of

---

[3]There is some analogy here with the vision outlined by Courgeau (2003, 2004) on the joint importance of dynamics (in his case, represented by event history) and multilevel approaches.

new organization that they might create by transforming their social niche into a new laboratory (thus restructuring the inter-organizational level) would not establish easy inter-organizational ties with their previous laboratory. In addition, observations suggest that this "independence" takes them, over time, close to nowhere in terms of further achievements.

In this chapter, I first look at basic characteristics of superposed levels of collective action as approached by the linked design in network analysis. I then argue that efforts to synchronize the temporalities of these levels create the energy for intra- and inter-organizational mobility as possible emancipation from constraints imposed by one's prior affiliations. This mobility in turn produces relational turnover for these members and this turnover is managed by the creation of the new relational infrastructure, i.e. a specific form of social status. Indeed, actors can experience organizational mobility and relational turnover (OMRT) as constraints and opportunities; to some extent they attempt to use OMRT to reshape this structure using such social forms and relational infrastructure. Using the energy created by multilevel structures requires attempts to use these social forms and relational infrastructure to challenge and change existing organizational structures. This chapter assumes that some uses of social forms such as niches and status are both instruments of restructuration attempts across levels and building blocks for cross-level synchronization. In the example of the construction or emergence of status as a social form in the dynamics of an intra-organizational advice network, provided in a case study, producing status for selected actors also allows the latter to reshape a system of places in this organization via the creation of new social "positions." Thus movement is shown to lead to a reshuffling of members of the organization across a new set of places and to a new kind of stability.

Finally OMRT created by multilevel structures and the synchronization of their different temporalities is construed as context for social processes helping members manage the dilemmas of collective action that characterizes the organizational society. It is important to mention that as costs of creation and maintenance of social forms (niches and status as relational infrastructure), synchronization costs will thus include human and social resources invested in adapting the social processes of one level to those at levels above and below. In particular examples will be provided of social processes such as collective learning or regulation using the metaphor of the 'multilevel spinning top' applied to institutional change and emergence. In addition, as already mentioned, incurring synchronization costs will be rewarding (in terms of managing constraints, learning and regulation) for some players; for others, they will be sunk costs. Such differences are only slightly visible in current studies of social inequalities. A dynamic and multilevel network approach to social life changes the measurements of these socio-economic costs and inequalities precisely by introducing systematic positioning, mobility, and relational turnover into the picture. Combining the work of Harrison White (1970) and Tom Snijders (1996, 2005) helps make these synchronization costs measurable and more generally redefine the social costs of living in an organizational and market society.

Multilevel Structures: Superposed Levels of Collective Agency

The multi-level dimension of social phenomena can be approached as the superposition of two systems of interdependencies, one inter-organizational, the other inter-individual. Attempts at solving this problem of joint examination include Breiger's "dual" approach (1974) of bipartite or two-mode networks. When a fixed set of actors belongs to a fixed set of organizations, it is possible to derive multiple memberships from inter-individual networks (assuming that a connection exists between two individuals because they belong to the same organization), and from inter-organizational networks (assuming that a connection exists between two organizations because they share common members). The typical example is that of "interlocking" directorates, i.e. connections created between two companies when one or multiple individuals simultaneously belong to the boards of both companies. The networks, derived at two different levels, can also be reconstituted in a multi-level structure. However, this structure provides relatively poor insights into social phenomena because relationships are assumed and are symmetrical by construction.

A second important contribution in multilevel network analysis is that of Fararo and Doreian (1980). They generalize Breiger's (1974) and Wilson's (1982) formalisms in order to craft a "formal theory of interpenetration" of distinct entities such as individuals and groups. Seen from the perspective of their tripartite structural analysis our approach uses a network (call it P) of relations among persons, a network (call it G) of relation among groups, and a network (call it A) of affiliations of persons to groups. Unlike in Breiger's (1974) approach, only A is an affiliation network; P and G are networks of social relations and interdependencies (such as getting advice from a colleague, or agreements among organizations to share equipment, respectively). Fararo and Doreian's article points out many kinds of relations among levels (consider, for example, AGAT, the network of ties between people whose organizations have agreements to share equipment). Similar ideas are extended and used below, in particular to identify "overlaps" between the two kinds of networks (P and G via A) and reconstitute individual strategies of management of resources originating from both levels. Articulation of distinct levels of action can thus be partly accounted for, beyond bipartite structures, using a method called *structural linked design* (Lazega et al. 2008) that brings together networks of different levels using individuals' (mono or multiple) affiliation ties. Statistical analysis of such datasets pioneered by Wasserman and Iacobucci (1991) has reached a high level of sophistication (Wang et al. 2013), with multiple examples provided in this volume.

An Empirical Case of Co-constitution Without Conflation

In this approach, each complete network is examined separately, and then combined with that of the other level thanks to information about the membership of each individual in the first network (inter-individual) to one of the organizations in the second

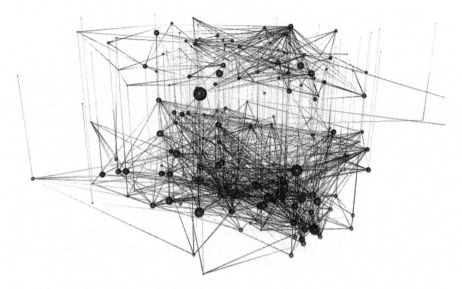

Fig. 3.1 Real-life multilevel network (Lazega et al. 2008) based on a linked-design approach studying an inter-individual network (*bottom* of the figure), an inter-organizational network (*top* of the figure) and vertical affiliation ties for the individuals in the organizations

network (inter-organizational). Work undertaken until now within this framework shows that dual/multiple positioning in superimposed systems of interdependencies makes it possible to formulate precise hypotheses about the relationship between members' complex positions in the structure and their achievements (measured at the individual level). It is especially the case when this positioning is articulated with the strategies of the actors. In this structural contextualization of action, the two levels of collective agency (one inter-individual and one inter-organizational) are in co-constitution of each other, but without being conflated (Archer 1982).

This approach can be illustrated using a case study in the sociology of science. In this case, the "elite" of French cancer researchers in 1999 was examined at both the inter-individual and the inter-organizational levels (Lazega et al. 2004, 2008, 2013; Barbillon et al. 2015). Figure 3.1 provides a graphical illustration of the structural linked design method.

In this context, we identified the systems of superimposed interdependencies, of the strategies of the actors who manage these interdependencies, and of their achievements measured at the individual level. No deterministic order is presupposed between position, strategy, and achievements, only an analytic one. This approach is particularly sensitive to the existence of inequalities between competing actors because these inequalities can render a given strategy more or less effective or "rewarding," depending on dual positioning as measurement of opportunity structure. This principle of dual-positioning individual actors (in the network of their inter-individual relationships and in the network of relationships between the organizations to which they belong) has two advantages.

Affiliations, Overlaps and Fish/Pond Relative Status

Firstly, dual positioning helps to construct new typologies of positions in the system, allowing for the characterization of individuals and the organizations in which they work in the same "dual entity." Dual positioning can correspond, for example, to a form of relative status, or double structural characteristics of the individual. It can be constructed, for example, by measuring both the centrality of the individual (in the inter-individual networks) and the centrality of the organization (in the inter-organizational networks) to which he or she belongs. Here the status of an actor is measured by his/her indegree centrality in the advice network of these researchers.

In metaphorical terms, members are identified, thanks to centrality scores, as big or little "fish"; organizations are identified likewise as big or small "ponds." This produces an endogenous partition of the population into four classes that are baptized, for a more intuitive understanding of this dual positioning, big fish in a big pond, big fish in a small pond, little fish in a big pond and little fish in a small pond (BFBP, BFSP, LFBP and LFSP). Belonging to one of the four categories locates actors in a meso-social space of opportunity structures, simultaneously inter-individual and inter-organizational. Measuring relative status of members and organizations in those terms provides a uniform basis for the interpretation of our results in the reconstitution of strategies of mobilization and articulation of heterogeneous resources at different levels.

Relational Strategies in Cross-Level Interdependencies

Secondly, this localization identifies strategies that individuals use to appropriate, to accumulate, and to manage both their own resources and the resources of their organizations. Actors vary in their capacity to use organizations as "tools with a life of their own". Some use a great deal of the resources of their organization, others much less. In particular, systems of interdependencies at different levels are controlled by actors of different hierarchical levels. Likewise, we can measure the overlap of relationships between individuals by those of their organizations. Information about in-degrees and out-degrees can also be used because incoming and outgoing ties are important in measurement of overlap between the relationships of the individual and that of organizations. It then becomes possible to articulate these relational strategies to the achievements of actors. It is in this respect that the contribution of a structural linked design is most original. As information about the relative status and relational strategies of individuals are used concurrently, we can eventually examine the achievement of individuals with explanatory variables different from those used in classic ecological analysis – which, to our knowledge, rarely measures the position of an actor in superposed systems of interdependencies and derived dual systems.

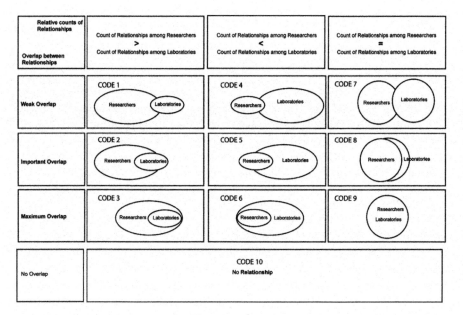

Fig. 3.2 Ten types of situations of overlap between ties of researchers and ties of their respective laboratories

In our case in point, all the researchers in this elite population are high performers in terms of the number of published articles. However when looking at their ways of managing their resource interdependencies at two different levels, especially by actors in categories other than the BFBP (i.e. the BFSP and all the Little Fish) we identify different relational strategies. The connection existing between membership in a class and strategies can be read in the level of overlap between the researcher's relationships and those of his/her laboratory, for outgoing as well as incoming ties. Figure 3.2 illustrates ten types of situations of overlap between ties of researchers and ties of their respective laboratories. Members' relational strategies are identified by types of overlap between interpersonal and inter-organizational networks.

A researcher may be cited (in these advice networks) by colleagues belonging to a laboratory that may or may not have inter-organizational ties with his/her own laboratory. The comparison of differences between these two types of relationships provides indications about the level of overlap between the two kinds of networks and about the behavior of actors in their organizations, thus offering insight into their strategies. In this case, we interpret incoming choices as indicators, for the laboratories, of their importance from a functional point of view, and, for researchers, of their prestige in terms of professional authority. We interpret outgoing ties as indicators of access. In the case of the laboratories, outgoing ties can be read as measures of access to exterior resources; for the researchers, they measure access to sources of learning and of personal support.

Overlaps, Relational Infrastructures, Entrapment or Emancipation

Using this typology, we can establish a correspondence between fish/pond category (BFBP, etc.), level of overlap understood as strategy, and achievement. Results show, firstly, that there are combinations that articulate little (or no) common prestige and little (or no) joint access to the same organizational resources. One could call these combinations "independent" strategies. It is not difficult to imagine concrete examples of behavior that reflects independent strategies. For example, a researcher representing an entire discipline in a scientific council might negotiate, in the name of the collective interest that he/she represents, to obtain resources for his/her own individual projects. Second, there are combinations that articulate little (or no) shared prestige but many of the common resources. One could call these combinations "individualist" strategies (benefiting from common resources but not sharing their prestige). Third, there are combinations that articulate a great deal of shared prestige but little (or no) common organizational resources. One could call these combinations "collectivist" strategies (constructing common prestige by using resources different from those of one's colleagues). Finally, there are combinations that articulate a great deal of shared prestige and common organizational resources. One could call these combinations "fusionist" strategies. The reconstitution of this typology of strategies yields insights into the relationship between position, strategy, and achievement.

Our analyses show that collectivist strategies are used by the big fish more often than by the little fish. In other words, the bigger the fish, the greater the overlap between the relationships of researchers and the relationships of their respective laboratories. Big fish know how, and are able, to use patronage to accumulate resources in their laboratory. Among the LFBP, the majority have strongly individualist strategies. The LFSP have no fusionist strategies and a very high proportion of independent strategies. Among this group, one finds a nearly complete separation between the relationships of researchers and those of laboratories, whether for outgoing or incoming ties. Their laboratories may also offer resources to which they do not have direct access or that they do not use. The LFSP often find themselves, relationally speaking, "trapped outside" their own organization, unable to build new relational infrastructures using this organization's resources. Following an independent strategy does not seem to benefit anyone, especially not the junior researchers who use it quite often.

Big fish do not seem more prone to use individualist strategies than the little fish. The only marked difference is the more frequent use of collectivist strategies, but also of fusionist strategies (although in very small numbers). The difference in the use of independent strategies is between the little and the big fish. Little fish – perhaps because of lower access to laboratory/organizational resources – follow an independent strategy much more often than big fish (66 % compared to 34 %). Also it is not the BFBP that most often use collectivist and fusionist strategies, but the BFSP; the latter are more often directors who can easily "sacrifice" their resources for the collective or, on the contrary, use the resources of the laboratory for their own interest, sometimes, for example, taking credit for other members' work. But due to the scarcity of resources of their smaller organization (sometimes combined with their own seniority), they find themselves "trapped inside" and also unable to build new relational infrastructures outside (if this is a goal of theirs at all).

Finally, one can measure the way in which actors' strategies are associated with achievement levels for researchers who are not BFBP, i.e. who are endowed with less social resources. Among researchers with increasing impact factor scores who were LF, the individualist strategy is by far the most efficient, especially for those in a big pond, in order to have a chance to catch up. One may explain this catching up by the fact that some LF, whether in big or small ponds, have learned, over time, to use the resources of their organization more efficiently to start building new relational infrastructures. This means that the LF benefit from building an individual network outside of the domain established by the network of their boss or laboratory. The same individualist strategy is counterproductive for the BFSP. The latter can attain very high levels of achievement (measured at the individual level) if he/she is the only one in the little pond to be able to appropriate the necessary resources and enter competition with the BFBP.

Dual Opportunity Structures, Asynchronies and "Emergence"

This specific result deserves to be highlighted. In this particular population, many junior members try to create ties outside the relational "territory" of their organization (and outside the network of their boss) in order to gain autonomy in their work. Here individualist strategies are rewarding in terms of achievement for actors who are not BFBP. They help them manage organizational constraints to try to reshape their opportunity structure. Of course actors do not always have an interest in leaving to create new collectives because support from their own current organizational environment can enrich them considerably with all sorts of resources. This is the case for example for members who benefit from a "network lift from dual alters" (as defined in Lazega et al. 2013).

If synchronization is necessary for the organization to benefit from the individual actions of its members, especially from individual actions that take place outside the organization, creating asynchronies is sometimes what helps individuals break free from patronage. Thus collective action at two vertically interdependent levels of agency can also be a story of "emancipation" from the influence of the other level, whether by catching up with this other level as it stands, or by creating a new emergent relational infrastructure (or sometimes more modestly, a new relational sub-structure) by investing in social forms, whether niches or status. The lag between the two can be considered the main source of change at both levels: structuration at one level drives structuration at the other in mostly conflicting, chaotic, and unequal ways. Time to adjust and adapt is not always available; enormous waste and disorganization may characterize the multilevel structuration process. When agents with status or entire niches "emancipate" and create their own organizations at the inter-organizational level, they try to take advantage of spatial and temporal gaps between agency at different levels. In the culture of our empirical case, structure and agency work together because some (young) members try to challenge the vested interests of their seniors or colleagues. In the example of 'field-configuring events' such as trade fairs (Favre et al. 2015, Chap. 12, in this volume), firms try to create or maintain themselves in socio-economic niches in their industry. Inter-organizational networks strongly influence inter-individual networks but not equally across all kinds of ties: long-term ties between individual members are influenced by the inter-organizational structure, while short-term ties much less so.

Emergent Corporate Entities: The Energy for/from Organized Mobility and Relational Turnover

Multilevel networks with collective agency at each level measure the meso-social order and the behavioral consequences and performance outcomes of actors (in the previous case, individual actors) in such superimposed systems of interdependencies. They show how, and the extent to which, new collective actors can be brought together (as a social construction, as opposed to just "emerging") out of previously existing ones, via relational and entrepreneurial emancipation from patronage beyond the boundaries of preexisting organizations.

Building and maintaining social forms as relational infrastructures is not an investment that takes place in a vacuum. Therefore synchronization costs must also include efforts that are spent to position oneself in the social space so as to be able to build or maintain these social forms. This positioning can be very complex. For example, creating ties to others beyond or outside the domain of one's organization can be a preparation for mobility (Lazega 2000). Indeed movements following paths that Harrison White (1970) calls "vacancy chains" can be seen as forms of rotation across systems of places that are often socially organized circuits, themselves constitutive of mobility. White calls such movements "mobility in loops" (1970:380). From his structural perspective, loops or systems of places are not all necessarily visible to actors involved, or even to managers of organizations who track, measure and sometimes steer other people's careers.

Internal or external labor markets were the first contexts identified by White for such circuits. The latter are also the focus of attention of citizens and professional observers daily: revolving doors for high status actors circulating from government to business, or the other way around, for example from investment banks to the Treasury; workers subjected to employment "flexibility" struggling to make such moves a reality step by step, and to keep limbos between jobs as short as possible; managers rotating their employees and themselves from one service to the other in the company, as in the case of associates assigned to different partners and clients of the firm in successive and heterogeneous task forces; directors moving from one corporate board to the other in a closed chain, or managers from one firm to the other (Checkley and Steglich 2007); sales representatives participating each year in dozens of similar and recurrent trade fairs of their industry (Brailly et al., forthcoming, 2015; Chap. 10; Favre et al., Chap 12, in this volume), or artists and gallery owners in the global art fairs circuit (Yogev and Grund 2012); or maids in the international labor markets (Gatmaytan 1997).

Around and beyond labor markets, there are also many such circuits: migrants in richer countries attract people from the same place of origin and sometimes return back to these places once they have acquired some status or once they have been overused sweeping floors and digging holes; students can spend semesters as part of their curriculum in universities of different countries before they come back to their alma mater; wider residential forms of mobility of individuals and their entire communities can be looked at, by geographers and sociologists, in the long run, as "mobility in loops" of neighborhoods, not to mention life cycle-related mobility when young adults move together into new places, then to bigger places when they have children, then to smaller ones when the children leave.[4]

The sociological and network literature has also looked, independently, at turnover in personal relational networks. An increasingly rich body of literature describes and models relational turnover using statistical tools designed for understanding network dynamics (Snijders 1996, 2005). Relational turnover is defined here as the set of changes observed in an actor's relationships between two moments in time (addition of new relationships, disappearance of previous relationships, maintenance of relationships, etc.). Dynamic models of co-evolution of behaviour and networks are based on analyses of this relational turnover in members' profiles and in the composition and structure of the collective. When we close our eyes and ignore conflicts of interests, is it because we became friends with people who tend to do the same thing and influence us in that direction, or is it because we chose, to begin with, friends among people who, like us, close their eyes when confronted with such a situation? It is often both, but each effect has a relative weight that can only be measured by observing and analysing behavioural changes and relational turnover over time. Without such analyses of relational turnover, explanations of concerted ignorance as social process remain untested.[5] Changing structural forms trigger changes in social processes downstream. All the main social phenomena – such as solidarity and exclusions, social control and conflict resolution, learning and socialization, regulation and institutionalization – have a dynamic relational dimension, depend on relational infrastructures, established or emergent, and reshape opportunity structures.

---

[4]The term "place" is used here in a general sense to refer to a location that can be occupied by a single person in any formally organized circuit that can be geographical and/or organizational. It is to be distinguished from the term "position" (White et al. 1977), i.e. a set of structurally equivalent actors that we call a social niche (Lazega 2001) when the ties between actors in the position are dense. A position makes sense in a system of positions (or niches when the positions are dense) that differs from the system of places while always combined and coevolving with it (Lazega forthcoming). Space (contiguity) and network (connectivity), for example, are both different and related.

[5]Snijders' work in many ways inaugurates a new epistemology in the social sciences, whereby research measures, formalizes, and models the co-evolution between behaviour and interdependencies, between interdependencies and conflicts between actors, individual and collective, an approach in which one confronts models with reality and its measurements, i.e. where models, measurements and problematics truly co-evolve.

Thinking of actors as mobile suggests again that building social forms in (spite of) relational turnover increases the costs of synchronization for some actors more than for others. Once the social forms have been created, actors are in a better position to reshape their opportunity structure and reduce the costs of mobility across a new set of places. This is easier to see at the intra-organizational level, as exemplified below in a situation where centrality is synonymous of stability as in the eye of a storm. Synchronization costs must therefore be defined as efforts to build or maintain social forms, but measurements of such efforts must contextualize them, and keep track of and weigh the differential effect of socio-economic positions and mobilities on the outcomes of very different efforts invested by heterogeneous and unequal actors.

Often overlooked in the literature is the systematic, recursive, and transformative link between the two realities (mobility across systems of places and relational turnover) and its implications for social life. There are connections between these movements, as actors switch places in these circuits, and change, at least in part, in their respective sets of relationships, that can be called their respective relational capital. There is also an effect of the latter change on the evolution of the system of places itself, an evolution that is only visible if places are not considered as purely contextual and exogenous, but as endogenized by members and thus as endogenous to the mechanisms under examination. The connection between movement and relational capital is often explored in part and in depth in specific areas of social life. Migration networks are, for example, prototypical: because separations of movers and stayers in migrations across continents are often devastating for individuals and social communities, the focus in such studies is rightly on coping with costs of leaving families behind, marginality, loneliness, creation and management of new relationships by individuals striving for social mobility and assimilation, their own or that of their children. Synchronization costs are then measured at the individual level. But the mechanics of this link and the effects of such movements on the system of places itself, its structure and governance, i.e. on the stability and change of the system and the opportunity structure that it represents for its members, also deserve to be explored, along with their social costs. Hence the measurement of synchronization costs at the level of emergent relational infrastructures.

"OMRT structuration" or transformation is a possible label for the complex dynamics that drive actors – individual and organizational – to change part of their relational and social capital as they switch places in such relatively closed, partly overlapping loops, whether formally institutionalized or still emergent, thus triggering social processes that may, under specific circumstances, reshape the initial opportunity structure of some, but not all, members of the setting. Each domain of social and economic life, and every corresponding field of research in the social sciences, has its OMRT structuration processes. We define OMRT structuration as the dynamic link between places and positions. We use the label "organized" to qualify mobility because both social actors and the social system create paths and rules for movements that are not allowed to be random.

Whether physical or social or both, these articulated movements and changes represent an important basis of social structure, order and inequalities in the organizational society. They are created by the social organization of these *milieux* and end up, under conditions that remain to be spelled out, restructuring these *milieux*, taking some members Somewhere and others Nowhere. This is not simply a recursive movement between two separate poles influencing each other because they compete in doing the same thing. OMRT dynamics involve more complex evolutions because they impact fundamental social processes (such as socialization, particularistic solidarity and discrimination, social control and conflict resolution, regulation and institutionalization, etc.). Indeed these processes all have a relational dimension and all depend on structural forms that facilitate their deployment (Lazega 2001, 2003, 2012).

As seen in the previous section, the energy for OMRT comes from multilevel structures to begin with. If organizations are open systems, then they are part of inter-organizational systems of interdependencies (observed as networks) and as such have dynamics with a certain level of closure. Movement makes sense from below and from above: from the perspective of individual actors who orient their actions to multiple levels when trying to reshape their opportunity structure, but also as driven by the fact that meso-social agency takes place in superimposed systems of interdependencies and collective agency. In such systems, the temporalities of each level are different. Actors try to take advantage of spatial and temporal gaps between agency at different levels. Each level must adjust and adapt to the evolution of the other level. Synchronization efforts, however, are more costly for one level than for the other, i.e. for actors without relational infrastructures than for actors who managed to build them. The level that is dominated will be forced to pay for the costs of synchronization. This can take the form of extra expenses of resources in catching up efforts.

In the organizational society, much energy is indeed spent catching up in status competitions imposed from above and/or self-imposed from below. Catching up with what? The answer is as much with catching up with the Joneses next door, as with keeping pace and adjusting to constraints coming from above to keep one's status. The power differentials generated by the multilevel structure of the organizational society are used as a source of energy through the promise of sharing of power and status. Each step of these catching up actions is what produces the energy for OMRT structuration.

From Place to Position to a New System of Places: A Spinning Top Model of Synchronization Benefits in Collective Learning

A second empirical illustration[6] can be useful to understand the necessity of looking at the dynamics of the network at each level in order to explore synchronization costs via relational infrastructure in an organizational context. This is a case study

---

[6]For a detailed presentation of the qualitative and quantitative study of this institution and its results, see Lazega et al. (2006, 2011, 2012; Lazega and Mounier 2009).

used to explore an intra-organizational relational turnover created by mobility. It is based on an organizational and longitudinal network study of advice-seeking among judges at a courthouse in a jurisdiction dealing with commercial litigation and bankruptcies in the French economy. These judges are elected with 14-years term limits. The court is composed of 20 (then 21 right after the second measurement of the network) specialized and generalist Chambers dealing with very heterogeneous forms of commercial litigation (company law, European community law, international law, unfair competition, multimedia and new technologies, etc.) and bankruptcies. Judges follow a work schedule that rotates them, on a yearly basis, from one Chamber to another. The rotation policy of judges across Chambers is meant to prevent corruption or conflicts of interests.

Tasks are complex and judges have discretion in many areas of business law. Disagreements abound about solutions for many legal problems. Commercial litigation is very diverse and conflict resolution often depends on knowledge of the specific industry and business in which the conflict takes place. These judges thus use each other for advice intensively in order to manage these uncertainties intra-organizationally, by tapping into the expertise and experience of their diverse set of colleagues.

In this study, 240 judges (all lay, voluntary and elected judges coming from the local business community) were interviewed altogether about their advice-seeking relationships within the court. Three measurements of this complete network were obtained over 5 years. Longitudinal analyses of the advice network among these lay judges, using Snijders' (1996, 2005) models, tease out a cyclical process of centralization, decentralization and recentralization of the network over time. Analyses and ethnography show that movements in this organizational system of places create forms of status that are used by specific members to change the system of places itself. It is useful to represent the dynamics of advice networks and of collective learning with the image of a spinning top. The metaphor represents cyclical dynamics through which individuals attain epistemic status over time to displace incumbent status holders at the top of the hierarchy and reproduce the persistent hierarchical organizational structure, while modifying the system of places.

In many organizations examined by researchers,[7] advice-seeking converges towards senior and recognized members and reflects a process of epistemic alignment on such members who gained the "authority to know," who provide social approval for specific decisions, and who contribute to the integration of the organization because they link the individual, group and organizational levels. This alignment is a key ingredient of intra-organizational collective learning. A status hierarchy provides a social incentive for actors to share their knowledge and experience with others, thus helping to explain the social organization of the learning process. Because advice networks are shaped by such status issues, they are

---

[7]For a review of the literature on advice seeking as social exchange, see Lazega (2014a).

usually highly centralized. They exhibit a pecking order that often closely follows the hierarchical structure of the organization. Members of formal organizations rarely declare that they seek advice from "people below" in this pecking order.

A spinning top model accounts for the dynamics of advice networks in organizations by providing a guiding metaphor for understanding intra-organizational collective learning: this process depends on the capacity of the organization to generate the pecking order that manages to remain stable while advice ties among other members of the organization are subject to rapid turnover – for example because of the rotation policy, because of career movement, because of the need to find new knowledge that old advisors cannot provide (Ortega 2001; Argote et al. 2005).

This spinning top heuristic brings together at least three components: a rotating body, a rotation axis, and a fragile equilibrium that depends, in parts, on characteristics of the previous components.[8] Time is taken into account through rotation movement and speed. We think of the rotating body as the learning organization. The rotation axis can represent the pecking order, i.e. the emergent hierarchy of members with epistemic status. These members have the "authority to know" in the organization. Rotation rules across intra-organizational boundaries and through status differences summarize formal structure. The fragile equilibrium created by the rotation movement represents the structural condition for learning collectively in the organization. This equilibrium itself depends on the stability of the rotation axis and the shape of the organization.

The endogenous evolution of advice networks is characterized by three interrelated moments (Lazega et al. 2006, 2011). Firstly, the centrality of members with high epistemic status varies over time. At first, it tends to be reinforced. Central members become increasingly central, in a Mertonian Matthew effect close to "preferential attachment": those who are sought out become increasingly sought out because they have built a reputation. Members who seek advice are increasingly under the impression that selecting these sources of advice is safe and legitimizes their knowledge claims, and that this choice signals an increase in relative status. Concentration of epistemic authority increases with the centralization of advice networks: learning becomes increasingly dependent on a smaller and smaller number of sources of authorized knowledge.

Secondly, however, in real life organizations, this centralization creates an overload for members with high epistemic status. They therefore tend to manage this overload by sharing a part of their epistemic status – through recommendations,

---

[8] We define these terms metaphorically and loosely: the rotating body represents the population of judges switching places once a year in a circular system of places as in a carrousel or in White's (1970) "mobility in loops." The rotation axis represents metaphorically a pecking order, i.e. a vertical differentiation between the judges and a form of epistemic status reached by the most central "epistemic leaders". This rotation axis can be pictured as the shaft of the spinning top providing the angular momentum thanks to which the spinning top stays up and represents vertical differentiation helping learning take place in a system where stability comes from movement.

i.e. by redirecting advice seekers to other sources. When advice provided by the very few super-central advisors becomes inaccessible or very rare, members turn to these other advisers, creating new epistemic stars. Sharing epistemic status, a form of delegation, increases the number of central advisers and decreases the centralization of the network. Thirdly, however, the increase in the number of central members with high epistemic status in the organization creates a problem of epistemic conflicts, consensus and coordination among epistemic authorities. If their co-orientation is easy, equilibrium is established. If not, conflicts between epistemic authorities trigger a reverse process of re-centralization. When the danger for collective action is that there are "too many chefs," i.e. epistemic leaders, some withdraw or retire, others are sidelined by one form or another of disqualification. As their numbers decrease, it becomes easier at the top to recreate consensus around a common definition of the situation, to provide coherent social benchmarks for homogeneous judgments of appropriateness and coordination.

These dynamics of centralization and decentralization in advice networks may not be purely endogenous (in the sense that overload through centralization leads to the super-central advisors creating new epistemic stars by redirecting advice requests to surrogates): indeed the patterning of advice relations can be influenced by the content of what one is seeking advice about, and by external events that may make one potential advisor a better source of advice than another. However the existence of this endogenous dimension of the process provides at least one mechanism explaining (see below) how a category of super-central elites is able to stabilize its position and stay at the top of the structure thanks to strong competition for epistemic authority and status.

This picture is heuristic for several reasons. First, it shows that time is important in allowing organizations to select members with epistemic status. Epistemic status builds up by reputation for expertise, by the capacity to provide quality control without raising too many controversies or conflicts of definition, by the trained capacity to speak legitimately on behalf of the collective. Acquiring this status takes effort and time. The authority to know is produced by long-term individual and collective investments that can be ruined if members with epistemic status leave or behave too opportunistically. The equilibrium reached by the spinning top thus suggests that members with status and epistemic authority in the organization have a strong incentive to keep their status and authority over time, even at some extra expense, to avoid the loss of the advantages attached to their relative standing.[9]

Second, this heuristic also suggests that the stability reached by the spinning top is fragile. The number of members with epistemic status varies over time. As already mentioned, we can think of several reasons why this number increases and decreases. One reason is that members tend to choose advisors that they perceive to

---

[9] About the costs of acquiring and maintaining status in organizations, see Frank (1985).

be the most popular (i.e. already chosen by a large number of colleagues). Members sought out by many other members tend to build a reputation; selecting them is perceived to be safe and legitimate. As emphasized by a micropolitical perspective, everyone seeks status and believes that they will reach a higher status; access to advisors higher up in the ladder becomes in itself a sign of relative status. This triggers the Matthew effect in which a member highly sought out in time t1 becomes even more intensively sought out in time t2.

Another reason is that this behavior creates an overload of requests for advice from a small number of highly central advisors with high epistemic status. Highly sought out advisors often manage this overload by delegating, i.e. referring the advice seeker to other advisors. This management of overload threatens the stability of the pecking order in the sense that it brings in new central advisors and requires coordination among the elites in order to avoid destructive status competition and definition conflicts between too many chefs. In turn, this strategy triggers either formal efforts of coordination among the elites or a new reduction in the number of advisors with high epistemic status through withdrawal of central advisors who become unavailable (due to retirement or delegitimization). This oscillation threatens the stability of the pecking order, with both positive and negative effects on intra-organizational learning.

Centralization of the advice network increases then decreases over time, as members with epistemic status try to avoid overload at the risk of accepting conflicts with other elite advisors. The existence of this oscillation was established using dynamic analyses of the evolution of this network. Figure 3.3 visualizes the evolution of this network using comparative statics.

An important outcome of these dynamics becomes apparent in this Figure. Highly central judges belonging to the core managed to use their relational infrastructure to create a new chamber for themselves in the chamber carrousel of this court, and to modify the division of work between chambers. Using both their formal and informal position and status, they manage to stay on top of the cyclical movement and to create a new formal place. This process suggests that when turnover is organized systematically in an organization, actors in a position to increase their status (thanks to an increase in stability paradoxically due to the movement itself) may also change the architecture of the whole organisation, i.e. create new places and new collective actors. OMRT processes have thus led some of these actors to reshape their setting as well as everyone else's opportunity structure in it. This reshaping may not be spectacular, but it is real and related to the fact that positions are not places and that the system of places can evolve.

Finally, the reasoning applied to examine a process of collective learning can also be applied to a process of regulation and to provide a new approach to the emergence of new institutions, for example a multilevel spinning top model of institutional emergence.

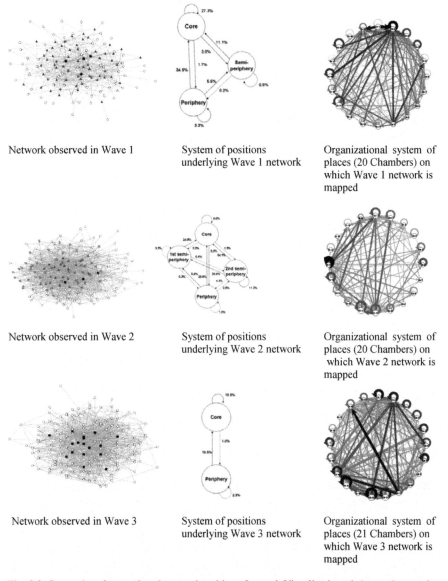

Network observed in Wave 1 — System of positions underlying Wave 1 network — Organizational system of places (20 Chambers) on which Wave 1 network is mapped

Network observed in Wave 2 — System of positions underlying Wave 2 network — Organizational system of places (20 Chambers) on which Wave 2 network is mapped

Network observed in Wave 3 — System of positions underlying Wave 3 network — Organizational system of places (21 Chambers) on which Wave 3 network is mapped

Fig. 3.3 Dynamics of networks, places and positions. Legend: Visualization of observed networks during the three waves of a longitudinal survey, the structure of blocks or system of positions underlying the network, and the carrousel of Chambers on which the network has been mapped with ties received. Thanks to Martin Mader for mapping the network on the system of chambers. Stochastic blockmodels (Snijders and Nowicki 2004) are taken from Lazega et al. (2011). They represent cyclical dynamics (centralisation – decentralisation – recentralisation) of change in a core-periphery structure characterizing the collective learning process in this organization. Network Wave 1, 3 blocks: 'Core' (4 *black squares*), 'semi-periphery' (*grey triangle*), and 'periphery' (*white circles*). Reduced graph three blocks, with intra- and inter-block densities. Network Wave 2, four blocks, 'core' (3 *black squares*), 'first semi-periphery' (*upward grey triangles*), 'second semi-periphery' (*downward grey triangles*), and 'periphery' (*white circles*). Reduced graph, four blocks, with intra- and inter-block densities. Network Wave 3, two blocks, 'Core' (17 *black squares*), 'Periphery' (*white circles*). Reduced graph, two blocks, with intra- and inter-block densities

It is indeed useful to frame a complex social phenomenon such as the emergence or the social construction of a new institution by taking into account that it takes place at several levels simultaneously. For example, the emergence of a judicial institution, the Unified Patent Court in Europe (Lazega 2012b), is an application of this multilevel spinning top model. It helps explain how a small network of institutional entrepreneurs with multiple and inconsistent forms of status uses, in its lobbying activity, multilevel networks and their dynamics to acquire the staying capacity and subsequent influence that is needed to frame, build and entrench a transnational institution. The image of a spinning top represents this process heuristically.

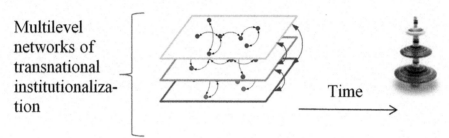

This image of a multilevel spinning top combines dynamic and multilevel perspectives on social phenomena such as the definition and institutionalization of new norms. It is possible to find in this metaphor mobility over time in a system of places and more or less supervised circulations between places at this intermediary level (as in many labor markets in which competition is made increasingly open as one goes down the social stratification); but also changing relationships between these intermediary levels as themselves driven by relational turnover created by mobilities (Lazega et al. 2006). This set of processes brings together networks of different levels in which individuals' affiliations are thus dependent of mobilities in loops. Evolution in a multilevel social space means that, from this perspective, dynamics are related to the third, intermediary level. To understand the dynamics of coevolution between collective action at two levels, it is necessary to bring in an intermediary – but nevertheless, in our view, generic third level.

In the case of this judicial institution, the main idea of this mechanism is that when such individual, oligarchic and dynamic positions of institutional entrepreneurs are stabilized by a supportive inter-organizational network (hence the crucial dynamics of the multilevel dimension of the process), these entrepreneurs are able to maintain their centrality and interactions long enough to surf on – if not to avoid altogether – the unpredictable and conflictual politics of an electoral process. This mechanism thus helps them succeed in their institutionalization efforts in spite of being a small collegial oligarchy – a process that may characterize the contemporary European 'democratic deficit': the multilevel structure helps actors keep their initial advantage of institutional entrepreneurs in selecting rules that will become priority rules for this institution. Here dynamics of multilevel networks represent a mechanism that mobilizes superposed levels of collective agency, interpersonal and inter-organizational at least, i.e. two meso levels that are added to the traditional national and international levels of agency and complexity.

Using these insights it is now possible to come back to the meaning of dynamics of multilevel networks and synchronization costs at the macro level.

Dynamics of Multilevel Networks, Synchronization Costs and Social Inequalities

Cross-level interaction between individuals and organizations is vital in the organizational society. This chapter first looked at basic characteristics of superposed levels of collective action as approached by linked design network analysis. Synchronization refers here to social coordination between the dynamics of each level in which actors are positioned. The issue of synchronization in the dynamics of such multilevel structures arises permanently, for example when individual and/or collective actors attempt to restructure the contexts of their interactions and manage the constraints that these contexts impose upon them through new efforts to redesign their opportunity structures at both levels simultaneously.

In a multilevel context where each level has its own temporality, synchronization costs are efforts – made by individuals and by organizations, in very asymmetrical ways – to keep in pace with each other by reshaping a structure of opportunity and constraints. To specify the nature of these costs, the Simmelian notion of 'social form' is a good approximation, i.e. a sedimented vertical or horizontal differentiation of the social world at the intermediary level. Such forms create a relational infrastructure that helps individual members or categories of stakeholders with coordination of their actions, with identification of their common interests, with selection of strategies and representatives. Social forms also help collectives with driving social processes that facilitate the management of dilemmas of collective action. In a Mertonian perspective (1957), social status and social niches can be identified as the main social forms that filter individual actions into social processes making collective action possible.

From a bottom-up perspective, social forms built or maintained at the lower level are also intermediary structures that can help actors create new organizations at the next, upper level in the hope to manage the constraints that this upper level imposes upon them. Thus intermediary levels between generic levels of collective agency are also generic, but as levers. Synchronization costs that are not part of such leverage efforts are usually sunk. Creating and maintaining such forms can transform these synchronization costs – as incurred by individuals and collectives in the organizational society – into rewarding investments. Status and organization provide a presence and staying capacity, if not necessarily a "seat at the table," at the higher level of collective agency: a chance to format collective action and benefit from investments in the political process.

Structuration at one level drives structuration at the other, often in conflicting and unequal ways. Time to adjust and adapt is available to some, but not to others; waste and disorganization may characterize the multilevel structuration process.[10] In organizational societies, management practices based on time pressure can marginalize or exclude, make or break careers, open or lose markets, determine the distribution of power and status, influence the social processes that create innovations, strengthen or weaken inequalities, introduce or prevent change. Synchronization between levels by building and maintaining social forms to reshape one's opportunity structure is much more costly for some than for others, especially for actors who are forced to be mobile – unless they can use this mobility to create new advantageous social forms. Stabilizing synchronization costs is rewarding for actors with a strong relational infrastructure when these costs are either shared or dumped on others.

The organizational society is characterized by complex multilevel governance systems and rapid forms of collective action at the meso-social level that "absorb society" and externalize social costs (Perrow 1991). Supposing that multiple levels of collective action are nested does not imply that they evolve symmetrically and in stable sync. High costs of synchronization (building social forms to create new corporate entities) can be transferred to the other level when one level has the power to do so, which is the most frequent situation. The co-evolution of two levels is complex, partly disconnected and asynchronous, raising the issue of who will incur these costs of synchronization. Measuring such costs hidden in these dynamics will help monitor opportunity hoarding (Tilly 1998) in the organizational society and perhaps explain the robustness and resilience of such multilevel structures.

Reasoning in terms of OMRT dynamics is important at this stage because it helps understand how both stability and change in the system are created precisely by the movement that it organizes, directly or indirectly. Our purpose is not to argue that there is more such mobility now than in the past, but to argue that much of the effect of such mobility on the structuring of collectives has not been measured, particularly in terms of social inequality. The new attention to these OMRT dynamics is needed because these processes take new forms in contemporary society (Archer 2013, 2014; Lazega 2014b) and involve hidden costs. Intensity and speed of change matter more in everything; members are exposed to increasingly

---

[10]Since this creates dynamics of multilevel networks with different levels of agency, a new family of models is needed to account for such dynamics. This family of models can be a multilevel extension of Snijders (1996) model of dynamics of networks, using characteristics of level 2 network as set of exogenous factors in the evolution of level 1 network, and the other way around. Intermediary level relational infrastructures can be modelled as niches and status, but also using affiliation two-mode data, based on exogenously defined groups. The co-evolution of both level networks is added to the co-evolution of behavior and relational choices. In terms of model specification, new 'independent' variables from inter-organizational networks operate at the inter-individual level, and vice-versa. It is also worth proposing a multilevel version of Snijders' model of dynamics of networks, for example by introducing dual alters or induced potentials, i.e. extended opportunity structures (Lazega et al. 2013), into this formalism.

open competition as they go down the social hierarchy; forms of social control become increasingly intrusive.

OMRT transformation can in turn further change the social processes that help members use other levels of agency to manage the dilemmas of collective action at their own level. Synchronization has costs of adaptation to the other level and the costs of adjustments in dual and asynchronous opportunity structures can be shifted or dumped "downwards", on the weakest parts of the system (Lazega 2013). The metaphor of the spinning top used above to combine organized mobility, relational turnover and the emergence of status, is heuristic because it expresses the fact that some actors' movements and mobility often contribute to (re)create the stability and wealth of other actors, including the latters' capacity to acquire and capitalize resources (including accumulating status). When various forms of mobility slow down or accelerate, new people are left behind and distanced from multiple perspectives, reproducing or creating new social inequalities and hierarchies. Those in better positions in these hierarchies, who know how to use organizations as tools with lives of their own, do better than others because they can use social forms to navigate or even reshape the prior system of places to their advantage.

Relational capital of individuals and social capital of organizations have always been important determinants of inequalities (Breiger 1990), but they become even stronger determinants when the capacity of societies to adapt to changes and environments that they themselves have created depends on their OMRT dynamics. In this context, the dynamics produced by multilevel structures lead to new forms of stability and inequalities at the meso-level of society. Some are able to benefit from OMRT and obtain returns on their investments in synchronization, while others face forms of individual or collective insecurity that is increased by their relative weakness in controlling the multilevel dynamics of collective action, and are thus led to invest in synchronization costs without returns. Measuring hidden and relative costs of synchronization in these dynamics is equivalent to monitoring opportunity hoarding in the organizational society and providing an organizational view of inequality-generating mechanisms (Tilly 1998). Understanding how OMRT dynamics accomplish the recursivity of the structural transformations that they create at several levels requires understanding how social forms (status sets and systems of niches) are used strategically to transform investments in synchronization into benefits – or are not used in this way, leading to further costs. In short, measuring synchronization costs will help redefine the social costs of living in an organizational and market society, especially in relational, structural and political terms.

Looking at the changes in a system of places itself as driven by OMRT, and as an inequality-generating mechanism, means that places are no longer considered exogenous in the social sciences.[11] Changes in social processes that help members manage the dilemmas of collective action also take place in contexts, for example

---

[11] Although institutional locations may seem more important than geographical ones, the social sciences may only be able to endogenize systems of places, i.e. these forms of division of work,

of governance, increasingly defined by OMRT dynamics and (de)structuration that can be driven by residential, educational, professional forms of mobility. These dynamics can transform collective learning and regulation, as seen in the examples above, into secondary socialization (Brailly 2014; Favre 2014; Montes 2014) that helps members of society deal with these dilemmas (Lazega 2003, 2012). Contemporary public statistical datasets are ill-suited for the measurement of OMRT dynamics, relational infrastructure and synchronization costs in interaction with social stratification in the organizational society. Without a better knowledge of the meso-social level, individual meso-level profiles and meso-level inequalities and mechanisms, sociology is at risk of becoming socially irrelevant, unable to deal with the complexity of institutional changes triggered by many contemporary challenges. In this respect, much remains to be done.

References

Archer, M. S. (1982). Morphogenesis versus structuration: On combining structure and action. *British Journal of Sociology, 35*, 455–483.
Archer, M. S. (Ed.). (2013). *Social morphogenesis*. Dordrecht: Springer.
Archer, M. S. (Ed.). (2014). *Late modernity: Trajectories towards morphogenic society*. Dordrecht: Springer.
Argote, L., Kane, A., & Levine, J. (2005). Knowledge transfer between groups via personnel rotation: Effects of social identity and knowledge quality. *Organizational Behavior and Human Decisions Processes, 96*, 56–71.
Barbillon, P., Donnet, S., Lazega, E., & Bar-Hen, A. (2015). *Stochastic block models for multiplex networks: an application to networks of researchers*, arXiv.org>stat>arXiv:1501.06444.
Bathelt, H., & Glückler, J. (2011). *The relational economy: Geographies of knowing and learning*. Oxford: Oxford University Press.
Berends, H., Van Burg, E., & van Raaij, E. M. (2011). Contacts and contracts: Cross-level network dynamics in the development of an aircraft material. *Organization Science, 22*, 940–960.
Brailly, J. (2014), Coopérer pour résister: Interactions marchandes et réseaux multiniveaux dans un salon d'échanges de programmes de télévision en Europe Centrale et Orientale. Doctoral dissertation, University of Paris-Dauphine.
Brailly, J., & Lazega, E. (2012). Diversité des approches de la modélisation multiniveaux en analyses de réseaux sociaux et organisationnels. *Mathématiques et Sciences Sociales, 198*, 5–32.
Brailly, J., Favre, G., Chatellet, J., & Lazega, E. (forthcoming, 2015). Embeddedness as a multilevel problem: A case study in economic sociology. *Social Networks* (in press).
Breiger, R. L. (1974). The duality of persons and groups. *Social Forces, 53*, 181–190.
Breiger, R. L. (Ed.). (1990). *Social mobility and social structure*. Cambridge: Cambridge University Press.
Brennecke, J. & Rank, O. (2015). Knowledge networks in high- tech clusters: A multilevel perspective on interpersonal and inter-organizational collaboration. In E. Lazega, & T. A. B. Snijders (Eds), *Multilevel network analysis: Theory, methods and applications* (pp. 273–293). Cham: Springer.

---

with the help of specialists of spatial and organizational movement, i.e. geographers (Bathelt and Glückler 2011; Glückler 2012, 2013; Glückler and Hammer, 2012, forthcoming).

Checkley, M., & Steglich, C. E. G. (2007). Partners in power: Job mobility and dynamic deal-making. *European Management Review, 4*(2007), 161–171.
Comet, C. (2007). Capital social et profits des artisans du bâtiment: le poids des incertitudes sociotechniques. *Revue Française de Sociologie, 48*, 67–91.
Courgeau, D. (Ed.). (2003). *Methodology and epistemology of multilevel analysis* (Collection methodos). Dordrecht: Kluwer Academic Publishers.
Courgeau, D. (2004). *Du groupe à l'Individu: Synthèse multiniveau*. Paris: Éditions de l'INED.
Crozier, M. (1963). *Le Phenomène bureaucratique*. Paris: Seuil.
Delarre, S. (2005). La reproduction des groupes d'entreprises comme entités socio-économiques stables. *Revue Française de Sociologie, 46*, 115–150.
Eloire, F. (2010). Une approche sociologique de la concurrence sur un marché Le cas.des restaurateurs lillois. *Revue Française de Sociologie, 51*(3), 481–517.
Fararo, T. J., & Doreian, P. (1980). Tripartite structural analysis: Generalizing the Breiger-Wilson formalism. *Social Networks, 6*, 141–175.
Favre, G. (2014). *Des rencontres dans la mondialisation. Réseaux et apprentissages dans un salon de distribution de de programmes de télévision en Afrique sub-saharienne*. Doctoral dissertation, University of Paris-Dauphine.
Favre, G., Brailly, J., Bhatellet, J., & Lazega, E. (2015). Inter-organizational network influence on long-term and short-term inter-individual relationships: The case of a trade fair for TV programs distribution in sub-Saharan Africa. In E. Lazega, & T. A. B. Snijders (Eds), *Multilevel network analysis: Theory, methods and applications* (pp. 295–314). Cham: Springer.
Frank, R. H. (1985). *Choosing the right pond: Human behavior and the quest for status*. Oxford: Oxford University Press.
Gatmaytan, D. B. (1997). Death and the maid: Work, violence, and the Filipina in the international labor market. *Harvard Women's Law Journal, 20*, 229–262.
Glückler, J. (2012). Organisierte Unternehmensnetzwerke: Eine Einführung [Introduction to organized corporate networks]. In J. Glückler, W. Dehning, M. Janneck, & T. Armbrüster (Eds.), *Unternehmensnetzwerke. Architekturen, Strukturen und Strategien* (pp. 1–18). Heidelberg: Springer Gabler.
Glückler, J. (2013). The problem of mobilizing expertise at a distance. In P. Meusburger, J. Glückler & M. el Meskioui (Eds.), Knowledge and the economy (pp. 95–109). Knowledge and space: Vol. 5. Dordrecht: Springer.
Glückler, J., & Hammer, I. (forthcoming). Organized networks and the creation of network goods, University of Heidelberg.
Granovetter, M. (1994). Business groups. In N. Smelser & R. Swedberg (Eds.), *Handbook of economic sociology*. Princeton/New York: Princeton University Press/Russell Sage Foundation.
Grossetti, M. (2011). «L'espace à trois dimensions des phénomènes sociaux. Echelles d'action et d'analyse», *SociologieS*, http://sociologies.revues.org/index3466.html
Hollway, J., & Koskinen, J. (2015). Multilevel bilateralism and multilateralism: States' bilateral and multilateral fisheries treaties and their secretariats. In E. Lazega, & T. A. B. Snijders (Eds), *Multilevel network analysis: Theory, methods and applications* (pp. 315–332). Cham: Springer.
Krackhardt, D. (1990). Assessing the political landscape: Structure, cognition, and power in organizations. *Administrative Science Quarterly, 35*, 342–369.
Lazega, E. (1996). Arrangements contractuels et structures relationnelles. *Revue Française de Sociologie, 37*, 439–456.
Lazega, E. (2000). Teaming up and out? Cooperation and solidarity in a collegial organization. *European Sociological Review, 16*, 245–266.
Lazega, E. (2001). *The collegial phenomenon: The social mechanisms of cooperation among peers in a corporate law partnership*. Oxford: Oxford University Press.
Lazega, E., & Pattison, P. (2001). Social capital as social mechanisms and collective assets: The example of status auctions among colleagues. In N. Lin, K. Cook, & R. Burt (Eds.), *Social capital: Theory and research* (pp. 185–208). New York: Aldine-de Gruyter.
Lazega, E. (2003). Rationalité, discipline sociale et structure. *Revue Française de Sociologie, 44*, 305–330.

Lazega, E. (2009). Theory of cooperation among competitors: A neo-structural approach. *Socio-Logica, Italian Journal of Sociology Online*, N° 1/2009.

Lazega, E. (2012a). Sociologie néo-structurale. In R. Keucheyan & G. Bronner (Eds.), *Introduction à la théorie sociale contemporaine*. Paris: Presses Universitaires de France.

Lazega, E. (2012b). Learning through lobbying: Mapping judicial dialogue across national borders among European intellectual property judges. *Utrecht Law Review*, 8(2, May). http://www.utrechtlawreview.org

Lazega, E. (2013). Analyses de réseaux et classes sociales. *Revue Française de Socio-Economie*, 10, 273–279.

Lazega, E. (2014a). Appropriateness and structure in organizations: Secondary socialization through dynamics of advice networks and weak culture. In D. J. Brass, G. (Joe) Labianca, A. Mehra, D. S. Halgin, & S. P. Borgatti (Eds.), *Volume on contemporary perspectives on organizational social networks* (Research in the sociology of organizations, Vol. 40, pp. 381–402).

Lazega, E. (2014b). 'Morphogenesis unbound' from the dynamics of multilevel networks: A neo-structural perspective. In M. S. Archer (ed.), *Late modernity: Trajectories towards morphogenic society* (pp 173–191). Dordrecht: Springer.

Lazega, E. (forthcoming). Dynamics of multilevel networks in social processes. In M. S. Archer (Ed.), *Social morphogenesis*. Dordrecht: Springer.

Lazega, E., & Mounier, L. (2002). Interdependent entrepreneurs and the social discipline of their cooperation: The research program of structural economic sociology for a society of organizations. In O. Favereau & E. Lazega (Eds.), *Conventions and structures in economic organization: Markets, networks, and hierarchies* (pp. 147–199). Cheltenham: Edward Elgar Publishing.

Lazega, E., & Mounier, L. (2009). Polynormativité et contrôle social du monde des affaires: le cas de l'interventionnisme et de la punitivité des juges du Tribunal de Commerce de Paris. *Droit et Société*, 71, 103–132.

Lazega, E., & Pattison, P. E. (1999). Multiplexity, generalized exchange and cooperation in organizations: A case study. *Social Networks*, 21, 67–90.

Lazega, E., & Penalva-Icher. (2011). Réseaux sociaux numériques et coopération entre concurrents. *Hermes*, 59, 43–49.

Lazega, E., Mounier, L., Stofer, R., & Tripier, A. (2004). Discipline scientifique et discipline sociale: Réseaux de conseil, apprentissage collectif et innovation dans la recherche française sur le cancer (1997–1999). *Recherches Sociologiques*, 35, 3–27.

Lazega, E., Lemercier, C., & Mounier, L. (2006). A spinning top model of formal structure and informal behaviour: Dynamics of advice networks in a commercial court. *European Management Review*, 3, 113–122.

Lazega, E., Jourda, M.-T., Mounier, L., & Stofer, R. (2008). Catching up with big fish in the big pond? Multi-level network analysis through linked design. *Social Networks*, 30, 157–176.

Lazega, E., Sapulete, S., & Mounier, L. (2011). Structural stability regardless of membership turnover? The added value of blockmodelling in the analysis of network evolution. *Quality & Quantity*, 45, 129–144.

Lazega, E., Mounier, L., Snijders, T. A. B., & Tubaro, P. (2012). Norms, status and the dynamics of advice networks. *Social Networks*, 34, 323–332.

Lazega, E., Jourda, M.-T., & Mounier, L. (2013). Network lift from dual alters: Extended opportunity structures from a multilevel and structural perspective. *European Sociological Review*, 29, 1226–1238.

Merton, R. K. (1957). *Social theory and social structure* (2nd ed.). Glencoe: Free Press.

Montes-Lihn, J. (2014). Apprentissage inter-organisationnel au sein des réseaux interindividuels: le cas de la conversion de viticulteurs à l'agriculture biologique. Doctoral dissertation, University of Paris-Dauphine.

Olson, M. (1965). *The logic of collective action*. Cambridge: Harvard University Press.

Ortega, J. (2001). Job rotation as a learning mechanism. *Management Science*, 47, 1361–1370.

Oubenal, M. (2013). Le processus social de légitimation des produits financiers: le cas des Exchange Traded Funds en France. Doctoral dissertation, University of Paris-Dauphine.

Penalva-Icher, E. (2010). Amitié et régulation par les normes: Le cas de l'investissement socialement responsable. *Revue Française de Sociologie, 51*, 519–544.

Perrow, C. (1991). A society of organizations. *Theory and Society, 20*, 725–762.

Pina-Stranger, A., & Lazega, E. (2011). Bringing personalized ties back in: Their added value for Biotech entrepreneurs and venture capitalists in inter-organizational networks. *The Sociological Quarterly, 52*, 268–292.

Selznick, P. (1949). *TVA and the grass roots: A study of politics and organization.* University of California Press.

Snijders, T. A. B. (1996). Stochastic actor-oriented models for network change. *Journal of Mathematical Sociology, 21*, 149–172.

Snijders, T. A. B. (2005). Models for Longitudinal Network Data. Chapter 11. In P. Carrington, J. Scott, & S. Wasserman (Eds), *Models and methods in social network analysis*. New York: Cambridge University Press.

Snijders, T. A. B. (2015). The Multiple flavours of multilevel issues for networks. In E. Lazega, & T. A. B. Snijders (Eds), *Multilevel network analysis: Theory, methods and applications* (pp. 15–46). Cham: Springer.

Tilly, C. (1998). *Durable inequality*. Berkeley: University of California Press.

Varanda, M. (2005). La réorganisation du petit commerce en centre-ville. L'échec d'une action collective. *Revue Française de Sociologie, 46*, 325–350.

Wang, P., Robins, G., Pattison, P., & Lazega, E. (2013). Exponential random graph models for multilevel networks. *Social Networks, 35*(1), 96–115.

Wasserman, S., & Iacobucci, D. (1991). Statistical modeling of one-mode and two-mode networks: Simultaneous analysis of graphs and bipartite graphs. *British Journal of Mathematical and Statistical Psychology, 44*, 13–44.

White, H. C. (1970). *Chains of opportunity: System models of mobility in organizations*. Cambridge: Harvard University Press.

White, H. C., Boorman, C. S., & Breiger, R. L. (1976). Social structure from multiple networks I. Blockmodels of roles and positions. *American Journal of Sociology, 81*, 730–780.

Wilson, T. P. (1982). Relational networks: An extension of sociometric concepts. *Social Networks, 4*, 105–16.

Yogev, T., & Grund, T. (2012). Network dynamics and market structure: The case of art fairs. *Sociological Focus, 45*(1), 23–40.

Part II
Methods

Chapter 4
Modeling Individual Outcomes Using a *Multilevel Social Influence* (MSI) Model: Individual Versus Team Effects of Trust on Job Satisfaction in an Organisational Context

Filip Agneessens and Johan Koskinen

Introduction and General Context

Over the last decades, social network analysis has become increasing popular (Borgatti and Halgin 2011: Figure 1). Part of this popularity can be attributed to the successful attempts to explain the attitudes and behavior of individuals by their social environment, i.e. the notion that individuals are influenced by the people they are connected to. Diverse theoretical arguments have been developed to explain these so-called *social influence*[1] mechanisms (e.g., Snijders et al. 2010). However, one general theoretical argument has been captured by the social capital concept (see for example: Adler and Kwon 2002; Nahapiet and Ghoshal 1998; Flap et al. 1998; Portes 1998; Lin 1999; Inkpen and Tsang 2005; Burt 1992), i.e. the idea that: "[...] Social structure is a kind of capital that can create for certain individuals or groups a competitive advantage in pursuing their ends. Better connected people enjoy higher returns" (Burt 2001: 32). Social influence and social capital research has tended to focus on either the individual position or the network-level structure (Gabbay and Leenders 1999). Empirical research trying to explain individual attitudes and

---

[1] We will use *social influence* to describe any social process where connections impact individual outcomes, and we reserve the concept *social contagion* to represent the adjustment of one's own behaviour to those of others (Friedkin 2001; Erickson 1988). Social influence can be contrasted to the other main type of social network studies, where the focus lies on *social selection* processes (de Klepper et al. 2010; Borgatti and Kidwell 2011, Agneessens and Wittek 2012). In the latter case, the main focus is on the question how ties emerge in between specific units or actors.

F. Agneessens (✉)
Surrey Business School, University of Surrey, Guildford, UK
e-mail: f.agneessens@surrey.ac.uk

J. Koskinen
Social Statistics Discipline Area, University of Manchester, Manchester, UK

© Springer International Publishing Switzerland 2016
E. Lazega, T.A.B. Snijders (eds.), *Multilevel Network Analysis for the Social Sciences*, Methodos Series 12, DOI 10.1007/978-3-319-24520-1_4

behavior has primarily been looking at the influence of the position that the person has within the network, while research that focuses on the global properties of the network as a whole in order to explain these individual differences has been somewhat less prominent. Although extensive research has been done at both the individual and the group level, little progress has been made in bringing together the effects of the individual's position and the global network properties into one approach.

In this chapter we will focus on conceptualizing *Multilevel Social Influence* (MSI) models that are able to explain individual differences in behavior and attitudes by considering the (individual level) network position, while simultaneously looking at the influence of the (group level) network structure. Such an approach requires a multilevel method, where both levels are explicitly modeled. However, while the network nature of the data offers the possibility of simultaneously investigating the impact of the network level and the individual level position, the complex network interdependence within a single network makes classic multilevel modeling unsuitable (Snijders and Bosker 2012). Unlike classic multilevel models, the interdependence of social networks makes the models more complex, as we need to control for both levels as well as for social contagion and network autocorrelation.

We therefore employ and extend the multilevel model, addressing these dependence issues formally by including team-level fixed and random effects and an autocorrelation component to account for dependencies between cases. This allows us to consider both individual-level and group-level effects jointly with individual-level and group-level effects derived from the network. As the networks are nested in teams and individuals are embedded in but not nested in the networks, we consider the network formally an intermediate level, a level ½. We set up the model as a Bayesian hierarchical model that lends itself to straightforward estimation using Markov chain Monte Carlo.

In the next section, we first discuss the general theoretical argument for considering both the group structure and the individual position from a social capital perspective, and the types of measures that can be considered. We subsequently discuss the statistical multilevel model and illustrate it by considering an organizational setting focusing on the importance of trust relations for employee job satisfaction. We consider how individual differences in patterns of being trusted by colleagues (within a team) might impact a person's satisfaction, while we, at the same time, also consider how the trust structure of the group (density and centralization) might impact the job satisfaction of all members of the group. We end the chapter with a discussion of potential further extensions of the model.

The *Multilevel Social Influence* (MSI) Arguments: Individual Network Position and Network Structure

Because of the vast amount of research that focuses on social influence and uses social capital theory, a comprehensive summary of the field would be outside the scope of this chapter. We refer the interested reader to review articles (see for example: Adler and Kwon 2002; Nahapiet and Ghoshal 1998; Flap et al. 1998; Portes 1998; Lin 1999; Inkpen and Tsang 2005) and instead will in the next section concentrate on some core ideas at both the individual and group level in order to explain the benefits of a *Multilevel Social Influence* (MSI) approach.

Individual Network Position

As discussed before, being in a specific position in a network might influence individual-level outcomes (often formulated as bringing benefits to individuals). Structural measures that have been used to capture network position and their impact on attitudes and behavior include: degree centrality, closeness centrality and brokerage (or structural holes). Other aspects that have been considered include a focus on the resources of the alters, the diversity of alters, and the level of homophily or similarity between ego and alter.

Centrality

Centrality measures, such as degree and closeness, are often used to capture the extent to which a person has direct (or indirect) access to the resources from others in the group, but can also indicate how much a person is being influenced by or is influencing others (e.g. Brass and Burkhardt 1992; Brass 1984). In an organizational context for example, centrality is often used to explain differences in performance (e.g. Sparrowe et al. 2001; Lazega 2001; Cross and Cummings 2004).

Structural Holes/Brokerage

Burt's structural holes argument (Burt 1992) has focused on the bargaining position that results from being the connection between two actors who are themselves not connected. As a result the actor is in a beneficial position when having to bargain about the exchange of information, which can ultimately be reflected in a higher position of power and influence. Moreover, in line with Granovetter's "Strength of Weak Ties" theory (1973), it has also been argued that such open structures are (more) likely to provide unique information.

Resourcefulness of Ego's Connections

Some studies have incorporated the resourcefulness of the alters explicitly by measuring the extent to which alters around an actor possess more or less useful characteristics (e.g., Lin et al. 1981; Hurlbert 1991). For example, Hurlbert (1991) investigated whether having direct access to highly educated persons makes people more satisfied with their life, than being linked to lower educated alters.

Heterogeneity Among Ego's Connections

Another approach has been to capture the diversity or heterogeneity of the alters in ego's surrounding (Marsden 1987; Burt 1983). As different categories of people are more likely to belong to different social circles (cf. Granovetter 1973), being connected to others with different (rather than the same) characteristics is likely to capture access to more diverse or unique sets of information or other resources (Burt 1983; Marsden 1987; Reagans and McEvily 2003). Some studies have for example looked at diversity in education, race, or age (Marsden 1987; Campbell et al. 1986). Heterogeneity has often been captured by Blau's Index of Qualitative Variation (UCINET, Borgatti et al. 2002; Blau 1977).

Homophily/Heterophily on an Independent Characteristic

This measure incorporates the level of homophily-heterophily, i.e. similarity or dissimilarity in characteristics between ego and his or her connections (cf. Reagans and McEvily 2003; McPherson et al. 2001). Dissimilarity between ego and alter on some characteristic can indicate access to more unique resources and qualities, not (yet) possessed by ego (cf. Cross and Cummings 2004; Bantel and Jackson 1989; Pelled et al. 1999). However, at the same time similarity on crucial characteristics (e.g. Kandel 1978; Marsden 1988; Ibarra 1992; Bacharach et al. 2005) can be beneficial to people because it enables easier understanding of each other's behavior. Because of the ability to place oneself in the position of a similar alter, similarity on some major characteristics has also been shown to reduce relational conflict (Pelled 1996). A widely used measure in this respect is the External-Internal (EI)-index (Krackhardt and Stern 1988).

Network Level Structure

While much of the social capital literature has focused on the social influence of individual position, studies that have looked at the network level have primarily focused on: the level of cohesion (density); the level of centralization; and the level of subgroup formation (fragmentation).

Cohesion

Cohesive groups are often argued to benefit from the sharing of resources among its members. Groups that are highly cohesive – i.e. have a high density – are likely to exchange information, leading to shared visions about the aims and the way in which such aims should be obtained (Sparrowe et al. 2001; Molm 1994; Hansen et al. 2005; Podolny and Baron 1997).

Cohesion also enables individuals to combine forces, provide collective sanctions ensuring that obligations and promises are kept and norms are adhered to (Coleman 1988: S107). By ensuring that norms are enforced and free-riding is prevented, high density is likely to generate trust (Coleman 1988, 1990) and reduces the need for costly monitoring and transaction costs (cf. Oh et al. 2004: 863; Adler and Kwon 2002). However, cohesion can also have disadvantages, as highly dense networks have been shown to prevent ties with others outside the team, thereby reducing the inflow of new information (Oh et al. 2004).

Centralization

Groups with a centralized communication network have often been claimed to be more productive especially when performing simple tasks because in centralized networks information can follow a shorter path length and coordination is clearer (Leavitt 1951; in Cummings and Cross 2003: 198). However, for more complex tasks, decentralized communication networks seem to work better (Shaw 1964; see: Cummings and Cross 2003; Katz and Martin 1997: 319–321), because non-routine and complex tasks require a higher degree of coordination (cf. Van de Ven et al. 1976; Hansen 1999). Moreover, decentralized networks are more efficient in dealing with crises, especially if the network consists of strong ties (cf. Cummings and Cross 2003).

Fragmentation

The degree to which a group is divided into clear subgroups has often been considered to have negative effects. Fragmentation disables the spread of information and might even indicate conflict between different groups and a strong subgroup identity (Krackhardt 1999).

Why Use Multilevel Social Influence?

In section "Individual network position" we provided general reasons for the relevance of individual position in order to explain individual behavior and attitudes, while in section "Network level structure" we focused on the network level structure. In this section we explain the core rationale for integrating both perspectives (individual social capital and group social capital) into a single *Multilevel Social Influence* (MSI) model. We propose three main arguments why such models are needed (see also Chap. 1).

Find Persistent Results Over Groups

One basic reason for studying multiple networks simultaneously is that one is generally not interested in describing the social processes that go on in a specific case (such as the specific processes happening in a single school class or one team in an organization). Rather, when performing fundamental research, one is interested in general processes, i.e., the aim is to find out whether and to what extent general patterns exist in groups of a specific kind. In order to be able to generalize to groups or networks of a specific kind, one needs to ensure that social processes are similarly prevalent in these different, multiple networks. For example, in the case of school children, we might want to know if, in general, friendship relations in classrooms impact student's happiness, or increases their chances of being successful.[2]

Wrongly Assume that it is Individual Effect When it is a Group Effect

Second, since both the individual position and the network structure of the network as a whole might impact one's attitudes and behavior, it is important to avoid making an ecological fallacy (cf. Snijders and Bosker 2012). Using a multilevel model provides the possibility to incorporate group-level characteristics and hence disentangle the relative importance of "individual social capital" from "collectively-owned social capital."

Figure 4.1 illustrates the situation where the individual position is indeed important for job satisfaction, while there is no effect at the group level.

However, considering Fig. 4.2, using only the individual level network position, we might wrongly assume that people who are very central in a network are more satisfied with their work, whereas in reality all people in a high density network are more satisfied. In this case the group-level (density) effect is relevant, while the individual degree centrality is in reality not important, as the cohesion is impacting all its members to the same extent. However, not including the group-level effect (density) will make us incorrectly conclude that central people are more satisfied.

---

[2] An additional reason for combining these results emerges when one deals with networks of small sizes and need to ensure that the model has enough power. Note that since we focus on social influence with an individual characteristic as the dependent variable, the model has N observations only (the number of individuals), and not $(N*(N-1))$.

4 Modeling Individual Outcomes Using a *Multilevel Social Influence* (MSI)...

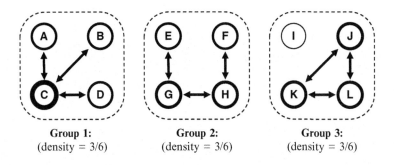

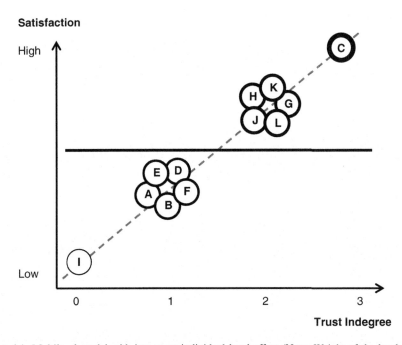

Fig. 4.1 Multilevel model with important individual level effect (Note: Weight of the border of the node reflects job satisfaction)

However, as mentioned before, unlike classic multilevel models, the complex interdependence between the employees in the network require us to adjust the multilevel models for this interdependence.

Effects are Different in Different Situations – Cross-Level Interactions

A third major reason for studying multiple networks is that we might be interested in understanding when specific processes might differ under specific conditions

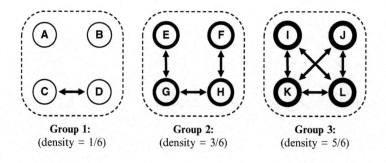

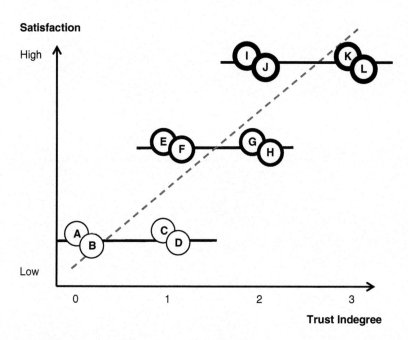

Fig. 4.2 Multilevel model with important group level effect

(Lazega et al. 2008). A cross-level effect, i.e., a combination of individual position and network-level characteristics, might generate more interesting insights. In those cases, the impact of an individual's position in the group might depend on the network structure of the group as a whole. As Brass noted: "For example, a researcher might ask, to what extent does an actor's centrality within a highly central clique in a decentralized network affects that actor's power?" (Brass 2003: 291).

Figure 4.3 shows an example in which being more central in a low density network has a large positive effect on satisfaction, while in the denser network centrality has an opposite effect.

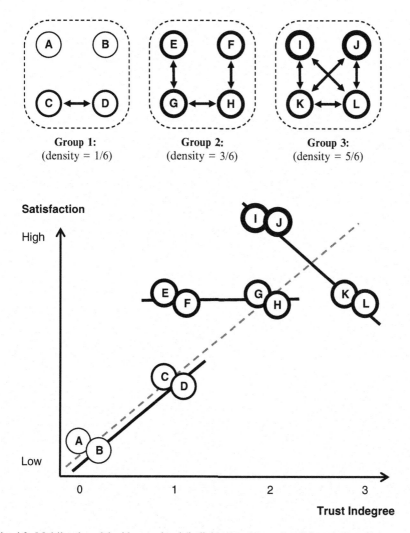

Fig. 4.3 Multilevel model with cross level (individual and group level) interaction effect

To illustrate the details of the *Multilevel Social Influence* (MSI) model we will discuss the practical aspects of the model with an example about job satisfaction and trust among 27 teams.

Trust Networks on Employee Job Satisfaction: An Example

We now turn to an empirical example that focuses on the impact of trust networks on job satisfaction among employees. Job satisfaction is a particularly well-suited example for illustrating the interplay of individual, network, and structure. While an individual's job satisfaction is essentially a personal characteristic, it can be partly influenced by the group context (in this case, the network structure of the group). Moreover the level of satisfaction might be impacted by the social contacts within the group (social influence at the individual level) and therefore requires a relational perspective, where both levels are explicitly modeled.

Theoretical Arguments

Existing research has identified a variety of factors that impact job satisfaction (Spector 1997). In this chapter we will solely focus on the influence that social networks have on job satisfaction. We will provide a selective reading of the literature and only focus on some theoretical arguments that are relevant for the social influence model discussed below.

Social network studies have provided considerable evidence for the impact of instrumental relations (communication), as well as affective relations (friendship and social support) on job satisfaction (e.g., Roberts and O'Reilly 1979; Baldwin et al. 1997; Flap and Volker 2001; Hurlbert 1991; Umberson et al. 1996; Requena 2003; Venkataramani et al. 2013).

Trust and Job Satisfaction

Trust relations can be expected to be particularly vital for job satisfaction because they are essential for the exchange of information and other resources (see Hurlbert 1991; Umberson et al. 1996; Requena 2003; Agneessens and Wittek 2008; Kramer 1999; Tsai and Ghoshal 1998).

One argument that explains the effect of trust on job satisfaction relies on the mediating role of emotional support. Since "intimacy, reassurance and sharing confidences" are central components for emotional support (Harlow and Cantor 1995: 329), trust might be an essential condition for the occurrence of social support. Emotional support in turn has been shown to provide a buffer against stressful situations (e.g., Thoits 1982; House 1981), and therefore is likely to prevent a potential decrease in job satisfaction. Taking these different components together, it seems that trust is an essential component that needs to be present between people in order for it to generate the emotional support needed to ensure high job satisfaction.

Close relations have been claimed to provide sources of social support (Agneessens et al. 2006), but trust also enables access to crucial information at work (Hurlbert 1991; Umberson et al. 1996; Requena 2003). In many cases the transfer of fine-grained, long-lasting and costly information would not be thinkable without trust (Uzzi 1996: 681). Moreover, trust ensures that one will not be taken advantage of (i.e. that favors will be returned) and that the advice will not be misused. Trust is the basis for being more willing to share advice and forgo self-interest (Podolny and Baron 1997). Such a situation is likely to encourage more critical reflection and open exchange of ideas without ending up in a conflict situation (Jehn and Shah 1997).

Hence, being considered trustworthy by others will enable the employee to get access to more resources and more open discussion, and this makes an employee feel more integrated in the organization, and is likely to increase his performance and satisfaction.

Individual and Group Level Effects

Following the arguments in this section and in sections "Individual network position" and "Network level structure" at an individual level we can expect people with a high level of incoming trust relationships (i.e., being trusted by a lot of others) to be more likely to have a higher job satisfaction. We will test this by incorporating the in-degree centrality in the trust network.

An alternative argument might focus on the idea that trust relationships in a team benefits all its team members simultaneously. Hence, being integrated in a group where a lot of trust relationships exist might benefit the team as a whole. A cohesive (dense) group might lead to less time being spent on monitoring each other (Langfred 2004; Dirks 1999), and therefore a higher level of job satisfaction among all the members of the group. We will simultaneously test this group level and individual level effect by incorporating both in the multilevel model.

Finally we also decided to incorporate the variation in in-degree centrality as a second group-level characteristic. Given a specific level of trust in a group, a high level of in-degree centralization in the trust network might be an indication of agreement about who can be trusted and who is not to be trusted.

Data and Measurement

Data was collected in two knowledge-intensive organizations. In total 31 teams were surveyed, including 235 employees. The unit non-response rate was 9.8 %. If we excluded the teams with less than 4 members responding, we ended up with 27 teams with 201 employees (Figs. 4.4). Descriptive statistics can be found in Table 4.1.

The survey consisted of a face-to-face interview of about half an hour. It included measures on gender, age, networks, job satisfaction and performance. The trust relation was measured using the following question: "Consider your relation with each of your colleagues, and consider the opposite nouns "distrust-trust". To what extent do you associate your relation with your colleague with distrust or trust?"

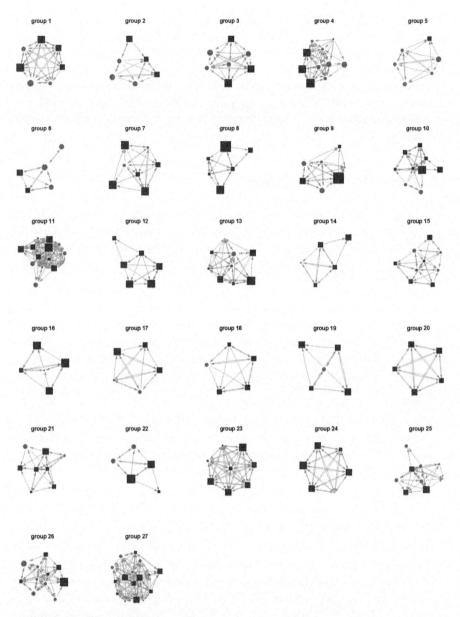

Fig. 4.4 Graphical representation of 27 teams (Note: Trust ties, with size of nodes representing level of job satisfaction and the symbol of the nodes representing gender)

The answer was on a 7-point scale with endpoints "distrust" (−3) and "trust" (+3), with the number 0 in the middle (de Lange et al., 2004; Agneessens, 2006). We dichotomized the network, and considered a trust relation when a value +1 or higher was selected.

Table 4.1 Descriptive statistics for the members of the 27 teams

		Mean	Sd	Min	Max
Job satisfaction	N = 201	49.93	18.49	6	100
Gender		0.62	–	0	1
Age		42.59	9.29	21	65
Hierarchy		0.12	–	0	1
Indegree trust		63.24	25.11	0	100
Size team	M = 27	7.46	3.29	4	15
Density		63.24	15.35	46	100
Var indegree		18.17	7.94	0	33.9

Model for the Analysis of Job Satisfaction and Trust in Teams

We now turn to the *Multilevel Social Influence* (MSI) model. We elaborate our conceptualization of the network as an intermediate level between the level of the individuals and the level of the team. In a standard nested multilevel model, dependencies between individuals within a level are straightforward to capture through random effects (see e.g. Goldstein 1995; Snijders and Bosker 2012). Thus, we have idiosyncrasies at the individual level captured by an error term, and we have, again, idiosyncrasies at the team level captured by another error term. While we could classify individuals by their membership to network ties and thus induce variance terms as in a standard multilevel model (Koskinen and Stenberg 2012), this would treat the network mostly as a nuisance and would typically make unrealistic assumptions about how these errors relate to each other.

There is a long, and theoretically informed, tradition of modeling network-dependencies between outcomes explicitly, through network effects and network autocorrelation models (Erbring and Young 1979; Doreian 1982; Duke 1993). An excellent review of the network autocorrelation model and the network effects model, how they are defined and what distinguishes them is given in Marsden and Friedkin (1993). We propose to incorporate these models into the multilevel framework through conceptualizing the network as an intermediate level. In the same way that individual-level covariates may be derived from level two variables, and level two covariates may be derived from level one variables, network measures may be construed either as individual-level predictors or group-level predictors. The explicit dependencies implied by the network autocorrelation and the network effects models then account for the lack of independence 'within' the network level. While in the standard multilevel framework it is straightforward (most of the time) to partition variance so that variation may be attributed to different levels, this is less straightforward with the network level. We explore here the interplay of the group-level effects and the network-level effects.

Combining the team networks furthermore permits us to investigate network-level effects for small networks. Recall that the sizes of the teams range from 4 to 15 and the densities range from 0.46 to 1.00. Additionally, combining the networks in one joint model, we need to consider the potential for heterogeneity in network-level effects.

A Bayesian inference framework provides a convenient and principled approach for dealing with the complex interdependencies between our different levels. Zhang et al. (2013), for example, leverage the Bayesian framework when developing a network effects model for binary outcomes with multiple feedback parameters.

Model Formulation

Let y be the vector of job satisfaction scores for the N individuals $i \in V = \{1,\ldots,N\}$, and X be an $N \times p$ matrix of individual-level covariates. The standard linear regression across all teams is given by $y = X\beta + \varepsilon$. The standard assumption of i.i.d. errors $\varepsilon \sim N_N\left(0, \sigma^2 \mathbf{I}_N\right)$ is unrealistic as individuals are grouped into teams (level 2) and embedded in networks of trust (level ½), the latter level which is itself nested in level 2. We design a set of fixed and random effects for both of these levels.

Denote the set of groups $G = G(V) = \{1,\ldots,M\}$ and let the $N \times M$ design matrix D have element $D_{ig} = 1$ if $G(i) = g$ and zero otherwise, with the group sizes $n_g = \sum_{i=1}^{N} D_{ig}$. Within each group the trust network is represented by its $n_g \times n_g$ binary adjacency matrix $A^{[g]}$ and the row-normalised adjacency matrix $W^{[g]}$ (we normalise by dividing $A_{ij}^{[g]}$ by $\max\left(1, A_{i+}^{[g]}\right)$ but other normalisations are possible, see Leenders 2002; we adopt the notational convention that indices of $A^{[g]}$ are unambiguous given the indices in V, rather than using a different index set for individuals in groups). The weights may be collected in a global block-diagonal weight matrix W, with $W^{[1]}, \ldots, W^{[M]}$ on the diagonal. We shall use the operator $\oplus$ for the construction of block-diagonal matrices, so that $W = \oplus_{g=1}^{M} W^{[g]}$.

Level 2 Fixed Effects and Random Effects

On the group-level we include the team-size as a fixed effect predictor $n = \left(n_g\right)_{g=1}^{M}$, with the associated parameter γ. Average team job satisfaction is modelled using the group-level random effect $u \sim N_G\left(0, \upsilon^2 \mathbf{I}_G\right)$.

Level 1 Fixed and Random Effects

The individual level covariates X_i are

X_{i1}: intercept
X_{i2}: gender
X_{i3}: age
X_{i4}: hierarchy

The associated vector of coefficients is denoted β. The level one random errors as usual $\varepsilon \sim N_N\left(0, \sigma^2 \mathbf{I}_N\right)$.

Level ½ Fixed and Random Effects

We construct three 'fixed' effects for the network-level V_i

$V_{i1} = A^{[g]}_{+i}/(n_g - 1)$: the normalised trust in-degree of i, $G(i) = g$
$V_{i2} = A^{[g]}_{++}/[n_g(n_g - 1)]$: the density of the trust network $G(i) = g$
$V_{i3} = \sqrt{\sum_{i:G(i)=g}(V_{i1} - V_{i2})^2}$: centralisation in network g

Note that while V_{i1} enter as an individual-level covariate in the model, the global network properties enter as team-level covariates. The associated 3×1 parameter vector is denoted η.

To capture network dependence, we consider two interactions with levels 1 and 2. This first is to allow for correlated errors of individuals that have a trust tie by adding the effect:

$$\xi = \rho W \xi + \varepsilon$$

for a network correlation parameter $\rho \in pos(W)$. The range space $pos(W) = \cap_g pos(W^{[g]})$, where $pos(W^{[g]})$ is defined as $\rho \in (-1, 1)$ such that $\Pi_{j=1,\ldots,n_g}\left(1 - \rho \lambda^{[g]}_j\right) > 0$, where $\lambda^{[g]}_j$ is the jth eigenvalue of $W^{[g]}$. This defines a conditional model $y\,|\,\beta, \gamma, u, \eta, \rho, \sigma^2 \sim N(X\beta + \gamma Dn + Du + V\eta, \Sigma)$, where $\Sigma = C\sigma^2 I_N C^T$, with $C = (I_N - \rho W)^{-1}$.

The second network dependence effect we consider is the network effects parameter α. This is the familiar network autocorrelation through the outcome variable, defining the model:

$$y = \alpha W y + X\beta + \gamma Dn + Du + V\eta + \varepsilon$$

Similar to the network autocorrelation model, this defines a conditional model $y\,|\,\beta, \gamma, u, \eta, \alpha, \sigma^2 \sim N(C(X\beta + \gamma Dn + Du + V\eta), \Sigma)$, where $C = (I_N - \alpha W)^{-1}$, and $\Sigma = C\sigma^2 I_N C^T$. To guarantee that the variance covariance matrix is positive definite, $\alpha \in pos(W)$.

It may be a strong assumption assuming that the values of the network-level effects are the same across the different groups. We may allow both parameters to vary at the group level by assuming a hierarchical prior. For the first parameter the random effects autocorrelation is assumed to be

$$\rho^{[g]} \sim N_{pos(W^{[g]})}(\mu_\rho, \tau_\rho),$$

which is a normal distribution truncated to the interval $pos(W^{[g]})$. In the conditional model this means that $C = \oplus_{g=1}^{M} (\mathbf{I}_N - \rho^{[g]} W^{[g]})^{-1}$. For the second parameter we let

$$\alpha^{[g]} \sim N_{pos(W^{[g]})} (\mu_\alpha, \tau_\alpha).$$

Prior Distributions and Estimation

We chose conjugate priors for the regressors $(\beta, \gamma, \eta) | \sigma^2 \sim N\left(\mu_\beta, \frac{\sigma^2}{\kappa_0} \mathbf{I}_p\right)$, $\sigma^2 \sim$ InvGamma $(q_0/2, q_0\sigma_0^2)$, and here $\mu_\beta = 0$, $\kappa_0 = 100$, $q_0 = 2$, $\sigma_0^2 = 2$. For $\upsilon^2 \sim$ InvGamma $(r_0/2, r_0\upsilon_0^2)$, here with $r_0 = 4$, $\sigma_0^2 = 4$. For the correlation parameters $\rho \sim N_{pos(W)}(\tilde{\mu}_\rho, \tilde{\tau}_\rho)$, with $\tilde{\mu}_\rho = 0$ and $\tilde{\tau}_\rho = 1$, $\alpha \sim N_{pos(W)}(\tilde{\mu}_\alpha, \tilde{\tau}_\alpha)$, with $\tilde{\mu}_\alpha = 0$ and $\tilde{\tau}_\alpha = 1$. For the random effects correlation parameters we set $\mu_\rho | \tau_\rho \sim N_{pos(W)}(0, \tau_\rho^2/2)$, and $\tau_\rho^2 \sim$ InvGamma $(2.5/2, 2.5\tau_{\rho 0}^2)$, $\tau_{\rho 0}^2 = 0.1$ and $\mu_\alpha | \tau_\alpha \sim N_{pos(W)}(0, \tau_\alpha^2/2)$, and $\tau_\alpha^2 \sim$ InvGamma $(2.5/2, 2.5\tau_{\alpha 0}^2)$, $\tau_{\alpha 0}^2 = 0.1$.

Estimation is carried out using a Metropolis-Hastings MCMC scheme with 100,000 iterations (50,000 for the models of Table 3) where 10 % of values are discarded for thinning and 20 % removed as burn-in. To get an assessment of the fit across such different model specifications, we use Gelman et al.'s (2004, p. 175) omnibus test statistic $\chi^2 = \sum_i \chi_i^2$, where

$$\chi_i^2 = \frac{\left(y_i - \frac{\sum_{t=1}^{T} y_i^t}{T}\right)}{V(y_i^t)}$$

and y_i^t is a replicate observation for $i \in V$ drawn from the posterior predictive distribution.

Results

The main hypothesis of the paper relate to the effects of the level ½ fixed effects η, how the network position and composition affects job satisfaction. In models 1 through 9 reported in Table 4.2, we test these effects controlling for different combinations of level ½ and level 2 dependencies. These effects are robust in the sense that with high posterior probability across all models (a) the coefficient for trust indegree (η_1) is negative; (b) the coefficient for trust density (η_2) is positive; (c) the coefficient for trust centralisation (η_3) is positive.

4 Modeling Individual Outcomes Using a *Multilevel Social Influence* (MSI)... 97

Table 4.2 Multilevel network regressions of job satisfaction for 27 teams

		M1		M2		M3		M4		M5		M6		M7		M8		M9	
		Mean	Sd	Mean	Sd	Mean	Sd	Mean	Sd	Mean	Sd	Mean	Sd	Mean	Sd	Mean	Sd	Mean	Sd
Intercept	β_1	37.62	13.13	40.57	12.40	37.29	11.30	34.92	15.32	39.45	11.86	38.73	13.19	37.13	11.52	40.47	12.52	33.85	15.57
Gender	β_2	−5.20	2.75	−6.19	2.71	−5.76	2.67	−4.89	2.64	−6.41	2.61	−5.36	2.84	−5.75	2.71	−6.02	2.74	−4.75	2.76
Age	β_3	0.02	0.14	0.01	0.14	0.01	0.14	0.03	0.14	0.01	0.14	0.01	0.14	0.02	0.14	0.01	0.14	0.03	0.14
Hierarchy	β_4	9.59	3.57	9.26	3.65	9.51	3.66	9.38	3.56	9.33	3.67	9.65	3.64	9.57	3.65	9.24	3.53	9.47	3.57
Indegree	η_1	−0.14	0.06	−0.14	0.06	−0.15	0.06	−0.14	0.06	−0.14	0.06	−0.15	0.06	−0.15	0.06	−0.14	0.06	−0.14	0.06
Density	η_2	36.14	13.38	31.98	13.52	30.75	11.71	35.46	16.13	35.93	12.01	35.60	13.29	32.24	11.85	31.83	13.33	36.70	15.63
Centralization	η_3	19.07	7.64	18.92	7.28	15.49	6.52	18.76	10.16	18.96	6.49	18.91	7.83	16.59	6.72	18.77	7.46	20.40	10.01
Network corr	ρ	0.17	0.10																
	μ_ρ			0.11	0.21							0.16	0.10			0.08	0.11		
	τ_ρ^2			0.31	0.45											0.10	0.09		
Network eff.	α					0.12	0.07							0.10	0.07				
	μ_α							−0.01	0.07									−0.01	0.07
	τ_α^2							0.02	0.01									0.02	0.01
Group size	γ									−1.42	0.44	−1.36	0.53	−1.32	0.44	−1.36	0.45	−1.07	0.63
Level 2 var	υ^2									2.44	3.39	2.17	3.10	2.08	2.85	2.22	3.59	1.74	1.98
Level 1 var	σ^2	280.80	27.65	270.80	28.00	280.80	28.68	259.70	27.88	281.60	29.56	280.90	28.90	281.00	28.70	270.20	28.53	257.90	27.27
GOF stat	$\chi^2(\chi_i^2)$	184.00	6.70	154.00	6.70	186.00	6.70	167.00	6.60	186.00	6.80	182.00	6.70	184.00	6.70	168.00	6.80	167.00	6.60

Models 1 and 5 both account for the dependence within teams, but the former captures this purely through network autocorrelation and the latter through the team-level random intercept. The fit of M5 is not better than that of M1 and an autocorrelation of $\rho = 0.17$ is considerable compared to the level 2 variance (posterior probability that $\rho > 0$ is 0.95). The network correlation through the outcome variable, α, does not seem to account for much given that it is near to zero with high posterior probability across all models it is included in (M3 and M7). This suggest that there is no 'contagion effect' above what is captured by the level ½ fixed effects η.

Allowing ρ and α to vary across teams (M2, M4, M8, and M9) weakens any evidence for a common network effect, μ_ρ or μ_α. While, for example, there are teams with a discernible positive correlation effect $\rho^{[g]}$, in a predictive sense (see Fig. 4.5), the higher level parameter μ_ρ is close to zero. The posterior probability that $\mu_\rho > 0$ is 0.81, given data, for M2. Twenty-one out of the 27 teams have a predicted mean for $\rho^{[g]}$ greater than zero. That random variation for $\rho^{[g]}$ picks up some of the heterogeneity across groups is not manifested (as one would expect) in a radical change in ν^2 but rather in improved fit (the best fitting model is M2).

In Fig. 4.5 (panel b) we examine the extent to which $\rho^{[g]}$ accounts for the variation between groups by plotting the predictive distributions of $\rho^{[g]}$ from M2 ordered by $E(u^{[g]} \mid W,y,x,n)$ from M5. The u-shape reveals that the groups that 'deviate' from

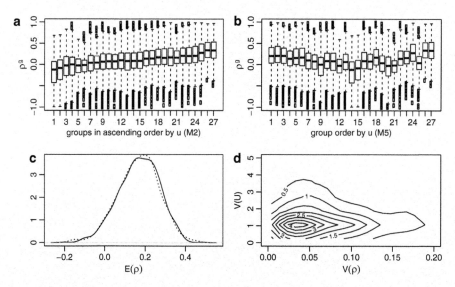

Fig. 4.5 Posterior analysis of variance: (**a**) posterior predictive distributions of $\rho^{[g]}$ (M2) ordered according to network mean; (**b**) posterior predictive distributions of $\rho^{[g]}$ (M2) order according to expected value of random intercept according to M5; (**c**) comparing the posterior distribution of ρ for M1 (*solid*) and M6 (*dashed*); (**d**) bivariate posterior distribution of τ_ρ^2 and ν^2 (from M8)

the grand mean are indeed the ones where the network autocorrelation is greatest. Considering the modest variation on level two (2.44 in M5) and the fact that ρ is not affected if both ρ and $u^{[g]}$ are included, as in M6, the variation on level ½ appears to be more important (Fig. 4.5 panel c). The association between v^2 and τ_ρ^2 is negligible as illustrated in Fig. 4.5 panel d. We may (tentatively) conclude that there is some heterogeneity of network level effects across teams but there is not enough information in data to fully quantify this.

While models M1 through M9 demonstrate the robustness of the fixed network-level effects and how these and the team-level random effect account for the network autocorrelation ρ, these models do not demonstrate how the effects relate to influence. Clearly, there is no network effect α given that the derived measures are taken into account (M3) but is there an influence or contagion effect that they explain away? To this end we shall parse out the effects of M7 into sub-models M7:A through M7:D. The results are provided in Table 4.3.

Model M7:A is a model where the only effect of the network-level is the autocorrelation through the outcome variable. The point estimate of the parameter α is 0.16 and it is greater than zero with a posterior probability of 0.995, indicating strong evidence for within-team influence. This conclusion is virtually unchanged once the team-level random intercept is included in M7:B, suggesting that the strength of the influence effect is un-confounded by between-team differences. However, introducing the network-level measure in-degree (V_{i1}), eliminates the influence effect α in the sense that the magnitude is reduced and the posterior uncertainty is increased. The support for a positive α drops to 0.9 for M7:C (the posterior is provided in Fig. 4.6a). The feedback loop modelled by α is thus

Table 4.3 Multilevel network regressions of job satisfaction for 27 teams. Interdependence of network level fixed effects and the contagion parameter

		M7:A		M7:B		M7:C		M7:D	
		Mean	Sd	Mean	Sd	Mean	Sd	Mean	Sd
Intercept	β_1	47.77	9.05	48.27	9.10	59.15	10.07	35.11	12.03
Gender	β_2	−5.04	2.75	−5.11	2.86	−5.68	2.72	−5.21	2.78
Age	β_3	0.12	0.14	0.11	0.14	0.09	0.14	0.06	0.14
Hierarchy	β_4	8.94	3.70	9.05	3.75	8.87	3.63	9.51	3.73
Indegree	η_1					−0.08	0.05		
Density	η_2							17.34	10.71
Centralization	η_3							16.48	6.92
Network eff.	α	0.16	0.07	0.16	0.07	0.10	0.08	0.10	0.07
Group size	γ	−1.11	0.39	−1.12	0.40	−1.36	0.44	−1.30	0.45
Level 2 var	v^2			1.82	2.11	2.88	4.89	2.03	2.77
Level 1 var	σ^2	294.92	29.52	296.62	29.34	292.35	32.95	290.04	30.27
GOF stat	$\chi^2\left(\check{\chi}_i^2\right)$	192.40	7.85	186.82	7.40	187.54	6.93	184.51	7.07

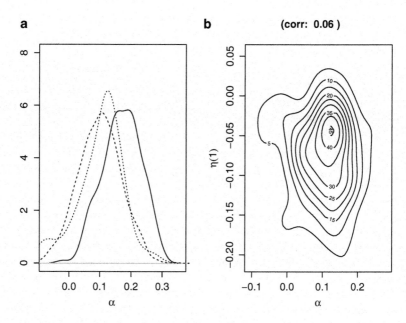

Fig. 4.6 Posterior analysis of network fixed and feedback effects: (**a**) posterior distributions of α for M7:A (*solid*), M7:C (*dotted*), and M7:D (*dashed*); (**b**) bivariate posterior distribution of α and η_1 for M7:C

confounded by including a derived measure of the conduits of this feedback. The parameters α and η_1 are however virtually independent a posteriori as seen in Fig. 4.6b. Comparing the estimate η_1 for M7:C and M7 reveals that the indegree-effect on its own does not supplant the influence evidenced by α in M7:A and M7:B, as the 95 % posterior credibility interval for η_1 is $(-0.19, 0.009)$ in M7:C. Similarly, in M7:D, when only the derived network-level measures for the team-level, network density and network centralisation, are included, this attenuates the network effect (α) but also diminishes the effect of the fixed, global network measure density; there is little evidence for an effect of network density on job satisfaction in M7:D.

Interpreting M7 and models M7:A through M7:D jointly, there is evidence for network autocorrelation (α) but this is explained away by the individual in-degree and the global network measures. There is however only an effect of individual in-degree and the global network measures on job satisfaction when they are included together (as in M7). Thus the exact nature of the network influence on job satisfaction is that the density of the trust network contributes positively to job satisfaction but people that are trusted more than others in their team tend to have lower job-satisfaction.

Discussion and Conclusions

We have argued for the need for a more integrated approach to study the effects of individual network position and global network structure on individuals, their attitudes and opinions. Focusing on 201 employees in 27 groups as a specific empirical example, we have demonstrated how individual attributes, the group structure (density and centralization), and the position of the person in the trust network (in-degree centrality) combined can explain job satisfaction. By carrying out the *Multilevel Social Influence* (MSI) analysis across different groups, we were able to identify the contribution of individual network position relative to the contribution of the network structure at the team level. Together these elements explained the network dependencies within teams.

The model proposed here is generic, in the sense that other types of individual network position measures (such as heterogeneity or brokerage) as well as group-level network properties (such as fragmentation) can in principle also be modeled. The challenge with these more complex properties is, however, that one needs to ensure that the proper control variables are included at both the individual and group level.

Given the recent possibilities for collecting large-scale data and the trend in collecting data from multiple sets of actors, it is becoming increasingly feasible (and necessary) to look at both individual position and the structure of the set of actors at the same time, enabling the possibility to disentangle the relative importance of "individual social capital" from "collectively owned social capital". As more multiple network analysis studies and large-scale data becomes available more interesting and generalizable results become possible, where micro and meso can be combined, rather than focusing on a case study based on a single network. The nature of the empirical example investigated here (few, rather small groups) did not allow us to fully explore the possibilities of assessing heterogeneity in network processes across different contexts. This should be a target of future research.

Acknowledgments We would like to thank Tom Snijders for comments on an earlier version and the sociology students (Ghent University) and Daniëlle De Lange for help with the practical data collection.

References

Adler, P. S., & Kwon, S. W. (2002). Social capital: Prospects for a new concept. *Academy of Management Review, 27*, 17–40.

Agneessens, F. (2006). *Social capital in knowledge intensive teams: The importance of content, structure and resources for performance of researchers at university*. PhD dissertation. Ghent University, Ghent.

Agneessens, F., & Wittek, R. (2008). Social capital and employee well-being: Disentangling intrapersonal and interpersonal selection and influence mechanisms. *Revue Française de Sociologie, 49*, 613–637.

Agneessens, F., & Wittek, R. (2012). Where do intra-organizational advice relations come from? The role of informal status and social capital in social exchange. *Social Networks, 34*, 333–345.

Agneessens, F., Waege, H., & Lievens, J. (2006). Diversity in social support by role relations: A typology. *Social Networks, 28*, 427–441.

Bacharach, S. B., Bamberger, P. A., & Vashdi, D. (2005). Diversity and homophily at work: Supportive relations among white and African-American peers. *Academy of Management Journal, 48*, 619–644.

Baldwin, T. T., Bedell, M. D., & Johnson, J. L. (1997). The social fabric of a team-based MBA program: Network effects on student satisfaction and performance. *Academy of Management Journal, 40*, 1369–1397.

Bantel, K., & Jackson, S. (1989). Top management and innovations in banking: Does the composition of the top team make a difference? *Strategic Management Journal, 10*, 107–124.

Blau, P. M. (1977). *Inequality and heterogeneity*. New York: Free Press.

Borgatti, S. P., & Halgin, D. S. (2011). On network theory. *Organization Science, 22*, 1168–1181.

Borgatti, S. P., & Kidwell, V. (2011). Network theorizing. In P. Carrington & J. Scott (Eds.), *The Sage handbook of social network analysis* (pp. 40–54). London: Sage.

Borgatti, S. P., Everett, M. G., & Freeman, L. C. (2002). *Ucinet for Windows: Software for social network analysis*. Harvard: Analytic Technologies.

Brass, D. J. (1984). Being in the right place: A structural analysis of individual influence in an organization. *Administrative Science Quarterly, 29*, 518–539.

Brass, D. J. (2003). A social network perspective on human resources management. In R. Cross, A. Parker, & L. Sasson (Eds.), *Networks in the knowledge economy* (pp. 283–323). Oxford: Oxford University Press.

Brass, D. J., & Burkhardt, M. E. (1992). Centrality and power in organizations. In N. Nohria & R. G. Eccles (Eds.), *Networks and organizations: Structure, form, and action* (pp. 191–215). Boston: Harvard Business School Press.

Burt, R. S. (1983). Range. In R. S. Burt & M. J. Minor (Eds.), *Applied network analysis. A methodological introduction* (pp. 176–194). London: Sage.

Burt, R. S. (1992). *Structural holes: The social structure of competition*. Cambridge: Harvard University Press.

Burt, R. S. (2001). Structural holes versus network closure as social capital. In N. Lin, K. Cook, & R. S. Burt (Eds.), *Social capital: Theory and research*. New York: Aldine De Gruyter.

Campbell, K. E., Marsden, P. V., & Hurlbert, J. S. (1986). Social resources and socioeconomic status. *Social Networks, 8*, 97–117.

Coleman, J. S. (1988). Social capital in the creation of human capital. *American Journal of Sociology, 94*, S95–S120.

Coleman, J. (1990). *Foundations of social theory*. Cambridge: Harvard University Press.

Cross, R., & Cummings, J. N. (2004). Tie and network correlates of individual performance in knowledge-intensive work. *Academy of Management Journal, 47*, 928–937.

Cummings, J. N., & Cross, R. (2003). Structural properties of work groups and their consequences for performance. *Social Networks, 25*, 197–210.

De Klepper, M., Sleebos, E., van de Bunt, G., & Agneessens, F. (2010). Similarity in friendship networks: Selection or influence? The effect of constraining contexts and non-visible individual attributes. *Social Networks, 32*, 82–90.

De Lange, D., Agneessens, F., & Waege, H. (2004) Asking social network questions: A quality assessment of different measures. *Metodoloski zvezki, 1*(2), 351–378. mrvar.fdv.uni-lj.si/pub/mz/mz1.1/lange.pdf

Dirks, K. T. (1999). The effects of interpersonal trust on work group performance. *Journal of Applied Psychology, 84*, 445–455.

Doreian, P. (1982). Maximum likelihood methods for linear models: Spatial effect and spatial disturbance terms. *Sociological Methods & Research, 10*, 243–269.

Duke, J. B. (1993). Estimation of the network effects model in a large data set. *Sociological Methods Research, 21*, 465–481.

Erbring, L., & Young, A. (1979). Individuals and social structure: Contextual effects as endogeneous feedback. *Sociological Methods and Research, 7*, 396–430.

Erickson, B. H. (1988). The relational basis of attitudes. In B. Wellman & S. D. Berkowitz (Eds.), *Social structures* (pp. 99–122). New York: Cambridge University Press.

Flap, H., & Völker, B. (2001). Goal specific social capital and job satisfaction: Effects of different types of networks on instrumental and social aspects of work. *Social Networks, 23*, 297–320.

Flap, H., Bulder, B., & Völker, B. (1998). Intra-organizational networks and performance: A review. *Computational & Mathematical Organization Theory, 4*, 109–147.

Friedkin, N. E. (2001). Norm formation in social influence networks. *Social Networks, 23*, 167–189.

Gabbay, S. M., & Leenders, R. T. A. J. (1999). CSC: The structure of advantage and disadvantage. In R. T. A. J. Leenders & S. M. Gabbay (Eds.), *Corporate social capital and liability* (pp. 1–14). Boston: Kluwer Academic Publisher.

Gelman, A., Carlin, J., Stern, H., Dunson, D., Vehtari, A., & Rubin, D. (2004). *Bayesian data analysis* (Texts in statistical science). Boca Raton: Chapman & Hall/CRC.

Goldstein, H. (1995). *Multilevel statistical models* (2nd ed.). London: Edward Arnold.

Granovetter, M. S. (1973). The strength of weak ties. *American Journal of Sociology, 78*, 1360–1380.

Hansen, M. T. (1999). The search-transfer problem: The role of weak ties in sharing knowledge across organization subunits. *Administrative Science Quarterly, 44*, 82–111.

Hansen, M. T., Mors, M. L., & Lovas, B. (2005). Knowledge sharing in organizations: Multiple networks, multiple phases. *Academy of Management Journal, 48*, 776–793.

Harlow, R. E., & Cantor, N. (1995). To whom do people turn when things go poor: Task orientation and functional social contacts. *Journal of Personality and Social Psychology, 69*, 329–340.

House, J. S. (1981). *Work stress and social support*. Reading: Addison-Wesley.

Hurlbert, J. S. (1991). Social networks, social circles, and job satisfaction. *Work and Occupations, 18*, 415–429.

Ibarra, H. (1992). Homophily and differential returns: Sex differences in network structure and access in an advertising firm. *Administrative Science Quarterly, 37*, 422–447.

Inkpen, A. C., & Tsang, E. W. K. (2005). Social capital, networks, and knowledge transfer. *Academy of Management Review, 30*, 146–165.

Jehn, K. A., & Shah, P. P. (1997). Interpersonal relationships and task performance: An examination of mediating processes in friendship and acquaintance groups. *Journal of Personality and Social Psychology, 72*, 775–790.

Kandel, D. B. (1978). Homophily, selection and socialization in adolescent friendships. *American Journal of Sociology, 84*, 427–436.

Katz, J. S., & Martin, B. R. (1997). What is collaboration? *Research Policy, 26*, 1–18.

Koskinen, J. H., & Stenberg, S.-Å. (2012). Bayesian analysis of multilevel probit models for data with friendship dependencies. *Journal of Educational and Behavioural Statistics, 37*, 203–230.

Krackhardt, D. (1999). The ties that torture: Simmelian tie analysis in organizations. *Research in the Sociology of Organizations, 16*, 183–210.

Krackhardt, D., & Stern, R. N. (1988). Informal networks and organizational crisis: An experimental simulation. *Social Psychology Quarterly, 51*, 123–140.

Kramer, R. M. (1999). Trust and distrust in organizations: Emerging perspectives, enduring questions. *Annual Review of Psychology, 50*, 569–598.

Langfred, C. W. (2004). Too much of a good thing? Negative effects of high trust and individual autonomy in self-managing teams. *Academy of Management Journal, 47*, 385–399.

Lazega, E. (2001). *The collegial phenomenon. The social mechanisms of cooperation among peers in a corporate law partnership*. Oxford: Oxford University Press.

Lazega, E., Jourda, M.-T., Mounies, L., & Stofer, R. (2008). Catching up with big fish in the big pond? Multi-level network analysis through linked design. *Social Networks, 30*, 157–176.

Leavitt, H. J. (1951). Some effects of certain communication patterns on group performance. *The Journal of Abnormal and Social Psychology, 46*, 38–50.

Leenders, R. T. A. J. (2002). Modeling social influence through network autocorrelation: Constructing the weight matrix. *Social Networks, 24*, 21–47.
Leenders, R. T. A. J., & Gabbey, S. M. (1999). *Corporate social capital and liability*. Boston: Kluwer.
Lin, N. (1999). Building a network theory of social capital. *Connections, 22*, 28–51.
Lin, N., Vaughn, J. C., & Ensel, W. M. (1981). Social resources and occupational status attainment. *Social Forces, 59*, 1163–1181.
Marsden, P. V. (1987). Core discussion networks of Americans. *American Sociological Review, 52*, 122–131.
Marsden, P. V. (1988). Homogeneity in confiding relations. *Social Networks, 10*, 57–76.
Marsden, P., & Friedkin, N. (1993). Network studies of social-influence. *Sociological Methods & Research, 22*, 127–151.
McPherson, M., Smith-Lovin, L., & Cook, J. M. (2001). Birds of a feather: Homophily in social networks. *Annual Review of Sociology, 27*, 415–444.
Molm, L. D. (1994). Dependence and risk: Transforming the structure of social exchange. *Social Psychology Quarterly, 57*, 163–176.
Nahapiet, J., & Ghoshal, S. (1998). Social capital, intellectual capital, and the organizational advantage. *Academy of Management Review, 23*, 242–266.
Oh, H., Chung, M.-H., & Labianca, G. (2004). Group social capital and group effectiveness: The role of informal socializing ties. *Academy of Management Journal, 47*, 860–875.
Pelled, L. H. (1996). Demographic diversity, conflict, and work group outcomes: An intervening process theory. *Organization Science, 7*, 615–631.
Pelled, L. H., Eisenhardt, K. M., & Xin, K. R. (1999). Exploring the black box: An analysis of work group diversity, conflict, and performance. *Administrative Science Quarterly, 44*, 1–28.
Podolny, J. M., & Baron, J. N. (1997). Resources and relationships: Social networks and mobility in the workplace. *American Sociological Review, 62*, 673–693.
Portes, A. (1998). Social capital: Its origins and applications in modern sociology. *Annual Review of Sociology, 24*, 1–24.
Reagans, R. E., & McEvily, B. (2003). Network structure and knowledge transfer: The effects of cohesion and range. *Administrative Science Quarterly, 48*, 240–267.
Requena, F. (2003). Social capital, satisfaction and quality of life in the workplace. *Social Indicators Research, 61*, 331–360.
Roberts, K. H., & O'Reilty, C. A., III. (1979). Some correlates of communication roles in organizations. *Academy of Management Journal, 22*, 42–57.
Shaw, M. E. (1964). Communication networks. In L. Berkowitz (Ed.), *Advances in experimental psychology* (pp. 111–147). New York: Academic.
Snijders, T. A. B., & Bosker, R. J. (2012). *Multilevel analysis: An introduction to basic and advanced multilevel modelling* (2nd ed.). London: Sage.
Snijders, T. A. B., van de Bunt, G. G., & Steglich, C. E. G. (2010). Introduction to actor-based models for network dynamics. *Social Networks, 32*, 44–60.
Sparrowe, R. T., Liden, R. C., Wayne, S. J., & Kraimer, M. L. (2001). Social networks and the performance of individuals and groups. *Academy of Management Journal, 44*, 318–325.
Spector, P. E. (1997). *Job satisfaction: Application, assessment, causes, and consequences*. Thousand Oaks: Sage.
Thoits, P. A. (1982). Conceptual, methodological, and theoretical problems in studying social support as a buffer against life stress. *Journal of Health and Social Behavior, 23*, 145–159.
Tsai, W., & Ghoshal, S. (1998). Social capital and value creation: The role of intrafirm networks. *Academy of Management Journal, 41*, 464–478.
Umberson, D., Chen, M. D., House, J. S., Hopkins, K., & Slaten, E. (1996). The effect of social relationships on psychological well-being: Are men and women really so different? *American Sociological Review, 61*, 837–857.
Uzzi, B. (1996). The sources and consequences of embeddedness for the economic performance of organzations: The network effect. *American Sociological Review, 61*, 674–698.

Van de Ven, A. H., Delbecq, A. L., & Koenig, R. (1976). Determinants of coordination modes within organizations. *American Sociological Review, 41*, 322–338.

Venkataramani, V., Labianca, G., & Grosser, T. (2013). Positive and negative workplace relationships, social satisfaction, and organizational attachment. *Journal of Applied Psychology, 98*, 1028–1039.

Zhang, B., Thomas, A. C., Krackhardt, D., Doreian, P., & Krishnan, R. (2013). Contrasting multiple social network autocorrelations for binary outcomes, with applications to technology adoption. *ACM Transactions on Management Information Systems (TMIS) 3,* Article No. 18.

Chapter 5
Multilevel Models for Multilevel Network Dependencies

Mark Tranmer and Emmanuel Lazega

Introduction

Multilevel networks occur when a network of lowest level nodes, such as people and their personal ties, is embedded in a network of higher level nodes, such as organizations and their organizational ties. Given this multilevel network structure, it may be of substantive interest to investigate the way in which a level 1 nodal attribute, which can be regarded as a dependent variable, varies across the various components of a multilevel network. For example, how much does a performance score for a person vary by his or her network connections, and the connections of the organisations to which he or she is affiliated?

We explain how a type of multilevel model, called a Multiple Membership Multiple Classification (MMMC) model, can be used with such multilevel network data to estimate the relative share of variation in a lowest level nodal dependent variable across the various components of a multilevel network in which it is embedded. We illustrate the approach with an analysis of real multilevel network data for French cancer elites.

This chapter is organized as follows. We begin by briefly reviewing Network Autocorrelation Models (NAMs), as these are well-established models for network dependencies in single-level networks and thus provide a good starting point for

---

M. Tranmer (✉)
Social Statistics, School of Social Sciences, University of Manchester, Manchester M13 9PL, UK
e-mail: mark.tranmer@manchester.ac.uk

E. Lazega
Institut d'Etudes Politiques de Paris, SPC, CSO-CNRS, 19 rue Amélie, 75007 Paris, France
e-mail: emmanuel.lazega@sciencespo.fr

discussing node-level variable dependencies in single-level networks. This then provides the basis to introduce more recent alternative models for network dependencies, which enable different substantive questions about network dependencies from those that are usually the focus in a NAM analysis to be answered. We then introduce the Multiple Membership (MM) model, and explain how it can be used to model single-level network dependencies; in particular to investigate network variations in the dependent variable. Next, we explain how the MM model can be extended to a Multiple Membership Multiple Classification (MMMC) model for multilevel network dependencies, where the multiple classifications arise because there is more than one network, as well as the affiliations of level 1 units to level 2 units. Following this, we fit an MMMC model to our case study dataset on French cancer elites, and interpret the results. Finally, we draw conclusions about the research value of the MMMC model for multilevel networks and briefly discuss further extensions to the model.

Network Autocorrelation Models for Single Level Networks

A single-level network comprises a set of nodes and their connections, or ties. Often, a set of attributes of the nodes is available for such a network. We might regard one of these as a node-level (nodal) dependent variable, and others as node-level explanatory variables. We may wish to regress the nodal dependent variable on the nodal explanatory variables. If we fit an Ordinary Least Squares (OLS) regression model to such data, we ignore the fact that the nodes are connected; the underlying assumption of independence of units in an OLS regression analysis is not valid for connected nodes. We must take the network connections into account in our analysis: either because these are regarded as a nuisance, or because the network dependencies are of direct substantive interest.

Well-established models for network dependencies in single level networks are Network Autocorrelation Models (NAMs). These evolved from Spatial Autocorrelation Models (SAMs) – see, for example, Ord (1975) and Doreian (1980). The theoretical specification of NAMs and SAMs is the same, only the data input differs. In the SAMs, a spatial proximity or contiguity matrix is included for the areas in the analysis, where the areas are the units of analysis. For NAMs a social network matrix is used in place of the geographical information and the network nodes are the units of analysis. There are two types of NAMs: the network effects model and the network disturbances model. These are both defined below.

The network effects model is defined, for a single-level network, by:

$$y = \rho \mathbf{W} y + \mathbf{X} \mathbf{B} + \epsilon$$
$$\epsilon \sim N(0, \sigma_e^2) \tag{5.1}$$

The network disturbances model is defined by:

$$y = \mathbf{XB} + \epsilon$$
$$\epsilon = \rho \mathbf{W}\epsilon + \nu$$
$$\nu \sim N(0, \sigma_\nu^2) \tag{5.2}$$

In both Eqs. 5.1 and 5.2, the data include: a nodal dependent variable y, which is an attribute of the network nodes; explanatory variables $\mathbf{X}$, also attributes of the network nodes; and a weight matrix, $\mathbf{W}$, derived from the network adjacency matrix. The weight matrix, $\mathbf{W}$, is usually standardized so that the rows sum to 1, and the diagonal elements of the weight matrix are structurally set to zero. Estimation of Models 5.1 and 5.2 requires inversion of the weight matrix $\mathbf{W}$. Leenders (2002) reviews NAMs and gives a detailed discussion about how the weight matrices may be defined in different ways from the same original network matrix for such models. Model 5.1 and 5.2 will sometimes yield similar goodness of fit. The choice of whether to model the network dependence as a direct fixed effect, as in Model 5.2, or via a random effect through the error terms, as in Model 5.1, will depend on the research questions of the substantive study (Leenders 2002). Model 5.2 might be used to take into account network dependencies when they are regarded as a nuisance, whereas Model 5.1 allows for the direct association of values of the dependent variables for connected nodes (e.g. alters in an ego net), when estimating the value for the focal node (e.g. the ego in an ego net). In that sense, Model 5.1 can be seen as a type of peer-effect model. In Models 5.1 and 5.2, average network correlations between the focal and connected values of y (for Model 5.1) or the error term (for Model 5.2) are given by the correlation coefficient, ρ. NAMs can be fitted in R (R Core Team 2013) using the *sna* package (Butts 2010).

Multilevel and Multiple Membership Models

An alternative way of modeling network dependencies for a single-level network, particularly valuable for investigating network *variations* in a nodal dependent variable, is via a Multiple Membership (MM) model. An MM model is a type of multilevel model. Because multilevel models have only recently been used in the context of network dependence for nodal dependent variables, we begin with a general discussion of multilevel and multiple membership models before explaining, in section "Multiple Membership Models for Single-Level Network Dependencies", how these models may be used with social networks.

Since the 1980s, multilevel models have been used extensively in statistical analysis, including applications in the social sciences and health. For example, multilevel models have been applied to the analysis of school effectiveness to investigate variations in examination performance for pupils (level 1), in schools (level 2). Here, the dependent variable is the examination performance of the pupil, a level 1 variable, which may be related to attributes of the pupils (level 1 variables), as well as attributes of the schools (level 2 variables). These may be measured directly at the school level, such as whether the school was built in the last 30 years; or level 1 variables may be aggregated to the school level to be included as level 2 variables, such as the percentage of pupils taking free meals in the school. Furthermore, we can include cross-level interactions between pupil level and school level variables in this model framework; for example, to determine whether the percentage of pupils on free school meals in the school has a different association with examination scores for pupils who are allocated free school meals, as compared with pupils who are not.

When we have a multilevel population structure, such as pupils in schools, multilevel models are useful to take that structure into account in the analysis. Such models can be used when we regard the multilevel structure as a nuisance, for example as a model-based approach to take into account clustering in a multi-stage sampling design when estimating an overall population regression equation for individuals. However, more often multilevel models are extremely useful when the multilevel structure is of substantive interest. For example, based on our example above, using a multilevel model we could determine how much variation in examination score is estimated to be at the school level, and how much is estimated at the pupil level, and hence whether there is any evidence of similar (correlated) examination scores in the same school: that is, clustering. If so, we can then see how much of this clustering can be explained by characteristics of the pupils or the schools. Moreover, having allowed for the multilevel population of pupils in schools, we can identify particular schools from the model outputs for inference by examining the school-level residual terms from the multilevel model. For example, we can identify schools that are doing especially well in terms of estimated average examination performance, having controlled for pupil characteristics.

Multilevel models avoid the problems of the atomistic or ecological fallacy that would be likely to occur if we modeled data from a multilevel population at a single level. The atomistic fallacy would occur in our example if we carried out a single level analysis of pupil data and did not take into account the fact that each pupil attends a particular school and may therefore share a common experience with other pupils in that school, such as being subject to the same teaching policy within that school, or having the shared experience of studying within a modern building. The ecological fallacy would occur if we aggregated all the pupil information to the school level (level 2) and carried out a single-level analysis of school-level data, such as school means. In this case, through aggregation, we would lose information about variation in pupil's examination scores within the schools.

In theory, dummy variables can be created for the schools that pupils attend and added to a single-level regression model, but this is problematic in practice when there are a large number of schools in data to be analyzed, because there would then be a large number of coefficients for these dummy variables to be estimated in the model. In the multilevel approach, the school level appears in the random part of the model and variance (and often also covariance) components are estimated for these school-level random effects. For variance components, or "random intercepts", models there is one school-level variance component to be estimated for the school-level random effects for the constant term, rather than a large number of coefficients, as would be the case for dummy variables in the fixed part of a single-level regression model. The school-level variance component, alongside the pupil-level variance component, allows us to estimate the variation in examination scores between and within schools. Within the multilevel model framework, it is also possible to allow the explanatory variables to have random coefficients – for example we could investigate whether the school-level variation in examination performance is different for boys and girls; in other words, whether the association of examination score with gender is different in different schools.

We have described an example above for a two-level population of pupils (level 1) in schools (level 2). Further hierarchical levels could be added to the model – either between the school and pupil levels, such as classes within the school, or above the school level, such as the Local Education Authority, if these could be identified in the available data, and if there were sufficient numbers of units at each level. Usually, 10 or more units are needed for each level. Fewer than 10 units can often be treated as fixed effects in the model.

Hierarchical multilevel modeling as described above, where each lower-level unit is a member of only one unit above it, has become a standard statistical analysis technique in recent years, and such models can be fitted in multilevel software such as MLwiN (Rasbash et al. 2012) or HLM (Raudenbush 2004), as well as statistical software such as stata (Rabe-Hesketh and Skrondal 2008) and R (R Core Team 2013; Finch et al. 2014). Basic hierarchical models can also be fitted in more recent releases of SPSS (Heck et al. 2013). For a general overview of Multilevel Analysis, including more discussion of software, see Snijders and Bosker (2011).

More recent developments in multilevel analysis have been in realistically complex models for population structures that are non-hierarchical, such as cross-classified models. For example, two pupils who live in the same local area might each attend a different school, whereas two pupils from the same school might each live in a different local area. Here, areas and schools are non-hierarchical groups. However, we may have a substantive hypothesis regarding the way in which the local area in which the pupil lives and the school the pupil attends are each associated with their educational performance. In this situation we can use a multilevel model in which the areas and schools are cross-classified (Goldstein 1994).

Another realistically complex multilevel model is the Multiple Membership Model. Here, individuals can be members of multiple groups. For example, an individual might work and live in two separate areas, perhaps spending 30 % of a typical week in the work area and the remainder of their time at home. If we wish to associate that individual's health in the context of the air quality of their local area, we could choose the area where they live as the group in a simple two-level multilevel model, but we would then not recognize that the individual spends a fair proportion of the week in the area of their workplace, which may have different air quality to their area of residence. To allow multiple areas to be included in a model for individuals, as in this example, a multiple membership model can be used, where in our example the individual is a member of two groups: the place in which they live and the place in which they work. Membership weights, which we assume sum to one for each individual, reflect the time spent in the area in which they live and the area in which they work. For the example above these would be 0.7 (home) and 0.3 (work). This model still applies for people who live and work in the same area. In that case the individual would be a member of a single area with a weight of 1. Multiple membership models were first described in the literature by Hill and Goldstein (1998). Browne et al. (2001) extended these to multiple membership multiple classification (MMMC) models, explaining that several group memberships could apply to the same population of individuals. Although MMMC models are sometimes described as multilevel models, the word *classification* is preferred over *level*, because these classifications are not assumed to have any hierarchy, as is usually implied by *level*.

Multiple Membership Models for Single-Level Network Dependencies

Multiple membership models can be used to investigate network variations in a nodal dependent variable. For a binary-valued undirected adjacency matrix, row i of the matrix is ego i's alters. If we regard egos as groups and alters as the individuals in that group, and consider the first row of this matrix as an ego, any of the other $n-1$ nodes can potentially be alters in node 1's ego net (NB: Throughout this discussion, "ego net" is equivalent to "ego neighbourhood"). Often the network will comprise overlapping ego nets, where the same alter will appear in different ego nets and thus be a member of more than one of these groups. Node 1 may also be an alter in some of the other $n-1$ ego nets in the network. Using this approach we break down an $n \times n$ adjacency matrix in n groups: the ego nets. Define y_i as a dependent variable for each node in the network ($i = 1, \ldots, n$). We may then be interested in the extent to which this dependent variable varies between and within ego nets. The multiple membership model allows us to investigate this, given ego net overlap. We can fit MM models before and after the inclusion of nodal explanatory variables.

Each row of the adjacency matrix represents a node in the network, which can be an alter in the other $n-1$ ego nets in the network. We assign membership weights for this which are usually assumed to sum to 1 across the row. For example, if the first node of the network was an alter in three ego nets: say for nodes 3,7, and 11, then weights for membership of each of these ego nets are $\frac{1}{3}$, and all other weights in that row of the weight matrix- including the diagonal – are set to zero.

We can then write down a multiple membership model for this situation as:

$$y_i = \mathbf{x}_i'\beta + \sum_{j \in m(i)} w_{m_i,j} u_j + e_i$$

$$i = 1, \ldots, n$$

$$u_j \sim N(0, \sigma_u^2) \quad e_i \sim N(0, \sigma_e^2) \quad Cov(u_j, e_i) = 0 \qquad (5.3)$$

Here, y_i is an interval-scale dependent variable for each node in the network, where $i = 1,\ldots,n$, and n is the total number of nodes in the network. $\mathbf{x}'_i \beta$ is a set of nodal explanatory variables and their coefficients, in the fixed part of the model. $\sum_{j \in m(i)} w_{mi,j} u_j$ is a weighted sum of n random effects $u_j, j = 1,\ldots n$. Non-zero weights $w_{mi,j}$ are assigned when i is a member of j's ego net. e_i is an individual- (node-) level error term. The ego net random effects, u_j have zero mean and variance σ_u^2. The individual node-level random effects, e_i have zero mean and variance σ_e^2. The ego net and individual node-level random effects are assumed to be uncorrelated.

In the discussion so far, we have described a situation where there is one set of network groups in a single-level network: the ego nets within that network. We could also define other network subgroups such as cliques of a particular minimum size e.g. cliques of 3 or more individuals. It is possible to put more than one network subgroup in the multiple membership model framework. For example, we could include components in the model for cliques of varying sizes: 3 or more, 4 or more, and so on, to assess where the variations in the node-level dependent variable are with respect to these clique thresholds. As is the case for NAMs, we could also fit these models for directed adjacency matrices, where the rows would represent the outgoing ties for each node in the network and the columns represent their incoming ties. In this situation, we could define both outgoing and incoming tie weights, and include both an outgoing and an incoming component in the same model. We could also use valued adjacency matrices and make weights inversely proportional to the sum of the tie values in each ego net. Here, the value of the tie for each alter would be the numerator, resulting in larger tie values having larger ego net membership weights. Weighting schemes other than the inverse of the sum of ego net ties could also be used: for example, the weights could be made inversely proportional to the square root of the sum of the ties in each ego net.

In a standard nested hierarchical multilevel model, each lowest level unit is a member of one higher level unit with a weight of one. For example, each pupil goes to one school at a particular time point. When we fit a null model for this case we can calculate the variance partition coefficient from the estimated variance components at the individual and group level; for example, the estimated level 1 variance component for pupils and the estimated level 2 variance component for schools, when modeling variations in examination performance for the two-level hierarchy of pupils in schools. For a multiple membership model, lower level units are potentially members of multiple groups, with associated membership weights. Each individual has a (potentially) different group membership as determined by their membership weights. This means the variance partition coefficient cannot be calculated directly from the model estimates. One practical approach for estimating the proportion of variation between groups and individuals in the multiple membership model is to first scale the estimated group-level variance component by the average non-zero group membership weight, and then to calculate the variance partition coefficient on the basis of this scaled measure.

Explanatory variables can be added directly to the fixed part of the MM model; at the individual level, the group level, or both. In addition, if we hypothesized that some kind of overspill might occur in the explanatory variables, where the alter's values of these explanatory variables might be associated with the dependent variable of the ego, "peer effect" explanatory variables could also be created by multiplying the nodal values of explanatory connected to the focal node by their outgoing or incoming weights as appropriate, as indicated in Eq. 5.4. These peer effect explanatory variables could be added to the fixed part of the model.

$$\bar{x}_i = \sum_{j \in m(i)} w_{mi,j} x_i \qquad (5.4)$$

Tranmer et al. (2014) fitted a multiple membership model to a single-level social network of friendship based on adolescent health data from the US (Harris et al. 2009), where the individual nodal dependent variable was a pupil's examination score. Amongst the models they fitted was a multiple membership model, as described theoretically above, for the ego nets in the friendship networks. Having fitted this model, they found that some of the variation in examination score was estimated to be between ego nets. In other words, two pupils from the same ego net were more likely to have similar examination scores than two pupils from different ego nets. They also fitted models with network cliques in place of ego nets as the network groups, and again found evidence of between clique variation (and thus within clique similarity) of examination score. They also extended model 5.3 to include additional classifications for the schools the pupils attended, and the areas in which the pupils lived. This allowed an assessment of network, school, and area variations in the examination performance of pupils. When they compared a model that included only an individual level and school classifications with another model that included an individual level with both school and network classifications, they found that the latter had better statistical goodness-of-fit, and that the estimated school-level variance component decreased a little when a network component was included in the model. They concluded that some of the estimated school-level variation in the examination performance of pupils in the former model was attributable to the friendship networks of pupils, once this information was included in the latter model. By extending the model in this way, the MM model becomes a multiple membership multiple classification (MMMC) model, because there are now several sets of classifications included: for the networks, the schools, and areas of the population.

Tranmer et al. (2014) also fitted a series of NAMs to the adolescent health data to compare, empirically, the goodness of fit of these models with the MMMC models. For the NAMS they created dummy variables for the schools in the population. They found that the models had similar statistical goodness of fit to the MMMC models, but concluded these two types of models have different substantive uses. For example, NAMs can be used to control for network effects in estimating school differences in exam scores via the estimated coefficients of the school dummy variables in the model, whereas the MMMC model allows school and network variance components to be estimated when investigating variations in examination score, and, like the hierarchical models discussed above, also allows explanatory variables in the model to have random coefficients. The MMMC model can also be used with categorical response variables, such as a binary attribute, as the dependent variable, which is not straightforward in the NAM framework. Although both MMs and NAMs use the same information from the data, they treat it in very different ways. For example, estimation of the NAM parameters the inversion of the (row standardized) adjacency matrix of friendship connections, whereas the MMMC model uses this weight information directly without the need for matrix inversion.

Multiple Membership Multiple Classification (MMMC) Models for Multilevel Networks

A multilevel network with two levels can be defined as a set of n_1 level 1 nodes, and their connections (the level 1 network), and a set of n_2 level 2 nodes and their connections (the level 2 network). At each network level, the connections could be directed or undirected, binary or valued. The values of n_1 and n_2 are often not closely related. When level 1 nodes represent people and level 2 nodes represent organizations, the available data may have fewer level 2 nodes than level 1 nodes, and the affiliation of level 1 nodes to level 2 nodes might be known.

For example, Lazega et al. (2008) collected multilevel network data for French elite cancer researchers and the research laboratories to which they were affiliated, in the Île de France area. There are individual and collective forms of agency at these two levels. At the researcher level (level 1), the network describes advice-seeking, and there are $n_1 = 97$ nodes. At the laboratory level, the network describes collaborations among the laboratories, and there are $n_2 = 82$ nodes at this level. Information was also collected on researchers' affiliations with laboratories, where each researcher is affiliated with exactly one laboratory. This information therefore indicates which level 1 nodes are contained in which level 2 nodes. Lazega et al. (2008) were interested in how the performance scores of individual researchers, a level 1 network nodal variable, are associated with attributes of those researchers such as age, speciality, and fish/pond status, as well the laboratories in which they worked, given the multilevel network structure in which they are embedded. However they did not use a multilevel modeling approach to investigate this.

In Eq. 5.5, we define the MMMC model for a multilevel network with two levels in which the affiliations of level 1 nodes to level 2 nodes is known. As discussed earlier, in section "Multilevel and Multiple Membership Models", we will assume that the networks are grouped by ego nets. In the two-level network, there are two sets of ego nets: ego nets of researchers for the level 1 network, and ego nets of laboratories for the level 2 network. There is also another population grouping here: the affiliation of researchers to laboratories. The MMMC model for two sets of network connections and affiliations of level 1 nodes to level 2 nodes, may be defined as:

$$y_{i\ell} = \mathbf{x}'_i\beta + \sum_{j\in m(i)} w_{mi,j}u_j + \sum_{k\in p(\ell)} w_{p\ell,k}v_k + \eta_\ell + e_{i\ell}$$

$$i = 1,\ldots,n_1, \ \ell = 1,\ldots,n_2$$

Where n_1 is the number of level 1 nodes, and n_2 is the number of level 2 nodes;

$$u_j \sim N(0,\sigma_u^2) \ \ v_k \sim N(0,\sigma_v^2) \ \ \eta_\ell \sim N(0,\sigma_\eta^2) \ \ e_i \sim N(0,\sigma_e^2)$$

$$Cov(u_j,e_{i\ell}) = Cov(u_v,e_{i\ell}) = Cov(\eta_\ell,e_{i\ell}) = Cov(u_j,v_k) = Cov(u_j,\eta_\ell)$$
$$= Cov(v_k,\eta_\ell) = 0. \tag{5.5}$$

In the formulation of Model 5.5, the dependent variable, $y_{i\ell}$, is an interval-scale dependent variable for each level 1 node i, affiliated to level 2 node ℓ, which may be related to a set of explanatory variables with coefficients, β, via the term $\mathbf{x}'\beta$ in the fixed part of the model. Attributes of the level 1 and/or level 2 nodes, and cross-level interactions between these variables, could be used as explanatory variables in the model.

The ego nets at the two levels of the multilevel network are represented in the model by two weighted sums of random effects, $\sum_{j\in m(i)} w_{mi,j}u_j$ for the level 1 network, and for the level 2 network, $\sum_{k\in p(\ell)} w_{p\ell,k}v_k$. When the network groups are defined as ego nets, each row of the adjacency matrix for the level 1 network is the ego net of that particular node, so that the number of random effects for the level 1 network is n_1; similarly, for the level 2 network, there are n_2 random effects. To include the random effects of the alters of each ego in the model estimation process, a system of weights is used. If the ego net of the first researcher in the level 1 network has a total of n_{11} alters, then each alter in that ego's network is given a weight of $\frac{1}{n_{11}}$, so that the weights sum to 1 across the row, and these weights are thus row-standardized. A similar system is used for the level 2 network weights, based on the ego net membership at that level. In addition, a random effect, η_ℓ is included for the affiliations of researchers to laboratories. As is typical in multilevel modeling, the random effects are assumed to be normally distributed and uncorrelated with one another, allowing variance components for the different networks, and for the individual researcher level, to be defined and estimated. Because the random effects are assumed to be uncorrelated, it is possible to estimate the relative share of variation in the dependent variable for the individual level 1 nodes, the level 1 network ego nets, the level 2 network ego nets, and the affiliation of researchers to laboratories.

Empirical Case Study

To illustrate our approach, we use the well-known and well-researched French Cancer researchers dataset of Lazega et al. (2008). Full details of the data collection and variables can be found in Lazega et al. (2008) in their "big fish, small pond" analysis. More recently, this multilevel dataset has been analyzed by Wang et al.

(2013). These authors used a Multilevel Exponential Graph Model (MERGM) to investigate the multilevel network structure of the ties in these data. Here, we explain how to investigate multilevel network dependencies in a dependent variable that is an attribute of the level 1 nodes; the research performance of the individual cancer researchers.

Data

Lazega et al. (2008) collected and analyzed multilevel network data, where the first-level directed network nodes are individual cancer researchers and the second-level directed network nodes are laboratories. Attributes of the researchers (level 1 nodes) include research performance scores. The value of this score at the first time point in the study is the dependent variable, y_i, we investigate in our case study. Other attributes of the level 1 nodes include the researcher's age in years, speciality of the researcher, and whether s/he is a director of research or not. In addition, we know whether the researchers can be classified into four categories based on their level 1 network centrality ('fish') and the level 2 network centrality of the laboratory ('pond') in which they work. Four classifications are given: Big Fish, Small Pond; Little Fish, Small Pond; Big Fish, Big Pond; Little Fish, Big Pond. These explanatory variables were used the analysis that follows. The data we used for the analysis are based on 97 researchers in 82 laboratories.

Research Questions

Based on these data, we ask the following research questions:

1. Is any of the variation in performance score associated with the network connections of researchers, or the connections of laboratories to which the researchers are affiliated?
2. If so, what is the relative share of that variation? Is it mainly associated with networks of researchers, networks of laboratories, or the way in which researchers are affiliated to laboratories?
3. Is the network variation in performance score mainly associated with outgoing or incoming ties?
4. Is the variation in performance score all explained by the explanatory variables once these are added to the fixed part of the model?
5. If not, how is the relative share of the remaining variation associated with networks of researchers, laboratories, and the affiliations of researchers to laboratories?

6. Would we have come to the same conclusions about the way in which the covariates are associated with research performance score, if we had simply fitted a single-level model?
7. What do we learn, substantively, from the more complex MMMC models that would have not been possible with simpler models?

Data Preparation

The data comprise a vector of $n_1 = 97$ values for the dependent variable for the researchers; for the n_p explanatory variables, a $97 \times n_p$ matrix; and two directed binary adjacency matrices: one for the researchers, of dimension 97×97, and one for the $n_2 = 82$ laboratories, of dimension 82×82. Data manipulation for the weight matrices was carried out using R. To expand the laboratory (level 2 network) weight matrix and give it n_1 rows instead of n_2, those rows of weights for laboratories with more than one researcher were repeated in the dataset resulting in a 97×82 weight matrix for the laboratories, where the laboratory weight information was repeated for those rows of researchers in the data that were affiliated to the same laboratory. This is a standard way of preparing hierarchical multilevel data and an advantage of the multilevel approach is that it is quite straightforward to achieve. Dummy variables were created for the categorical explanatory variables. For example, the four-category Fish/Pond variable was added to the fixed part of the model as three dummy variables. All interval explanatory variables were standardized to have mean zero and standard deviation of 1.

Model Fitting Strategy and Software Details

We fitted Model 5.5 to the Lazega data, both as null models, and later with all explanatory variables added to the fixed part of the model. We fitted these models for both the outgoing tie networks of researchers and laboratories and the incoming tie networks. Thus, the fully specified model included, in the random part, a level 1 ego net classification, a level 2 ego net classification, laboratory level to which the researchers were affiliated, and an individual researcher level. We also fitted reduced versions of model 5.5 in which, for example, only one network level was specified. As we were using an Monte Carlo Markov Chain (MCMC) approach, we evaluated model goodness of fit with the DIC measure: the smaller the value of DIC, the better the model fit, having taken into account the number of effective parameters in the model (i.e. the model complexity). This measure allowed us to compare the statistical fit of the fully specified models with reduced models and with a baseline single-level model.

The MMMC models were fitted in R (R Core Team 2013) making use of the R2MLwiN package (Zhang et al. 2016), which invokes the MLwiN (Rasbash et al. 2012) software for multilevel modeling to obtain the results before returning them to the R environment. The model results presented here were all estimated via an MCMC algorithm (Browne 2009), using default flat priors for the fixed effects and a chain of 20,000 samples. In all models, standard diffuse (gamma) priors were assumed for the variance parameters.

Results

We now discuss the results of the MMMC models. We begin with null models for the outgoing tie networks.

Outgoing Tie Networks

The results in Table 5.1 suggest that the majority of the variation in research performance is between individual researchers. M1 is the baseline single-level model, which estimates the mean as zero and the variance at the individual as 1, as we would expect with a standardized dependent variable. M2 is a simple hierarchy of researchers in laboratories. The DIC suggests better goodness of fit than M1. For M1, with a single individual-level variance component, 100 % of the estimated variation in research performance is at the individual researcher level. Once we have more than one variance component estimated, we can compare the share of variation for each estimated component. For M2 there is 55 % variation at the individual researcher level and 45 % variation between laboratories. Even though most laboratories contain exactly one researcher in the data, a few laboratories contain more than one researcher, and hence it is possible to estimate a laboratory-level variance component. In M3 we include a variance component for ego nets of laboratories. The variance component for this, $\hat{\sigma}_v^2$ net.lab., is estimated as 0.307. However, we must first scale this component to make it comparable with the other estimated variance components. We do this by multiplying the estimate by the average (mean) non-zero ego net alter membership weight. Having done this, we see that 8 % of the variation in research performance is at the laboratory ego net level and 92 % at the individual level, and that, in terms of goodness of fit, this model is little better than the single-level model, M1. We now include the ego nets for single-level network of researchers in M4. Having scaled the estimated variance component for the ego nets of researchers by the average ego net membership weight, we see we can associate around 43 % of the variation in performance score with it and the remaining 57 % of variation at the individual level. The DIC for this model is lower than all previous models. This suggests that ego nets of researchers are associated with variation in performance score; thus, there is clustering of researcher performance scores within ego nets of researchers. Model 5 (M5) includes all components, and the DIC is the smallest for all models fitted in Table 5.1. This is a multilevel network model with components for laboratory

Table 5.1 Null models: outgoing tie networks

	M1	M2	M3	M4
Constant	0.000	−0.045	−0.046	−0.174
(s.e.)	(0.103)	(0.107)	(0.116)	(0.154)
$\hat{\sigma}_v^2$ net.lab.			0.307	
var. share %			8	
$\hat{\sigma}_u^2$ net.res.				2.046
var. share %				43
$\hat{\sigma}_\eta^2$ lab.		0.417		
var. share %		43		
$\hat{\sigma}_e^2$ res.	1.022	0.551	0.917	0.440
var. share %	100	55	92	57
DIC	278.26	250.09	275.33	229.35
	M5	M6	M7	
Constant	−0.180	−0.186	−0.159	
	(0.155)	(0.163)	(0.153)	
$\hat{\sigma}_v^2$ net.lab.	0.066	0.061		
var. share %	2	2		
$\hat{\sigma}_u^2$ net.res.	1.806	1.981	1.807	
var. share %	38	42	38	
$\hat{\sigma}_\eta^2$ lab.	0.053		0.073	
var. share %	7		9	
$\hat{\sigma}_e^2$ res.	0.410	0.435	0.413	
var. share %	53	56	53	
DIC	226.94	229.58	227.12	

ego nets, researcher ego nets and the affiliations of researchers to laboratories. We see in the results for M5 that most of the variation remains at the individual level (53 %), then the ego nets of researchers (38 %), then, to a lesser extent, affiliations of researchers of laboratories (7 %) then laboratory networks (2 %). In M6 and M7 we tried removing some of the multilevel network components from M5 to empirically compare these reduced models. We found, in M6, that by removing the laboratory affiliation information, the model fit is slightly worse compared with M5, and that there is a subsequent increase in the share of variation at the individual level (56 %) and networks of researcher levels (42 %). In M7 we removed the networks of laboratories component, and we see that the share of variation that had been associated with that level is now added to the laboratory affiliation component (9 %), and that the goodness of fit is almost as good as the fully specified model (M5).

Incoming Tie Networks

We now consider similar analyses based on the incoming tie networks of researchers and laboratories. The results are shown in Table 5.2. The first thing we notice is that

5 Multilevel Models for Multilevel Network Dependencies   121

Table 5.2 Null models: incoming tie networks

	M8	M9	M10	M11
Constant	−0.143	−0.022	−0.104	−0.045
(s.e.)	(0.164)	(0.114)	(0.146)	(0.113)
$\hat{\sigma}_v^2$ net.lab.	0.723		0.309	
var. share %	18		8	
$\hat{\sigma}_u^2$ net.res.		0.149	0.092	0.084
var. share %		3	2	1
$\hat{\sigma}_\eta^2$ lab.			0.324	0.409
var. share			34	42
$\hat{\sigma}_e^2$ res.	0.822	0.996	0.547	0.547
var. share	82	97	56	56
DIC	269.26	278.75	250.48	250.81

incoming ego nets for laboratories have a greater share of variation than incoming tie networks of researchers. We also notice that the goodness of fit measures of the incoming tie models in Table 5.2 are not as good as those involving outgoing tie networks of researchers in Table 5.1. Also, the relative share of variation is different. For example, in M9, we see that although most variation in performance is between individual researchers, 56 %, it is now the laboratories that have the next largest share 34 %, then, to a much lesser extent, the ego nets of laboratories based on their incoming ties 8 %, then the ego nets of researchers based on their incoming ties 2 %.

Allowing for Explanatory Variables

We next added covariates to the fixed part of the model. These are characteristics of the researchers, including speciality, age, fish/pond, and whether the researcher is a 'research director.' The results are given in Table 5.3. M12 is a single-level regression of the results for comparison with the multilevel network models for outgoing ties (M13) and incoming ties (M14). For M12 we see that various specialities are significantly associated with increases in performance score, compared with the baseline category (Diagnostics). Age and research director are not significantly associated with performance score in any of the three models. Some categories of fish/pond are significantly associated with different average performance scores in all models. The baseline category is big fish, big pond, and we see that in comparison little fish in small ponds have, on average, significantly lower performance scores compared with researchers who are big fish in big ponds. We also see in M13 and M14 that, having allowed for these explanatory variables, the variation above the individual level is reduced. Only the outgoing tie ego net variation for researchers in M13 retains any appreciable share of the variation in the performance score of the researchers. The total variation explained by the explanatory variables in the three models is around 20 % for the single level model (M12) with a total variance in the dependent variable conditional on the explanatory variables in the model estimated at 0.803, around 35 % for the outgoing ties model (M13), with a total variance in the

Table 5.3 MMMC models with selected covariates

	M12		M13		M14	
Constant	−0.213	(0.266)	−0.205	(0.267)	−0.294	(0.278)
Surgery/Radiology	−0.352	(0.410)	−0.658	(0.409)	−0.435	(0.419)
Haematology	0.887	(0.312)**	0.724	(0.308)*	0.810	(0.328)*
Tumour, Chemotherapy	0.078	(0.309)	−0.052	(0.297)	0.044	(0.317)
Pharmacology	−0.168	(0.363)	−0.101	(0.371)	−0.086	(0.379)
Molecular/Cellular	0.799	(0.297)**	0.423	(0.333)	0.606	(0.316).
Molecular/Genetics	0.906	(0.378)*	0.644	(0.358)	0.897	(0.389)*
Big fish, small pond	−0.143	(0.271)	−0.171	(0.247)	−0.141	(0.274)
Little fish, big pond	−0.123	(0.263)	−0.164	(0.230)	−0.106	(0.246)
Little fish, small pond	−0.611	(0.265)*	−0.584	(0.251)*	−0.519	(0.276).
Age (standardised)	0.097	(0.096)	0.068	(0.083)	0.118	(0.089)
Research Director	0.073	(0.186)	0.183	(0.174)	0.194	(0.185)
$\hat{\sigma}_v^2$ net.lab			0.079		0.053	
var. share			3		2	
$\hat{\sigma}_u^2$ net.res			1.145		0.055	
var. share			29		1	
$\hat{\sigma}_\eta^2$ lab.			0.115		0.288	
var. share			17		37	
$\hat{\sigma}_e^2$ res.	0.803		0.337		0.479	
var share.	100		51		61	
DIC	240.20		210.11		240.77	

Signif. codes: '**' 0.01; '*' 0.05; '.' 0.1

dependent variable conditional on the explanatory variables in the model estimated at 0.641, and around 21 % for the incoming ties Model (M14), with a total variance in the dependent variable conditional on the explanatory variables in the model estimated at 0.785. These results are consistent with DIC values; M13 gives the best goodness of fit of the two models, with M12 and M14 being essentially the same, higher, value of DIC.

Conclusions and Further Extensions to the MMMC Model

We have defined a Multiple Membership Multiple Classification (MMMC) model for estimating the relative share of variation for a level 1 nodal dependent variable embedded in a multilevel network, before and after controlling for explanatory variables. We have explained that MMMC models can be fitted in statistical software through the use of R and MLwiN. We have fitted this model to real multilevel network data for French cancer research elites.

Some of the variation of the performance scores of the researchers, an attribute of the level 1 nodes of this multilevel network, is particularly associated with the way in which researchers nominated other researchers in their ego net (their outgoing ties): around 40 % of the variation before allowing for explanatory variables. Having added characteristics of researchers as explanatory variables, this reduces the overall magnitude of the residual variation, but there is still a suggestion that some of this residual variation is associated with outgoing tie networks of researchers: around 29 % of the residual variation. We also find that if we had only fitted a single-level model we would have found more significant mean differences in the performance scores of researchers from different specialities. In particular, we would have found expertise in molecular topics to be associated with significantly higher mean performance scores than some of the other specialities. These differences do not persist when multilevel components are added to the models; we would reach a different conclusion regarding the variables in the fixed part of the model if we only fitted the single-level model and did not include the multilevel network components. Moreover, the MMMC models have enabled us to see that, having allowed for the full multilevel structure in the model, there is some evidence that incoming ego nets of researchers are associated with variations in research performance. Such a finding would not have been possible with simpler, single-level models.

Extensions to the MMMC models are possible, and further information can be obtained from them. Extensions include the possibility of random coefficients: to investigate, for example, whether the explanatory variables for researchers have stronger (or weaker) associations with the dependent variable in some ego nets, compared with others. Peer-effect explanatory variables could be added in this model framework. Other groupings could be included in the model framework such as a geographical dimension – different regions of France, for example, or a time dimension if the network information and attributes were available at different time points. Other network subgroups could be used in the models, such as cliques. More than one network subgroup definition could be used in the same model to investigate the association of networks of dependence and structure. The extent to which we can expect the corresponding model parameters to be identified will depend on the quality of the available data. The identification of model parameters will also depend on the extent to which the network matrices are different from one another, and their density. Further information that can be obtained from MMMC models include the residuals for the various ego net levels, and other levels specified in the models. These would allow the identification of "unusual" ego nets of researchers or laboratories, by ranking the residuals in a similar manner as has been done for schools in studies of school effectiveness, or hospitals in health studies.

Acknowledgements The Leverhulme Trust. Multilevel Network Modelling Group Leverhulme International Networks Scheme. Network Grant Reference Number: F/00120/BR. (2009–2013).

References

Browne, W. J. (2009). MCMC estimation in MLwiN. Centre for Mutltilevel Modelling, University of Bristol.

Browne, W. J., Goldstein, H., & Rasbash, J. (2001). Multiple membership multiple classification (MMMC) models. *Statistical Modelling, 1*(2), 103–124.

Butts, C. T. (2010). SNA: Tools for social network analysis. R package version 2.2-0.

Doreian, P. (1980). Linear models with spatially distributed data spatial disturbances or spatial effects? *Sociological Methods & Research, 9*(1), 29–60.

Finch, W. H., Bolin, J. E., & Kelley, K. (2014). *Multilevel modeling using R*. Boca Raton: CRC Press.

Goldstein, H. (1994). Multilevel cross-classified models. *Sociological Methods & Research, 22*(3), 364–375.

Harris, K. M., Florey, F., Tabor, J., Bearman, P. S., Jones, J., & Udry, J. R. (2009). The National Longitudinal Study of Adolescent Health: Research design. University of North Carolina, Chapel Hill. Available from http://www.cpc.unc.edu/projects/addhealth/design.

Heck, R. H., Thomas, S. L., & Tabata, L. N. (2013). *Multilevel and longitudinal modeling with IBM SPSS*. New York: Routledge.

Hill, P. W., & Goldstein, H. (1998). Multilevel modeling of educational data with cross-classification and missing identification for units. *Journal of Educational and Behavioral Statistics, 23*(2), 117–128.

Lazega, E., Jourda, M.-T., Mounier, L., & Stofer, R. (2008). Catching up with big fish in the big pond? Multi-level network analysis through linked design. *Social Networks, 30*(2), 159–176.

Leenders, R. T. A. (2002). Modeling social influence through network autocorrelation: Constructing the weight matrix. *Social Networks, 24*(1), 21–47.

Ord, K. (1975). Estimation methods for models of spatial interaction. *Journal of the American Statistical Association, 70*(349), 120–126.

R Core Team. (2013). R: A language and environment for statistical computing. R Foundation for Statistical Computing, Vienna.

Rabe-Hesketh, S., & Skrondal, A. (2008). *Multilevel and longitudinal modeling using Stata*. College Station: STATA Press.

Rasbash, J., Steele, F., Browne, W. J., Goldstein, H., & Charlton, C. (2012). A user's guide to MLwiN.

Raudenbush, S. W. (2004). *HLM 6: Hierarchical linear and nonlinear modeling*. Lincolnwood: Scientific Software International.

Snijders, T. A., & Bosker, R. J. (2011). *Multilevel analysis: An introduction to basic and advanced multilevel modeling*. London: SAGE.

Tranmer, M., Steel, D., & Browne, W. J. (2014). Multiple-membership multiple-classification models for social network and group dependencies. *Journal of the Royal Statistical Society: Series A (Statistics in Society), 177*(2), 439–455.

Wang, P., Robins, G., Pattison, P., & Lazega, E. (2013). Exponential random graph models for multilevel networks. *Social Networks, 35*(1), 96–115.

Zhang, Z., Parker, R., Charlton, C. M., & Browne, W. J. (2016). R2MLwiN: A package to run MLwiN from within R. *Journal of Statistical Software* (in press).

Chapter 6
Multilevel Network Analysis Using ERGM and Its Extension

Peng Wang, Garry Robins, and Petr Matous

Introduction

Exponential random graph models (ERGMs) posit network structure as endogenous based on the assumption that network ties are conditionally dependent, in other words, the existence of a network tie depends on the existence of other network ties conditioning on the rest of the network (Frank and Strauss 1986; Lusher et al. 2013; Snijders et al. 2006; Robins et al. 2007). ERGM specifications have evolved from the baseline Erdös-Rényi or Bernoulli random graphs (Erdös and Rényi 1960) to the most recent Edge-triangle models (Pattison and Snijders 2013) using various tie dependence assumptions. Pattison and Snijders (2013) summarized these assumptions in a growing hierarchical structure that provides guidelines for future ERGM specification developments.

In multilevel network contexts, ERGMs offer a statistical framework that captures complicated multilevel structure through some simple structural signatures or network configurations based on these tie dependence assumptions. But for multilevel network models, network ties are interdependent not only within levels but also across levels. The interpretations of ERGM parameters make hypothesis testing about multilevel network structure possible. Wang et al. (2013b) proposed

---

P. Wang (✉)
Centre for Transformative Innovation, Faculty of Business and Law, Swinburne University of Technology, Hawthorn, VIC, Australia
e-mail: pengwang@swin.edu.au

G. Robins
Melbourne School of Psychological Sciences, The University of Melbourne, Parkville, VIC, Australia

P. Matous
School of Civil Engineering, Faculty of Engineering and Information Technologies, The University of Sydney, NSW, Australia

ERGM specifications for multilevel networks, and demonstrated the features of multilevel ERGMs with simulation studies and modeling examples. Combining multilevel network structure and nodal attributes, Wang et al. (2015) proposed Social Selection Models (SSMs) where the existence of multilevel network ties are conditionally dependent on not only the existence of other network ties but also on nodal attributes. They demonstrated that nodal attributes may affect network structures both within and across levels.

In this chapter, we will first review the multilevel network data structure, multilevel ERGM and SSM specifications as proposed in Wang et al. (2013b, 2015). Then we will apply these models to a dataset collected among 265 farmers and their communication network in a rural community in Ethiopia. The modeling example highlights the features of these models and their theoretical importance, that is, within-level network structures are interdependent with network structures of other levels; and within level nodal attributes can affect multilevel network structures.

Multilevel Network Data Representation

Social network data consists of a given set of nodes, ties or relationships defined on the nodes, and various attributes of the nodes. A one mode network with n nodes can be represented by an n by n adjacency matrix $X = \{X_{ij}\}$ which is a collection of network tie variables such that $X_{ij} = 1$ if there is a tie between nodes i and j, otherwise $X_{ij} = 0$. For two-mode or bipartite networks with n nodes in one set and m nodes in the other, X becomes an n by m rectangular matrix. In ERGMs, X can be treated as a network random variable with its realization denoted by x, i.e. $X = x$. Multilevel social network data can have several sets of nodes where each set defines a level; ties are then defined within or between levels. In the simplest form as shown in Fig. 6.1, a two-level network can be seen as a combination of

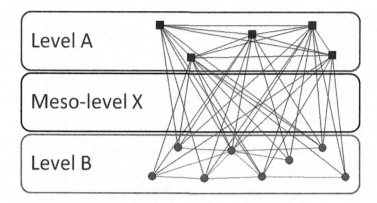

Fig. 6.1 A two-level network representation

two within-level one-mode networks (labeled here as A and B), and a bipartite meso-level network (X). Such network structure is not unusual in social networks. Examples include researcher advice ties and collaboration among their affiliated laboratories (Lazega et al. 2008; Wang et al. 2013b); interaction among employees and cooperation among their organizational units in a government institution (Zappa and Robins 2015); alliances among tribal clans and environmental dependencies among the forests they manage (Bodin and Tengö 2012).

The terminology of "levels" arises through such social science applications where the empirical context naturally suggests constructs at different but interconnected levels of analysis. The multilevel ERGM, however, does not require such a context. Rather it is applicable to more general data structures: at a minimum, two types of nodes with distinct types of tie within and between the different node sets (Wasserman and Iacobucci 1991). In our modeling example, the two "levels" are formed by classifying the 265 Ethiopian farmers into two groups of 87 entrepreneurial (level A) and 178 non-entrepreneurial (level B) farmers based on their activities. These can indeed be thought of as two levels in the sense that the entrepreneurial farmers provide the means whereby the social system accesses the wider agricultural economy in Ethiopia. Although all within- and between-level networks in our example are notionally communication ties, the content of communication may differ depending on whether it concerns entrepreneurial or non-entrepreneurial activities. The multilevel ERGMs described in the next section enable us to examine whether these communication structures differ within and between the two different types of farmers.

Multilevel ERGMs

Wang et al. (2013b) proposed ERGMs for multilevel networks by applying the hierarchy of dependence assumptions (Pattison and Snijders 2013). The resulting model combines the features of one-mode and bipartite ERGMs (Frank and Strauss 1986; Wasserman and Pattison 1996; Snijders et al. 2006; Skvoretz and Faust 1999; Agneessens and Roose 2008; Wang et al. 2009, 2013a), and highlights the interdependent nature of micro-, macro- and meso-level network ties. Using the notation introduced in the previous section, a multilevel ERGM can be expressed as

$$\Pr(A = a, X = x, B = b) = $$
$$\frac{1}{\kappa(\theta)} \exp \sum_Q \left\{ \begin{array}{l} \theta_Q z_Q(a) + \theta_Q z_Q(x) + \theta_Q z_Q(b) + \\ \theta_Q z_Q(a,x) + \theta_Q z_Q(b,x) + \theta_Q z_Q(a,x,b) \end{array} \right\}$$

where

- Q defines a network configuration where the tie variables within a configuration are assumed to be conditionally dependent.

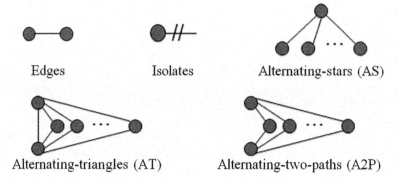

Fig. 6.2 ERGM specification for one-mode within-level (A or B) networks (z_Q (a) or z_Q (b))

- z_Q is a network statistic, or the count of the configuration of type Q. Using network X as an example, it takes the general form $z_Q(x) = \sum_x \prod_{X_{ij} \in Q} X_{ij}$
- θ_Q is the parameter associated with z_Q
- $\kappa(\theta)$ is a normalizing constant defined based on the graph space of networks of a given size and the actual model specification.

For a two-level network (A, X, B), z_Q (a) and z_Q (b) are within-level network statistics which may be defined based on ERGM specifications for one-mode networks such as those used by Snijders et al. (2006). Figure 6.2 lists some within-level graph configurations we use in our modeling example.

The number of Edges controls the density of a network distribution; the Isolate effect is helpful to model degree distributions in networks with isolated nodes; an alternating-star (AS) effect models the network degree distribution more generally, with a positive effect indicating degree centralization; the alternating-triangle (AT) effect models tendencies to network closure; and the alternating-two-path (A2P) parameter models the tendency for nodes to share multiple partners. The "Alternating" mechanism was introduced in Snijders et al. (2006) to alleviate ERGM degeneracy issues (Handcock 2003; Rinaldo et al. 2009), and hence improve model convergence.

For our empirical example, the AS, AT and A2P parameters in the A network (the entrepreneurial farmers) test whether some of the entrepreneurs are particularly popular or active among their peers (AS); whether there is network closure among the entrepreneurs (AT); and whether entrepreneurs tend to share entrepreneurial partners (A2P).

z_Q (x) are meso-level statistics which may follow ERGM specifications for bipartite networks such as those proposed by Wang et al. (2013a). Figure 6.3 provides the bipartite configurations we use in our modeling example where type A nodes are depicted as squares, and type B nodes are circles.

Similar to one-mode networks, the meso edge parameter controls the density of the meso-level network; alternating-stars A and B (ASA, ASB) are meso-level

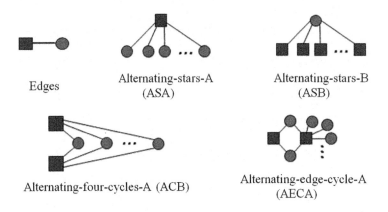

Fig. 6.3 Meso ERGM specifications

degree centralization effects; and alternating-four-cycles-B (ACB) is similar to the one-mode A2P, representing type A nodes' tendency to share multiple partners of type B. The ACB can also be interpreted as a bipartite closure effect; as in bipartite networks, the smallest closure that is not a tie is a four-cycle. The alternating-edge-cycle-A (AECA) represents interaction between bipartite closure and degree centralization: a brokerage effect where the central A-node in the AECA configuration can be seen as a broker between the closed meso-structure and the rest of the meso-network (Wang et al. 2013a).

For the farmers, the meso-network is composed of the ties between entrepreneurial and non-entrepreneurial farmers. The ASA parameter tests whether some entrepreneurial farmers are particularly active or popular among non-entrepreneurial farmers (and vice versa for ASB); the ACB parameter investigates whether entrepreneurs tend to share non-entrepreneurial partners; and the AECA parameter examines whether entrepreneurs who share non-entrepreneurial communication partners are also likely to have other non-entrepreneurial communication partners. For AECA, a negative parameter suggests that communications between entrepreneurs and non-entrepreneurs tend to pass within closed structures of shared partners, and that entrepreneurs operating within these cycles do not communicate with external non-entrepreneurs.

z_Q (a,x) and z_Q (b,x) are network statistics involving one of the within-level networks and the meso-level network. z_Q (a,x,b) are cross-level statistics involving tie variables from all three networks. Wang et al. (2013b) proposed statistics for non-directed networks such as those in Fig. 6.4. Wang et al. (2013b) also included directed multilevel networks, which we will not consider here. Here we extend the Wang et al. (2013b) non-directed statistic by introducing the Alternating-Star-A-X-Alternating-Star-B (ASAXASB) and the Alternating-four-cycle-AXB (AC4AXB) configurations that are particularly helpful in modeling the empirical data.

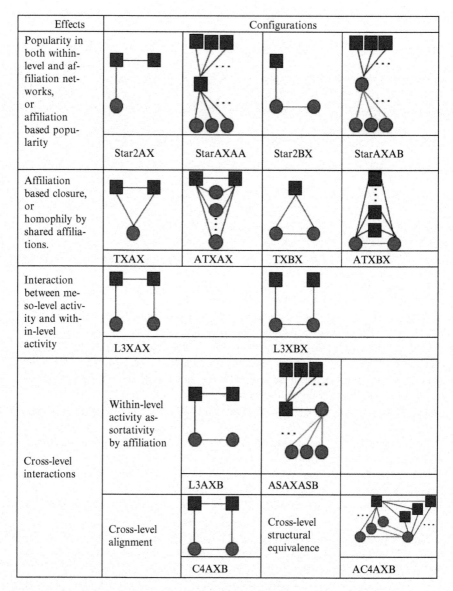

Fig. 6.4 Two-level ERGM specification for non-directed networks

Star2AX and Star2BX are effects testing whether active nodes in the one-mode network (A or B, respectively) are also active in the meso network. For instance, are entrepreneurs who are popular among entrepreneurs also popular among non-entrepreneurs? StarAXAA and StarAXAB are the "Alternating" versions of Star2AX and Star2BX, following Snijders et al. (2006) to enhance model convergence and limit degeneracy issues.

Triangle-XAX (TXAX) and Triangle-XBX (TXBX) represent the tendency for meso ties to be closed by within-level ties, i.e. the tendency for nodes with common affiliations to form ties. ATXAX and ATXBX are their "Alternating" versions. For instance, if two non-entrepreneurs share an entrepreneurial partner, are they also likely to communicate with each other?

L3XAX and L3XBX are three-paths that test whether nodes that are active or popular in the meso network are tied within levels. For instance, do entrepreneurs with many non-entrepreneurial partners tend to communicate with each other? The L3AXB effect tests whether there is a tendency for active or popular nodes in within-level networks to be affiliated in the meso network. For instance, do popular entrepreneurs tend to be partners of popular non-entrepreneurs? We call these effects cross-level assortativity effects as they represent degree correlations established by a tie of a different type. The ASAXASB effect is the "Alternating" version of the L3AXB effect, which helps model convergence in our modeling example.

The C4AXB effect represents a cross-level alignment structure where nodes with connected affiliations are also connected. This effect is of particular interest in two-level network models, as it tests whether having a connection in one level enhances the likelihood of forming a tie in the other level. If there is a tie between two entrepreneurs, is there also likely to be a tie between their non-entrepreneurial partners?

The AC4AXB configuration is the "Alternating" version of C4AXB, which can also be interpreted as cross-level structural equivalence, as it has two nodes of different types sharing the same partners (regardless of node type). Structurally equivalent nodes may share other properties such as various attributes or performance measures (Lorrain and White 1971; Burt 1976). The effect tests whether there is a tendency for entrepreneurial and non-entrepreneurial farmers to share the same patterns of ties within and across levels: in short, whether they occupy similar network positions.

Multilevel Social Selection Models

Social Selection Models (SSMs) incorporate nodal attributes as exogenous covariates to test the hypothesis whether network structures are affected by nodal attributes. Robins et al. (2001) proposed SSMs for one-mode networks; and Agneessens and Roose (2008) and Wang (2013c) described bipartite SSMs. Wang et al. (2015) proposed specifications for multilevel SSMs and demonstrated that multilevel network structures may be affected by attributes of nodes within the same level as well as of nodes from a different level. In this section, we review the general form of multilevel SSMs and some specifications used in our modeling example.

Nodal attributes can be binary, continuous, or categorical. Binary attributes use "1" to indicate a node "has" or "belongs to" a certain group, e.g., gender, organizational membership, "0" otherwise. Continuous attributes assign values to nodes based on various measurements, such as age, experience, and various performance measures. Categorical attributes divide the set of nodes into groups or categories that allow us to test the tendency of nodes with matching or mismatching categories to form ties. Let $Y^A = y^A$ and $Y^B = y^B$ denote the random variables representing attribute values for nodes from level A and B respectively. Each attribute random variable is a collection of attribute variables for individual nodes, i.e. $Y^A = \{Y_i^A\}$ and $Y^B = \{Y_i^B\}$. As extensions to multilevel ERGMs, the multilevel SSMs can be expressed as

$$\Pr\left(A = a, X = x, B = b \,|\, Y^A = y^A, Y^B = y^B\right) = \frac{1}{\kappa(\theta)} \exp \sum_{Q,\Lambda} \left\{\theta_Q z_Q(a, x, b) + \theta_\Lambda z_\Lambda\left(a, x, b, y^A, y^B\right)\right\}$$

where

- $z_Q(a,x,b)$ represents graph statistics involving only network tie variables as in multilevel ERGMs.
- $z_\Lambda(a, x, b, y^A, y^B)$ are statistics involving interactions among tie variables and attribute values. Here Λ represents configurations derived from dependence assumptions between network tie and nodal attribute variables (Robins et al. 2001). Using network A as an example, SSM statistics can be expressed in the general form of $z_\Lambda\left(a, y^A\right) = \sum_a \prod_{A_{ij}, y_i^A, y_j^A \in \Lambda} A_{ij} Y_i^A Y_j^A$
- θ_Q and θ_Λ are the associated parameters for their corresponding graph statistics.

Note that not all of $\{a, x, b, y^A, y^B\}$ are required to be present in SSMs, depending on the design of the study or availability of the relevant data.

The attribute variables are treated as fixed covariates in SSMs to test how attribute values may affect the formation of network ties. More interestingly, in the multilevel network context, we may test how attributes of nodes at one level may affect tie formation at the other level, as well as in the meso network.

Figure 6.5 lists some example SSM specifications for within-level one-mode networks as proposed by Robins et al. (2001).

The Activity effects for binary and continuous attributes test whether nodes of a particular type or higher attribute values tend to be more active in the network. The Binary interaction effect tests the tendency for nodes of the same type to form ties.

Activity	Activity	Matching
Interaction Binary	Difference Continuous	Mismatching Categorical

Fig. 6.5 SSM specification for one-mode networks

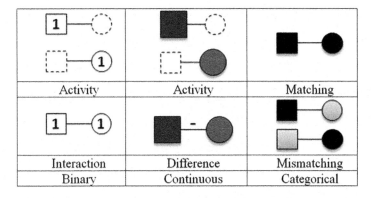

Fig. 6.6 Bipartite SSM specifications

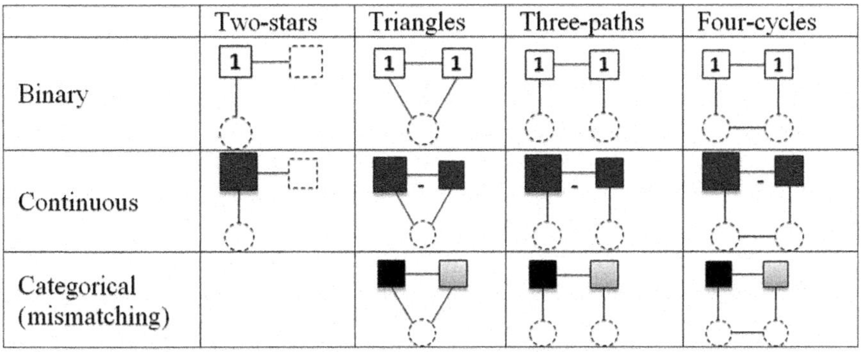

Fig. 6.7 Two-level SSM specifications

The "Difference" effect for continuous attributes can be interpreted as a homophily effect where a negative parameter estimate indicates nodes with similar attribute values tend to form a tie. The categorical "Matching" and "Mismatch" configuration tests whether nodes from the same or different categories tend to form more ties.

Figure 6.6 lists some bipartite SSM configurations used in our modeling example for the meso network (See also Wang 2013c). Interpretations of these configurations are very similar to their one-mode counterparts except that the two nodes involved in the dyad are from different levels.

Although they are not used in our examples, Fig. 6.7 lists some possible multilevel SSM specifications that involve attribute measures from one level (A). A more comprehensive list of configurations with attributes from both levels and their possible interpretations can be found in Wang et al. (2015). The two-star configurations represent the tendency for nodes of a particular type or nodes with a higher attribute to be popular or active in both within- and meso-level networks. The interpretations for the triangle, three-path and four-cycle effects are similar to the interpretations of their corresponding configurations in multilevel ERGMs, except they also focus on whether the nodes involved in the dyad both have the same attributes, or have similar attribute values, or belong to the same or different categories.

Estimation and Goodness of Fit

The normalizing constant $\kappa(\theta)$ for ERGMs or SSMs becomes intractable for even small networks, because the number of possible networks increases drastically as the number of nodes increases. Hence ERGM/SSM parameter estimation relies on network samples generated from Monte Carlo simulations. The model presented in this chapter is based on the output from MPNet software as an extension to PNet (Wang et al. 2009) which implements the Markov Chain Mote Carlo (MCMC) simulation and maximum likelihood estimation algorithms as described in Snijders (2002). The estimation algorithm calculates t-ratios at the end of estimations where models with t-ratios for all estimated parameters smaller than 0.1 in absolute values are considered as converged models. The t-ratios also serve as test statistics for the model's goodness of fit where a comparison between the observed graph statistics and the distribution of graphs simulated from converged models are made, and t-ratios smaller than 2.0 in absolute values indicate adequate fit to underlying graph statistics that are not explicitly included in the model.

A statistically significantly positive parameter estimate suggests the corresponding observed statistics are greater than expected from an ERGM graph distribution where the parameter value is set at 0. The significance of parameter size is determined by the ratio of the parameter value to its estimated standard error. We regard such ratios with an absolute value greater than 2.0 as significant parameter estimates.

Modeling Example: Networks of Entrepreneurial and Non-entrepreneurial Farmers in Ethiopia

We apply multilevel ERGMs to a dataset of 265 Ethiopian farmers from a rural community and their agricultural information-sharing network. Ethiopia, with about 80 % of its population directly employed in agriculture, is one of the poorest and most agrarian countries in the world (Central Statistical Agency 2004). The sector is dominated by small-scale subsistence farmers with plots characterized by low inputs and low outputs (Deressa 2007). Such farming families cultivate 95 % of Ethiopian cropland and account for 90 % of the national production (Deressa 2007). Farmers with no alternative sources of subsistence are the most vulnerable to the volatile climate and after unproductive harvests may become dependent on food-aid (Bewket 2007; Deressa 2007; Mojo et al. 2010). However, some farmers acquire additional sources of income outside their own farm, which can be used as a buffer in times of need. These activities may also open opportunities and expose them to people and information beyond the limited horizon of their village.

For the purpose of illustrating the multilevel ERGMs in this chapter, we use data collected in 2011 in an Ethiopian village. The farmers in this region used to have only a limited access to information outside of their local networks and as a result some quintessential farming practices, such as composting, have been unknown in the area until recently (Matous et al. 2013a, b, 2014). The farmers' information-sharing networks were elicited by a free list name generator with a prompt: "Please list all people that you can recall from outside of this household that you seek out for advice, you can learn from, or who can generally provide useful information regarding farming practices." The data and the context have been described in Matous and Todo (2015). In the surveyed village of 265 households, 87 households had some source of income outside their farm. These sources of income ranged from small-scale entrepreneurial activities such as opening a shop or producing alcohol and running a bar to occasional salaried work in the nearest city. In contrast, 187 farms had no external source of income and their subsistence was dependent on the crop from their farms. We call the former group entrepreneurs and the latter group non-entrepreneurs in this chapter and explore the differences and interdependencies between the networks of these two types of farming households in rural Ethiopia.

These two groups form the basis of the two-level structure of the undirected network model presented in this chapter. Level A is composed of the entrepreneurs and level B is composed of the non-entrepreneurs. The communication between the entrepreneurs and the non-entrepreneurs form the meso-level network X. Figure 6.8 depicts this multilevel network where entrepreneurs and non-entrepreneurs are represented by squares and circles respectively.

Dividing the farmers into two levels allows us to test whether the difference in the farmers' activities may result in different communication structures. We may hypothesize that the entrepreneurs have a higher exposure to the markets, broader social contacts, and more diverse information, whereas non-entrepreneurs are tied to their land. As the entrepreneurial farmers can be sources of external information and advice, they may operate as brokers between groups of non-entrepreneurial farmers to whom they provide advice. The multilevel ERGM presented below demonstrates how we may test such hypotheses. It should be noted that we were unable to obtain a converged single level one-mode ERGM to the entire network using current specifications (i.e. Snijders et al. 2006). It appears that using homogeneous network structural effects across both groups of framers is too strict a criterion. The two-level model does not require the possibly unrealistic assumption that the networking activities of the entrepreneurs and the non-entrepreneurs have to be similar.

There are several nodal attributes likely to affect the network structure that we included in the model:

- Education: A continuous attribute representing the number of years of education received by the household representatives. Highly educated farmers may be the source of advice.

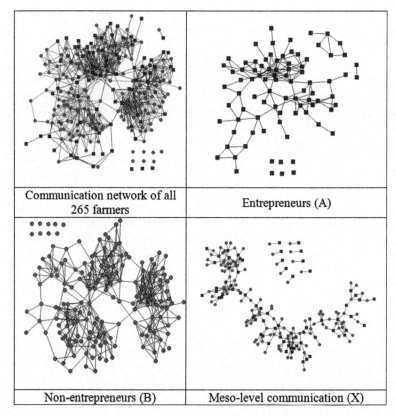

Fig. 6.8 Communication network among 265 Ethiopian farmers (Note that for network X, 61 isolated A nodes and 15 isolated B nodes are removed from the visualization)

- Land size: The area cultivated by each household indicates the socio-economic status of the household. Wealthy farmers may possibly be central in the village agricultural communication network.
- Religion: In this community, most farmers are either Christian or Muslim. Communication may more likely occur among members of the same religion who regularly meet in the village church or the village mosque for regular religious services.
- Region: There are three distinct areas or regions within this community separated by a small river and a road. We take geographical location into account by using a categorical variable, as farmers may be more likely to communicate with one another simply because they live closer to one another.

The inclusion of these attributes in our model allows us to take into account exogenous factors while modeling the endogenous social processes in this network.

In order to achieve model convergence, the network density was fixed throughout the model estimation; hence the density of the multilevel network is not modeled and we do not use the various edge parameters mentioned (for sake of completeness) in the previous figures. Table 6.1 lists parameter estimates of a converged multilevel ERGM with significant parameters shown in bold font. The model specification is selected based on goodness of fit (GOF) tests where a model is considered better if it provides adequate fit to more auxiliary graph statistics that are not part of the model. In the GOF tests, 131 relevant graph statistics were tested, including various ERGM configurations proposed to date (i.e. Snijders et al. 2006; Wang et al. 2013a, b), SSM configurations as in Robins et al. (2001), and Wang (2013c, 2015), and the global clustering coefficients, standard deviations and skewness of the degree distributions of within and meso networks. The final model provides an adequate fit to 128 of them, and the three poorly fitted statistics are listed in Table 6.2. We interpret the model parameters first, and then discuss what the GOF test results may further suggest about the network structure.

We begin our interpretation of the model with the networks A and B, the within-level parameter estimates for the entrepreneurs and non-entrepreneurs, respectively. The negative Alternating-star estimates for both networks indicate low degree centralization, so that high degree communication hubs do not emerge and the information sharing is relatively decentralized in this village. However, the positive Isolate parameter suggests that non-entrepreneurial farmers have a relatively high chance of being disconnected from each other (although they might still have connections with the entrepreneurs in the meso-level network X).

The positive Alternating-Triangle (AT) parameter estimates for both types of farmers suggests communication closure at both levels. The negative Alternating-2-path (A2P) parameter for non-entrepreneurs suggests that non-entrepreneurs are less likely to communicate with each other unless they have communication partners in common. In contrast, the A2P parameter is positive for the entrepreneurial farmers and near the border of statistical significance (with a ratio of the size of the estimate to its standard error of 1.87), which suggests that entrepreneurs tend to share communication partners whether they have a direct communication tie or not.

Moving on to the attributes effects within networks A and B, the positive Education activity parameter for the non-entrepreneurs suggests that the more educated individuals have more communication links. Formal education among non-entrepreneurs may increase their popularity as information providers or, alternatively, it may stimulate their information-seeking activity. There is no such effect for entrepreneurial farmers.[1] However, there is a significant homophily effect for the education levels for the entrepreneurs (negative Education difference parameter, i.e. entrepreneurs with similar levels of education tend to communicate with one another). This effect is not significant for the non-entrepreneurs, suggesting that their communication is more hierarchical in terms of education.

---

[1] Since the model adequately fitted the statistics of education activity for entrepreneurial farmers, we can consider such effect is not significantly different from 0.

Table 6.1 Multilevel ERGM estimates for the Ethiopian farmers

Networks	Effects	Parameter	Std. err.
Entrepreneurs (A)	AS	**−1.718**	**0.327**
	AT	**0.638**	**0.135**
	A2P	0.069	0.037
	Education difference	**−0.069**	**0.033**
	Region matching	**2.436**	**0.425**
	Religion matching	**0.868**	**0.413**
Non-entrepreneurs (B)	Isolates	**3.973**	**1.024**
	AS	**−2.632**	**0.393**
	AT	**1.147**	**0.080**
	A2P	**−0.113**	**0.017**
	Education activity	**0.023**	**0.008**
	Education difference	−0.017	0.013
	Land size activity	−0.012	0.023
	Region matching	**2.281**	**0.269**
	Religion matching	**0.378**	**0.086**
Meso-level advice between non-entrepreneurs and entrepreneurs (X)	ASA	0.065	0.207
	ASB	**0.813**	**0.302**
	ACB	**−0.716**	**0.171**
	AECA	−0.024	0.014
	Education difference	−0.013	0.022
	Land size activity A	**0.111**	**0.052**
	Land size activity B	−0.112	0.066
	Land difference	−0.073	0.072
	Region matching	**3.708**	**0.538**
	Religion matching	**0.620**	**0.208**
Entrepreneurs and meso-level networks (A and X)	StarAXAA	**1.265**	**0.344**
	ATXAX	**1.746**	**0.194**
	L3XAX	**−0.058**	**0.008**
Non-entrepreneurs farmer and meso-level networks (B and X)	StarAXAB	**1.320**	**0.383**
	L3XBX	**−0.046**	**0.013**
Cross-level (A, B and X)	ASAXASB	**0.117**	**0.018**
	AC4AXB	**−0.276**	**0.031**

Table 6.2 Poorly fitted graph statistics

Statistics	Observed	Mean	Std. dev.	t-ratio
TriangleXBX	254	108.13	26.10	5.59
ATXBX	218.56	92.76	19.67	6.40
ClusteringX	0.25	0.16	0.04	2.04

Both religion- and region-matching parameters for both within-level networks are strongly positive suggesting that information exchange is more likely to occur within the same part of the village and within the same religion.

The parameter estimates for the meso-level communication reveal some interesting differences between the entrepreneurs and the non-entrepreneurs. Firstly, the centralization effect is significant for the non-entrepreneurs but not for the entrepreneurs, which suggests centralization in the non-entrepreneurs' meso-level degree distribution and hence a disparity among the non-entrepreneurs' access to the entrepreneurs. Some non-entrepreneurs are particularly active in communicating with entrepreneurs. Secondly, the land size effects show that wealthier entrepreneurs with larger land have more connections with the non-entrepreneurs (indicated by positive Land size activity A), whereas the opposite may be true for the non-entrepreneurs. Wealthier entrepreneurs tend to be favored by non-entrepreneurs; whereas wealthy non-entrepreneurs may be less likely to communicate with entrepreneurs.

There are no meso-level homophily effects associated with education levels or land size in communication between the two types of farmers. Religion and region again play an important role in tie formation, i.e., entrepreneurs and non-entrepreneurs are more likely to be partners if they are from the same part of the village or belong to the same religious affiliation.

The negative Alternating-4-Cycle B (ACB) effect suggests that entrepreneurs tend not to share their non-entrepreneurial partners. It seems that the meso-level network is segmented by popular entrepreneurs. A possible interpretation is that the farmers engaged in trading with external markets have some level of "monopoly" over their own group of client farmers who are less likely to connect with other entrepreneurs. In contrast, however, as we will see below with the ATXAX effect, non-entrepreneurs may indeed be connected to two or more entrepreneurs when those entrepreneurs communicate with each other.

The Alternating-Edge-Cycle B (AECB) parameter is negative but not significant. Inclusion of AECB in the model provides good improvement on model GOF.

The interaction effects between the one-mode and bipartite networks are similar for both entrepreneurs and non-entrepreneurs with positive star association effects (StarAXAA and StarAXAB) and negative three-path effects (L3XAX and L3XBX). The positive star association effects suggest farmers popular amongst their peers are also popular with the other type of farmers. In contrast, the negative three-path effects suggest that popular farmers in the meso network are less likely to be linked to one another within-level. It seems that hubs in the meso network are also likely to be hubs in the within-level networks, but are less likely to communicate with one another. So, for instance, popular entrepreneurs (popular with both entrepreneurs and non-entrepreneurs) tend to communicate less with each other.

As noted above, the positive Alternating-Triangle-XAX (ATXAX) suggests that entrepreneurs who communicate with each other are also likely to communicate with the same non-entrepreneurs.

From the cross-level effects, the positive ASAXASB effect suggests that within-level popular actors are likely to be partners across levels. The alternating cross-level four-cycle (AC4AXB), which represents cross-level structural equivalence, is negative, suggesting that the entrepreneurs and non-entrepreneurs tend to be structurally different in this multilevel network, i.e. connecting to different groups of individuals. This is likely to be due to the difference in their activities with non-entrepreneurial farmers dedicated to the crop on their plots, whereas entrepreneurs are also engaged in trading and other activities. This result is not unexpected but emphasizes the desirability of modeling these two types of farmer at separate levels.

Although not suggested by the model parameters, the model GOF test shows the current model underfits the triangle structures (Triangle-XBX and ATXBX with t-ratios 5.59 and 6.40).[2] A model that includes one or both of these effects would be ideal; however, their inclusion in the model specification did not yield a converged model. This GOF result suggests that two linked non-entrepreneurs are also more likely than the model has predicted to communicate with one or more common entrepreneurs. Considering the negative three-path effects (L3XAX and L3XBX) in the model with the positive ATXAX effect and the underfitting of ATXBX, the results suggest that popular farmers in the meso-level network are less likely to communicate within levels unless they share partners in the meso level network.

In summary, this multilevel ERGM presents us with an interesting picture of how the communication network is segmented by farmer types, their popularity or activity, and their attributes. Controlling for religion, region, and education, non-entrepreneurs who are popular among their non-entrepreneurial peers tend to communicate across levels with popular entrepreneurs. Cross-level network closure is present: connected non-entrepreneurs are likely to share the same entrepreneurial partners; and connected entrepreneurs are likely to share the same non-entrepreneurial partners. There is also meso-level segmentation suggesting that entrepreneurs have sets of non-entrepreneurial "clients." Finally, the network has a tendency against cross-level structural equivalence or alignments: entrepreneurs and non-entrepreneurs do not occupy similar network positions. So, overall, although this a relatively small village that is influenced by classical demographic factors such as geospatial, religious and wealth segmentation, there are nevertheless additional self-organizing network processes that affect the flow of agricultural information. These include segmentation into relatively closed advice structures that restrict the flow of information between cliques of entrepreneurial and client non-entrepreneurial farmers. Without multilevel ERGMs, it would be difficult to uncover the structure of these social processes.

---

[2] Besides under-fitting the interaction triangle effects (TriangleXBX and ATXBX), the model also under-fitted the bipartite clustering coefficient as the ratio between the number of four-cycles and three-paths (Robins and Alexander 2004), as suggested by the t-ratio of 2.04.

Conclusion and Discussion

Based on conditional dependence assumptions among network ties, ERGMs for multilevel networks allow us to test the interdependent nature of network ties within and across levels. ERGM can thus reveal detailed multilevel social processes that are otherwise difficult to investigate with other methods.

In this chapter, we reviewed the generalized network structure for multilevel networks, the multilevel ERGM and SSM specifications as proposed in Wang et al. (2013a, 2015). We extend the model specifications with two new configurations that are the "Alternating" forms of cross-level three-paths and four-cycles and discussed their possible interpretations.

We apply the extended model specifications to a communication network among Ethiopian farmers. The resulting model provides an informative description of this farming community. There are similarities as well as clear distinctions between the entrepreneurial farmers and the rest. Without considering the meso- and across-level effects, we might argue that the two types of farmers have similar network behavior, i.e., both are active within their religion and region; both have flat degree distribution, and both tend to form network closures. The meso- and cross-level effects, however, show that the network is segmented by the farmer types, where popular meso-level nodes tend not to communicate within levels, but popular within-level nodes tend to communicate across levels through the meso-level network. The negative cross-level structural equivalence parameter further reflects such fine distinctions.

Similar to ERGMs, multilevel ERGMs have their limitations. Not all empirical networks will result in converged models. Issues of model degeneracy, lack of computational efficiency, and a possibility of inadequate representation of the modeled social processes may still be present. These issues call for further development of ERGM and its extensions. We see the current development of multilevel ERGMs as early steps towards a full elaboration of a branch of methodology for analyzing multilevel social network data.

Acknowledgements We thankfully acknowledge the ideas of Yoshihisa Kashima and the contribution of Yasuyuki Todo and Dagne Mojo in gathering of the data. The fieldwork was financially supported by the Ministry of Education, Culture, Sports, Science and Technology in Japan.

References

Agneessens, F., & Roose, H. (2008). Local structural properties and attribute characteristics in 2-mode networks: p* models to map choices of theater events. *Journal of Mathematical Sociology, 32*(3), 204–237.

Bewket, W. (2007). Soil and water conservation intervention with conventional technologies in northwestern highlands of Ethiopia: acceptance and adoption by farmers. *Land Use Policy, 24*(2), 404–416.

Bodin, Ö., & Tengö, M. (2012). Disentangling intangible social–ecological systems. *Global Environmental Change, 22*(2), 430–439.

Burt, R. S. (1976). Positions in networks. *Social Forces, 55*, 93–122.

Central Statistical Agency. (2004). *The Federal Democratic Republic of Ethiopia statistical abstract for 2003*. Addis Ababa: Central Statistical Agency.

Deressa, T. T. (2007). *Measuring the economic impact of the climate change on Ethiopian agriculture: Ricardian approach*. Washington, DC: The World Bank.

Erdös, P., & Rényi, A. (1960). On the evolution of random graphs. *Publications of the Mathematical Institute of the Hungarian Academy of Science, 5*, 17–61.

Frank, O., & Strauss, D. (1986). Markov graphs. *Journal of the American Statistical Association, 81*(395), 832–842.

Handcock, M. S. (2003). *In assessing degeneracy statistical models of social networks* (Working Paper No. 39). Center for Statistics and the Social Sciences, University of Washington.

Lazega, E., Jourda, M. T., Mounier, L., & Stofer, R. (2008). Catching up with big fish in the big pond? Multi-level network analysis through linked design. *Social Networks, 30*(2), 159–176.

Lorrain, F., & White, H. C. (1971). Structural equivalence of individuals in social networks. *Journal of Mathematical Sociology, 1*, 49–80.

Lusher, D., Koskinen, J., & Robins, G. (Eds.). (2013). *Exponential random graph models for social networks: Theory, methods, and applications*. New York: Cambridge University Press.

Matous, P., & Todo, Y. (2015). Exploring dynamic mechanisms of learning networks for resource conservation. *Ecology and Society, 20*(2), 36.

Matous, P., Todo, Y., & Mojo, D. (2013a). Roles of extension and ethno-religious networks in acceptance of resource-conserving agriculture among Ethiopian farmers. *International Journal of Agricultural Sustainability, 11*(4), 301–316.

Matous, P., Todo, Y., & Mojo, D. (2013b). Boots are made for walking: Interactions across physical and social space in infrastructure-poor regions. *Journal of Transport Geography, 31*, 226–235.

Matous, P., Todo, Y., & Ishikawa, T. (2014). Emergence of multiplex mobile phone communication networks across rural areas: An Ethiopian experiment. *Network Science, 2*(02), 162–188.

Mojo, D., Todo, Y., & Matous, P. (2010). Perception of farmers and agricultural professionals on changes in productivity and water resources in Ethiopia. *World Academy of Science, Engineering and Technology, 1*(66), 860–868.

Pattison, P., & Snijders, T. (2013). Modelling social networks: Next steps. In D. Lusher, J. Koskinen, & G. Robins (Eds.), *Exponential random graph models for social networks, theory, methods, and applications* (pp. 287–301). New York: Cambridge University Press.

Rinaldo, A., Fienberg, S., & Zhou, Y. (2009). On the geometry of discrete exponential families with application to exponential random graph models. *Electronic Journal of Statistics, 3*, 446–484.

Robins, G., & Alexander, M. (2004). Small worlds among interlocking directors: Network structure and distance in bipartite graphs. *Computational & Mathematical Organization Theory, 10*(1), 69–94.

Robins, G., Elliott, P., & Pattison, P. (2001). Network models for social selection processes. *Social Networks, 23*(1), 1–30.

Robins, G., Pattison, P., Kalish, Y., & Lusher, D. (2007). An introduction to exponential random graph (p*) models for social networks. *Social Networks, 29*(2), 173–191.

Skvoretz, J., & Faust, K. (1999). Logit models for affiliation networks. *Sociological Methodology, 29*(1), 253–280.

Snijders, T. A. (2002). Markov chain Monte Carlo estimation of exponential random graph models. *Journal of Social Structure, 3*(2), 1–40.

Snijders, T. A., Pattison, P. E., Robins, G. L., & Handcock, M. S. (2006). New specifications for exponential random graph models. *Sociological Methodology, 36*(1), 99–153.

Wang, P. (2013). Exponential random graph model extensions: Models for multiple networks and bipartite networks. In D. Lusher, J. Koskinen, & G. Robins (Eds.), *Exponential random graph models for social networks: Theory, methods, and applications* (pp. 115–129). New York: Cambridge University Press.

Wang, P., Pattison, P., & Robins, G. (2009). *PNet: A program for simulations and estimations of exponential random graph models*. Melbourne school of psychological sciences, University of Melbourne, Australia. http://sna.unimelb.edu.au/PNet

Wang, P., Pattison, P., & Robins, G. (2013a). Exponential random graph model specifications for bipartite networks—A dependence hierarchy. *Social Networks, 35*(2), 211–222.

Wang, P., Robins, G., Pattison, P., & Lazega, E. (2013b). Exponential random graph models for multilevel networks. *Social Networks, 35*(1), 96–115.

Wang, P., Robins, G., Pattison, P., & Lazega, E. (2015). Social selection models for multilevel networks. *Social Networks, 35*, 96–115.

Wasserman, S., & Iacobucci, D. (1991). Statistical modeling of one-mode and two-mode networks: Simultaneous analysis of graphs and bipartite graphs. *British Journal of Mathematical and Statistical Psychology, 44*, 13–44.

Wasserman, S., & Pattison, P. (1996). Logit models and logistic regressions for social networks: I. An introduction to Markov graphs and p*. *Psychometrika, 61*(3), 401–425.

Zappa, P., & Robins, G. (2015). Organizational learning across multi-level networks. *Social Networks* (in press).

Chapter 7
Correspondence Analysis of Multirelational Multilevel Networks

Mengxiao Zhu, Valentina Kuskova, Stanley Wasserman, and Noshir Contractor

Introduction

Social network analysis is concerned not only with social relations (Wellman 1988), but also more generally with attributes across pairs of social actors, which are referred to as *dyadic attributes* (Borgatti and Everett 1987, p. 243). These dyadic attributes range from shared affiliations to distances between cities to similarities in respondents' answers to items on a questionnaire. While most network studies have investigated one-mode networks (Borgatti and Everett 1987), social network approaches are easily extended to two-mode data, such as the relationship between employees and work teams with which they are affiliated (Wasserman and Faust 1994). In two-mode networks, different types of nodes (e.g., employees and teams) are represented as different modes. Unlike typical affiliation networks (for a primer on affiliation networks, please refer to Wasserman and Faust 1994;

M. Zhu (✉)
Educational Testing Service, Princeton, NJ, USA
e-mail: mzhu@ets.org; mengxiao.zhu@gmail.com

V. Kuskova
National Research University Higher School of Economics, Moscow, Russian Federation
e-mail: vkuskova@hse.ru

S. Wasserman
National Research University Higher School of Economics, Moscow, Russian Federation

Indiana University, Bloomington, IN, USA
e-mail: stanwass@indiana.edu

N. Contractor
Northwestern University, Evanston, IL, USA
e-mail: nosh@northwestern.edu

Borgatti et al. 2013; Newman 2010), where a second mode is just a subset of the first, we focus on the data with emergent properties of the second mode (e.g., teams are more than just subsets, because they perform additional emergent functions that go beyond uniting individual employees together). The relations in this network are the links between nodes of different modes. Over the years, a variety of tools and techniques have been developed for displaying, analyzing, and interpreting such data (e.g., Borgatti and Everett 1987; Doreian et al. 2004; Latapy et al. 2008; Roberts 2000).

However, most current two-mode network analysis techniques focus exclusively on the links between different modes, without considering dyadic attributes such as attribute similarity or nodes nested in networks at different levels. Despite recent advancements in network analysis methods, including extensions of multiple correspondence analysis (e.g., D'Esposito et al. 2014), there is clearly a need to further extend many of these approaches to multiple levels. The multilevel approach, recently popularized in fields such as management, combines the unit of observation with higher levels in which the focal unit is embedded (individuals in teams, teams in units, units in organizations; e.g., Phelps et al. 2012). This multiple level approach has been considered, for example, in studies on innovation (Berends et al. 2011) and knowledge management (Zhao and Anand 2013). Methods such as canonical correlation analysis have been used to evaluate two sets of variables simultaneously with the contingency table as input. For example Parkhe (1993) utilized this approach to study the relationships between a set of performance variables and a set of payoffs (e.g., Parkhe 1993). While it is a very useful technique and can be applied to multi-way contingency tables (Gilula and Haberman 1988), canonical correlation analysis is not designed for the study of network structure and composition variables, and this limitation is often acknowledged in studies using this technique (e.g., Berends et al. 2011; Payne et al. 2011; Zhao and Anand 2013). As these researchers noted, some research questions can neither be asked nor answered, because of the lack of methodology for analyzing relational data at multiple levels.

Consider, for example, individual actors nested within teams. Due to existing organizational structures or other a priori arrangements, actors are often nested within multiple teams that share one or more members, thus giving rise to affiliation data (Wageman et al. 2012). In such an arrangement, the actors are the lower level, the teams are the upper level, and the actors can be in more than one team. These types of data are multilevel and can be complex if the actor-nesting is not mutually exclusive. In many teams, especially self-assembled teams, individuals participate in more than one team (e.g., Denton 1997; Kauffeld 2006). In the meantime, individuals are socially connected to each other through previous collaborations or communications with each other. The dependencies among overlapping teams create an additional level of complexity in the analysis, with the presence of the aggregate effects of team members' interactions with one another (Klein and Kozlowski 2000). Further, there are theoretical reasons for understanding the effects of multiple team membership on productivity and learning at the individual and team level (O'Leary et al. 2011).

The need for a robust method for visualizing and modeling multilevel relational data becomes even more challenging as data sets become richer and larger. Consider, for example, big data, and the need to have exploratory and data reduction tools to deal with it. According to McAffee and Brynjolfsson (2012), about 2.5 exabytes of data are created every day, and this number doubles approximately every 40 months (an exabyte is 1000 times a petabyte, which is equivalent to about 20 million cabinets' worth of text. Walmart alone generates approximately 2.5 petabytes of data an hour from customer transactions). While insights gathered from analyzing big data can allow companies to substantially outperform the competition (McAfee and Brynjolfsson 2012), these insights can only be unleashed when we have a better understanding of how to use analytics and methodological tools for data reduction (LaValle et al. 2011). In addition to the size, the most notable thing about big data is the embedded relationality: patterns of connections between individuals, groups of people, relationships between them, or just the structure of information, such as presence of latent factors within the set (Boyd and Crawford 2011). Network approaches are a logical choice to discern these insights, and in this regard, multiple correspondence analysis can prove to become a useful tool, especially when multi-level relationships are embedded within the data. In this regard, the approach we propose can be used as a preliminary data analysis tool, allowing us to look at the structure of the data for the purpose of determining more advanced models that could fit that structure.

To address some of the issues outlined above, this study provides two examples, which model teams of individuals using network methodology. The most straightforward way to represent team membership is to use one-mode networks, where nodes represent individuals, and links among individuals indicate joint participation in one or more teams. This one-mode representation captures the overlapping team membership, but unfortunately, fails to preserve the team structures. For instance, links in a one-mode network between A, B and C fail to convey information about whether A, B, and C were together on one team or if A and B were on one team, C on another team, and B and C on yet another team. Instead, we use affiliation networks to represent teams and individuals, with links representing team membership. There are many representations of an affiliation network, including as an affiliation network matrix, bipartite graph, hypergraph, or simplicial complex (Borgatti and Halgin 2011; Faust 2005; Skvoretz and Faust 1999). Each of these representations contains exactly the same information, and any one representation can be derived from the other. This study uses bipartite networks, in which the two types of nodes represent teams and individuals. The social relations between individuals can then be easily represented using one-mode networks with nodes representing individuals and links representing relations between individuals.

Understanding the associations between and among variables in complex social systems, which exist, for example, in multiple nested groups, can be difficult, and there is a paucity of theoretical models that yield precise hypotheses. Hence we argue for the use of exploratory network analysis techniques as a useful theoretical preamble (and/or data reduction strategy) to more confirmatory approaches such as specifying *p*/ERGM* models (Holland and Leinhardt 1981; Wasserman and Robins 2005). This exploration is especially useful in narrowing the potentially unwieldy combinatorial space for model specification. Hence we propose a method for exploration of multilevel relational data that distills the number of possible hypotheses and generative mechanisms that can be subsequently tested using confirmatory methods such as *p*/ERGM*.

We use correspondence analysis (Wasserman and Faust 1994) and its extension, multiple correspondence analysis (Greenacre 2010), which enable us to analyze multiple relations and attributes at both individual and team levels. Correspondence analysis incorporates the interactions among observations and can be extended to more than two sets of variables; here, we show how it can be used on a much larger number. The results from correspondence analysis can also be presented graphically, using a plot rather than numbers alone. Relations among various variables as well as observed raw data can be shown in the same plot, essentially providing a much richer graphical output. Because of these advantages, correspondence analysis can be used as an important exploratory tool to examine the features of the dataset and the relations among variables of interest.

In this article, we present a brief history of this exploratory network analysis approach, provide theory for extending correspondence analysis to multiple levels, and then provide two illustrative examples from individuals playing in teams in massively multiplayer online games (MMOG). The first example is of combat teams made up of individuals from United States playing the MMOG EverQuest II. We explore the impact of among various individual-level and team-level attributes on team performance, while considering team affiliations and social relations among individuals. We use this example to show how multiple correspondence analysis can be used for hypotheses generation, and later for confirmatory testing with more advanced methods. The second example considers another MMOG, Dragon Nest, with individuals, this time in China, playing in multiple combat teams. We use the example to demonstrate the utility of our methodology to discern cultural differences in team assembly and performance, showing how comparative analysis of large datasets could unearth cultural differences.

Methodology

Existing Methods for Analyzing Affiliation Network Data

Bipartite networks are one way to represent affiliation networks as including two types of nodes as well as relationships between those two types of nodes (Wasserman and Faust 1994). Figure 7.1 illustrates a bipartite network of six children and the three parties they attend. The affiliations between individuals and teams are in-between links. For example, a link between *Allison* and *Party 1* indicates that *Allison* went to *Party 1*. This relationship system can have other

Fig. 7.1 Bipartite graph as example representation for multilevel networks (From Wasserman and Faust 1994, with modifications)

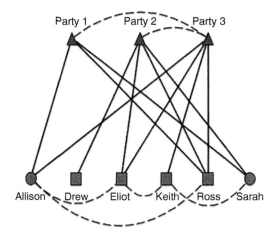

relations as well as attributes, such as one-mode relational ties: If we label two levels as A and B, we can have AA and BB ties, in addition to AB ties. Also, there could be more than two levels. In the example shown, we can add a third level, alliances (e.g., multiple parties sharing the same theme) and include relational ties within and between all levels (it is not shown on the graph, but can be easily inferred as one more level for alliances between parties). For such structures, there are two types of variables: Q composition (or attribute) and R structure (or relational) variables. Such a dichotomy of composition and structure variables is rather common in data analysis, where one or more response variables are predicted as a function of a collection of explanatory variables. In the example in Fig. 7.1, $g = 6$ and refers to the number of children; $h = 3$ refers to the number of parties. We consider the variables measured on each of the $g(g-1)/2$ dyads in case of a one-mode network, or the $g * h$ dyads (in the case of a two-mode network with two levels). The number of dyads changes corresponding to the number of modes and levels, and we consider N pairs of possible inter-actor relationships (where N is, for example, equal to $g(g-1)/2$ or $g * h$) as the rows of a matrix and consider the variables that are measured on the N rows. As a result, these dyadic pattern matrices have N rows and the number of columns equal to the levels of composition variables taken together.

Ideally, representation of multilevel data should facilitate the visualization of all three kinds of patterning described above: the AB structure, the A level structure, and the B level structure. While simplicial complexes and hypergraphs (for details, please see Wasserman and Faust 1994) provide representations, a common approach is to convert the two-mode network into two one-mode networks: one shows how actors are linked to each other in terms of events, and the other, how events are linked together in terms of actors. However, neither provides an overall picture of the total A, B, and AB structures. Bipartite graphs display the AB structure but they do not provide a clear image of the associations among A actors or B actors.

This limitation is resolved with Galois lattices (Wasserman and Faust 1994), which meet all three requirements in a clear visual model (Fig. 7.2 presents the

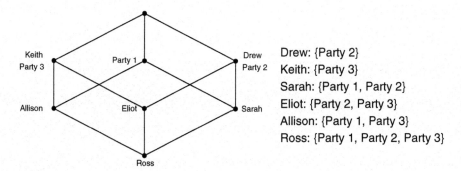

Fig. 7.2 Galois lattice as example representation for multilevel networks (From Wasserman and Faust 1994)

previous example as a Galois lattice). The nodes in Galois lattices are points in a multidimensional space, each representing a subset of actors and events. Reading from the bottom up, there is a line or sequence of lines ascending from a child to a party if he or she attended that party. If two children's ascending lines reach the same party node, then they both attended that party. On the other hand, if two children's ascending lines can only reach the top (null) node, then it means that they did not attend any party together, (e.g., Keith and Drew in the example in Fig. 7.2). In a similar way, the relations between the parties can be read through the descending lines that reach children.

Despite the obvious clarity, focus on subsets, and ability to display complementary relationships between the A's and the B's, the Gallois lattice method has a number of disadvantages. First, the usual display becomes complex as the number of actors and events increases. Second, there is no unique best visual. The vertical dimension represents degrees of subset inclusion relationships among points, but the horizontal dimension is arbitrary. As a result, constructing good measures is problematic. Third, unlike graph theory, properties and analyses of Galois lattices are not well developed.

Correspondence Analysis and Multiple Correspondence Analysis

Correspondence analysis and its extension, multiple correspondence analysis, were originally developed as a multivariate statistical technique for analysis of categorical data (Greenacre 2010; Wasserman et al. 1990). In the 1980s, researchers started to apply this method to analyze the one-mode and two-mode social network structures. For a detailed review and comparison with other statistical methods, such as canonical analysis, refer to, e.g., Borgatti and Everett 1987; Faust 1997; Wasserman and Faust 1994; Wasserman et al. 1990. Many applications of correspondence analysis and multiple correspondence analysis have focused on visualizing and displaying structures in networks (e.g., D'Esposito et al. 2014; Roberts 2000). Recently (D'Esposito et al. 2014), extensions of correspondence analysis have allowed studies to take into account the nature of the relational data (e.g., structural (dis)similarity of actors or events) and nodes' attributes. In this study, we apply correspondence analysis and especially multiple correspondence analysis to multiple and multilevel networks by focusing on the relations between attribute variables at both the same and different levels, while considering and controlling for the network relations between nodes from different modes.

For a two-mode network with A actors as one mode and B actors as another mode, correspondence analysis is a method for visually representing both the rows and the columns of a two-mode matrix in a map, where points representing the A actors are placed together if they are tied to the same B actors; points representing the B actors are placed close together if they are tied to the same A actors; and A points and B points are placed together if those A's are tied to those B's. Correspondence analysis includes an adjustment for marginal effects. As a result, A's are placed closed to B's to the extent that these B's were tied to few other A's, and these A's are tied to few other B's. One of the advantages of this method is that it allows studying correlations between the scores in rows and columns. Using reciprocal averaging, a score for a given row is the weighted average of the scores for the columns, and the weights are the relative frequencies of the cells (Wasserman and Faust 1994).

Mathematically, a bipartite network B with g nodes on the first mode and h nodes on the second mode can be represented using a $g \times h$ matrix $\mathcal{M}$, where $m_{ij} = 1$ if node i from the first mode is affiliated with node j from the second mode and $m_{ij} = 0$ otherwise. For example, in Table 7.1, the bipartite network is represented as follows.

Correspondence analysis takes the affiliation matrix as an input and represents the relations between nodes in both modes as well as the relations in a low-dimensional map. Results then identify multiple factors, which help to cluster nodes from both modes based on the affiliation relations. Nodes from each mode are assigned a set of scores, which can be used to cluster these nodes. For a bipartite network of individuals and teams, the results of the correspondence analysis summarize relations among individuals and teams in a dimension much lower than the dimension of the network itself.

Given a $g \times h$ matrix $\mathcal{M}$ as input to the correspondence analysis, a set of $W = \min(g-1, h-1)$ scores are generated for each row and column, with a set of W

Table 7.1 An example of affiliation matrix for bipartite network

	Team 1	Team 2	Team 3
Person a	1	1	0
Person b	1	0	1
Person c	1	0	1
Person d	0	1	0

numbers measuring the correlation between the rows and columns (Wasserman and Faust 1994). The scores satisfy the following relations:

$$\eta_k u_{ik} = \sum_{j=1}^{h} \frac{m_{ij}}{m_{i+}} v_{jk} \tag{7.1}$$

$$\eta_k v_{jk} = \sum_{i=1}^{g} \frac{m_{ij}}{m_{+j}} u_{ik} \tag{7.2}$$

where, u_{ik} is the row score for row i on dimension k; v_{jk} is the column score for column j on dimension k. η_k^2 is called the *principal inertia*, and the u and v scores are called the *principal coordinates*.

Standard coordinates $\tilde{u}$ and $\tilde{v}$ (Greenacre 1984) can then be calculated by rescaling the principal coordinates:

$$\tilde{u}_{ik} = u_{ik}/\eta_k \tag{7.3}$$

$$\tilde{v}_{jk} = v_{jk}/\eta_k \tag{7.4}$$

These scores are called standardized scores because the weighted mean is equal to 0 and the weighted variance is equal to 1.

The results from the correspondence analysis are often presented by plotting the coordinates using just the first two dimensions (Nenadic and Greenacre 2007; Wasserman and Faust 1989). Each mode is represented in this two dimensional space, with points for each level of both modes. Let us label the first mode as *actors* and the second mode as *teams*. Actors are placed close to each other in this space if they are similar. Teams are placed close to each other in this space if the teams are similar. Specific actors and teams are placed close to each other if those actors involved are closely related to those teams. As an example, Fig. 7.3 shows the plotted correspondence analysis for the bipartite person-team network data as shown in Table 7.1. It can be observed from this plot that Person b and Person c are close to each other, and the data show that both of them are members of both Team 1 and Team 3.

In addition to demonstrating the structural features of the system of teams and individuals, correspondence analysis can also be used to study the relations of attributes of teams and individuals. This requires an extension of the standard correspondence analysis, to what is called *multiple correspondence analysis* (Nenadic and Greenacre 2007; Wasserman et al. 1990). To include attribute variables from many modes, the nonzero relations in the original $g \times h$ matrix $\mathcal{M}$ are represented as dyads and rows in the new matrix. All attribute variables need to be transformed to categorical variables and be represented by indicator vectors as columns in the new matrix. This new matrix is called the *multiple indicator matrix* (Wasserman et al. 1990). Multiple indicator matrices can be developed in a similar way when the relations studied in the models are one-mode networks.

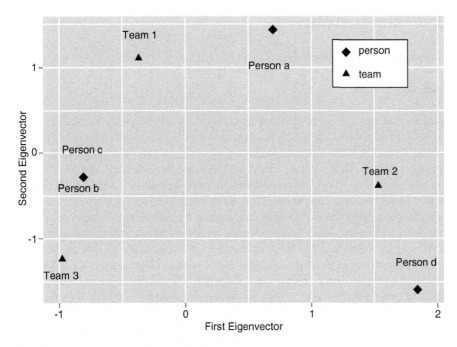

Fig. 7.3 Correspondence analysis for the bipartite network data

Table 7.2 Example of multiple indicator matrix

Dyads	Person gender female	Person gender male	Team performance high	Team performance medium	Team performance low
(a, 1)	0	1	1	0	0
(b, 1)	1	0	1	0	0
(c, 1)	0	1	1	0	0
(a, 2)	0	1	0	1	0
(d, 2)	0	1	0	1	0
(b, 3)	1	0	0	0	1
(c, 3)	0	1	0	0	1

Consider the multiple indicator matrix created based on the network where individuals belong to different teams (Table 7.2). In this example, *Person a*, *Person c*, and *Person d* are males, and *Person b* is female. Performance of *Team 1* is the highest, performance of *Team 2* is midlevel, and performance of *Team 3* is the lowest.

The correspondence analysis on this newly constructed, multiple indicator matrix is called *multiple correspondence analysis*. The results can be interpreted similarly as for simple correspondence analysis.

Illustrative Examples

Example 1: EverQuest II

Data and Sample

Data for this example were obtained from the Massively Multiplayer Online Game (MMOG) EverQuest II (EQ2). It is a fantasy-based game, centered on performance of combat teams, with multiple players nested within teams. The choice of the data is important for several reasons. First, EverQuest is a large dataset, which highlights the relevance of our proposed method in light of the discussion of "big data" above; indeed, large datasets can be analyzed using multilevel correspondence analysis. Second, the nesting feature is important because it indicates that there is more than one level in this example. Server records for the game include player attributes, activities, and relations. Data were collected in two stages: We used relational data among players using the US-based game server between September 5–11, 2006. We collected attribute data such as gender and affiliation with an in-game organization called a guild for the same set of individuals at around 6 p.m. on September 4, 2006. Data from the EQ2 game world data is extremely large and hence analytically intractable. However, the game world is partitioned into smaller island/continent zones. The zones are relatively independent of each other, and, over a short time period, there are no significant player transfers between them. To make the analysis more feasible, teams were identified and sampled by zone. Figure 7.4 shows Zone Everfrost in the EverQuest II game world. The dataset used in this study contains 192 players in 189 teams.

Figure 7.5 contains the bipartite graph of teams and individuals, from the Zone Everfrost, with spring embedding layout (Borgatti et al. 2002). The illustration demonstrates that the individuals and teams in the Zone Everfrost form one big connected subset and several smaller ones.

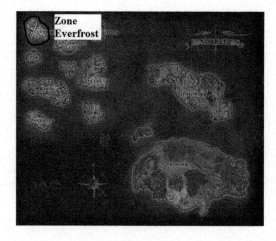

Fig. 7.4 Zone Everfrost in EverQuest II

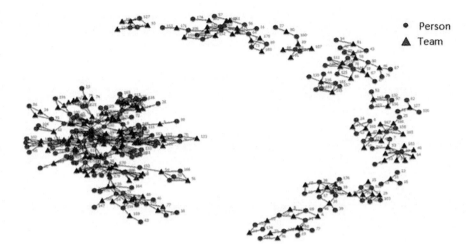

Fig. 7.5 Affiliation network of individuals and teams in Zone Everfrost with spring embedding layout

Variables

There are several types of variables collected in this sample: performance variables, individual- and team-level attributes, and relational variables.

Individual-level attributes include gender (avatar gender, not necessarily the user gender; male/female), age (user age), level (measure of general ability in the game), guild affiliation (whether or not a player belongs to one of the in-game organizations), and expertise. In EverQuest II, there are four prototype classes: Fighter, Priest, Mage, and Scout. They each have special expertise and serve different roles in a team.

Team-level attributes include team size (number of players in a team, with a minimum of two and maximum of six); team level (system-calculated level for the team, representing the general ability of the team); team life span (the length of time the team has been active). There are also expertise diversity, age diversity (coefficient of variation), gender diversity, and guild diversity. In most analyses used as examples in this study, we reported results on guild diversity.

This measure is calculated using the Blau's index (Blau 1977) for each team,

$$D = 1 - \sum_{i=1}^{n} p_i^2$$

where n is the total number of guilds and p_i represents the percentage of team members who are in the ith guild.

Team performance variables are derived from the original six built-in metrics in the game: number of monsters killed, number of encounters, earned experience points, total level gain, number of quests completed, and the number of deaths (a negative measure of performance). *F1* is the short-term performance; it captures the number of monsters killed, number of encounters, earned experience points, and total level gain. *F2* is the long-term performance variable; it captures the number of quests completed by the team. *F3* is the negative performance variable; it captures the number of deaths of team members. Performance variables are categorized into three levels: high, mid, and low indexed as 3, 2, and 1 respectively and used as a suffix to the type of performance metric. Thus, for example, in the indicator matrix, F13 indicates high short-term performance, F21 indicates low-level long-term performance, and F31 indicates low-level negative performance.

Other relational independent variables. There are two other player-to-player relations available in the dataset. One is the communication relation constructed by using the one-on-one message exchange activities (AA1). Another is previous collaboration relations, constructed using data from the previous month's log record on who played with whom on the same team (AA2).

We present three example analyses in this study. The first two are simple, but illustrative, models to predict performance from team-level attributes (specifically guild diversity) and individual-level attributes (specifically guild affiliation) respectively. Greater variation in attribute variables implies greater ability to "explain" performance. The third example explores the association between individual attributes (specifically guild affiliation) and social relations (specifically prior communication and collaboration).

Analytic Method

Correspondence analysis was done using R package *ca* (Nenadic and Greenacre 2007) for the bipartite network of Zone Everfrost. Standardized scores from the first two dimensions in Fig. 7.6 above were plotted using R package *ggplot2* (Wickham 2012). The results show several clusters: one big cluster and several smaller ones. This is consistent with the observation of the bipartite network depicted in Fig. 7.5. The correlations and distances among these clusters are measured more mathematically in the correspondence analysis. Among the 12 variables, results from two variables and the performance factors are shown here as examples.

Results

To demonstrate interpretation of results from correspondence analysis, we present three examples using this dataset. The first two examples uses team performance as dependent variable and explanatory variables related to the in-game organization guilds. Two measures, one at the team level and one at the individual level, are analyzed with three measures of performance. The first case is demonstrated with two plots, one with and one without the observed raw relational data, to illustrate how the relational data can be included in the plots. All other plots in this chapter will not include such data. The third example uses multiple network relations

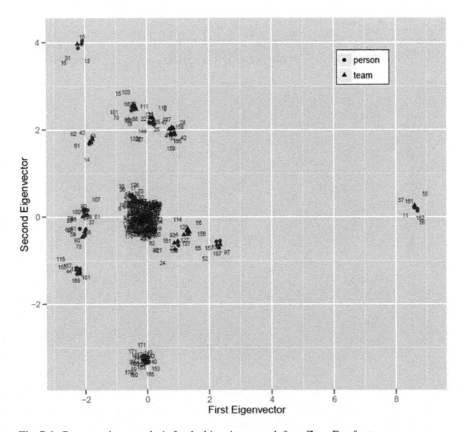

Fig. 7.6 Correspondence analysis for the bipartite network from Zone Everfrost

(i.e., previous collaboration and chat) and an individual-level variable indicating if a player is affiliated with a guild or not. The data are analyzed to discover potential relationships between guild affiliation and social interactions. Results from three analysis models are reported: one model for each network (e.g., collaboration and chat) and one that includes both networks. The results are demonstrated in plots without inclusion of the raw original data.

Team Performance and Team Guild Diversity: Fig. 7.7 shows the plot of the first two dimensions from the results of the multiple correspondence analysis with the original data. Figure 7.8 shows the same results without the original individual-level data, where the relations among the variables are easier to see. Later in the chapter, we show figures similar to Fig. 7.8, but for each of them, a figure similar to Fig. 7.7 can be created. The circles are the raw data of team affiliations, triangles are attribute variables, and the squares are the performance variables.

Table 7.3 shows the numerical breakdown of the analysis. The first two dimensions explained 45.9 % of the total observed variance. The locations of the data points and the locations of the variables show the relations among them. When data points or variables are near to each other, it indicates closer relations.

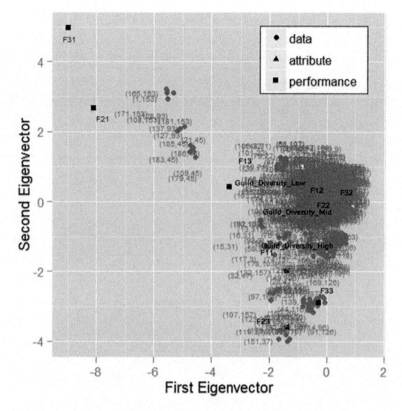

Fig. 7.7 Multiple correspondence analysis of guild diversity and performance with ties data

From the plot, most data points are clustered around the midlevel guild diversity and all three performance factors are at midlevel (F12, F22, and F32). Some teams have low long-term performance, shown by the small cluster near F21, or high long-term performance, shown by the cluster near F23.

Low guild diversity is closer to high and medium short-term performance (F13 and F12), rather than low short-term performance (F11). Low guild diversity is also closer to medium-level long-term performance (F22), rather than low long-term performance (F21). High guild diversity is also close to medium short-term performance (F12). Taken together these results suggest that, when the dependencies among observations are considered, teams with members from diverse guilds have higher short-term performance but lower long-term performance. These exploratory insights should stimulate theoretical explorations leading to hypotheses generation as well as offer opportunities for data reduction.

Team Performance and Individual Guild Affiliation: Next we explored the association of an individual level attribute, specifically guild affiliation, and team performance. Each dyad in the multiple correspondence matrix includes one node from each mode. Attributes at the individual level can be included in the same way

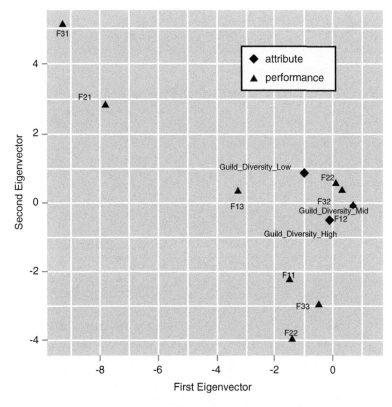

Fig. 7.8 Multiple correspondence analysis of guild diversity and performance

Table 7.3 Multiple correspondence analysis of guild diversity and performance; principal inertias (eigenvalues)

Dimension	Value	Percent variance explained	Cumulative percent variance explained	Screen plot
1	0.13	23.70	23.70	**************************
2	0.12	22.10	45.90	************************
3	0.08	14.70	60.60	***************
4	0.07	13.00	73.60	*************
5	0.05	9.80	83.50	*********
6	0.04	7.60	91.00	*****
7	0.03	5.30	96.30	**
8	0.02	3.70	100.00	

as the team-level variables were in the previous example. Figure 7.9 shows the plots of the first two dimensions from the correspondence analysis; Table 7.4 shows the numerical breakdown of the analysis. The first two dimensions explain 50.7 % of the total variance.

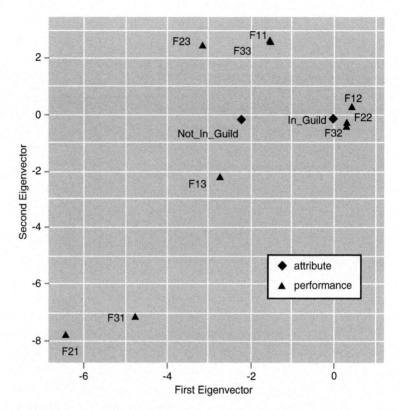

Fig. 7.9 Multiple correspondence analysis of guild affiliation and performance

Table 7.4 Multiple correspondence analysis of individual guild affiliation and performance; principal inertias (eigenvalues)

Dimension	Value	Percent variance explained	Cumulative percent variance explained	Screen plot
1	0.13	26.9	26.9	*************************
2	0.11	23.8	50.7	**********************
3	0.07	14.8	65.5	************
4	0.06	12.5	78.0	*********
5	0.05	11.3	89.3	********
6	0.03	6.5	95.8	***
7	0.02	4.2	100.0	

As shown in both Fig. 7.9, belonging to a guild is associated with mid-level short-term, long-term, and negative performance. Individuals not in a guild face more uncertainty. They may have either very high or very low short-term performance (about equal distance to F11 and F13) and they usually encounter more deaths (closer to F33 than F31).

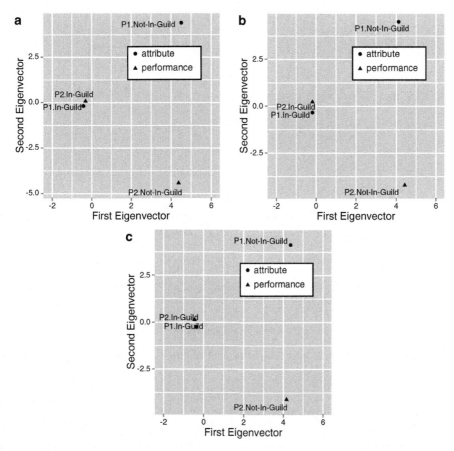

Fig. 7.10 Multiple network analysis results. (**a**) Guild membership and chat relation; (**b**) Guild membership and collaboration relation; (**c**) Guild membership and both relations

Multiple Network Analysis: Our third example with this dataset demonstrates the application of correspondence analysis to multiple networks. We use examples with the two-mode network team affiliation network (AB), two one-mode network relations (chat relation [AA1] and collaboration relation [AA2]), and two attribute variables, an individual level attribute (guild membership) and a team level attribute (team performance). We first explore the association of guild membership and the two one-mode network relations taken individually and then together. As shown in Fig. 7.10a, players in a guild tend to chat with other players in guilds; players not in a guild are not likely to chat with each other. Circles denote Node i's attributes in the Node i and Node j dyad; triangles denote Node j's attributes in Node i and Node j dyad.

Similar results are observed with the collaboration relation, presented in Fig. 7.10b. Players in guilds tend to collaborate with others in guilds. Players who do not belong to a guild are not likely to collaborate with each other. When both

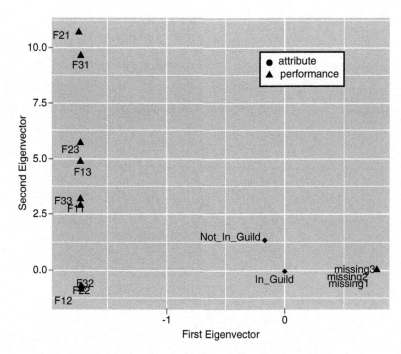

Fig. 7.11 Multiple correspondence analysis of guild affiliation and performance controlling for multiple network relations

relations are included together with guild membership, we found (see Fig. 7.10c) that they point in the same direction as the effects for each relation (i.e., guild members collaborate with and chat with others in guilds). In other words, the effects of each of the two relations while controlling for the other are similar to the effects of the other relation. Using the analogy of regression models, it means that the interaction effects are in the same direction as the main effects. For all three analyses, the first two dimensions explain 100 % of the total variance, because there are only two levels for one of the variables, and additional dimensionality is not possible. Hence, we omit the tables for principal inertias/eigenvalues.

Next, we conducted a multiple correspondence analysis with the team affiliation network (AB), the chat relation (AA1), the collaboration relation (AA2) and the two attribute variables, individual level guild affiliation and team level performance. Figure 7.11 shows the plot of the first two dimensions; and Table 7.5 shows the numerical breakdown of the analysis. The first two dimensions explain 66.3 % of the total variance. It is instructive to compare the association of guild affiliation and performance in Fig. 7.11 controlling for the two one-mode relations (chat and collaboration) with the association of guild affiliation and performance, shown in Fig. 7.9, that did not control for the two one-mode relations. The associations of guild affiliation and performance observed in Fig. 7.9 disappear in Fig. 7.11, when controlling for the two one-mode relations. This suggests that at least part of the

Table 7.5 Multiple correspondence analysis of individual guild affiliation and performance controlling for multiple network relations; principal inertias (eigenvalues)

Dimension	Value	Percent variance explained	Cumulative percent variance explained	Screen plot
1	0.56	54.3	54.3	**************************
2	0.12	12.0	66.3	**********************
3	0.11	10.9	77.2	************
4	0.07	6.6	83.8	*********
5	0.06	5.7	89.5	********
6	0.06	5.6	95.1	***
7	0.03	3.0	98.1	
8	0.02	1.9	100	

previously observed relation between guild affiliation and mid-level performance are captured by the frequent chat and collaboration between individuals belonging to guilds. Thus, if we control these relations, the previously observed relationship disappears.

It is important to consider the stability of the results. One source of instability is sampling variability. We have no reason to suspect this being a source of lack of stability of the solution because it is highly unlikely, given the data, that any one point contributes substantially greater to the solution. Further, we did not perform hypothesis testing, so that source of the lack of stability can also be eliminated. Sampling variability could also occur because, given the large size of the overall dataset, we randomly sampled from a wider population (Greenacre 2010). However, we repeated the analysis several times with different subsamples and obtained very similar results. For parsimony, we are not reporting the results here, but we have confirmed that the results are consistent. Yet another source of stability stems from the potential inadequacy of using the two-dimension plot to capture the association among the variables of interests. As suggested in Greenacre and Hastie (1987) and Roberts (2000), the quality of these two-dimension plots are generally "pessimistic," especially for multiple correspondence analysis, despite the fact that sometimes, the first two dimensions account for a seemingly not very high portion of the total inertia (such as 50.7 %, as in Table 7.4).

Developing Hypotheses from Preliminary Results

Multiple correspondence analysis, as described above, is a useful tool for hypotheses generation and subsequent testing with other more sophisticated confirmatory methods, such as p*/ERGM models (Robins et al. 2007a; Wang et al. 2013; Wasserman and Pattison 1996). Here its use is demonstrated on the example of the results in Fig. 7.9, relating individual guild affiliation with team performance.

As shown in Fig. 7.9, guild affiliation is associated with mid-level short-term and long-term performance (F12, F22), and also with mid-level negative performance (F32). When not in guilds, individuals can exhibit very high or very low short-term performance, and they usually show higher negative performance (face more deaths). In other words, belonging to a guild is associated with a mid-level performance, without any extremes of excellent results or higher deaths. Theoretically this might suggest that affiliating with an organization (in this case, a guild) serves to moderate a freelancer's performance. Affiliation buffers against very poor performance by leveraging the benefits of coordinating with, and gaining insights from, other guild members. But it might also stymie very high performance because of the costs incurred in coordinating with others. Therefore, a hypothesis deduced from this curvilinear reasoning would be as follows:

Hypothesis 1: Belonging to a guild reduces the chances of extreme high or low performance.

To test this hypothesis, we fitted exponential random graph models (p^* models, Wasserman and Pattison 1996) using MPNet software package. The essence of p* modeling is comparing the network under consideration with a series of random networks generated on the same set of nodes, to evaluate which network statistics are statistically more or less likely to result in a distribution of networks in which the observed network is very likely to occur. Model coefficients are logit-coefficients, with the dependent variable indicating the log odds of a tie between two existing nodes. Positive coefficients indicate that an attribute is more likely to appear in the observed network than could be expected by chance; negative coefficients indicate the opposite (Robins et al. 2007b).

We fit three models separately for the interaction between the individual attribute, guild affiliation, and the short-term team performance measure. Results are presented in Table 7.6, and we focus on interpreting results related to attribute variables. It can be seen from the table that, across all three performance levels, guild affiliation has positive effects, i.e., individuals with guild affiliation are more likely to join teams than those without guild affiliation. This effect needs to be controlled when considering the interaction effects of individual guild affiliation and team performance. We also control the effects of team performance in all three models using the three team performance effect terms. After controlling the structure effects (XEdge and XStar2A, i.e., density of the affiliation network and the stars in the affiliation network), the converged p* model results show that, across all three performance levels, there are negative and significant relationships (at $p < .1$ level) between guild affiliation and performance. A negative relationship, as explained above, means that the tie is less likely in the observed network than in a randomly generated network with the same nodes. Across the three performance levels, we find, that the association of guild affiliation with high-level and low-level performance are less likely to be observed than with mid-level performance (with parameters of and for low- and high-level performance vs. for mid-level performance). These results indicate that belonging to a guild reduces the chances of extreme performance on either end, supporting, in effect, Hypothesis 1.

The relationships explored and confirmed may not always seem intuitive. In fact, common sense indicates that guild affiliation – belonging to a group – may

Table 7.6 p* model results: guild affiliation and performance

Effects	Estimates	Standard errors
Low-level performance		
XEdge	−3.41	0.25
XStar2A	−0.20	0.05
Individual in-guild effect	0.18	0.20
Team low-level performance effect	0.61	0.37
In-guild low-level performance matching effect	−0.57	0.35
Mid-level performance		
XEdge	−3.63	0.36
XStar2A	−0.20	0.05
Individual in-guild effect	0.21	0.35
Team middle-level performance effect	0.31	0.30
In-guild middle-level performance matching effect	−0.09	0.31
High-level performance		
XEdge	−3.39	0.27
XStar2A	−0.21	0.05
Individual in-guild effect	0.21	0.22
Team high-level performance effect	0.19	0.31
In-guild high-level performance matching effect	−0.56	0.31

Note: t-statistics = (observation − sample mean)/standard error; SACF (sample autocorrelation)

increase one's performance. In our example, this is clearly not the case. Multiple correspondence analysis results, presented in Fig. 7.9, prompted us to test a more nuanced claim about the nature of the relationship between guild affiliation and performance. We then considered possible theoretical explanations and formulated this reasoning into a hypothesis and tested it with a more sophisticated confirmatory network analytic technique. This illustrates how the use of MCA as an exploratory tool to assist hypothesis formulation, especially with large datasets or multiple attributes, substantially simplifies the analysis process. While we conducted the confirmatory test using the same data sample, a stronger claim could be made if the results were tested on different samples and found to be consistent. On the other hand differences across data sets might prompt a second level of theorizing about explanations for potential differences. The second example reported below illustrates exploration of those differences.

Example 2: Dragon Nest

The second example helps us explore the impact of cultural differences on how teams form and perform. We begin by reviewing theoretical considerations of cultural differences that can inform an exploratory analysis; next, we utilize the analytical methods described above, to explore cultural differences by comparing the predominantly US-based EQ2 data with the predominantly Chinese data collected from the MMOG Dragon's Nest.

Hinds et al. (2011) lament that cultural differences are often ignored in the studies of global collaboration and recommend a more explicit and nuanced inclusion of cultural differences in studies of teams. They suggest that studies of collaboration in teams could benefit from consideration of cultural differences. A cultural dimension potentially influencing how teams form and perform is tightness-looseness (Gelfand et al. 2011). This dimension distinguishes cultures on the basis of the degree to which they have many social norms and low tolerance for deviant behavior (tight) versus few social norms and higher tolerance for deviant behavior (loose). Forming teams based on social norms are more likely to occur in tight cultures, such as China, with many social norms and low tolerance for deviant behavior than among those in loose cultures, like the US, where individuals might be more likely to form teams driven by performance considerations.

Data and Sample

Data for this example were obtained from the MMOG Dragon's Nest (DN), a fantasy game where players form teams in order to advance their characters and travel into dungeons. Unlike the EQ2 dataset, where players were predominantly from US, players in DN were predominantly from China. This offered the opportunity to uncover the influence of cultural differences on how teams form and perform.

This dataset has the same characteristics as EQ2 – a sample of "big data," with a nesting of levels reflecting players being members in multiple teams. The data were collected during 1 week, January 24–30, 2011, from Zone 101 of the game, and the dataset contained information on 304 persons from 217 teams. One distinguishing feature of this dataset is that teams are smaller, 2–4 people, so selecting a partner is perhaps more strategic than in EQ2.

Variables

Variable selection was very similar to the way it was carried out in the first example. Variables of interest included guild diversity (categorical, three-level variable), individual guild affiliation (binary – either in-guild or not-in-guild), team performance (categorical, three levels, equivalent to the short-term performance in the first example). The only network relation examined here was the person-team two-mode network.

Analytic Method

Correspondence analysis was performed in the same manner as in the first example, using R packages *ca* (Nenadic and Greenacre 2007), *ggplot2* (Wickham 2012).

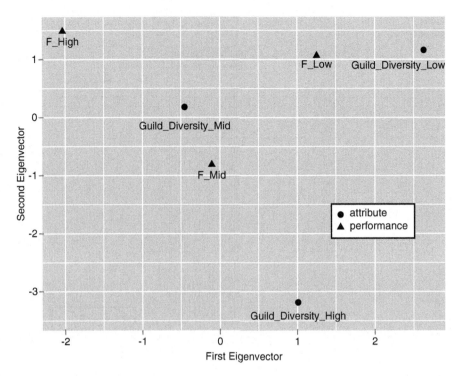

Fig. 7.12 Multiple correspondence analysis of guild diversity and performance

Because the primary purpose of this example was to demonstrate the cultural differences that could be discovered using multiple correspondence analysis, we focus more on the comparison with the first example than with the explanation of the analytic techniques already described previously.

Results

Team Performance and Guild Diversity: As in the first example, we plotted the results of the first two dimensions obtained using multiple correspondence analysis, presented below in Fig. 7.12. Triangles are attribute variables, and the squares are the performance variables. The first two dimensions explained 66.4 % of the total observed variance. Similar to the first example, the locations of the variables show the relations among them; when variables are near to each other, it indicates closer relations.

From the plot it is clear that unlike the EQ2 example, where most data points were clustered around the mid-level guild diversity, and all three performance factors were at mid-level, the data in this example is more evenly distributed between different performance levels. In other words, something other than performance alone keeps people affiliated with their respective guilds. This could serve as a demonstration of the cultural context described above: people in tight cultures

Table 7.7 Multiple correspondence analysis of guild diversity and performance; principal inertias (eigenvalues)

Dimension	Value	Percent variance explained	Cumulative percent variance explained	Screen plot
1	0.37	36.30	36.30	************************
2	0.31	30.10	66.40	******************
3	0.20	19.00	85.40	*****
4	0.15	14.60	100.00	

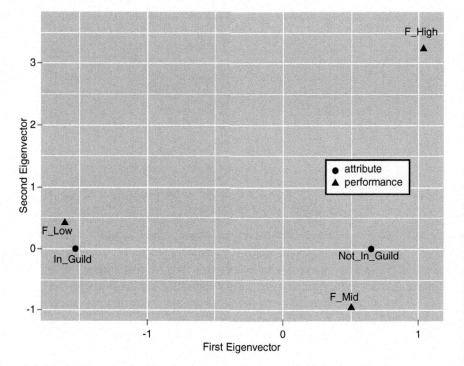

Fig. 7.13 Multiple correspondence analysis of guild affiliation and performance

(as this is an example comprised mostly of Chinese players) tend to form teams based on social norms, rather than expectations of performance typical for loose cultures (as in the US-based EQ2 example).

Table 7.7 shows the numerical breakdown of the analysis. The first two dimensions explained 66.4 % of the observed variance, and unlike the EQ2 example with eight dimensions, there were only four dimensions in total, which, again, could possibly account for cultural differences between tight and the loose cultures.

Team Performance and Individual Guild Affiliation: Similar to the EQ2 example, attributes at the individual level were included in the analysis in the same way as the team-level variables. Figure 7.13 shows the plot of the first two dimensions from the correspondence analysis; Table 7.8 shows the numerical breakdown of the analysis.

Table 7.8 Multiple correspondence analysis of guild affiliation and performance; principal inertias (eigenvalues)

Dimension	Value	Percent variance explained	Cumulative percent variance explained	Screen plot
1	0.44	54.50	54.60	************************
2	0.25	31.20	85.70	**********
3	0.11	14.30	100.00	

Again, as in the previous example, it is clear that there are pronounced differences in the way that people form teams, and that this influences how they perform. Here, the affiliation with the guild actually results in lower performance, with a midlevel performance associated more closely with not being in a guild. As results in Table 7.8 show, there are actually only three dimensions to the data, with the first two dimensions explaining over 85 % of the variance. Here, again, it is apparent that social norms dictate how people form into teams, which is quite different, culturally, from the EQ2 example where performance dictated how people formed teams.

As a result, we were able to use multiple correspondence analysis as a preliminary data analysis tool to explore cultural differences between how teams form and perform in the US and China. More specifically, using MCA, one can explore large datasets before engaging in time-consuming tasks of testing more complex models with control variables.

Conclusions

In this study, we illustrate the advantages of using correspondence analysis as an exploratory method for analyzing relational data at multiple levels using examples from two massively multi-player online games. Correspondence analysis incorporates relations among the observations and includes both the relational ties and attributes at multiple levels. The results from correspondence analysis can also be visually represented in easily accessible plots. Relations among various variables as well as observed raw data can be shown in the same plot although in some cases it might be useful to suppress visualizing the raw data. The plots display more information than just means and standard errors as seen in regression model results. With these advantages, correspondence analysis can be used as an important exploratory tool to examine the features of multilevel network datasets and the relations among variables of interest. The insights drawn from this exploratory technique serve as a theoretical and data reduction preamble for further analysis that can then be carried out using other more sophisticated confirmatory methods, such as p^*/ERGM models (Frank and Strauss 1986; Robins and Pattison 2005; Wasserman and Pattison 1996). As we have demonstrated with our examples, generating hypotheses from MCA results and testing them by fitting p^* models is much more streamlined with the use of MCA. Ideally, with the proliferation of big data, the confirmatory tests can be analyzed using separate but similar data sources. The proliferation of big data also increases the opportunity of using MCA to explore differences such as data gathered across different cultures.

This method also has some limitations. For instance, correspondence analysis requires categorical (or frequency) data. Some information is unavoidably lost during the transformation. The plots created using the scores from the first two dimensions are a projection of the higher dimensional data, which can lead to misinterpretation by the human eye. Furthermore, the magnitude of distances between points in the display does not indicate connections in the relation network. As with many exploratory approaches, the visualization of the results can be viewed in different ways by different people. Given the preliminary nature of this study, we recognize these limitations. Our goal is not to draw conclusions about the relationships of the study variables, but to use correspondence analysis as a way of developing hypotheses and models that can then be tested using subsequent techniques, such as p*/ERGM.

Acknowledgements The authors wish to acknowledge the Army Research Laboratory W911NF-09-2-0053 and the Army Research Office W911NF-12-1-0176 that contributed to the development of materials presented in this chapter. The views and conclusions contained in this document are those of the authors and should not be interpreted as representing the official policies, either expressed or implied, of the Army Research Laboratory or the Army Research Office or the U.S. Government. The U.S. Government is authorized to reproduce and distribute reprints for Government purposes notwithstanding any copyright notation here on. The book chapter was also prepared within the framework of a subsidy granted to the Higher School of Economics, Moscow, by the Government of the Russian Federation for the implementation of the Global Competitiveness Program.

References

Berends, H., van Burg, E., & van Raaij, E. M. (2011). Contacts and contracts: Cross-level network dynamics in the development of an aircraft material. *Organization Science, 22*, 940–960.
Blau, P. (1977). *Inequality and heterogeneity*. New York: Free Press.
Borgatti, S. P., & Everett, M. G. (1987). Network analysis of 2-mode data. *Social Networks, 19*, 243–269.
Borgatti, S. P., & Halgin, D. S. (2011). Analyzing affiliation networks. In P. Carrington & J. Scott (Eds.), *The Sage handbook of social network analysis* (pp. 417–433). London: Sage Publications.
Borgatti, S., Everett, M. G., & Freeman, L. C. (2002). *Ucinet for Windows: Software for social network analysis*. Harvard: Analytic Technologies.
Borgatti, S. P., Everett, M. G., & Johnson, J. C. (2013). *Analyzing social networks*. Thousand Oaks: SAGE Publications Limited.
Boyd, D., & Crawford, K. (2011). *Six provocations for big data*. Retrieved from http://papers.ssrn.com/sol3/papers.cfm?abstract_id=1926431
De Stefano, D., D'Esposito, M. R., & Ragozini, G. (2014). On the use of multiple correspondence analysis to visually explore affiliation networks. *Social Networks, 38*, 28–40.
Denton, H. G. (1997). Multidisciplinary team-based project work: Planning factors. *Design Studies, 18*, 155–170.

Doreian, P., Batagelj, V., & Ferligoj, A. (2004). Generalized blockmodeling of two-mode network data. *Social Networks, 26*, 29–53.
Faust, K. (1997). Centrality in affiliation networks. *Social Networks, 19*, 157–191.
Faust, K. (2005). Using correspondence analysis for joint displays of affiliation networks. In P. J. Carrington, J. Scott, & S. Wasserman (Eds.), *Models and methods in social network analysis* (pp. 117–147). New York: Cambridge University Press.
Frank, O., & Strauss, D. (1986). Markov graphs. *Journal of the American Statistical Association, 81*(395), 832–842.
Gelfand, M., et al. (2011). Differences between tight and loose cultures: A 33 nation study. *Science, 332*, 1100–1104.
Gilula, Z., & Haberman, S. J. (1988). The analysis of multivariate contingency tables by restricted canonical and restricted association models. *Journal of the American Statistical Association, 83*(403), 760–771.
Greenacre, M. (1984). *Theory and applications of correspondence analysis*. London: Academic.
Greenacre, M. (2010). *Correspondence analysis in practice*. London: CRC Press.
Greenacre, M., & Hastie, T. (1987). The geometric interpretation of correspondence analysis. *Journal of the American Statistical Association, 82*, 437–447.
Hinds, P., Liu, L., & Lyon, J. (2011). Putting the global in global work: An intercultural lens on the practice of cross-national collaboration. *The Academy of Management Annals, 5*, 135–188.
Holland, P. W., & Leinhardt, S. (1981). An exponential family of probability distributions for directed graphs (with discussion). *Journal of the American Statistical Association, 76*, 33–65.
Kauffeld, S. (2006). Self-directed work groups and team competence. *Journal of Occupational and Organizational Psychology, 79*(1), 1–21.
Klein, K. J., & Kozlowski, S. W. (Eds.). (2000). *Multilevel theory, research, and methods in organizations: Foundations, extensions, and new directions*. San Francisco: Jossey-Bass.
Latapy, M., Magnien, C., & Del Vecchio, N. (2008). Basic notions for the analysis of large two-mode networks. *Social Networks, 30*(1), 31–48.
LaValle, S., Lesser, E., Shockley, R., Hopkins, M. S., & Kruschwitz, N. (2011). Big data, analytics and the path from insights to value. *MIT Sloan Management Review, 52*(2), 21–31.
McAfee, A., & Brynjolfsson, E. (2012). Big data: The management revolution. *Harvard Business Review, 90*(10), 60–66.
O'Leary, M., Mortensen, M., & Woolley, A. (2011). Multiple team membership: A theoretical model of its effects on productivity and learning for individuals and teams. *Academy of Management Review, 36*, 461–478.
Nenadic, O., & Greenacre, M. (2007). Correspondence analysis in R, with two- and three-dimensional graphics: The ca package. *Journal of Statistical Software, 20*(3). Retrieved from http://www.jstatsoft.org/v20/i03/
Newman, M. (2010). *Networks: An introduction*. Oxford: Oxford University Press.
Parkhe, A. (1993). Strategic alliance structuring: A game theoretic and transaction cost examination of interfirm cooperation. *Academy of Management Journal, 36*, 794–829.
Payne, G. T., Moore, C. B., Griffis, S. E., & Autry, C. W. (2011). Multilevel challenges and opportunities in social capital research. *Journal of Management, 37*, 491–520.
Phelps, C., Heidl, R., & Wadhwa, A. (2012). Knowledge, networks, and knowledge networks a review and research agenda. *Journal of Management, 38*(4), 1115–1166.
Roberts, J. M. (2000). Correspondence analysis of two-mode network data. *Social Networks, 22*(1), 65–72.
Robins, G., & Pattison, P. (2005). Interdependencies and social processes: Dependence graphs and generalized dependence structures. In P. J. Carrington, J. Scott, & S. Wasserman (Eds.), *Models and methods in social network analysis*. New York: Cambridge University Press.
Robins, G. L., Snijders, T., Wang, P., Handcock, M. S., & Pattison, P. E. (2007a). Recent developments in exponential random graph (p*) models for social networks. *Social Networks, 29*(2), 192–215.
Robins, G., Pattison, P., Kalish, Y., & Lusher, D. (2007b). An introduction to exponential random graph (p*) models for social networks. *Social Networks, 29*(2), 173–191.

Skvoretz, J., & Faust, K. (1999). Logit models for affiliation networks. *Sociological Methodology, 29*, 253–280.

Wageman, R., Gardner, H., & Mortensen, M. (2012). The changing ecology of teams: New directions for teams research. *Journal of Organizational Behavior, 33*(3), 301–315.

Wang, P., Robins, G., Pattison, P., & Lazega, E. (2013). Exponential random graph models for multilevel networks. *Social Networks, 35*(1), 96–115.

Wasserman, S., & Faust, K. (1989). Canonical analysis of the composition and structure of social networks. *Sociological Methodology, 19*, 1–42.

Wasserman, S., & Faust, K. (1994). *Social network analysis: Methods and applications*. Cambridge: Cambridge University Press.

Wasserman, S., & Pattison, P. E. (1996). Logit models and logistic regressions for social networks: I. An introduction to Markov graphs and p*. *Psychometrika, 61*(3), 401–425.

Wasserman, S., & Robins, G. (2005). An introduction to random graphs, dependence graphs, and p*. In P. J. Carrington, J. Scott, & S. Wasserman (Eds.), *Models and methods in social network analysis* (pp. 148–161). New York: Cambridge University Press.

Wasserman, S., Faust, K., & Galaskiewicz, J. (1990). Correspondence and canonical analysis of relational data. *Journal of Mathematical Sociology, 1*, 11–64.

Wellman, B. (1988). Thinking structurally. In B. Wellman & S. D. Berkowitz (Eds.), *Social structures: A network approach*. Cambridge: Cambridge University Press.

Wickham, H. (2012). *ggplot2* [Computer software]. Retrieved from http://ggplot2.org/

Zhao, Z. J., & Anand, J. (2013). Beyond boundary spanners: The 'collective bridge' as an efficient interunit structure for transferring collective knowledge. *Strategic Management Journal, 34*, 1513–1530.

Chapter 8
Role Sets and Division of Work at Two Levels of Collective Agency: The Case of Blockmodeling a Multilevel (Inter-individual and Inter-organizational) Network

Aleš Žiberna and Emmanuel Lazega

Introduction

Explorations of the vertical, multi-level dimension of social phenomena following a linked-design approach (Lazega et al. 2008) improve knowledge of multi-level conflicts and interdependencies, and additionally of the manner in which actors at each level manage these interdependencies. Superimposed systems of interdependencies are in fact superimposed levels of collective agency, inter-individual and inter-organizational, that co-constitute each other (Breiger 1974) but must not be conflated. In this chapter, we use blockmodeling at both levels separately and jointly to further explore the articulations between such superimposed systems of interdependencies and collective agency, inter-individual and inter-organizational. Specifically, we present an application of blockmodeling (Žiberna 2014) to a multilevel network of elite cancer researchers in France, the data for which was gathered by Lazega et al. (2008). This network is multilevel, as it includes two levels of units and agency: individuals (here researchers as level-one units) and organizations (here laboratories as level-two units) and affiliation ties between and among them. Therefore this network is composed of a one-mode (advice-seeking) network of researchers, a one-mode (collaboration) network of laboratories, and a two-mode network tying the researchers to the laboratories in which they are employed.

A. Žiberna (✉)
Faculty of Social Sciences, University of Ljubljana, Kardeljeva ploščad 5, 1000 Ljubljana, Slovenia
e-mail: ales.ziberna@fdv.uni-lj.si

E. Lazega
Institut d'Etudes Politiques de Paris, SPC, CSO-CNRS, 19 rue Amélie, 75007 Paris, France
e-mail: emmanuel.lazega@sciencespo.fr

While this multilevel network has already been analyzed with this method (Žiberna 2014), the analysis presented in that study was done with the aim of presenting the generality of the method and not with the aim of getting as much insight as possible into the structure of this multilevel network. Here we present a more applied and exploratory blockmodel analysis of this network, enhanced by substantive insights. In addition, the analysis presented here uses some of recent advances in blockmodeling relatively sparse networks (Žiberna 2013a).

Three approaches for adding insights into the global structure of this multilevel network are used. The first is a separate analysis of each level and a comparison of results, both in terms of similarity of structure and in terms of whether the partition of the researcher network is similar to the partition of the laboratory network in which these researchers are employed. The second approach tries to convert this multilevel problem to a classical one-level blockmodeling problem by converting or reshaping one of the one-mode networks (for one level, in this case the network of laboratories) to the other level. The meaning of this "reshaped" network as indirect ties among researchers is discussed, as are the methods for joint analysis of the original researcher network and this indirect researcher network. The third approach is what we call a true multilevel approach. With this approach we blockmodel the whole multilevel network, that is, we jointly blockmodel the network of researchers, the network of laboratories, and the two-mode network joining the researchers and laboratories. The results of this analysis are relatively well-fitting blockmodels for each level (researchers and laboratories) together with ties among groups of individuals and groups of organizations.

Multilevel Networks

We define multilevel networks here as a networks where we have units from at least two levels of collective agency, ties among units of the same levels and ties among units of different levels. This corresponds to the fourth definition from the document "What Are Multilevel Networks" prepared by the Multi-level Network Modeling Group (MNMG) (2012) and to definition used in Lazega et al. (2008), Wang et al. (2013) and Snijders (Chap. 2, this volume).

Therefore, we define multilevel networks here as networks composed of one-mode networks for each level and two-mode networks that "join" units from different levels. In this chapter we will limit ourselves to only two levels and only one relation per level and one relation for ties among levels.[1] For such two-level networks with N lower-level units and M higher-level units, the data could have the following structure (the dimensions of the matrices are given in the square brackets):

- a network of individuals or first-level units represented by a matrix $N1_{[N \times N]}$
- a network of institutions or second-level units represented by a matrix $N2_{[M \times M]}$

---

[1] For a more general version of the described approaches see Žiberna (2014).

- a two-mode (affiliation) network tying individuals to institutions, or ties between first- and second-level units represented by a matrix $TM_{[N \times M]}$

The discussion in this chapter is limited[2] to the case where two-mode networks represent partitions of "lower" level units into "higher" level units, that is each "lower" level unit is tied to exactly one "higher" level unit, while each "higher" level unit is tied to at least one "lower" level unit. Such networks can of course be also analyzed using other methods. Iacobucci and Wasserman (1990) were the first to suggest the analysis of such networks (although not in a multilevel context) and (Wasserman and Iacobucci 1991) also presented a method for the statistical modeling of such networks, although they did not apply it to a real dataset. More than a decade later the importance of a multilevel view was advocated by Brass et al. (2004) and Lazega et al. (2004, 2006, 2008, 2013). Recently, Wang et al. (2013) extended exponential random graph models to multilevel networks. The same dataset is used for demonstration purposes in Wang et al. (2013) and Žiberna (2014). This is of course the same dataset that is analyzed in this chapter.

Additional methods and applications (e.g. Bellotti 2012; Snijders et al. 2013) can be found for combinations of only one-mode networks at one level and a two-mode network connecting this level to another level. Such networks can be seen as a special case of multilevel networks as defined here where no relations are collected for one level.

Blockmodeling

Blockmodeling is used for partitioning network units into clusters and, at the same time, partitioning the set of ties into blocks (White et al. 1976; Doreian et al. 2005a, p. 29). Blockmodeling can be also seen as a data reduction technique for obtaining a simplified model for relations among units (Borgatti and Everett 1992), and is also the foundation for building role structures (Boorman and White 1976; White et al. 1976). Several approaches to blockmodeling exist, such as conventional blockmodeling (e.g. Breiger et al. 1975; Burt 1976; see Doreian et al. 2005a, pp. 25–26 for definitions), generalized blockmodeling (Doreian et al. 1994, 2005a) and stochastic blockmodeling (Holland et al. 1983; Anderson et al. 1992; Snijders and Nowicki 1997). While generalized blockmodeling is used in this chapter, separate analysis and conversion to one-level blockmodeling, at least, can be easily implemented using other approaches.

In generalized blockmodeling the criterion function is optimized when searching for the optimal partition given the selected equivalence and network (Batagelj et al. 1992a, b; Doreian et al. 1994). How the criterion function is computed

---

[2] See Žiberna (2014) (including footnotes) for needed modifications in the case of other types of two-mode networks.

for single-relational networks is described in works where different approaches to generalized blockmodeling are presented (e.g. Doreian et al. 2005a; Žiberna 2007, 2013a). Here we are using blockmodeling for sparse networks based on structural equivalence with differential weighting of inconsistencies for null and non-null blocks suggested by Žiberna (2013a). How these criterion functions are combined is described in the next chapter and in more detail in Žiberna (2014, pp. 48–51).

Multilevel Blockmodeling[3]

The ultimate goal of multilevel blockmodeling is to find a blockmodel (groups and the ties among them) for the whole multilevel network; that is, to partition the units at all levels into groups by taking all available information into account and determining the ties among these groups.

In this chapter, three general approaches are discussed:

(a) a separate analysis of each mode and a comparison of the results;
(b) the conversion of the multilevel problem into a classical one-level blockmodeling problem (hereafter "the conversion approach"); and
(c) a true multilevel approach.

These are not really alternative approaches since at least the first one (separate analysis) should be the first step in any blockmodeling analysis of multilevel networks. The separate analysis approach (a) represents a good exploratory technique and can guide a more complex analysis and show whether more complex approaches are even justified. The conversion approach (b) is appropriate when we want to focus on a certain level while using information from the other level(s) to improve the partition and/or when the other level(s) can be used as indirect relations for units of the level in focus. In contrast, the multilevel approach (c) should be used when we already have some knowledge about the network structure. It can provide us with novel insights into the ties among clusters from different levels. It can also help us search for such clusters at individual levels in such a way that the ties among them are relatively "clean." Use of the first and at least one of the other two approaches is also in line with the idea of Lazega et al. (2013) that it "is important to examine both levels separately and jointly."

---

[3]This section is a slightly modified version of the section with the same title form Žiberna (2014, pp. 48–51) Reprinted from Social Networks, Vol 39, Aleš Žiberna, "Blockmodeling of Multilevel Networks," 46–61, Copyright (2014), with permission from Elsevier.

A Separate Analysis of Each Mode and a Comparison of the Results

The simplest way to analyze a multilevel network using blockmodeling is to blockmodel each level separately and then compare the results. The comparison can be done in several ways:

(a) forcing the partition obtained at one level onto the other level and analyzing the fit; or
(b) obtaining the partitions on both levels and comparing them.

Both options are complementary and ideally both should be used. The first option in (a) means that, after obtaining a partition on a given level, this partition is forced onto another level. This can be done by either reshaping the partition to the level onto which it is to be forced or reshaping the one-mode network of the level on which the partition is to be forced to the level on which the partition was obtained. Both reshapings are done through the use of the two-mode networks joining the two levels.

The reshaping is most straightforward when the two-mode network essentially represents a partition of units of the first level into classes defined by the second level and we are reshaping the second-level partition to the first level. In such cases, the second-level partition can be reshaped to the first level simply by assigning to the units of the first level the class (cluster) of the units of the second level to which these units belong.

Similarly, we can easily reshape the network of the second level to the first by assigning the tie of the second-level units to pairs of first-level units that are associated with these second-level units. This can be simply obtained by pre- and post-multiplying the matrix representing the second-level network by the matrix representing the two-mode network (transposed when needed) as presented in Eq. (8.1).

$$\mathbf{N2}^* = \mathbf{TM} \times \mathbf{N2} \times \mathbf{TM}' \tag{8.1}$$

The reshaped network represented by matrix N2* actually represents indirect ties between units of the first level through the ties among second-level units to which these first-level units are associated. Such a transformation is also undertaken by Lazega et al. (2013), where they call neighbors in the resulting network "dual actors."

The transformations are a little more complicated in the other direction or when first-level units are tied to more than one second-level unit. In such cases, some averaging, voting, or aggregation rules are required.

After a partition at one level is obtained and a suitable reshaping has been applied, we can see how this partition fits the other level. That is, we can check whether the pattern of ties of the second network is well explained by this partition and therefore by the structure of the first-level network. We could say that we are performing a kind of pre-specified blockmodeling (Batagelj et al. 1998) and checking the fit of the pre-specified partition (and possibly a blockmodel image) to a network. If the fit is good (significantly better than random), we can say that the structures of both networks are associated. In addition, we can check whether the blockmodel images are similar at both levels. If they are, this indicates that not only are the groups on one level associated with the groups on the other level, but so too is the pattern of ties among groups.

The second option (b) is to compare partitions obtained at both levels. This is done by reshaping one of the partitions for it to be compatible with the other and using some classical indices for comparing partitions to compare them, such as the Rand Index (Rand 1971) or Adjusted Rand Index (ARI) (Hubert and Arabie 1985). Obviously, larger values of these indices indicate a stronger association among the partitions and therefore among the global structures of the one-mode networks at different levels. All values of ARI over 0 indicate that the association is greater than would be expected by chance.

This approach is a good exploratory technique, since it is simple to perform and allows an estimation of the association of group structures across levels, and therefore it should always be the first step in the analysis. These comparisons allow us to determine whether there is some similarity in the structure of the two networks and whether the similarity is only in the partitions or also in the pattern of ties among groups. Where no similarity is found, more complex analyses are probably not justified. In case of only partition similarities, the single-relational version (explained in the next subsection) of the conversion approach is most likely unsuitable.

Of course, this approach also has limitations especially since all partitions are only based on one level, and since the ties between groups of different levels cannot be modeled, only observed. However, this does not limit its usefulness as an exploratory technique.

Conversion of the Multilevel Problem to a Classical One-Level Blockmodeling Problem

The first approach suggested here that takes information about both levels into account is to convert this multilevel problem to a one-level problem. This approach is appropriate in cases where we believe that the partitions at different levels are practically the same (after reshaping) and we want to use as much information as possible to find these partitions. In fact, when using this approach only a partition at one level is obtained, which can then be reshaped if desired to obtain a partition at another level. Therefore, we should only use it if we find in the separate analysis stage that partitions for these two levels are similar, or if one partition at least approximately fits both levels.

In this approach we reshape the network from one level to the other and then partition both networks at this "other" level simultaneously. We can treat the reshaped network as an additional (indirect) relation in the "other" level network.[4] We can then proceed in two ways. The first one is to somehow aggregate these two relationships by using some function like maximum (other options include minimum, average and sum) on the values from both relations for the same tie. This option only makes sense if the two relations measure similar concepts or have a similar structure in terms of both partitions and patterns of ties among groups; for example, if we can consider one network person's direct access to some resources and the other network person's indirect access through institutional exchange. In some cases, it might be sensible to find a partition at one level using this approach, but not on the other; for example, it might make sense to assume that employees can access resources through their firm's connections, but not vice versa.[5] In this case, when partitioning the employees it would be sensible to include their firms' connections to better estimate their position in some network, but it would not make sense to estimate the firms' positions also using their employees' connections.

The second option is to blockmodel the multi-relational network directly. This simply means that we perform blockmodeling on both relations (single-relational networks) simultaneously by constraining them to the same partition. Blockmodeling multirelational or multiple networks (jointly) was advocated in early works on blockmodeling (Breiger et al. 1975; White et al. 1976; Arabie et al. 1978) but neglected until recently in generalized blockmodeling literature (Doreian et al. 2005a). The technical details of this option are discussed by Žiberna (2014, sec. 3.1) with slightly different notation.

The advantages of this approach are that is it still relatively simple to perform and that it uses all available information (on both) levels to obtain a partition at the selected level. However, as discussed above, this only makes sense in certain cases. The approach also has several disadvantages, the first being that some information is lost in the aggregation, especially if the single-relational approach (aggregating relations prior to the blockmodeling analysis) is used. Second, the choice of suitable weights can be problematic when a multi-relational version is used. Finally, the approach only obtains one[6] partition that is then reshaped to different levels. This means that the ties between groups at different levels are fixed and cannot be observed or modeled.

---

[4]Since single-relational networks are represented by matrices, the multi-relational networks are represented by multiway matrices as used by Borgatti and Everett (1992).

[5]We do not imply that firms can (never) access resources through employees' (personal) networks.

[6]We could use different levels as a "base" level, that is the level to which other levels are reshaped. The partitions obtained using different base levels might then slightly differ when reshaped to the same level, especially if in the two-mode network units from both sets of nodes can have many ties (to nodes of the other set).

Fig. 8.1 Combining all networks into a "joint" network. The redundant part is written in *gray*

N1	TM
TM'	N2

The True Multilevel Approach

The purpose of this approach is to partition units of both levels simultaneously with some restrictions on the two-mode network, that is, on ties between levels. The idea is to join both one-mode and two-mode networks (for all levels) into one "joint" network. The one-mode "within-level" networks are on the diagonal "blocks" of this "joint" network and the two-mode network is on the off-diagonal "blocks", transposed where needed, as depicted in Fig. 8.1. It is sufficient to include the two-mode network only below or only above the diagonal since these are duplicated elements.

We can then specify suitable approaches and equivalences (allowed block types and possibly their positions) for each of these one-mode and two-mode networks separately. Then we can blockmodel this "joint" network based on these specifications with the restriction that units from different levels cannot be in the same cluster. The technical details of blockmodeling the "joint" network[7] are discussed in Žiberna (2014). Suitable specifications for one-mode networks can be found in the relevant literature (e.g. Doreian et al. 2005a; Žiberna 2007); in this chapter we only discuss them in the empirical section.

While generalized blockmodeling of two-mode networks has also been covered (Doreian et al. 2004, 2005b), some suitable specifications for the two-mode network are discussed here. When specifying equivalences for two mode networks we should have in mind that we want to obtain clear connections among groups at both levels. This means that it is preferable that most blocks in the two-mode network be null (empty, without any ties), since this makes the connections between the groups at different levels clearer. Preferably, such blocks would have no inconsistencies (no ties). The goal of very few or even no inconsistencies in null blocks can be achieved by heavily penalizing the inconsistencies in the null blocks or equivalently penalizing less the inconsistencies in other blocks (Doreian et al. 2005b, pp. 260–261; Žiberna 2013a).

This approach has several advantages: it takes all available information (all one-mode and two-mode networks) into account; that no aggregation is necessary; and that ties between levels can be modeled.

However, it also has several drawbacks. In conceptual terms, the main disadvantages are that there are no clear guidelines concerning what are appropriate weights for different parts of "joint" network, that is, for both one-mode networks and for the

---

[7]Which is usually treated as a multirelational network.

two-mode network. In the event of equal weights, in principle the parts with larger inconsistencies have a bigger influence on the results. As the inconsistencies are dependent on the equivalences (or allowed block types and their positions), network sizes, pattern of and number of clusters, all these factors influence the appropriate weighting.

Additional disadvantages are tied to optimization problems, especially as a local search with a single exchange and move as allowed "moves" is currently used for optimization. First, finding an optimal partition using the direct approach is in most cases an NP-hard problem (Batagelj et al. 2004, p. 461). The multilevel approach is even more time-demanding as there are more units in a multilevel network than in single-level networks.

Another problem lies in the fact that currently a local search with allowed transformations being a single exchange and a single move is used (see e.g. Batagelj et al. 1992a, p. 127 for details). This is problematic since in the multilevel approach quite hard constraints are usually desired for a two-mode network, typically by preferring null blocks and making ties in null blocks relatively costly. If the current partition is such that ties between a certain higher level unit and some lower level units are in a non-null block, moving just the higher level unit (since only one move at a time is allowed) would most likely move several ties in the two-mode network to the null block and would therefore be very costly, to a such an extent that the move would most likely not be selected. In the current implementation, we attempt to circumvent this problem by brute force, namely by using many random starting partitions with a local search. The option would be not to use very strict or costly restrictions on the two-mode network in the first stage in order not to make such moves too costly. If this results in an under-structured two-mode network (too many ties in the null block or too few null blocks), the resulting partition can be further optimized with more stringent (and costly) constraints on the two-mode network. Of course, it would be better to use an adapted tabu search (Brusco and Steinley 2011) or similar algorithm that would temporarily allow costly moves or probably even better the direct multiobjective blockmodeling (Brusco et al. 2013).

Analysis of a Multilevel Network of Cancer Researchers in France

We examine here the multilevel network of cancer researchers in France (Lazega et al. 2008) using multilevel blockmodeling. The analyzed multilevel network is composed of two levels, a level of researchers and a level of research laboratories. The networks and other data used are described in more detail in the following subsection. Generalized blockmodeling offers a wide range of possible analyses. In this paper we choose a more exploratory approach. This means that we do not search for a certain group structure (i. e. cohesive groups,[8] hierarchy, core-periphery structure, ...), but allow any "pattern" of ties among groups. As this network is relatively sparse, we are using binary blockmodeling according to structural equivalence with different weights for inconsistencies of null and complete blocks, the approach proposed suggested by Žiberna (2013a) as the most appropriate for blockmodeling sparse networks in cases where as clean as possible null blocks are desired.

All of the analysis was performed using the development version of package blockmodeling (Žiberna 2013b) for R statistical environment (R Core Team 2013).

Data Description

The multilevel network of the elite of cancer researchers in France was gathered and analyzed by Lazega et al. (2004, 2006, 2008, 2013). Several networks of researchers and several networks of laboratories were collected together with a two-mode network of researchers' membership in laboratories (laboratories). For this chapter and analyses, the same kind of aggregation as performed by Lazega et al. (2008) was used.

This gave us the following networks:

- A network of researchers aggregating five sub-networks: (1) Discussion network for the global orientation of future lines of research; (2) Advice network for finding the right contacts for institutional support for the project; (3) Advice network for finding the right contacts for funding the project; (4) Advice network for the recruitment of collaborators; (5) Network of colleagues to whom to send manuscripts before submitting them to journals.
- A network of laboratories aggregating seven sub-networks: (1) A network of laboratories with which one's laboratory has set up common research programs; (2) A network of laboratories with which one's laboratory has written joint responses to tender offers; (3) A network of laboratories from which one's laboratory has recruited postdocs and researchers; (4) A network of laboratories with which one's laboratory shares technical equipment; (5) A network of laboratories with which one's laboratory shares experimental materials (plasmides, etc.); (6) A network of laboratories where one's laboratory has recruited administrative and technical personnel; and (7) A network of laboratories with which one's laboratory has exchanged invitations to conferences or seminars.
- A two-mode network of laboratories and researchers: A membership matrix of laboratories × researchers.

---

[8]The same network was analyzed using a pre-specified approach assuming cohesive groups structure within each level in the example section of the paper presenting blockmodeling of multilevel networks (Žiberna 2014).

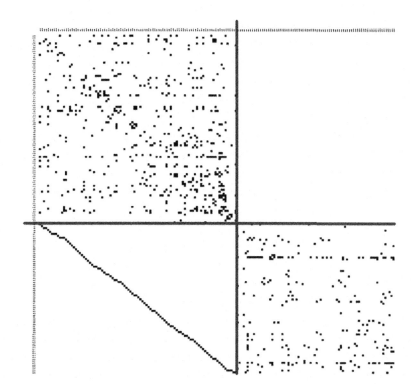

Fig. 8.2 Matrix representation of the whole (multilevel) network – researchers are *up/left*, laboratories are *down/right* (Žiberna 2014; Reprinted from Social Networks, Vol 39, Aleš Žiberna, "Blockmodeling of Multilevel Networks," 46–61, Copyright (2014), with permission from Elsevier)

In this application we are using data on 78 laboratories and 98 researchers, namely all cases where we have data on pairs of researchers and laboratories (or larger groups since there can be more than one researcher per lab). While some laboratories and researchers have no outgoing ties, they were not excluded since they were nominated by others.

First, both networks (and the ties between them) are presented graphically in Fig. 8.2 using a matrix representation. Both levels are here presented in one matrix. The blue lines separate sets of units from different levels and, at the same time, also the networks from different levels. In the diagonal blocks, the two one-mode networks are presented. The upper left section of the matrix contains the network of researchers, while the lower right shows the network of laboratories. The units from these two networks (researchers and laboratories), and therefore the two networks themselves, are tied through a two-mode network showing which researchers work in which laboratories. This network is positioned in the lower right part of the matrix. The upper left part is left empty for clarity reasons, although it might be as well populated with the transpose of the two-mode network from the lower right part. This representation does not reveal much about the structure of both one-mode

Table 8.1 Basic network statistics (Žiberna 2014)

	Researcher	Laboratories
Size	98	78
Density	0.059	0.039
Average in-degree	5.745	3.013
Centralization – degree	0.139	0.220
Centralization – in-degree	0.117	0.118
Centralization – out-degree	0.190	0.381
Centralization – betweenness	0.122	0.244
Clustering coefficient	0.266	0.184
Reciprocity	0.367	0.083

Reprinted from Social Networks, Vol 39, Aleš Žiberna, "Blockmodeling of Multilevel Networks," 46–61, Copyright (2014), with permission from Elsevier

networks (blockmodeling methods are used for this later in the chapter), however the structure of the two-mode network is quite clear (also due to the fact that researchers from the same laboratories are grouped together). Each laboratory is tied to one or more researchers, while each researcher is tied to exactly one laboratory. As mentioned previously, the two-mode network represents a partition of researchers into laboratories.

In Table 8.1 some basic statistics of both networks (network of researchers and network of labs) are presented. Some important differences between the networks can be observed. Density, reciprocity and to a lesser extent clustering coefficients are larger in the network of researchers than in the network of laboratories. This might indicate that the blockmodeling analysis might more appropriate for the network of researchers as there is more "grouping" in this network. Out-degree centralization and betweenness centralization are larger in the network of laboratories. The high out-degree centralization is the result of two laboratories reporting many more ties than other laboratories. Based on this, we cannot expect a similar structure in both networks and especially not the same blockmodels and equivalences, yet we cannot rule out some similarities in structure such as similar partitions, the same equivalences with different blockmodels (image matrices), etc.

Lazega et al. (2008) reported on several variables measured on researchers and laboratories, however in this chapter we only use age, whether the researcher is located in the Paris region or not, laboratory size, whether the researcher is also a laboratory director, and performance measures for two time points. We also use the specialties of the researchers are also measured via a categorical variable with seven categories assigned by an expert[9] in which each researcher was assigned to only one main, dominant category based the analysis of the content of his/her publications as downloaded from PUBMED, and used in Lazega et al. (2013).

---

[9] We thank David Lazega for creating this variable.

In addition, we also use the Fish/Pond status and multilevel relational strategies determined by Lazega et al. (2008). While these were also derived based on the multilevel network,[10] they offer a different view than blockmodeling. Blockmodeling looks for groups of units with a similar position in the network; in other words, that have ties to equivalent other units. The Fish/Pond status is somewhat similar; however it measures the position in the network only based on centrality scores (degrees for individuals, degrees and size for organizations). Multilevel relational strategies, on the other hand, focus on the comparison of the researchers and the laboratories networks from the perspective of the individual researchers. These comparisons are used to measure the overlap between the network of the organization and that of the individual. Different categories of overlaps are used as indicators of strategies used by the individual to manage his/her relational capital as differentiated – when appropriate – from the relational capital of his/her organization.

To estimate the overlap of the network of researchers and the network of laboratories the network of laboratories was reshaped to fit the network of researchers. This reshaped network of laboratories is actually a network among researchers where a tie between two researchers means that their laboratories are tied. The overall overlap measured as the percentage of researchers' ties that have "support" in the network of laboratories is 29.2 %. If we take the opposite direction and reshape the network of researchers to laboratories by creating a tie between two laboratories if at least some researchers from those laboratories are connected and compute the overlap as the percentage of laboratories' ties that have "support" in the network of researchers, we obtain 18.1 %. However, here we are focusing on the first case where we are mainly interested in the support for the researchers' ties in the network of laboratories. Another way to assess the tie similarity of the networks is through the association coefficient Cramer's V, which is 0.216 for the network of researchers and the reshaped network of laboratories. The small overall overlap and small association coefficient indicate that the networks are quite different. While it is possible that some common structure is present in both networks, it is not very likely. In particular, the image matrices are expected to be very different.

Separate Analysis

The first and simplest way to analyze multilevel networks is to analyze each level separately and then compare the results. While this is the simplest analysis, it can provide relatively rich results especially in terms of similarity of structures and should always be the first step of the analysis.

---

[10]The Fish/Pond status also takes into account the size of the laboratories (in addition to the multilevel network).

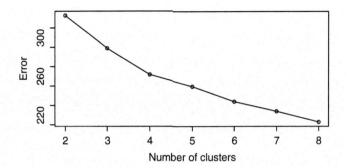

Fig. 8.3 Errors for blockmodeling of the network of researchers by different numbers of clusters

Network of Researchers

As mentioned, binary blockmodeling according to structural equivalence with different weights for inconsistencies of null and complete blocks is used. In compliance with suggestions given in Žiberna (2013a), the weights for different block types are set to 1 for null block and $1/(1-d)$ for complete blocks, where d is the density of the analyzed network (0.059).

As the appropriate number of clusters is not known, numbers of clusters from two to eight were tested and the corresponding errors are presented in Fig. 8.3. Networks/matrices partitioned according to solutions with 4 to 7 clusters are presented in Fig. 8.4. We excluded partitions with less or more clusters based on the desired level of complexity and the results in Fig. 8.3. Based on Figs. 8.3 and 8.4, the most appropriate number of clusters is 4, 5 or 6 clusters. We opted to present the 4-cluster solution, as the least complex one. The same procedure for determining the appropriate number of clusters was used in the analysis of the networks of laboratories and in the conversion approach (presented in later in the paper), although there the figures similar to Figs. 8.3 and 8.4 are omitted and only the network partition according to the selected number of clusters is presented.

The image in Fig. 8.5 represents the densities of the resulting blocks. If we used the descriptions used by the authors studying Slovenian co-authorship networks (Kronegger et al. 2011; Mali et al. 2012),[11] the four-cluster partition decomposes the network into a bridging core, two cores and a semi-pheriphery.

In Table 8.2 we explore whether this partition can be associated with exogenous variables, in Table 8.3 with Fish/Pond status, and in Table 8.4 with relational strategy. We can see that the first cluster, the "bridging core," has representatives of all specialties except hematology. It has the largest percentage of laboratory directors (73 % compared to 48 % in the whole network). These are fundamental researchers combined with the "hot" specialty at the time (diagnostics, prevention

---

[11]With perhaps less stringent demands in terms of densities. For related issues, see Lazega et al. (2011).

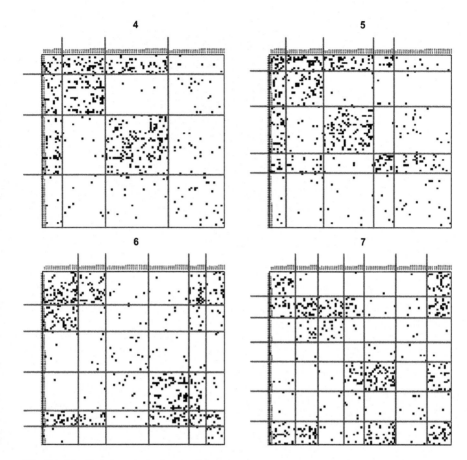

Fig. 8.4 Partitioned network of researchers

and epidemiology) and focusing on solid tumors. Most (9/11) of its members are Big fish in Big ponds with mixed multilevel relational strategies.

The next core is the highest performance cluster. The majority of researchers specialize in either hematology (43 %) or pharmacology (22 %). This core is comprised mainly of researchers from the "provinces". All benefit in terms of IF scores from 20 years of success of French hematology (Lazega et al. 2004). They are mainly big fish in big or small ponds with mixed relational strategies.

The last core is the largest cluster. It is composed of researchers mainly from large laboratories in the Paris region beginning to study solid tumors with molecular genetics, with the lowest performance results because this approach had not yet succeeded in providing results at the time of the study (it would later on, a decade after the network study). They are also mainly big fish in big or small ponds but mixed with a higher proportion of little fish than the previous core positions. Their multilevel relational strategies are mixed, mainly independent or collectivist, that is, strategies that were previously shown not to be associated with high levels of individual performance.

Fig. 8.5 Image of the 4-cluster partition for the network of researchers

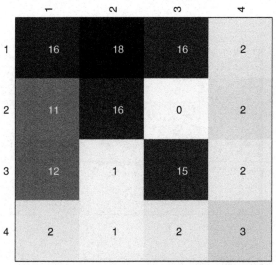

* all values in cells were multiplied by 100

Table 8.2 Averages of exogenous variables by clusters obtained for by blockmodeling the network of researchers

	1	2	3	4	All
Frequency	11	23	34	30	98
Age	48.91	45.48	50.06	48.00	48.21
Paris (1) vs provinces	0.36	0.17	0.76	0.47	0.48
Laboratory size	26.91	22.65	31.33	32.07	29.00
Research director (status)	0.73	0.43	0.55	0.47	0.52
Performance1	26.11	31.78	26.10	28.54	28.20
Performance2	36.58	44.43	33.06	42.25	39.00
Diagnostics, prevention, epidemiology	0.27	0.13	0.24	0.13	0.19
Surgery, radiology	0.09	0.09	0.03	0.10	0.07
Hematology	0	0.43	0.03	0.17	0.16
Solid tumor, chemotherapy	0.18	0.04	0.24	0.17	0.16
Pharmacology	0.18	0.22	0.06	0.03	0.10
Molecular cellular	0.18	0	0.21	0.40	0.22
Molecular genetics	0.09	0.09	0.18	0	0.09

The (semi-)periphery is the last cluster. It is composed of the largest percentage of researchers exploring solid tumors with molecular and cellular research in the largest laboratories. They are mainly little fish both in big and small ponds. Their multilevel relational strategies are mainly independent, with a few individualistic ones. This category mixes little fish in big ponds who will later catch up with the highest performers and little fish in smaller ponds who will tend not to catch up.

8 Role Sets and Division of Work at Two Levels of Collective Agency: The... 189

Table 8.3 Fish-pond status by clusters obtained for by blockmodeling the network of researchers

Fish-pond status	Cluster				Sum
	1	2	3	4	
Big Fish in Big Ponds (BFBP)	9	8	11	3	31
Big Fish in Small Ponds (BFSP)	0	7	12	0	19
Little Fish in Big Ponds (LFBP)	1	5	7	12	25
Little Fish in Small Ponds (LFSP)	1	3	3	15	22
NA	0	0	1	0	1
Sum	11	23	34	30	98

Table 8.4 Multilevel relational strategy of researchers (four categories) by clusters obtained for by blockmodeling the network of researchers

Relational strategy	Cluster				Sum
	1	2	3	4	
Independent	2	5	15	22	44
Individualist	3	7	5	6	21
Collectivist	4	6	10	2	22
Fusional	2	5	3	0	10
NA	0	0	1	0	1
Sum	11	23	34	30	98

Network of Laboratories

The same procedure applied to the network of researchers is also applied to the network of laboratories. The weights for different block types are again set to 1 for null blocks and $1/(1-d)$ for complete blocks, where d is the density of the network of laboratories ($d = 0.039$). Numbers of clusters from two to eight were tested and the four-cluster solution was selected. The partitioned network and corresponding image are presented in Fig. 8.6.

The four-cluster partition decomposes the network into a (semi-)periphery, a bridging core and two cores. It has very similar structure as the researchers' partition.

In Tables 8.5, 8.6, and 8.7 we explore whether this partition can be associated with other variables. The first cluster is the bridging core. This is the smallest and the highest-performing cluster where a large percentage of laboratories, mostly around Paris, specialize in fundamental research (a particularly rewarding specialty for impact factor scores) using molecular/cellular genetics research (80 %). Practically all researchers from the laboratories of this cluster are big or little fish, but in big ponds, and employ relational strategies that independent or (mainly) individualist, the latter being associated most often with highest impact factor scores.

The next two clusters are cores. The first one among these (cluster 2) has no researchers from pharmacology. As in the previous cluster, here most laboratories (although fewer than before) are big ponds, and the researchers are big or little fish. The second (cluster 3) is the least performing cluster in this system, where practically no researchers from these laboratories specialize in molecular research. This

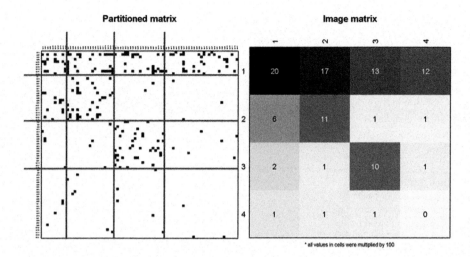

Fig. 8.6 The network of laboratories partitioned into four clusters

Table 8.5 Averages of exogenous variables by clusters for the network of laboratories partitions

	1	2	3	4	All
Freq	10	19	20	29	78
Age	50.40	47.39	48.36	48.67	48.50
Paris (1) vs provinces	0.80	0.58	0.30	0.47	0.49
Laboratory size	44.20	25.95	25.60	30.38	29.85
Research director (status)	0.55	0.62	0.57	0.53	0.57
Performance1	34.24	32.28	20.71	25.77	27.14
Performance2	55.07	44.90	29.45	33.64	38.06
Diagnostics, prevention, epidemiology	0.10	0.11	0.20	0.26	0.19
Surgery, radiology	0	0.05	0.17	0.03	0.07
Hematology	0	0.16	0.19	0.21	0.16
Solid tumor, chemotherapy	0.10	0.24	0.15	0.17	0.17
Pharmacology	0	0	0.27	0.09	0.10
Molecular cellular	0.40	0.29	0	0.24	0.21
Molecular genetics	0.40	0.16	0.02	0	0.10

Averages are computed as averages of average laboratory values among the interviewed researcher

is also the most "provincial" cluster. This cluster (3) is composed of laboratories where one notices the highest proportion of researchers with a "fusional" multilevel relational strategy, i.e. with perfect overlap between the inter-individual network of the researcher and the inter-organizational network of the laboratory in which this researcher is affiliated.

The last cluster is a periphery. No researchers from these laboratories specialize in genetic/molecular research. Most researchers from laboratories in this cluster are

Table 8.6 Fish-pond status by clusters (of researchers' laboratories) for the network of laboratories partition

Fish-pond status	Cluster				
	1	2	3	4	Sum
Big Fish in Big Ponds (BFBP)	6	13	11	1	31
Big Fish in Small Ponds (BFSP)	0	1	4	14	19
Little Fish in Big Ponds (LFBP)	4	6	9	6	25
Little Fish in Small Ponds (LFSP)	1	5	2	14	22
NA	0	0	0	1	1
Sum	11	25	26	36	98

Table 8.7 Multilevel relational strategy of researchers (four categories) by cluster (of researchers' laboratories) for the network of laboratories partition

Rel. strategy	Cluster				
	1	2	3	4	Sum
Independent	4	11	10	19	44
Individualist	5	5	6	5	21
Collectivist	1	9	3	9	22
Fusional	1	0	7	2	10
NA	0	0	0	1	1
Sum	11	25	26	36	98

big or little fish but all in small ponds and all employ relational independent or collectivist strategies. These are the laboratories with researchers who will not catch up with the BFBP over time.

Comparison

Here the partitions obtained at both levels separately are compared. To facilitate the comparison, the laboratories' partition is first reshaped to researchers (each researcher is "assigned" the cluster of their lab). The two to eight cluster laboratories' partitions were compared to the two to eight cluster researchers' partitions using the Adjusted Rand Index (ARI) (Hubert and Arabie 1985). All ARIs were close to 0, the highest being 0.11. Therefore, the association there among partitions based on different levels is low. This does not give much hope with regard to more complex analyses.

Both the networks nevertheless have a similar structure – they are both comprised of one bridging core that connects all cores, two cores, and one (semi)periphery.

Another way to compare partitions among levels is to use a partition from one level and apply it to another level. For example, we could force the laboratories' partition onto the network of researchers and check the fit. For illustration the four-cluster laboratories' partition obtained in the previous sub-subsection is forced onto the network of researchers. As before, when computing the ARI here also we must

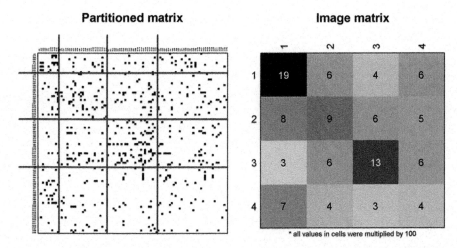

Fig. 8.7 The network of researchers partitioned according to the 4-cluster laboratories' partition and the corresponding image

first reshape the laboratories' partition to the researchers. The network of researchers partitioned according to this partition and the corresponding image are shown in Fig. 8.7. No clear structure emerges, although it is clear, especially from the image matrix, that the pattern of ties is not random. Especially if we focus on the diagonal blocks (intra-cluster ties) we can see that the "bridging core" has the highest density of intra-cluster ties, followed by the other two cores and the (semi)periphery has the lowest density of intra-cluster ties, as we would expect based on the laboratories' image matrix.

The error for this partition (using the same model as when blockmodeling researchers network) is 464.7 which is relatively close to the "maximal" error of 556.9 or average error of a randomly generated partition (504.8) and much further from the optimal result obtained in the sub-subsection 0, which is 271.3 for the four-cluster partition. This indicates that, while there is some similarity among the structure of both networks, it is very small as this error is closer to "maximal" and even "random" error than to the optimal one.

A similar analysis could also be performed for other partitions. In the case of applying a researchers' partition to the network of laboratories, reshaping this partition is a little more problematic although several approaches are reasonable. Another option to circumvent this is to reshape the network of laboratories to the researchers which is less complicated. Further discussion of this exceeds the scope of this chapter.

Conversion of the Multilevel Problem to a Classical One-Level Blockmodeling Problem

In this subsection the multilevel problem was converted to a one-level problem, namely to a single set of units. In particular, here the network of laboratories was converted to researchers' "space"[12] by defining a new relation between researchers based on ties between laboratories. In this new relation (let us call it "institutional"), two researchers are tied if their laboratories are tied (or if they are members of the same lab). Further analysis varies on how we combine this network with the "original" network of researchers. The first option is to create a new single-relational ("extended") network where two researchers are tied if they are tied directly ("original" network of researchers) or through their laboratories ("institutional" network). Such networks are also discussed by Lazega et al. (2013) in terms of extended opportunity structures. Another approach is to combine these two relations into a multi-relational network (of researchers).

Single-Relational Network

The same pre-specified blockmodel as was applied to the network of researchers in the previous section ("Separate analysis") was applied to this "extended" network. The weights for different block types are again set to 1 for null blocks and $d/(1-d)$ for complete blocks, where d is now the density of the "extended" network of researchers ($d = 0.090$). In the lack of a clear "elbow" on the "error plot" (plot of errors by number of clusters) a four-cluster solution was again selected mainly based on the examination of partitioned networks at different numbers of clusters, and based on selection of this number in the separate analysis. The "extended" network of researchers and its "components" (the "original" network of researchers plus the "institutional" network of researchers) and the corresponding images (block densities) are presented in Fig. 8.8 (partitioned matrices on the left and image matrices on the right). In Tables 8.8, 8.9, and 8.10 we can see that the obtained clusters differ in researchers' specialties, Fish-pond statuses, and, to a lesser extent, researchers' relational strategies.

Multi-relational Network

Another approach to jointly blockmodel the "original" network of researchers and the "institutional" network of researchers is to combine these two relations into a multi-relational network (of researchers). Within each relation the same approach as before was used, that is, binary blockmodeling according to structural equivalence with different weights for inconsistencies of null and complete blocks. The weights for different block types are again set to 1 for null block and $1/(1-d)$ for complete

---

[12]Conversion of the network of researchers to the laboratories' "space" is also possible, although more complex.

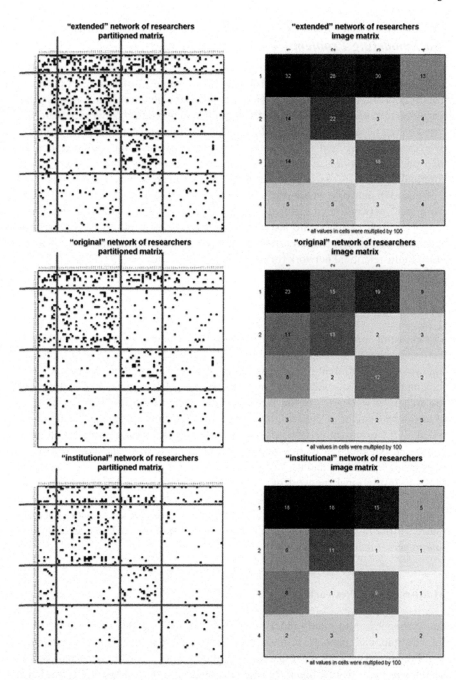

Fig. 8.8 The "extended" network of researchers and its "components" (the "original" network of researchers and the "institutional" network of researchers) – partitioned into 4 clusters and the corresponding images

8 Role Sets and Division of Work at Two Levels of Collective Agency: The...

Table 8.8 Averages of exogenous variables by clusters of the "extended" network of researchers partition

	1	2	3	4	All
Freq	10	34	22	32	98
Age	50.90	46.33	47.73	49.62	48.21
Paris (1) vs provinces	0.40	0.64	0.36	0.44	0.48
Laboratory size	31.70	32.85	24.95	26.97	29.00
Research director (status)	0.70	0.42	0.50	0.56	0.52
Performance1	33.44	36.81	20.95	22.68	28.20
Performance2	44.65	50.53	29.22	32.06	39.00
Diagnostics, prevention, epidemiology	0.10	0.15	0.23	0.22	0.19
Surgery, radiology	0	0	0.23	0.06	0.07
Hematology	0.20	0.24	0.05	0.16	0.16
Solid tumor, chemotherapy	0.20	0.06	0.27	0.19	0.16
Pharmacology	0.10	0	0.14	0.19	0.10
Molecular cellular	0.20	0.33	0.09	0.19	0.22
Molecular genetics	0.20	0.21	0	0	0.09

Table 8.9 Fish-pond status by clusters of the "extended" network of researchers partition

Fish-pond status	Cluster				
	1	2	3	4	Sum
Big Fish in Big Ponds (BFBP)	9	15	4	3	31
Big Fish in Little Ponds (BFLP)	0	7	8	4	19
Little Fish in Big Ponds (LFBP)	1	7	8	9	25
Little Fish in Little Ponds (LFLP)	0	4	2	16	22
NA	0	1	0	0	1
Sum	10	34	22	32	98

Table 8.10 Multilevel relational strategy of researchers (four categories) by clusters of the "extended" network of researchers partition

Rel. strategy	Cluster				
	1	2	3	4	Sum
Independent	2	13	13	16	44
Individualist	4	6	4	7	21
Collectivist	2	11	2	7	22
Fusional	2	3	3	2	10
NA	0	1	0	0	1
Sum	10	34	22	32	98

blocks, where d is the density of the appropriate relation ($d = 0.059$ for "original" network and $d = 0.045$ for "institutional" network). In this case both relations were equally weighted. Another option would be to weight relations proportional to their "random" errors (average errors of blockmodels based on 1000 randomly generated partitions). In this concrete case both options produce the same results at the selected number of clusters.

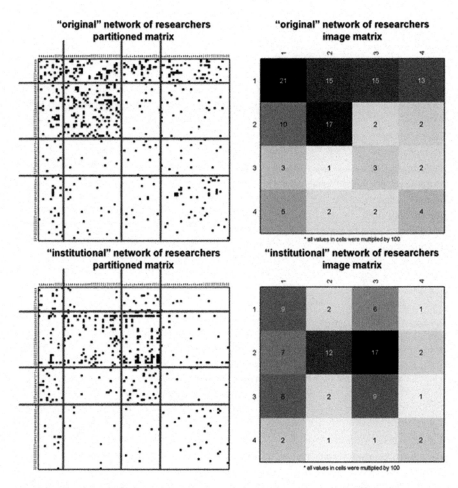

Fig. 8.9 Partitioned multi-relational network of researchers and the corresponding images

The four-cluster solution was selected for similar reasons as in the single-relational approach. Both relations partitioned according to this solution and the corresponding images are presented in Fig. 8.9 (partitioned matrices on the left and image matrices on the right). While certain patterns of ties can be observed in both relations, we could hardly say that the blockmodel is a good fit. Secondly we can also observe that the pattern of ties among groups is not the same in both relations. For example, cluster 3 is the least intra-connected cluster in the "original" network and it has practically no incoming ties from cluster 2, while in the "institutional" network it is more intra-connected and the block from cluster 2 to cluster 3 is the densest block in the relation. In Tables 8.11, 8.12, and 8.13 we can see that the groups differ quite significantly in "geography" (Paris vs. Provinces), researchers' specialties (e.g. cluster 1 is very much centered around hematology and cluster 2

Table 8.11 Averages of exogenous variables by clusters of the multi-relational network of researchers partition

	1	2	3	4	All
Freq	13	30	20	35	98
Age	47.25	47.43	46.45	50.20	48.21
Paris (1) vs provinces	0.33	0.80	0.30	0.37	0.48
Laboratory size	27.83	32.87	32.00	24.37	29.00
Research director (status)	0.50	0.57	0.40	0.54	0.52
Performance1	26.20	36.48	24.96	23.65	28.20
Performance2	43.76	48.04	35.13	31.82	39.00
Diagnostics, prevention, epidemiology	0.08	0.20	0.20	0.20	0.19
Surgery, radiology	0.08	0	0.20	0.06	0.07
Hematology	0.42	0.07	0.15	0.17	0.16
Solid tumor, chemotherapy	0.17	0.10	0.10	0.26	0.16
Pharmacology	0.17	0	0.05	0.20	0.10
Molecular cellular	0.08	0.37	0.25	0.11	0.22
Molecular genetics	0	0.27	0.05	0	0.09

Table 8.12 Fish-pond status by clusters of the multi-relational network of researchers partition

Fish-pond status	Cluster				Sum
	1	2	3	4	
Big Fish in Big Ponds (BFBP)	8	15	5	3	31
Big Fish in Small Ponds (BFSP)	1	6	1	11	19
Little Fish in Big Ponds (LFBP)	3	6	10	6	25
Little Fish in Small Ponds (LFSP)	0	3	4	15	22
NA	1	0	0	0	1
Sum	13	30	20	35	98

Table 8.13 Multilevel relational strategy of researchers (four categories) by clusters of the multi-relational network of researchers partition

Rel. strategy	Cluster				Sum
	1	2	3	4	
Independent	1	10	15	18	44
Individualist	5	6	4	6	21
Collectivist	2	11	0	9	22
Fusional	4	3	1	2	10
NA	1	0	0	0	1
Sum	13	30	20	35	98

around fundamental molecular research) and Fish/Pond statuses (e.g. cluster 1 and to a lesser extent cluster 2 are composed mainly of Big Fish in Big Ponds).

A True Multilevel Approach

The true multi-relational approach is an approach where we partition the multilevel network structured as presented in Fig. 8.2. As described in previously, the whole multilevel network (matrix presented in Fig. 8.2) is partitioned simultaneously, with the restriction that units from different levels cannot be in the same cluster. In terms of Fig. 8.2 this means that clusters and blocks cannot "cross" the thick line partitioning the matrix into four blocks. Again we used binary blockmodeling according to structural equivalence with different weights for null and complete block, but otherwise no pre-specification were used. The weights of null and complete blocks were first determined for each relation/network separately, that is, for the network of researchers, the network of laboratories, and the two-mode network joining them. For all networks the initial weights were 1 for null block and $1/(1-d)$ for complete blocks, where d is the density of the appropriate relation/network ($d = 0.059$ for the network of researchers, $d = 0.039$ for the network of laboratories, and $d = 0.013$ for the two-mode network).

The role of the two-mode network is to "tie" the two levels together. In this network we want as many completely or nearly completely null blocks as possible to make the comparison of the researchers' and laboratories' clusters easier, although we do not want to force the researchers' and laboratories' clusters to match perfectly (e.g. by forcing all researchers from laboratories from a given cluster of laboratories to be in the same cluster of researchers). Using the same model as for the other two networks is also appropriate for this task.

For a true multilevel approach, we have to somehow allow for an appropriate contribution of both levels and of the two-mode network. In the suggested approach, this is achieved through appropriate weighting. Here we decided to weight the relations (that is, both levels and the two-mode network) inversely proportional to the "random" error, that is the average error obtained when forcing 1000 random (non-optimized) partitions to selected network/relation. Therefore, the following weights were initially used: 1 for the network of researchers, 2.520 for the network of laboratories and 6.851 for the two-mode network. However, this weight of the two-mode network was too strong, which was evident from obtaining only the minimal number of non-null blocks (four) and no errors in the null blocks, so we decided to halve the weight of this network to 3.426. With this weighting we still obtained very few errors in the null blocks, however the fit is not so "perfect" anymore and thus facilitates a better fit of the other two networks/relations.

Since when using this approach finding the global (and not local) optimum is more problematic, at least 10,000 random starting points were used (instead of the 1000 used in the other examples).

Due to the time complexity of the algorithm, the size of the multilevel network and space limitations of this chapter, we fixed the number of clusters to four at both levels. These two numbers were selected based on the results of the separate analysis stage. The partitioned multilevel network and corresponding image is presented in Fig. 8.10. The upper left part of the matrices shows ties among researchers (the parts

8 Role Sets and Division of Work at Two Levels of Collective Agency: The...

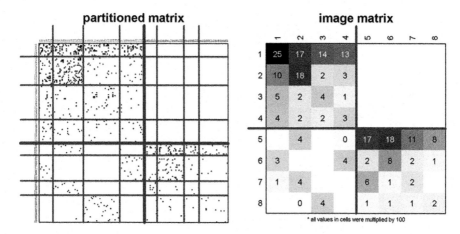

Fig. 8.10 Partitioned multilevel network and the corresponding image

are separated by (wider in case of the original matrix) lines), the lower right part shows the ties among laboratories, and the lower left part the ties among laboratories and researchers, that is, which laboratories employ which researchers.

Blockmodeling the whole multilevel network, i.e. both researchers and laboratories networks jointly while taking into account the ties among researcher and laboratories, gives us an interesting overview of the system. Although the partitioning of the individual levels is not as clear as in the separate analyses, the benefit of this approach is that we now have relatively clear "ties" among researchers' and laboratories' clusters, which were however not fixed in advance. In terms of the overall structure we can still observe the existence of a core-periphery system with bridging cores, cores and (semi)peripheries. The bridging cores are researchers' cluster 1 and laboratories' cluster 5. However as it is evident from the partitioned two-mode network, these two clusters (1 and 5) are not connected (there are no ties in the block from cluster 5 to cluster 1), meaning that no researchers from the researchers' bridging core (cluster 1) are employed in the laboratories from laboratories' main bridging core (cluster 5). Most of the researchers' from this cluster (1) are employed in laboratories from laboratories' cluster 6 (an ordinary core) while two are employed in laboratories from laboratories' cluster 7 (periphery) (there are only two "dots" in the block from cluster 7 to cluster 1). Similarly, most laboratories from the clusters' main bridging core (cluster 5) employ researchers from researchers' cluster 2 (also an ordinary core). The most expected tie is the one from researchers' cluster 3 (periphery) to laboratories' cluster 8 (also periphery). These and other ties within and between clusters are evident form Figs. 8.10 and 8.11.

The association among both the (researchers' and laboratories') partitions and other variables is examined in Tables 8.14, 8.15, and 8.16. While both researchers' and laboratories' clusters differ in terms of these variables, for most clusters no clear "profile" can be found. Perhaps the most "profiled" cluster is the researchers'

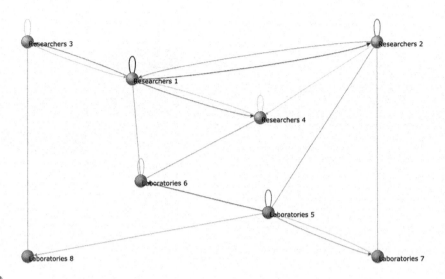

Fig. 8.11 The multilevel image graph. Researchers' clusters are *yellow/white* and the laboratories' clusters are *green/gray*. The *ties* represent the densities of the blocs. The ties with values less than 0.025 were removed (values 2 or lower in image matrix on Fig. 8.10) for clarity

Table 8.14 Averages of exogenous variables by clusters for the multilevel network partition

	Researchers					Laboratories				
	1	2	3	4	All	5	6	7	8	All
Freq	13	28	34	23	98	12	25	14	27	78
Age	47.50	48.54	49.38	46.43	48.21	47.58	47.70	48.11	49.86	48.50
Paris (1) vs provinces	0.33	0.82	0.29	0.43	0.48	0.83	0.36	0.79	0.31	0.49
Laboratory size	28.50	29.57	25.76	33.35	29.00	39.00	33.56	21.64	26.59	29.85
Research director (status)	0.50	0.61	0.50	0.43	0.52	0.46	0.53	0.71	0.57	0.57
Performance1	27.50	31.11	24.86	29.98	28.20	33.84	27.21	28.72	23.29	27.14
Performance2	41.90	45.54	31.37	40.78	39.00	57.78	36.98	38.37	30.13	38.06
Diagnostics, prevention, epidemiology	0.08	0.32	0.09	0.22	0.19	0.17	0.20	0.36	0.09	0.19
Surgery, radiology	0.08	0	0.09	0.13	0.07	0	0.12	0	0.09	0.07
Hematology	0.42	0.07	0.21	0.09	0.16	0.08	0.16	0.21	0.18	0.16
Solid tumor, chemotherapy	0.17	0.07	0.29	0.09	0.16	0.17	0.12	0.04	0.30	0.17
Pharmacology	0.17	0	0.21	0.04	0.10	0	0.12	0	0.18	0.10
Molecular cellular	0	0.29	0.12	0.39	0.22	0.33	0.20	0.25	0.15	0.21
Molecular genetics	0.08	0.25	0	0.04	0.09	0.25	0.08	0.14	0.02	0.10

Averages for the laboratories' clusters are computed as averages of the average laboratory values among the interviewed researchers

Table 8.15 Fish-pond status by clusters of researchers and laboratories from the true multilevel partition

Fish-pond status	Researchers					Laboratories				
	1	2	3	4	Sum	5	6	7	8	Sum
Big Fish in Big Ponds (BFBP)	9	13	3	6	31	8	15	5	3	31
Big Fish in Little Ponds (BFLP)	1	7	10	1	19	1	1	6	11	19
Little Fish in Big Ponds (LFBP)	2	5	8	10	25	4	10	3	8	25
Little Fish in Little Ponds (LFLP)	0	3	13	6	22	1	6	2	13	22
NA	1	0	0	0	1	0	1	0	0	1
Sum	13	28	34	23	98	14	33	16	35	98

Table 8.16 Multilevel relational strategy of researchers (four categories) by clusters of researchers and laboratories from the true multilevel partition

Rel. strategy	Researchers					Laboratories				
	1	2	3	4	Sum	5	6	7	8	Sum
Independent	1	6	20	17	44	3	16	5	20	44
Individualist	5	8	6	2	21	4	7	3	7	21
Collectivist	2	11	7	2	22	6	4	5	7	22
Fusional	4	3	1	2	10	1	5	3	1	10
NA	1	0	0	0	1	0	1	0	0	1
Sum	13	28	34	23	98	14	33	16	35	98

core cluster 2, in which over 50 % of researchers specializing in fundamental research mainly work in laboratories located around Paris. As mentioned above, this researchers' cluster is tied to laboratories' clusters 5 (bridging core) and 7 (periphery) that also exhibit (although to a lesser extent) specialization in the same area and are also composed mainly of laboratories from around Paris.

In terms of Fish-pond status the clearest structure is in the bridging core clusters, where for the researchers (cluster 1) most members are Big Fish in Big Ponds and for the laboratories (cluster 5) most laboratories are Big Ponds. In terms of relational strategies cluster memberships are in most cases again mixed, although it is quite clear that the share of researchers employing an independent strategy is much larger in clusters 3 and 4 than in clusters 1 and 2 and also in laboratories from clusters 6 and 8 (compared to those from laboratories in clusters 5 and 7). For researchers' clusters the share of independents is larger for more peripheral clusters.

Comparison of the Results Using Different Approaches

In this section, several approaches were used on the two-level network of cooperation among researchers and laboratories. Although different approaches are not designed to produce the same results, some results from different approaches are compared in this section. Of course, not every possible comparison is presented here.

One of the results that is common to all approaches is that the result is a core-periphery-like structure (similar to those found by Kronegger et al. (2011) for Slovenian scientists) consisting of a bridging core, usually two simple cores, and a periphery. However, while both levels have similar structure, the multilevel approach in particular showed that the members of the researchers' bridging cores are not employed by laboratories from the laboratories' bridging core.

The most similar pair of four-cluster partitions of researchers are the researchers' partition from the true multilevel approach and the laboratories' partition reshaped to researchers from the same analysis. As these are both based on the same analysis this is not really interesting. More interesting is that the next largest similarity is among the researchers' partition from the multirelational conversion approach and the researchers' partition from the true multilevel approach.

In Table 8.17 the similarities between all of these partitions (the four-cluster partitions of researchers and the four-cluster partitions of laboratories) is measured by the Adjusted Rand Index (ARI). We can observe that most of the separate analysis partitions (especially for the researchers) are only slightly more similar to the other partitions than expected by chance. The similarity among other partitions (those that take both levels into account) is larger.[13] This is expected as these in some way already multilevel analyses take the same data (although with different level of aggregation) into account. We can also see that the partitions from the analysis that take both levels into account are more similar to the laboratories' single-level analysis partition than to the researchers' single-level analysis partition. This is different from the results obtained by Žiberna (2014, sec. 5.5) where at least the multilevel researchers' partition was more similar to the researchers' separate analysis partitions. However, there the focus was on finding cohesive subgroups and not on a general model of the network.

The characteristics of the obtained clusters in terms of the researchers' specialties (see Tables 8.2, 8.5, 8.8, 8.11, and 8.14) reveal that the cores (including bridging cores) in results based (more) on the researchers' networks seem to be more centered around hematology or solid tumors (coupled with fundamental research), while in the results based on the laboratories' network especially the bridging cores are characterized by a higher proportion of researchers working in fundamental research. The added value of this true multilevel analysis is to show that the division of work at the level of individuals and the division of work at the level of laboratories can complement and strengthen each other in the case of a segment of the population (hematologists and fundamental researchers), while this reinforcement does not work for others. This interpretation is consistent with the analysis of variations in performance levels (though measured by IF scores, always a questionable measurement) in this population. This is consistent also with substantive results (Lazega et al. 2004) explaining how this specialty -clinical hematology working on patients with leukemia- combined with fundamental research, became the most successful

---

[13]Even these similarities would be deemed very low by Steinley (2004); however he used these indices with a different purpose.

Table 8.17 Similarity of the four-cluster partitions of researchers obtained with different approaches measured by ARI

	Researchers	Laboratories	Single conversional	Multi conversional	Researchers – ML	Laboratories – ML
Researchers: researchers – separate analysis	1	0.058	0.081	0.094	0.071	0.025
Laboratories: laboratories – separate analysis	0.058	1	0.175	0.213	0.118	0.165
Single conversional: single-relational conversional approach (extended researchers network)	0.081	0.175	1	0.406	0.245	0.168
Multi conversional: multi-relational conversional approach	0.094	0.213	0.406	1	0.534	0.330
Researchers – ML: researchers partition from the true multilevel analysis	0.071	0.118	0.245	0.534	1	0.699
Laboratories – ML: laboratories partition from the true multilevel analysis	0.025	0.165	0.168	0.330	0.699	1

specialty in cancer research at the time, especially by imposing to hematologists, immunologists, and their laboratories a massive process of collective learning and alignment on the new methods of molecular biology. This alignment can also be a measure either of top-down power of the hierarchy forcing the researchers to comply, or a measure of bottom-up social discipline characterizing their milieu and profession – both controlled for the specificities of leukemia as a type of cancer.

This meeting of top-down and bottom-up pressures towards alignment, combined with the complementary character of the division of work across levels, was not present yet for the other specialties in their fight against different kinds of cancers (especially solid tumors), which may be why this effect is not noticeable for them in these multilevel analyses.

Discussion

Here we will try to shed some light on the mixing of "applied" and fundamental specialties which has been shown to lead to new scientific breakthroughs and on the relation between the two levels. As this mixing is best viewed when taking both levels into account while acknowledging the differences between them, only the results of the multirelational conversion approach and the true multilevel approach are discussed here.

We start with the analysis of the true multilevel results, which is in a sense a less restrictive model. In the researchers' network we can see that the "applied" researcher (mostly hematologist, but also researchers of solid tumors/chemotherapy and pharmacology) (bridging core) cluster 1 is highly connected to fundamental researchers' cluster 2. The connections go in both directions, although it seems that there is more activity[14] from the "applied" researchers' side (more ties go from applied to fundamental researchers than vice versa).

In the laboratories' networks the situation is actually quite similar, however the more connected and the more active group here is the more fundamental research (with some solid tumors and diagnostics, prevention, epidemiology) cluster (cluster 5). Here it is clear that the connections to the "applied" laboratories cluster (cluster 6) are mostly recognized[15] by the "fundamental" cluster. We can therefore see that the "active" group is not the same in both networks, which suggests a form of complementarity between both networks. The researchers from "active" laboratories perhaps do not need to be so active to get access to resources or vice versa.

The two fundamental clusters, one from the researchers' network and one from laboratories' network, are also connected, meaning that about half of the researchers who form the researchers' fundamental cluster (2) are employed in laboratories from the fundamental cluster (cluster 5) and the other half in another similar fundamental cluster (cluster 7). The difference between these two fundamental laboratory clusters are in the "applied" specialties with which they are associated, as well as localization and institutional affiliation. In the more active, bridging core of the fundamental laboratories cluster (cluster 5), fundamental research is mostly

---

[14]We use activity to refer to the outgoing ties, so the more active units are those having more outgoing ties.

[15]We use "recognized" since the direction of ties on the laboratories level is more an indication of who recognized the tie than of the pure direction of ties ("actions").

coupled with solid tumors (and diagnostics, prevention, epidemiology), while in the less active laboratories' fundamental cluster (cluster 7), fundamental research is coupled more with hematology (and diagnostics, prevention, epidemiology). This could be explained by the fact that the ties between solid tumors and fundamental research were being developed precisely at that time (and perhaps more "action" was observed therefore in that area) – although a breakthrough related to solid tumors would have to wait for at least one more decade.

The same could be observed in the results of the multirelational conversion approach. This model is in a sense similar to the true multilevel approach where the researchers' and the laboratories clusters' are fixed to be the same (meaning that the cluster of laboratories can be defined as cluster of laboratories that employ researchers from a given cluster and vice versa). The clusters from this approach are very similar to the researchers' cluster from the true multilevel approach. Therefore, the situation described above for researchers applies also here. In these analyses we can however again see how the lower "activity" of the researchers' fundamental cluster (2) is compensated by (or perhaps not needed due to) the high activity of their laboratories.

Conclusions

In this chapter we reviewed several approaches to blockmodeling multilevel networks and used them to analyze the multilevel (inter-individual and inter-organizational) network of French cancer researchers and laboratories. First we analyzed both levels separately and compared the results. Then we converted the laboratories' network to the "institutional" network of researchers and analyzed both networks simultaneously on the level of researchers. Finally, we used the true multilevel approach to analyze both networks (of researchers and of laboratories) together with ties between the levels, simultaneously.

In terms of pure blockmodeling analysis the main result is that the structures of both researchers and laboratories networks follow a core-periphery like structure (similar to those found by Kronegger et al. (2011) for Slovenian scientists) consisting of a bridging core, usually two simple cores, and a periphery. However, while both levels have similar structure, the separate analysis shows that the partition of the researchers and that of the laboratories do not match. Using the true multilevel approach it is possible to obtain a reasonable fit of the blockmodel while maintaining clear connections among researchers and laboratories partitions. This analysis showed that the members of the main researchers' bridging core are not affiliated to laboratories from the laboratories' bridging core.

This perhaps at first surprising result becomes more understandable if we take into account additional variables, especially researchers' specialties, reflecting one dimension of the division of work in this domain of research. We notice that while bridging cores for individual networks are composed primarily of researchers focusing on more "applied" research (clinical research and Diagnostics, Prevention,

Epidemiology) with some support from the fundamental researchers, the bridging cores for the laboratories' network are composed primarily of laboratories where most researchers focus on fundamental research. This could be explained by the fact that the two levels do not manage the same resources. The researchers' network represents advice networks, exchange of knowledge, where typically the teams are created by "applied" researchers (a mix of MDs and MDs-PhDs) working in a certain specialty and gathering in more fundamental researchers (PhDs). On the other hand the laboratories' network is in large part a network of circulation of more "material" resources, where the main "suppliers" are the laboratories focused on fundamental research. Therefore, as the two networks are tied by different ties, the partitions based on them differ.

To sum up, the suggested approaches enable a true multilevel blockmodeling analysis of multilevel networks. This approach opens up new perspectives that could be of interest for network analysts. For example, it could be useful to further explore the meaning of the conversion and extension practiced above. Each blockmodel represents a system of roles (White et al. 1976) and therefore a form of division of work that is likely to change over time in fields of organized collective action such as that examined here. As shown in Lazega et al. (2013), conversion is a form of extension of the reach of individuals in terms of access to resources that can be complementary to their own, thus strengthening the probability that this form of relational capital increases the focal actors' performances. Actors reason in multilevel ways (Lazega and Mounier 2002) and they know when their organization provides access to new resources that they did not have before. Therefore they have an incentive to follow that extension route. However the creation of this route drives changes in the network of the members and thus also changes in the previous role set and division of work. The methods presented here are useful for generating hypotheses about the direction taken by change in the division of work characterizing the system. This extension is a minimal approach to the dynamics of adjustments of one level to the other, with possible progress for our understanding of the relatively unequal costs of such adjustments to the other level, and of the parties who will incur such costs. The fact that researchers are relatively strongly connected and play the same role in the system can coexist with the fact that the laboratories to which they belong are sometimes strongly connected and play the same role in the system, and sometimes not. This begs the question of the conditions under which this multilevel "consistency" emerges. Because the combinatorial possibilities for "multilevel roles" (combining one role from each level, for example) could be very rich, more work is needed in conceptualizing such a "multilevel regular equivalence."

In addition, over time, this multilevel approach would make it possible to follow the extent to which systems having a strong overlap between partitions make it more difficult for researchers with specific strategies to leave their initial organization or inter-organizational context in order to create their own organizational structure. In this dynamic perspective, much remains to be done too.

In this chapter we have shed some light on this subject. We have shown that while the systems of roles is similar at both levels (core-periphery-like structures), the roles are occupied by different units (the "bridging" researchers are not employed by the "bridging" laboratories). Based on this outcome, we also speculate that the systems are driven by different forces. For the researchers network, the driving force could be "applied" researchers (mainly MDs in hematology and solid tumor specialists) making significant discoveries with the help of other, mainly fundamental, researchers (PhDs). On the other hand, the laboratory system is driven by the activity of mostly fundamental laboratories from the Paris region, where investments traditionally were more massive. However, the systems are by no means independent. The complementary nature of the systems could be indicated by the relatively lower "activity" (number of outgoing ties) of the researchers employed by the laboratories from the most "active" cluster. Actually, the strategy of these more active laboratories might be to build ties to resources so that their researchers do not need to invest so much time in this task. If so, the strategy seems effective as the researchers from these laboratories belong to the highest performing group of researchers.

Acknowledgements Section "Multilevel Blockmodeling" and pars of section "Analysis of a Multilevel Network of Cancer Researchers in France" are a modified version of parts from Žiberna (2014, pp. 48–51). Reprinted from Social Networks, Vol 39, Aleš Žiberna, "Blockmodeling of Multilevel Networks," 46–61, Copyright (2014), with permission from Elsevier.

References

Anderson, C. J., Wasserman, S., & Faust, K. (1992). Building stochastic blockmodels. *Social Networks, 14*, 137–161.
Arabie, P., Boorman, S. A., & Levitt, P. R. (1978). Constructing blockmodels: How and why. *Journal of Mathematical Psychology, 17*, 21–63.
Batagelj, V., Doreian, P., & Ferligoj, A. (1992a). An optimizational approach to regular equivalence. *Social Networks, 14*, 121–135.
Batagelj, V., Ferligoj, A., & Doreian, P. (1992b). Direct and indirect methods for structural equivalence. *Social Networks, 14*, 63–90.
Batagelj, V., Ferligoj, A., & Doreian, P. (1998). Fitting pre-specified blockmodels. In C. Hayashi, K. Yajima, H. H. Bock, N. Ohsumi, Y. Tanaka, & Y. Baba (Eds.), *Data science, classification, and related methods* (pp. 199–206). Tokyo: Springer.
Batagelj, V., Mrvar, A., Ferligoj, A., & Doreian, P. (2004). Generalized blockmodeling with Pajek. *Metodološki Zvezki, 1*, 455–467.
Bellotti, E. (2012). Getting funded. Multi-level network of physicists in Italy. *Social Networks, 34*, 215–229.
Boorman, S. A., & White, H. C. (1976). Social structure from multiple networks. II. Role structures. *American Journal of Sociology, 81*, 1384–1446.
Borgatti, S. P., & Everett, M. G. (1992). Regular blockmodels of multiway, multimode matrices. *Social Networks, 14*, 91–120.
Brass, D. J., Galaskiewicz, J., Greve, H. R., & Tsai, W. P. (2004). Taking stock of networks and organizations: A multilevel perspective. *Academy of Management Journal, 47*, 795–817.
Breiger, R. (1974). The duality of persons and groups. *Social Forces, 53*, 181–190.

Breiger, R., Boorman, S., & Arabie, P. (1975). Algorithm for clustering relational data with applications to social network analysis and comparison with multidimensional-scaling. *Journal of Mathematical Psychology, 12*, 328–383.

Brusco, M., & Steinley, D. (2011). A tabu-search heuristic for deterministic two-mode blockmodeling of binary network matrices. *Psychometrika, 76*, 612–633.

Brusco, M., Doreian, P., Steinley, D., & Satornino, C. B. (2013). Multiobjective blockmodeling for social network analysis. *Psychometrika, 78*, 498–525.

Burt, R. (1976). Positions in networks. *Social Forces, 55*, 93–122.

Doreian, P., Batagelj, V., & Ferligoj, A. (1994). Partitioning networks based on generalized concepts of equivalence. *The Journal of Mathematical Sociology, 19*, 1–27.

Doreian, P., Batagelj, V., & Ferligoj, A. (2004). Generalized blockmodeling of two-mode network data. *Social Networks, 26*, 29–53.

Doreian, P., Batagelj, V., & Ferligoj, A. (2005a). *Generalized blockmodeling*. New York: Cambridge University Press.

Doreian, P., Batagelj, V., & Ferligoj, A. (2005b). *Generalized blockmodeling*. Cambridge: Cambridge University Press.

Holland, P. W., Laskey, K. B., & Leinhardt, S. (1983). Stochastic blockmodels: First steps. *Social Networks, 5*, 109–137.

Hubert, L., & Arabie, P. (1985). Comparing partitions. *Journal of Classification, 2*, 193–218.

Iacobucci, D., & Wasserman, S. (1990). Social networks with 2 sets of actors. *Psychometrika, 55*, 707–720.

Kronegger, L., Ferligoj, A., & Doreian, P. (2011). On the dynamics of national scientific systems. *Quality and Quantity, 45*, 989–1015.

Lazega, E., & Mounier, L. (2002). Interdependent entrepreneurs and the social discipline of their cooperation: A research programme for structural economic sociology in a society of organizations. In O. Favereau & E. Lazega (Eds.), *Conventions and structures in economic organization* (pp. 147–199). Cheltenham: Edward Elgar.

Lazega, E., Mounier, L., Stofer, R., & Tripier, A. (2004). Discipline scientifique et discipline sociale: Réseaux de conseil, apprentissage collectif et innovation dans la recherche française sur le cancer (1997–1999). *Recherches Sociologiques, 35*, 3–28.

Lazega, E., Mounier, L., Jourda, M.-T., & Stofer, R. (2006). Organizational vs. personal social capital in scientists' performance: A multi-level network study of elite French cancer researchers (1996–1998). *Scientometrics, 67*, 27–44.

Lazega, E., Jourda, M.-T., Mounier, L., & Stofer, R. (2008). Catching up with big fish in the big pond? Multi-level network analysis through linked design. *Social Networks, 30*, 159–176.

Lazega, E., Sapulete, S., & Mounier, L. (2011). Structural stability regardless of membership turnover? The added value of blockmodelling in the analysis of network evolution. *Quality and Quantity, 45*, 129–144.

Lazega, E., Jourda, M.-T., & Mounier, L. (2013). Network lift from dual alters: Extended opportunity structures from a multilevel and structural perspective. *European Sociological Review, 29*, 1226–1238.

Mali, F., Kronegger, L., Doreian, P., & Ferligoj, A. (2012). Dynamic scientific co-authorship networks. In A. Scharnhorst, K. Börner, & P. Besselaar (Eds.), *Models of science dynamics, understanding complex systems* (pp. 195–232). Berlin: Springer.

Multilevel Network Modeling Group. (2012). *What are multilevel networks*. University of Manchester. Available at: http://mnmg.co.uk/Multilevel%20Networks.pdf

R Core Team. (2013). *R: A language and environment for statistical computing*. Vienna, Austria. Available at http://www.R-project.org/

Rand, W. M. (1971). Objective criteria for the evaluation of clustering methods. *Journal of the American Statistical Association, 66*, 846–850.

Snijders, T. A. B., & Nowicki, K. (1997). Estimation and prediction for stochastic blockmodels for graphs with latent block structure. *Journal of Classification, 14*, 75–100.

Snijders, T. A. B., Lomi, A., & Torló, V. J. (2013). A model for the multiplex dynamics of two-mode and one-mode networks, with an application to employment preference, friendship, and advice. *Social Networks, 35*, 265–276.

Steinley, D. (2004). Properties of the Hubert-Arable adjusted rand index. *Psychological Methods, 9*, 386–396.

Wang, P., Robins, G., Pattison, P., & Lazega, E. (2013). Exponential random graph models for multilevel networks. *Social Networks, 35*, 96–115.

Wasserman, S., & Iacobucci, D. (1991). Statistical modeling of one-mode and 2-mode networks – Simultaneous analysis of graphs and bipartite graphs. *British Journal of Mathematical and Statistical Psychology, 44*, 13–43.

White, H. C., Boorman, S. A., & Breiger, R. L. (1976). Social structure from multiple networks. I. Blockmodels of roles and positions. *American Journal of Sociology, 81*, 730–780.

Žiberna, A. (2007). Generalized blockmodeling of valued networks. *Social Networks, 29*, 105–126.

Žiberna, A. (2013a). Generalized blockmodeling of sparse networks. *Metodološki Zvezki, 10*, 99–119.

Žiberna, A. (2013b). Blockmodeling 0.2.2: An R package for generalized and classical blockmodeling of valued networks. Available at: http://www2.arnes.si/~aziber4/blockmodeling/

Žiberna, A. (2014). Blockmodeling of multilevel networks. *Social Networks, 39*, 46–61.

Part III
Applications

Chapter 9
Comparing Fields of Sciences: Multilevel Networks of Research Collaborations in Italian Academia

Elisa Bellotti, Luigi Guadalupi, and Guido Conaldi

Introduction

Much of the work done in the sociology of science observes scientific communities from a micro perspective, focusing on interactions in laboratories. By doing this, researchers try to uncover the impact of social and cultural norms in the everyday production of scientific results. Other studies approach the topic from a macro perspective, analyzing scientific organizations and the reciprocal influence they have with wider society. Less attention has been paid to the meso-level of interactions within and between scientists and the environments they work in. Methodologically, the gap in the literature can be filled using the recent advancements in multilevel analytical approaches, especially by the combination of multilevel analysis with social network analysis. This combination allows us to model structural effects on individual behaviors, where these effects are at work at different levels of social interactions, between individuals, groups, and organizations.

Linking the effects of interactions between scientists to the structural constraints that may emerge from working in large and complex institutional settings, and measuring these effects on individual and institutional behaviors is extremely interesting, as it offers an additional piece of the intellectual jigsaw that a simple look at individuals, or at organizations, cannot provide. Several analytical approaches have been developed for the analysis of data that describe social networks in multilevel

---

E. Bellotti (✉)
Department of Sociology, University of Manchester, Manchester, UK
e-mail: elisa.bellotti@manchester.ac.uk

L. Guadalupi
Institute for Research on Innovation and Services for Development (IRISS), National Research Council (CNR), Napoli, Italy

G. Conaldi
Centre for Business Network Analysis, University of Greenwich, London, UK

structures, as detailed in Snijders' chapter in this book. Generally speaking, these approaches have in common the assumption that what matters are the concrete interactions between individuals and/or organizations, that these interactions are structured in social networks, and that networks of lower levels (i.e., individuals) are nested within networks of higher levels (i.e.: organizations).

In this chapter we want to identify a suitable approach that can be applied to the study of scientific collaborations. In other words, we are interested in modeling the multilevel structure of scientific work, looking at social networks of collaborations between scientists, and at how these networks are embedded in disciplinary and organizational levels. Once the relational structure of scientific collaboration is described, we want to see if it plays a role in scholars' successes. We adopt the structural approach of Lazega et al. (2008) and analyze the local system of public funding to academic disciplines in Italy using bipartite networks. Such analysis has been already done for two academic areas: physics (Bellotti 2012) and philosophy (Bellotti 2014). Here we extend the analysis to all the areas of research in Italian Academia, in order to compare the results across different scientific fields. By doing this, we observe the variability of structural effects across disciplinary areas that we expect to be organized in different but comparable ways. In particular, the previous analyses of physicists and philosophers showed in both cases the overarching importance of academic ranks and of brokerage roles in obtaining research funding. There were also some other interesting effects, like the less impacting but still significant importance of working with a long-term established group of colleagues, and the advantages of working in specific sub-disciplines (Bellotti 2012, 2014).

Here we want to see if those results replicate across other disciplinary areas, or if some interesting differences can be found. For this purposes, we analyze 10 years (2001–2010) of the Italian Ministry of University and Research funding of Projects of National Interest (Prin) across all the disciplinary areas of academia. The micro-level (collaborations between scientists), macro-level (collaborations between institutions and between disciplines) and meso-level (the combination of network measures at a micro and macro level) of interactions are first independently analyzed, and the results are used to model the total amount of money researchers have received over the decade against the variables that meaningfully describe the network structures of collaborations to research projects. All the network measures are calculated in Ucinet (Borgatti et al. 2002) while the regression models for the 14 disciplinary areas are calculated in R, using the lnam function (linear network autocorrelation model) in the SNA package (Butts 2007).

The chapter is organized as follows. In the next section we describe some of the approaches that are available to study multilevel and bipartite networks. We briefly introduce multilevel analysis models, and specifically HLMs (Snijders and Bosker 2012), Mixed Membership Models (Browne et al. 2001; Erosheva and Fienberg 2011), and affiliation networks (Breiger 1974). While these modeling strategies focus on hierarchical dependencies, the problem of horizontal dependencies is dealt by a network disturbance model (White et al. 1981; Dow et al. 1983, 1984), which is more suitable when data present a network structure. These models are the essential antecedents to multilevel analysis of networks (MAN) (Tranmer et al. 2014), and multilevel network analysis (MNA) that uses ERGM models (Wang et al. 2013), which can be considered the two main analytical strategies for the study of multilevel networks. Most of these approaches have been extensively described in Snijders (Chap. 2, this volume), and when appropriate we limit our discussion to the reference to his chapter.

We then move on to describe the structure of the data we want to analyze, and we explain why, in our case, the mainstream models of MAN and MNA are not applicable, which points us towards the adoption of a network disturbance model. Once the analytical strategy is in place, we move on to illustrating the results of the univariate analysis of the elements that describe the micro-, macro- and meso-levels of scientific collaborations. These elements are then modeled in a linear regression where the dependent variable represents the total amount of money each researcher has earned in the 10 years under analysis, and where the effects on the standard errors stemming from the network autocorrelation are controlled by using the network disturbance model (White et al. 1981; Dow et al. 1983, 1984), which in our case is done by following the solution proposed by Leenders (2002). Results are discussed by focusing on the similarities and differences among the 14 disciplinary areas, and on the autocorrelations effects. We discuss the results in the discussion section, reflecting upon the contribution of a multilevel analytical approach, and we conclude the chapter indicating the limits of our approach, and possible future developments.

Multilevel Approaches to the Study of Social Networks

Multilevel approaches to the study of social networks stem from two complementary analytical perspectives: multilevel analysis and affiliation networks. As detailed in Snijders (Chap. 2, this volume) multilevel analysis, and in particular the hierarchical linear model (HLM), is a methodology that looks at variability in data where the source of variability depends on the nested nature of data, for example, pupils studying in different classrooms of the same school, or living in different neighborhoods (see also Snijders and Bosker 2012). A level is defined as a "system of categories for which it is reasonable to assume random effects" (Snijders, Chap. 2, this book: 6), where residuals (measured for a sample), or random errors (measured for a population) are expected to be correlated for people belonging to the same group. As discussed by Snijders (Chap. 2, this volume) an interesting extension of multilevel models are mixed membership models (Browne et al. 2001), which allow for individuals (or any first-level object of analysis) to belong to multiple second level groups.

Affiliation networks on the other hand, deal with the duality of people in groups (Breiger 1974). These are types of networks with two different sets of nodes, where one set can only interact with the other. They represent situations in which nodes from one level are members of the nodes at a higher level, for example, individuals who may be grouped in organizations, which in turn may have an influence on the probability that individuals interact. Such approach has been at the center of attention for social network researchers since it was first advanced by Breiger (1974), who describes the properties of two-mode networks. Fararo and Doreian (1984) extend Breiger's formalism to tripartite networks, where, for example, people are embedded in groups and groups in organizations; they then generalize the conceptual basis and the matrix formalisms of bipartite graphs to tripartite networks, and produce a set of matrix equations and operations that can be applied in the study of empirical networks. Both multilevel models and affiliation networks thus look at group dependencies, or dependencies nested from one level to another, although the former are statistical models, while the latter are graph theoretical structures.

While multilevel approaches deal with hierarchical dependencies, traditional social network analysis, or the cross-sectional analysis of one-mode networks, is interested in horizontal dependencies within a single level, with only a single set of nodes. Its scope is to study the structure of relationships between (for example) individuals and look at the effects that these may have on their behavior (or, alternatively, to look at how individual behavior may affect the position in a network). In order to account for network dependencies, social network analysis has adopted methods originally developed for spatial correlations (Cliff and Ord 1975; Ord 1975) that deal with the problem of autocorrelation, or Galton's problem (Naroll 1961, 1965; Schaefer 1974). In spatial terms the problem of autocorrelation consists in the non-independence of the residuals, which are more similar for proximal areas than for distant areas, and therefore do not follow a Gaussian (normal) distribution (Wang et al. 2014). Similarly, in a social network two individuals may exhibit similar characteristics for the very fact of being related: they may have influenced each other, or they might have established the relationship because of the pre-existing similarity (Steglich et al. 2010).

Social network analysis has thus extended the models for spatial dependencies in three main analytical strategies for the analysis of relational dependencies. The first is the network disturbances model, which corresponds to the spatial disturbance model in geography (Doreian 1992; Anselin and Hudak 1992). In this model the structure of the network is not assumed to have any direct influence on the variables that measure some aspects of individuals, but only to influence the error terms.

$$Y = X\beta + \varepsilon \tag{9.1a}$$

$$\varepsilon = \rho W \varepsilon + v \tag{9.1b}$$

The Eq. (9.1a) is a classic OLS, but the error term (9.1b) contains the matrix W representing the network structure (e.g., a $N \times N$ adjacency matrix), the parameter ρ representing the strength of dependence among the error terms, and the vector v representing the Gaussian distributed residuals.

The second model is the network effects model, also known in the geographical literature as the spatial effects model (Doreian 1992). Here the network is assumed to have a direct effect on an individual-level outcome variable. In the Eq. (9.2) ρW is thus included among the explanatory variables rather than in the error term. Here the random errors are normally distributed $\left(\varepsilon \sim IN\left(0, \sigma^{\wedge 2}I\right)\right)$.

$$Y = \rho WY + X\beta + \varepsilon \qquad (9.2)$$

The third model is proposed in Doreian (1992) and incorporates both the network effect and the network autocorrelation of the disturbance term, which is considerably more complex (for a complete discussion of this last model, and of the estimation procedures, see Doreian 1992).

Given the longstanding tradition of multilevel analysis and bipartite and one-mode networks analyses, it was just a matter of time before researchers started combining them. This was intended to combine single-level horizontal network dependencies (one-mode) with hierarchical group dependencies (multilevel and two-mode). In other words, methods are now available for combining network data with group affiliations, as well as network data stemming from relations at various levels of analysis. Snijders extensively explains the various approaches available for such analysis (p2, latent space models, ERGM, SAOM: see Snijders, Chap. 2, this volume). He also reviews the specific models for multilevel network analysis, which aim is to go beyond the analysis of a single network and to generalize results for a population of networks (Snijders, Chap. 2, this volume: 18). One of the most promising approaches is the family of Exponential Random Graph Models for multilevel networks (MNA, Wang et al. 2013), which consider each network tie as a random variable, and model how ties are patterned. These models deal specifically with situations in which we have relations between nodes at one level (e.g., individuals); relations between nodes at another level (e.g., organizations); and affiliations that link one mode to the other (individuals to organizations), where multiple affiliation is allowed (individuals can belong to more than one organization at a time). Stemming from the same family of models, Autologistic Actor Attribute models (ALAAM, see Daraganova and Robins 2013) are instead specifically designed to predict some characteristics of nodes (represented by an endogenous binary variable where $1 =$ presence and $0 =$ absence of such characteristics) assuming the network structure as exogenous and fixed.

A different way of analyzing the effects of social networks on individual characteristics, while also taking into account group dependencies, is the Multiple-Membership Multiple Classification (MMMC) modeling approach proposed by Browne et al. (2001) and discussed and applied in Tranmer et al. (2014), which is a useful approach for the multilevel analysis of networks (MAN). The approach combines mixed membership models (Browne et al. 2001), which allow individuals' multiple affiliations, with social networks measured at one level only (in Tranmer and colleagues' example from 2014, relationships between individuals nested in schools and geographical areas). The network structure and the groups' affiliations are used as exogenous factors that are expected to have effects on the individual-level educational attainment. This approach is very similar to the autocorrelation models (spatial and disturbance) presented above, but it has the advantage that is able to introduce group dependencies as random effects, while in the former they could only be accounted for in the models as fixed effects via a set of indicator (dummy) variables (Tranmer et al. 2014: 446).

Whether to use an autocorrelation model or a MMMC model depends, according to the authors, on the type of substantive research questions. If it is believed that the network of relations between actors, as well as the group dependencies, have a direct effect on the individuals' characteristics under measure (the dependent variable), then MMMC are preferable. If instead the network represents a nuisance, as it has an influence only on the correlation of the random errors, then the network disturbance model is indicated (Tranmer et al. 2014: 446).

Borrowing the notation of Wang et al. (2013: 213) we can summarize the various approaches presented so far in Table 9.1, where we label the macro-level network (i.e., organizations, grey square nodes) as network A, the micro-level network (i.e., individuals, black circular nodes) as network B, and the meso-level bipartite network (affiliations) as network X. Given the various possibilities, the next step is to identify which modeling strategy to adopt for the analysis of scientific collaborations. The choice depends on the theoretical justification of the approach, and the suitability

Table 9.1 Summary of multilevel data structures

Model	Data structure □ = A level │ = X level ● = B level	Description	Dependencies	Dependent variable
HLM		A cross-level nested structure, with all B nodes with degree one in X, and A and B empty	Nodes in B are expected to show correlated residuals if they have a node in A in common	A variable describing nodes' characteristic in B
Mixed membership models		A cross-level nested structure, with all B nodes with degree ≥ 1 in X, and A and B empty	Nodes in B are expected to show correlated residuals if they have one or more nodes in A in common	A variable describing nodes' characteristic in B
Affiliation network		A cross-level nested structure, with all B nodes with degree ≥ 1 in X, and A and B empty	Nodes in B are expected to increase the chances of interaction if they have one or more nodes in A in common	A variable describing nodes' characteristic in either A and/or or B. A network configuration describing ties' characteristic in X

(continued)

Table 9.1 (continued)

Model	Data structure ▢ = A level │ = X level ● = B level	Description	Dependencies	Dependent variable
Network disturbance and network effect models		A single level structure, with B nodes with either 0 or ≥1 in B	Nodes in B are expected to show correlated residuals (disturbance) or correlated attributes (effect) if adjacent in B	A variable describing nodes' characteristic in B. A network configuration describing ties' characteristic in B
MMMC (MAN)		A cross level structure, with all B nodes with degree ≥1 in X, either 0 or ≥1 in B, and A empty	Nodes in B are expected to show correlated residuals if they are if adjacent in B, and/or have one or more nodes in A in common	A variable describing nodes' characteristic in either A and/or B. A network configuration describing ties' characteristic in either B and/or X
MNA		A cross level structure, with all B nodes with degree ≥1 in X, all B nodes with either 0 or ≥1 in B, and all A nodes with either 0 or ≥1 in A	Nodes in B are expected to show correlated residuals if they are if adjacent in B, and/or if they have one or more nodes in A in common, and/or if these nodes in A are adjacent	A categorical variable describing nodes' characteristic in either A and/or B (ALAAM). A network configuration describing ties' characteristic in either B and/or A and/or X (ERGM)

of the data. In the next section we move on to the description of the structure of our data and the substantive questions that guide our analysis, which justify our analytical strategy.

The Database of PRIN Projects

The data analyzed in this chapter refer to the Italian academic funding line for Research Projects of National Interest (PRIN). This is a yearly competition organized by the Italian Ministry of Universities and Research (MIUR) that for some disciplines, especially humanities, represents the main (although not the only) source of research funding. PRIN projects are inter-organizational collaborations between researchers based in different universities, where each project is led by a national coordinator, and involves various local units. These are normally based in different institutions, although there can be exceptions in which coordinators of local units of one project may belong to the same department.

The PRIN scheme is a form of co-funding between MIUR and universities: every year, researchers obtain a budget from their universities to cover 30 % of a research project's cost, with the other 70 % provided by MIUR if the project is selected. Projects must be submitted for a specific disciplinary area. These disciplinary areas are:

1. Mathematical and Computer Science;
2. Physics;
3. Chemistry;
4. Environmental Sciences;
5. Biology;
6. Medicine;
7. Agriculture and Veterinary;
8. Architecture and Civil Engineering;
9. Industrial and Computer Engineering;
10. Ancient Studies, Literature and Philology, History and Art;
11. History, Philosophy, Pedagogy and Psychology Sciences;
12. Juridical Studies;
13. Economics and Statistics;
14. Political and Social Sciences.

Each of them is internally subdivided into sub-disciplinary sectors that distinguish, for example, between theoretical and experimental physics, or between ancient and modern philosophy. The topic of the project must be related to the disciplinary area in which is proposed and eventually funded; however, unit coordinators can be affiliated to various sub-disciplinary sectors, or even to different disciplinary areas. Thus, for example, it is possible to have a project where historians of ancient philosophy work with logicians or moral philosophers to analyze certain philosophical constructs in specific historical periods, or where mathematicians work with computer scientists to develop algorithms, and so forth.

Information on funded projects is available from the MIUR website (www.miur.it). Every funded project for every year (since 1996, although our analysis starts from 2001) is listed in a pdf file containing the name and university affiliation of researchers together with their role (national coordinator, local unit coordinator), the amount of funded money for each unit, and the title of the project. This is followed by a general account of the aim of the research, a statement about innovations in the topic of enquiry, a list of criteria for the verifiability of the project's outcomes, and finally a detailed description of each research team's duties. Across all the areas, 19,453 researchers have been funded during the 10 years under analysis.

The rank of the scientists (full professor, associate professor and researcher) and the sub-disciplinary affiliation (e.g., theoretical physics, material physics, etc. for the physics macro-area) are obtainable from the same MIUR website. The rank refers to the position occupied by every scientist in 2010. To take into account people's promotions, rank was also recorded in 2001, which is the earliest information available from MIUR's website (which is also the reason why our analysis does not go back beyond 2001); using this information we constructed a binary variable indicating if people changed rank between 2001 and 2010.

We only recorded information for scientists funded during the period under analysis and therefore included in the PRIN dataset. Scientists who have not been funded in this period are not recorded in our dataset, because although we could retrieve their attribute information from the MIUR website, the fact that they have not been funded should not be considered as a sign of unsuccessful bidding. They might not have entered a proposal for this line of funding or they might have been funded elsewhere. They therefore cannot be used as a control group against which to compare the successful scientists.

For this analysis, every scientist is given an identification number. We then created an individual variable for the following attributes: university affiliation, sub-discipline affiliation, rank, change in rank, role within the project (as national or local coordinator), and the total amount of funding received between 2001 and 2010, where this last information represents our dependent variable. We did this for all the disciplinary areas (14), thereby obtaining an attribute file for each of them. The unique identification numbers of all researchers (with the title of the projects in which they participated) were listed in a linked file and organized in a dataset consisting of ten bipartite networks of 'people by funded projects', one for each year from 2001 to 2010. Again, we did this for all the disciplinary areas, so for each of them we have ten bipartite 'people by project' networks.

Every researcher, being national coordinator, local coordinator, or research group member, can only work on one PRIN project at a time. The same limit applies to PRIN bids: when a group submits a proposal, all the members are restricted to that one bid; they cannot place their name on several projects in order to have more chances to be funded. All projects are funded for 24 months. Each year's network is thus reduced to a number of disconnected stars (with ties between scientists and the specific project they work on). Summing up the ten bipartite matrices, the resulting network shows overlap among the stars, as researchers move from one project to the next one (and in some cases, from one collaborative group to another) through the years. We obtained 14 of these overall networks, one for each disciplinary area.

Although scientists may move from one university to another, this is not common in Italy, where people tend to be appointed and spend their entire career in the same university, often the place where they obtained their PhD (Beltrame 2008). Over the entire population of scientists funded by MIUR (19,442), only 1.5 % have changed university in the 10 years under analysis (302). Therefore, although there are three distinct sets of nodes (people, projects, universities), the data do not form a tripartite network. Relations are only defined by individual collaborations on research projects, while institutional affiliation constitutes an attribute of individuals. Likewise, researchers become affiliated to a sub-discipline when they first get appointed in a permanent position in Italian Academia. Although they could potentially change disciplinary affiliation when obtaining a promotion, this very rarely happens (161 out of 19,442, or 0.8 %, in the 10 years under analysis), thus multiple sub-disciplinary affiliation is not allowed in our data.

While multiple affiliations are not allowed, it is still possible to apply matrix algebra and extract the university-by-project matrix, moving from the individual to the institutional level of collaboration. Similarly, we can extract the sub-discipline by project matrix, which represent another interesting institutional macro-level. This has been done by transforming the university affiliation attribute vector, and the corresponding sub-discipline one, into two-mode binary university-by-people and discipline-by-people matrices. These matrices are multiplied by the two-mode binary people-by-project matrix, obtaining a two-mode valued university-by-project matrix, and a two-mode valued discipline-by-project matrix. Transposing the people-by-project, the university-by-project and the discipline-by-project matrices yields a person-by-person valued network, a university-by-university valued network, and a discipline-by-discipline valued network (where in all of them the cells indicate the number of projects in common). We did this for all 14 macro areas, thus obtaining three networks for each of them. All networks are undirected.

The Multilevel Structure of PRIN Data

The original structure of the dataset, as we mentioned above, consists of a series of bipartite 'people by project' networks, one for every disciplinary area and for every year under analysis. Summing up all the years, we obtain 14 networks of overlapping stars, one for each discipline, in which black rounded nodes represent scientists and light grey triangles represent projects (Fig. 9.1). In Fig. 9.1 each scientist's macro affiliation (as noted above, multiple affiliation is not allowed) are also visualized. Dark grey square nodes represent universities and white downward

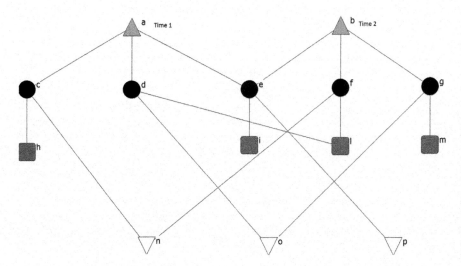

Fig. 9.1 Bipartite 'people by project' network with university and sub-discipline affiliation

9 Comparing Fields of Sciences: Multilevel Networks of Research... 223

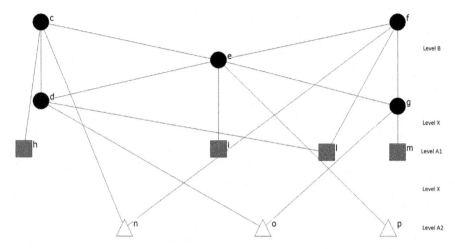

Fig. 9.2 One-mode 'people by people' network (projects in common) with university or discipline affiliation

triangles represent sub-disciplines. The bipartite networks are then transformed into one-mode 'people by people' networks, where the ties represent the number of projects two scientists have in common. This constitutes the first level of analysis (level B in Table 9.1), while universities and sub-disciplines constitute the second, higher level of the analysis (level A1 and A2 in Table 9.1), nesting individual researchers into groups. The ties connecting individuals to universities and to disciplines represent the X level (Fig. 9.2).

The data structure illustrated in Fig. 9.2 suggests two possible analytical approaches. The first is MMMC, where group dependencies (universities and sub-disciplines) are introduced as random variables; the second is the network disturbance model, where group affiliations are operationalized as fixed effects via dummy variables (belonging/not belonging to a group), while effects of the network of collaborations of individuals is expected to influence the dependence among the error terms as in Eq. (9.1b). As discussed, the choice of whether to use one or the other depends on the research question and the feasibility of the data (Tranmer et al. 2014).

In our case, we want to see if the position of scientists in the network of research collaborations, together with individual attributes, have an effect in increasing the total amount of funding each researcher receives in the 10 years under analysis, where the dependent variable (money) is continuous. If we only had individual attributes (being a national coordinator, rank, changes in rank, disciplinary affiliation), without knowing anything about collaborations, we could fit a standard OLS regression. We do know however that when researchers collaborate in a project, they often distribute the total amount of funding in equal parts across the local units. This is not always the case, as the money required for the tasks of the local units may vary: some units may need more staff time allocation, or more expensive equipment. But when such differences are excluded, researchers collaborating on the same project will end up with the same amount of funding. If people continue collaborating together project after project, they will eventually accumulate a similar amount of overall funding. If they change research groups, the similarity will not be as high, but we will still expect it to be greater than between two scientists who have never collaborated with each other. Therefore we expect that the network of collaborations between scientists will impact the correlation between the individual error terms, which can be controlled by using the network disturbance model.

We could also assume that if two scientists work in the same sub-discipline, or in the same university, their overall amount of funding would be correlated. This would certainly be possible, and the logic of the MMMC model would lead to including random group (A1 and A2) effects. In order to fit a full MMMC model we thus would need first of all to include some ego network structures as random effects, for example dyads and cliques as in Tranmer et al. (2014), the former likely to be nested in the latter. Then we would need to introduce university affiliation and discipline affiliation as random effects, and look at the potential autocorrelation of random errors of individuals not only collaborating with each other, but also working in the same discipline and/or in the same university.

While fitting a MMMC model could potentially be possible and even advisable, here we decided for the network disturbance model. We wanted to analyze the impact of individual attributes, ego network structural properties, ego network homophily, and structural properties of the macro network of university and disciplinary collaborations and the meso-level of "fish and ponds" all together. For such a complicated model the network disturbance model seems a simpler, although limited, option. Network disturbance models also assume a continuous dependent variable, which is our case.

One of the limits of fitting a network disturbance model, as we said, is that it normally accounts for group dependencies by adding these as fixed effects (i.e., dummy variables for affiliations to groups). This can be problematic when there are many groups, which is our case given the number of universities in Italy (94), as well as the number of sub-disciplines, which varies across disciplinary areas (medicine, for example, includes 50 sub-disciplines, while mathematics and computer science only have 10). Our proposed solution is to use some properties that summarize the network structure of the respective one-mode networks, university-by-university and sub-discipline-by-sub-discipline networks, where ties are the number of projects in common. These networks, derived from the combination of the bipartite 'people by project networks' and the affiliation vector people-by-university and people-by-discipline (as described in the previous section), are visually represented in Fig. 9.3, and constitute the multilevel structure of our data, where level A1 are universities and level A2 disciplines. Note that ties in B are valued, as they represent the number of projects people have in common; ties in X are either 0 or 1 from B to A1 and A2 (as every scientist can only be affiliated to one university and one sub-discipline), but can be ≥ 1 from A1 and A2 to B, as several scientists may work in the same university and in the same sub-discipline; and ties in A1 and A2 are valued, as they represent the number of projects universities or sub-disciplines have in common.

9 Comparing Fields of Sciences: Multilevel Networks of Research...

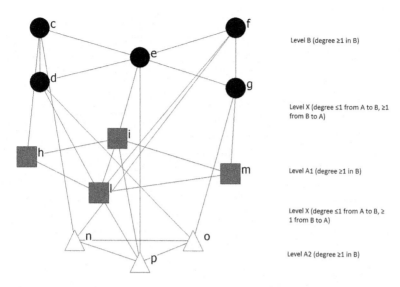

Fig. 9.3 Multilevel structure of individuals, universities and sub-disciplines

Given the fact that we analyze the outcomes at the individual level, in terms of the total amount of funding received over the years, a multilevel ERGM (MNA) is not suitable, as it analyzes relational (dyadic) outcomes.

In our case, the characteristics of level A1 (universities) and level A2 (disciplines) are on the explanatory side, not the dependent side. We do expect a structural effect with universities encouraging their researchers to work with other successful institutions, and researchers collaborating with central sub-disciplines (for example, most projects in physics will need a theoretical physicist, thus that sub-discipline will be more central in the sub-disciplinary network). Therefore we calculate some descriptive network measures that summarize the properties of the networks at the A1 and A2 level.

All 14 university-by-university networks, one for each disciplinary area, present a clear core-periphery structure, indicating that in each discipline there is a set of successful institutions everybody wants to collaborate with, that tend to collaborate more with each other (note that the institutions in the core vary across disciplines, as universities may excel in different specific areas). We measure belonging to a core institution for each scientist as a dummy variable, and we introduce it as fixed effect in our network disturbance model, to account for group dependencies. For sub-disciplines the networks are more scattered around clusters of sub-disciplinary collaborations. We thus use the values of flow betweenness (Freeman et al. 1991), which indicates how much each sub-discipline contributes to connecting the network of collaborations between sub-disciplines. We attribute the normalized values of flow betweenness of each sub-discipline to each researcher affiliated to it, and again we introduce it as fixed effect in our network disturbance model. To reiterate, both the network measures that describe the characteristics of the A1 and

A2 level are only included as fixed effects, without being accompanied by a random error term, a limitation required by the network disturbance model.

Individual attributes and structural properties of ego networks of the B level constitute what we call the micro-level; the core-periphery properties of the institutional networks and the flow betweenness values or the disciplinary network of the A1 and A2 level represent the macro-level. Following Lazega et al. (2008), we also model a meso-level that links the properties of B with the ones of A1 and A2 (level X). In their article, the authors categorize researchers and institutes as fishes and ponds according to their corresponding degree centrality values. Similarly here we consider as "big fish" scientists with a valued degree above the median of their own disciplinary areas (as the distribution is always skewed). Valued degree at the B level indicates the number of collaborations each scientist participated in over the 10 years of our analysis (note that individuals can collaborate with alters more than one time). As the network of universities is redundant with the network of individuals, it does not make sense to use degree values to distinguish between ponds. Therefore, the distinction is calculated on the number of scientists belonging to the same discipline and working in the same institution, regardless of being funded or not, the assumption being that an organization with a higher number of scientists offers a larger potential pool of contacts. We consider big ponds universities with a number of appointed scientists above the mean (as the distribution is not skewed). Combining information about fishes and ponds, we derive the same four categories of Lazega et al. (2008): big fishes in big ponds (BFBP), little fishes in big ponds (LFBP), big fishes in little ponds (BFLP), and little fishes in little ponds (LFLP). In this way we cluster together individuals and institutions with similar nested characteristics.

Univariate Analysis of Micro, Macro and Meso Characteristics

Hunting for funding is a highly competitive task in a scientist's life. It is necessary because it is impossible to do research without financial support and because it increases the chances of promotion and of appointing junior staff. In the end, financial support means publication of results, and publications are the measure of job performance in academia. The MIUR website does not provide detailed information on unsuccessful bids, only on successful ones. It does however provide such information at an aggregate level, indicating for each year (from 2001) the number of successful bids over the total number of proposals (Fig. 9.4). Thus we can see, for example, that mathematics and computer science (area 1) and chemistry (area 3) were more successful in 2002 than in 2001 and even more successful in 2003 than in 2002. 2003 also saw an increase in the successful proposals in earth sciences (area 4), agriculture and veterinary (area 7), juridical studies (area 12) and economics and statistics (area 13). Chemistry was even more successful in 2004, which also saw a large increase in political and social sciences, whose percentage of successful bids rose up to 82 %. In 2005 we see a further increase in earth sciences,

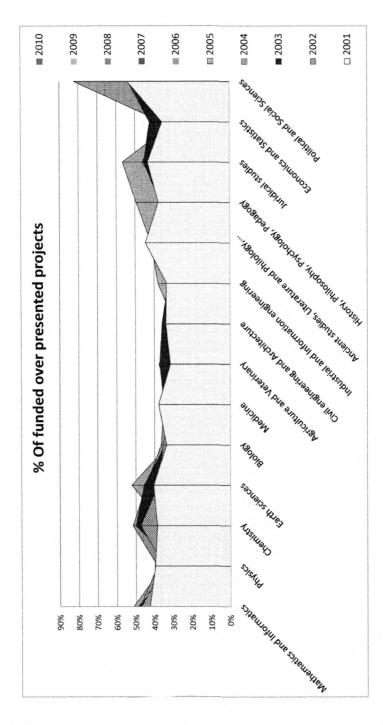

Fig. 9.4 Percentage of successful over total presentations

Table 9.2 Number of people funded in each disciplinary area

Area	Number of funded people
Medicine	3411
Industrial and computer engineering	1994
Biology	1991
Agriculture and veterinary	1542
Ancient studies, literature and philology, history and art	1509
Civil engineering and architecture	1324
History, philosophy, psychology, pedagogy	1311
Juridical studies	1219
Chemistry	1198
Economics and statistics	1067
Physics	957
Political and social sciences	676
Mathematics and computer science	653
Earth sciences	590
Total	*19,442*

industrial and informatics engineering (area 9), history, philosophy, psychology, pedagogy (area 11) and juridical studies. From 2006 funding has diminished in all disciplines, never reaching the success level of the first half of the decade. Table 9.2 summarizes the number of people funded in each disciplinary area.

The Micro-level: Individual Attributes

The individual attributes of each scientist funded across the 10 years represent, together with the structural properties of the level B network (the network of collaborations between scientists), our micro-level of analysis. The first important property to look at is the role within the project. Each project is organized around various local units. The project file in the MIUR database only reports the name of the local coordinator, while the names of the other people involved in the group are not available. Within these groups, one unit must act as the national coordinative unit, and its leader is in charge of the administrative aspects of the project and is the reference person for MIUR. While being a coordinator is a sign of prestige in a research group, being the national coordinator usually also means receiving the largest part of the funding, as it requires a greater investment of staff time for managing the grant. Figure 9.5 shows the percentage of researchers who have been national coordinators at least once in each disciplinary area (out of the total number of scientists who have been funded). A high number of national coordinators (as for example in earth sciences, where 54 % of researchers have been national coordinators at least once) indicates that a discipline revolves around many

9 Comparing Fields of Sciences: Multilevel Networks of Research... 229

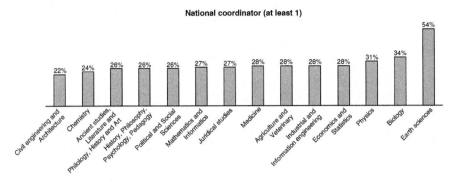

Fig. 9.5 Percentage of researchers who have been national coordinators at least once (out of the total number of researchers who have been funded)

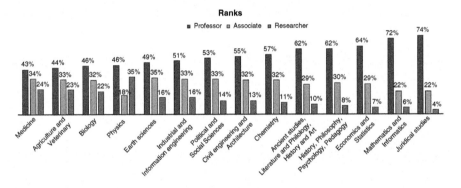

Fig. 9.6 Percentage of funded people in each rank for each discipline

group leaders; a low number (i.e. civil engineering and chemistry) suggests that the disciplines has fewer leaders who control most of the projects. Note that people could have been national coordinators as many as six times over the 10 years under analysis.

Rank is also very important. As we can see from Fig. 9.6, all the disciplines are dominated by full professors, who represent the largest percentage of funded researchers. However, this percentage varies across the disciplines, with 74 % of funded people being full professors in juridical studies, compared to only 43 % in medicine. The higher the percentage of full professors, the lower the percentage of researchers. The percentage of associate professors varies less across disciplines, ranging from 18 % in physics to 35 % in earth sciences, and constituting the second largest group of funded people in all disciplines but physics, where the percentage of researchers is higher.

The rank itself does not tell us whether people got funded because of their high rank, or if they were promoted to higher ranks because they got funded. We thus compared the rank of people at the beginning and at the end of the period under

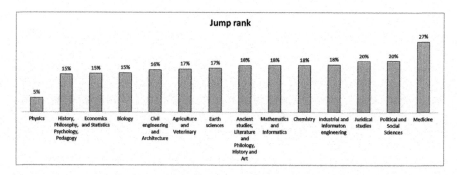

Fig. 9.7 Percentage of people gaining promotions over the total of funded people

analysis and recorded this information in a binary variable, with 1 indicating a promotion and 0 otherwise. Overall there is notable variation across disciplines (Fig. 9.7), with 27 % of people gaining a promotion in medicine (moving from researcher to associate professor, from associate to full professor, or from researcher to full professor), a percentage that drops to the minimum of 5 % in physics. We still cannot disentangle the direction of causality, but the information suggests that while in disciplines like physics the rank could explain the rate of success, in others it might be the rate of success facilitating promotions.

The Micro-level: Individual Networks

Rank, promotions, and coordination roles represent the individual attributes of scientists. We now move to analysis of the micro-level of collaborations on PRIN projects (level B). Three measures are used to observe the position of scientists in the structure of research collaborations. The first is the Yule's Q, a measure of homophily which accounts for projects' interdisciplinarity. Scientists funded via PRIN projects can collaborate with colleagues from the same sub-discipline, from other sub-disciplines in the same disciplinary area, and from different disciplinary areas. The number of people each scientist works with who belong to a different sub-discipline represents the interdisciplinarity of his/her egonet, or the degree to which the egonet of each scientist is heterogeneous. This is measured via the Yule's Q index, which scales the diversity of an egonet not only over the total number of alters in it, but also over the total number of people affiliated to a category. In other words, the egonet of collaborations of a scientist is more heterogeneous the more the disciplines of her collaborators are different from her own; but also the more s/he collaborates with people in disciplines which are underrepresented in the whole network. The values range from -1 (all collaborators belonging to the same sub-discipline as ego) to $+1$ (all collaborators belonging to a sub-discipline different from ego).

The second measure is the average degree of the egonet (ties are valued). The higher the average degree, the more individuals tend to collaborate with others over the years. This means creating more or less stable groups that either develop long-term research plans and ask for funding for follow-up projects, or simply decide where to invest their research efforts as a group over the years. Maintaining collaborations can be a good strategy as it creates a successful track record that may favor subsequent funding. However, it could also be the case that researchers prefer to, or are forced to, change the composition of their research group over time: in this way, they end up occupying a brokerage position between different groups of people, increasing the number of personal contacts with people who would be otherwise disconnected. We measure this tendency by counting the number of times people find themselves in a brokerage position in their egonets and dividing by the number of projects each researcher collaborates on (since the more projects an individual works on, the more brokerage possibilities s/he might have). Scaled brokerage thus constitutes our third micro-level network measure.

Average degree and brokerage are not mutually exclusive mechanisms: scientists might collaborate with one group 1 year, add new people to the original group 2 years later, and eventually move to collaborate with a third group after another 2 years. In this case, a scientist would find herself in the position of being the only link between groups one and two and group three. These mechanisms resemble those theorized by Burt (2005), who distinguishes between brokerage and closure in organizational settings, where brokerage favors the development of new ideas and closure the delivery of settled projects. In Burt's theory, both mechanisms are valuable: when combined, they maximize the advantage for actors in terms of developing dense egonets, as this facilitates the development of trust and behavioral control, while giving brokers different and exclusive perspectives from less connected people.

We model the success of these mechanisms in the next section to test which of the two is more successful for obtaining money. Here we assume a direction of causation from the structure to the level of funding (i.e. brokers attract more funding), but it could also be that a high level of funding attracts new people, resulting in a higher average degree of collaborations or a higher number of structural holes. Disentangling the direction of causation can only be tested with temporal analysis, where one can see if it is the position in the structure of collaboration that leads to the amount of funding received or if it is the amount of funding that stimulates further collaborations. However, this latter direction of causation would imply a greater effect from closure than from brokerage, as we would expect that successful collaborations favor the establishment of further projects with the same group of people rather than a drastic change of research groups.

Table 9.3 summarizes the average values of Yule's Q, brokerage and density of all disciplinary areas. Regarding the first measure, it is evident that some disciplines, like mathematics, tend to establish collaborations not only in the same disciplinary area, but also in the same sub-discipline. Medicine, on the other hand, is highly interdisciplinary. Along with medicine only chemistry and physics are characterized by heterogeneous collaborations, while for all the others the tendency

Table 9.3 Average values of Yule's Q, brokerage scores and average degree in each disciplinary area

Disciplinary area	Yule's Q	Scaled brokerage	Average degree
Mathematics and computer science	−0.76	1.57	1.00
Physics	0.40	1.47	1.12
Chemistry	0.37	4.39	1.26
Earth sciences	−0.68	1.38	1.18
Biology	−0.10	1.13	1.18
Medicine	0.76	2.23	1.04
Agriculture and veterinary	−0.47	2.15	1.06
Civil engineering and architecture	−0.63	2.97	1.03
Industrial and computer engineering	−0.56	1.58	1.04
Ancient studies, literature and philology, history and art	−0.58	1.59	1.21
History, philosophy, psychology, pedagogy	−0.60	1.69	1.13
Juridical studies	−0.64	2.33	1.04
Economics and statistics	−0.53	1.66	1.01
Political and social sciences	−0.34	2.03	1.08

is toward homophily (although values are close to equal balance between in-group and out-group ties for biology). Looking at the average brokerage scores per discipline, we notice that chemistry is the one where people tend to broker the most, while biologists seem to prefer to work in groups with fewer structural holes. Chemistry is also the discipline with most cohesive groups, confirming the possibility that brokerage and closure can be complementary structural mechanisms, while mathematics is the discipline were the average degree is lowest.

The Macro- and Meso-levels

As we explained before, the university-by-university and discipline-by-discipline networks, with the number of projects in common, constitute the macro levels (level A1 for universities and level A2 for disciplines). All the university networks are characterized by core/periphery structures calculated using the coreness routine in Ucinet (suitable for valued data). Ucinet automatically sets a cut-off point to distinguish between the core and the periphery. The percentage of people working in core universities (Fig. 9.8) varies across disciplines, from 34 % in juridical sciences to 77 % in agriculture and veterinary. A high percentage indicates the tendency of scientists to collaborate with others who work in equally successful universities, while a low one means that researchers collaborate with people working in institutions more successful than theirs.

The level of sub-disciplinary collaboration is analyzed using normalized flow betweenness, which measures the contribution of each node to all the possible

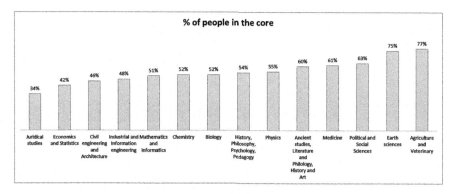

Fig. 9.8 Percentage of people working in core universities

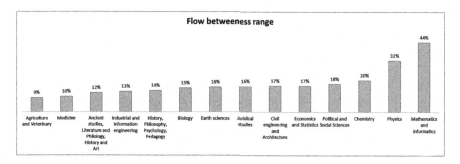

Fig. 9.9 Range of flow betweenness of sub-disciplines

maximum flows by taking into account the values of the ties, and dividing by the total flow through all the pairs. We assigned to each researcher the corresponding sub-disciplinary normalized flow betweenness value, thus aggregating them in the macro-level of sub-disciplinary groups. Figure 9.9 shows the values of centralization for the 14 macro areas, which indicates how much the network in each area is centralized around one or few sub-disciplines (Freeman 1979). The higher the value (which ranges from $0 =$ no centralization to $1 =$ maximum centralization), the more the network resembles a star.

The categorization into fishes and ponds constitutes the meso-level of analysis, or level X. Figure 9.10 illustrates the distribution of these four categories across the various disciplines, indicating predominance in all of them of BFBP and LFLP. This means that there are not many people working in little ponds, which is expected given the fact that the size of the pond is determined by the number of people appointed in a specific sub-discipline in every university.

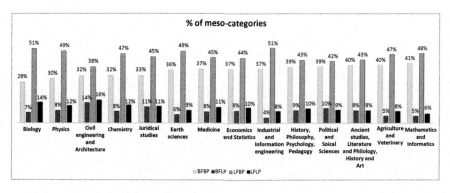

Fig. 9.10 Percentage of people in meso-categories

Modeling Funding Achievements

While in most of sociology of science studies academic success is measured in terms of publications and impact factor, in this study it is represented by the total amount of funding a researcher has received in the 10 years under analysis. So far, we have analyzed the individual and network characteristics in terms of getting connected with other researchers, without taking into account the amount of money received for every projects scientists work on. While it is likely that participating in a higher number of projects means obtaining more funding, this might not be always the case, as a scientist can participate in fewer but better funded projects. Therefore for each disciplinary area we model the amount of money obtained by every researcher against the variables that emerged as important at the micro-, macro-, and meso-level of analysis. We model each level hierarchically, in order to measure its influence separately from the other levels. We correct for potential lack of independence between cases using the network disturbances model (Leenders 2002), and we then compare the values of ρ across disciplines.

At the individual level, we expect national coordinators, full professors, and individuals who gained promotions to be more successful in obtaining money for research. Here the direction of causality must be taken with caution, as it could be that previous success in obtaining funding increases individuals' credibility and helps them to convince other people to join their projects in subsequent years; similarly, the capability of obtaining funding might contribute to career advancement.

H1. National coordinators are likely to obtain a larger amount of money for research than researchers who never lead a research group.

H2. Full professors are likely to obtain a larger amount of money for research than other ranks.

H3. Scientists who gained promotions are likely to obtain a larger amount of money than scientists who were not promoted.

At the micro-level (level B) of collaborations on research projects we expect projects with a lower level of interdisciplinarity to be more successful, therefore with lower values of Yule's Q indexes. This is because all disciplines but three seem to prefer homogenous collaborations. Again, direction of causality cannot be robustly tested, as it could be the case that people who received funding for homogenous collaborations continue in the same direction. We also want to measure the successful rate of researchers occupying a brokerage position or being involved in dense egonets: following Burt (2005), we expect both brokerage scores and egonet average degree to impact on the total amount of funding. If the direction of causality were reversed, we would expect closure to be the most successful strategy.

H4. Scientists with lower Yule's Q index values for sub-disciplines are likely to obtain a larger amount of money for research than the ones with higher values.

H5. Scientists with higher ego brokerage scores and/or higher egonet average degree are likely to obtain a larger amount of money for research than scientists with low values in one or both measures.

At the macro-level, given the fact that core institutions are the ones establishing more collaborations, we expect scientists working in them to be more successful than the ones working in peripheral universities (level A1). Likewise, we expect people working in central sub-disciplines to be more successful (level A2). Here the direction of causality is more robust, as given the low level of mobility of Italian researchers it is very unlikely that a scientist decides to move to a core institution attracted by the higher level of funding. Similarly, sub-disciplinary changes are very rare.

H6. Scientists working in core institutions are likely to obtain a larger amount of money for research than researcher working in peripheral ones.

H7. Scientists affiliated to central sub-disciplines are likely to obtain a larger amount of money for research than scientists affiliated to peripheral ones.

At the meso-level (level X), which combines the size of the egonets (degree) with the size of departments scientists work for (number of appointed scientists in the respective sub-discipline), we expect big fish in big ponds to be more successful than other categories, given the fact that in order to be a big fish scientists must have collaborated to more research projects than the median (therefore with a higher possibility of obtaining more money), and that big ponds might be considered more prestigious institutions, therefore attracting a higher level of funding. The direction of causality could be partially affected by the previous amount of funding, as successful projects can be part of the criteria of evaluation for proposals; however, being appointed in a big pond due to the previous amount of received funding is again very unlikely given the low mobility of Italian scientists.

H8. Big fish in big ponds (BFBP) are likely to obtain a larger amount of money for research than little fish in big ponds (LFBP), big fish in little ponds (BFLP) and little fish in little ponds (LFLP).

In all models the dependent variable is the log of the total amount of money awarded to each scientist during the observation period (as the distribution is skewed). In the first model we introduce the dummy variable of being a national coordinator. In the second model we introduce three variables related to rank as dummies: associate professor, researcher, and having had a promotion. In the third model we introduce the Yule's Q values for sub-disciplines, brokerage scores and egonet average degree (-1 scores for Yule's Q and 0 values for brokerage and closure being constant). In the fourth model we introduce a dummy for being in the network core, and the sub-discipline flow betweenness values. In the fifth model, the meso categories are introduced as three dummies: BFLP, LFBP, and LFLP – with BFBF acting as our reference category. All explanatory variables that were not coded as dummies were centered and rescaled by dividing by their standard deviations to ensure comparability of the regression coefficients. In all models the individual networks of collaborations (level B) are included to control for their potential effect on the correlation of the error terms, although in line with the network disturbance model the characteristics of the A1 and A2 level are only included as fixed effects, without being accompanied by a random error term. All the individual collaboration networks were rescaled to give to each relation a weight proportional to the share of the total number of collaborations entertained by a scientist that such relation represents. The disciplinary area of medicine could not be modeled at all, while for biology we could only fit the first three models. For industrial and computer engineering and ancient studies, literature and philology, history and art the fifth model (which contains all the variables) could not be fitted. We suspect that the problem lies in the large size of these networks, but further investigation is required.

Results

In this section we discuss the main results of our analysis by comparing them across the 14 disciplinary areas. The full set of results for each area, the descriptives, the correlations and the models' diagnostics are available from the corresponding author. Here we concentrate on the similarities and differences in the variability explained, in the significance of variables, and in the ρ values across the disciplinary areas. Figure 9.11 summarizes the total amount of variance explained by the full (5th) model in each area, where all the variables are estimated. This model explains a minimum of 37 % variance for physics, but up to 51 % for chemistry. In Fig. 9.12 we can see how much variance is explained by each model in each disciplinary area.

The first model, which takes into account how many times scientists have been in the role of national coordinators, explains between 14 % (in economics and statistics) and 25 % (in industrial and information engineering) of the variance, and the coefficients are always positive and significant. This is expected and confirms Hypothesis 1: the national coordinator is in most of the cases the one who sets up the project and obtains the largest part of the funding (Table 9.4). The second

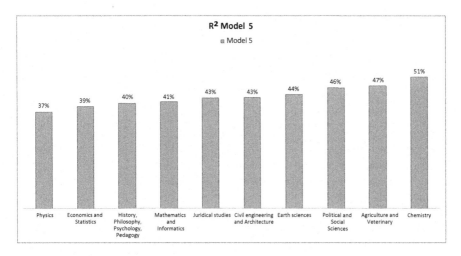

Fig. 9.11 Percentage of R^2 explained in each disciplinary area by the full model

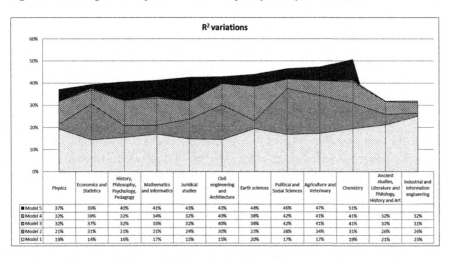

Fig. 9.12 R^2 variations for each model in each disciplinary area

model includes the scientists' ranks and promotions. This increases the R^2 by a minimum of 1 % in industrial and information engineering to a maximum of 21 % in political and social sciences. Being an associate professor or a researcher significantly decreases the amount of money granted compared to full professors in all the disciplinary areas but physics and biology where researchers significantly gain more money, confirming Hypothesis 2. Also, in all the disciplinary areas but mathematics and computer science, physics, and biology there is a significant positive correlation between being funded and obtaining promotions, confirming Hypothesis 3 (Table 9.4).

Table 9.4 Coefficients' values and significance for Model 1 and 2

Discipline	Model 1 Nat. coord	Model 2 Associate	Researcher	Jumprank
Mathematics and computer science	0.342***	−0.818***	0.091	−0.370***
Physics	0.408***	−0.209***	0.144***	−0.167**
Chemistry	0.426***	−0.243***	−0.348***	0.611***
Earth sciences	0.414***	−0.320***	−0.238**	0.783***
Biology	0.316***	−0.200***	0.519***	−0.142***
Agriculture and veterinary	0.420***	−0.037	−0.036	0.739**
Civil engineering and architecture	0.480***	−0.168***	−0.245***	0.757***
Industrial and computer engineering	0.395***	−0.112***	−0.182***	0.559***
Ancient studies, literature and philology, history and art	0.478***	−0.188***	−0.232**	0.620***
History, philosophy, psychology, pedagogy	0.461***	−0.215***	−0.344***	0.653***
Juridical studies	0.463***	−0.345***	−0.647***	0.762***
Economics and statistics	0.491***	−0.135**	−0.170*	0.714***
Political and social sciences	0.575***	−0.243***	−0.355***	0.842***

$*p < .05; **p < .01; ***p < .001$

The third model adds the egonet variables of the micro-level of collaborations, and the R^2 increases by a minimum of 4 % (political and social sciences) to a maximum of 15 % (earth sciences). Homophily of sub-disciplines in collaboration networks is significant for mathematics and computer science, chemistry, industrial and information engineering and ancient studies, which means that the more scientists collaborate with others in the same sub-discipline, the better funded they are. For these areas Hypothesis 4 is confirmed. On the contrary, for earth sciences the more scientists collaborate interdisciplinary, the better funded they are. The real difference, however, is made by brokerage roles: in all the disciplinary areas being a broker is not only positively significant, but the coefficients indicating the amount of money brokers obtain compared to non-brokers are all very high. Brokerage scores are positively and significantly accompanied by closure in all disciplines but physics, civil engineering and political and social sciences, while cohesion is negatively significant for industrial and computer engineering (Table 9.5). Hypothesis 5 is thus confirmed for the areas where cohesion is positively significant.

The fourth model introduces the macro variables of coreness of the University and of betweenness of the sub-disciplines. Both values are positively significant only for chemistry and industrial and computer engineering, while working in a core institution is positively significant also for mathematics and computer science, and negatively significant for physics and working in a central sub-discipline is significant also for economics and statistics (Table 9.6). However, the model does not add any more explanation of the variance in any disciplinary area. Generally speaking, Hypothesis 6 is not confirmed.

The fifth and final model, or full model, introduces the variables of the meso-level, which increase the variance's explanation by a minimum of 1 % in economics

9 Comparing Fields of Sciences: Multilevel Networks of Research...

Table 9.5 Coefficients' values and significance for Model 3

	Model 3		
Discipline	Yules' Q	Broker	Av. degree
Mathematics and computer science	−0.094*	3.104***	0.621***
Physics	0.004	2.387***	0.084
Chemistry	−0.065*	2.799***	0.499***
Earth sciences	0.125**	1.967***	0.668***
Agriculture and veterinary	−0.028	3.504***	0.399**
Civil engineering and architecture	−0.019	2.466***	−0.096
Industrial and computer engineering	−0.046**	1.506***	−1.601***
Ancient studies, literature and philology, history and art	−0.071**	2.408***	0.505**
History, philosophy, psychology, pedagogy	−0.046	2.762***	0.629***
Juridical studies	−0.009	2.596***	0.500*
Economics and statistics	0.011	2.819***	0.549***
Political and social sciences	−0.027	1.657***	0.162

$* p < .05; ** p < .01; *** p < .001$

Table 9.6 Coefficients' values and significance for Model 4

	Model 4	
Discipline	Core	Flow Btw
Mathematics and computer science	0.159**	−0.033
Physics	−0.308*	−0.00
Chemistry	0.095**	0.145**
Earth sciences	0.027	0.010
Agriculture and veterinary	−0.002	−0.051
Civil engineering and architecture	0.053	−0.041
Industrial and computer engineering	0.074***	0.214***
Ancient studies, literature and philology, history and art	0.069	0.094
History, philosophy, psychology, pedagogy	0.077	−0.087
Juridical studies	−0.004	−0.061
Economics and statistics	0.062	0.150**
Political and social sciences	0.109	0.056

$* p < .05; ** p < .01; *** p < .001$

and statistics to a maximum of 11 % for juridical sciences. Overall, scientists working in little ponds (small departments) are significantly more successful than their colleagues working in big ponds, apart from mathematics and computer science and physics, where little fish earn less money than big fish in big ponds. Little fish in big ponds are also less fortunate in agriculture and veterinary and in history, philosophy, psychology, and pedagogy (Table 9.7). Hypothesis 8 is thus not confirmed.

Finally we looked at the values of the parameter ρ in each model and for each disciplinary area, which represent the correlation strength of dependence in the random errors. If the value is significant, it means that the similarity of the amount of money received by each scientist to the amounts received by people s/he

Table 9.7 Coefficients' values and significance for Model 5

Discipline	Model 5		
	BFLP	LFBP	LFLP
Mathematics and computer science	−0.065	−0.511***	−0.641***
Physics	0.041	−0.413***	−0.349***
Chemistry	0.546***	0.049	0.620***
Earth sciences	0.256	−0.108	0.366***
Agriculture and veterinary	0.310***	−0.202**	0.239***
Civil engineering and architecture	0.371***	0.035	0.344***
History, philosophy, psychology, pedagogy	0.531***	−0.150*	0.440***
Juridical studies	0.721***	−0.034	0.767***
Economics and statistics	0.277**	−0.017	0.227**
Political and social sciences	0.529***	0.092	0.553***

$* p < .05; ** p < .01; *** p < .001$

Table 9.8 Values of the ρ parameter for each model in each disciplinary area

Discipline	Model 1	Model 2	Model 3	Model 4	Model 5
Mathematics and computer science	−0.003	−0.003	−0.004	−0.004	−0.004
Physics	−0.048	−0.058	−0.039	−0.041	−0.059
Chemistry	−0.110	−0.080	−0.058	−0.062	−0.082
Earth sciences	−0.046	−0.050	−0.086	−0.083	−0.081
Biology	0.618***	0.612***			
Agriculture and veterinary	−0.001	−0.001	−0.001	−0.001	−0.001
Civil engineering and architecture	−0.001	−0.001	−0.002	−0.002	−0.002
Industrial and computer engineering	0.532***	0.546	0.709***	0.714***	
Ancient studies, literature and philology, history and art	−0.001	−0.001	−0.002	−0.002	
History, philosophy, psychology, pedagogy	−0.001	0.564***	−0.001	−0.001	−0.002
Juridical studies	−0.002	−0.002	−0.002	−0.002	−0.002
Economics and statistics	−0.001	−0.001	−0.002	−0.002	−0.002
Political and social sciences	−0.004	−0.004	−0.004	−0.004	−0.004

$* p < .05; ** p < .01; *** p < .001$

collaborates with explains part of the variance that does not depend from our other independent variables. As we can see in Table 9.8, ρ values are all very minimal and not significant, apart from biology (for which we could only fit up to the second model) and industrial and computer engineering (for which we could not fit the full model). The value is also significant for the second model for history, philosophy, psychology, and pedagogy, although we suspect such values to be an anomaly which requires further investigation.

Discussion

The analysis of the influence of micro, macro, and meso factors on the rate of success of research funding proposals indicates some interesting elements that suggest possible underlying mechanisms which facilitate a successful funding rate. The roles of national coordinators and of brokers are extremely important in obtaining money in every disciplinary area. Along with ranks and promotions, which account for a good portion of variance explanation, what makes a difference for Italian scientists is their ability to establish research collaborations, either by attracting people to work under them (as national coordinators) or by attracting people who do not otherwise collaborate with each other (as brokers). However, disciplinary differences seem to be explained either by individual attributes or by egonets structures, and only rarely by both. The R^2 in disciplines like physics, history, philosophy, psychology and pedagogy, mathematics and computer science and earth sciences is relatively low in the second model (where ranks and promotions are introduced), while it increases 10 % or more in the third model (where egonets variables are introduced). This suggests that for these disciplines the micro structure of collaboration, as in with whom people collaborate, is more important than the position in the professional rankings. On the contrary, disciplines like political and social sciences, economics and statistics, and agriculture and veterinary, and see a higher impact of ranks and promotions compared to egonets properties, indicating that individual attributes count more.

Interestingly, the macro-level of university and sub-disciplines collaborations, represented by descriptive measures of the respective networks, does not explain any of the variance in any disciplinary area. This means that the fact that a department is successful in getting funding does not mean that its scientists will obtain, on average, more money than the ones who work in institutions with fewer collaborations. Likewise, working in sub-disciplines which are more requested for collaborations (as they occupy a central position in the sub-discipline network) do not overall increase the total amount of received funding. Results of the final model, which introduces the meso-level categorizations, suggest that scientists working in large departments may suffer from internal competition more than people working in small departments, and this is especially important for chemistry and juridical studies. Given the fact that the meso-level is measured, on our case, by combining micro-level egonet properties (number of collaborations) with macro-level institutional properties, we can conclude that it is important to take a meso-level of nested characteristics into account, as without this last level of analysis we would have missed the importance of macro-level properties.

Finally, the adoption of the network disturbance model has proven to be useful in testing for the effects of network autocorrelation. In our case, the network effect does not explain any further variance. This suggests that the similarities in the amount of funding between adjacent people do not influence the rate of success. Biology and industrial and computer engineering are worth further investigation, as we could not explain why the autocorrelation effect is significant in these cases. As we already mentioned, the high value in the second model for history, philosophy, psychology, and pedagogy is difficult to explain. We measured the impact of the individual variables (Associate, Researcher, Jumprank) on the ρ, but it becomes significant only when we input the three variables together. Despite these odd results, which require a deeper analysis, the absence of significance of ρ in all other cases suggests that our models are robust, and the error terms are not disturbed by the network effect.

Conclusions

In this chapter we analyzed the mechanisms that lie beyond the structure of research project collaborations in Italian academia. In line with previous results, we found that individual attributes (being a national coordinator, a full professor, and having being promoted) play a role in getting funded. It is however the position of being a broker across otherwise unconnected research groups that makes a difference in the total amount of funding received by a scientist over the years under analysis, in some cases combined with egonet closure. These results confirm not only the previous ones for physicists (Bellotti 2012) and philosophers (Bellotti 2014), but also the importance of looking at individual network properties when analyzing scientific collaborations. Leadership is a characteristic that seems to be related both to career achievements (becoming a full professor) and to the capability of attracting multiple research groups for scientific collaborations.

The importance of adopting a multilevel perspective is indicated by the relevance of the meso categories, which nest individual network data with organizational properties. Despite the lack of impact of macro categories (university and sub-disciplinary affiliations), results -which the analysis of individual characteristics would not be able to account for- show the necessity of controlling for these various nested levels. Also, the similarities of significant properties in explaining successful funding across the various disciplinary areas suggest common structural mechanisms that dominate this specific line of funding in Italian academia.

Our analytical approach is not without limits and problems. In some cases, specifically medicine, biology, ancient studies and industrial and computer engineering, the full model could not be fitted. In the case of the former two disciplinary areas not even the previous, simpler model could be computed. We suspect that the reasons lie in the size of these networks, which obviously poses a problem and a challenge for multilevel analysis. Furthermore, the lack of congruence between nodes in each time observation means that dynamic network analysis (SAOM) cannot be performed on our data. This is another serious limit, as the direction of causality could not be untangled. We cannot therefore explain if it is the previous success in being funded that attract more collaboration and facilitates promotions or vice versa.

Another problem relates to the analysis of the macro-level of sub-disciplinary collaborations, which is limited by the type of variable that describes it. We use flow betweenness because as far as we know it is the only measure of betweenness centrality that deals with valued data. However, this measure is difficult to interpret in the case of research collaborations. We wanted to grasp the characteristic of a discipline that is in high demand among other sub-disciplines (for example, every project in physics is likely to need a theoretical physicists), but flow betweenness, as in the measure of the contribution of each node to all the possible maximum flows between pairs of nodes, does not fully capture this property. Also, the properties of the macro-level of collaborations, represented by coreness and flow betweenness, are only introduced as fixed effects, in line with the requirements of the network disturbance model. It would be interesting to include the effects of their respective groups following the logic of multilevel analysis, but this is not, at this stage, easily combined with our already complicated model.

Finally, both brokerage and closure may be strategically pursued by researchers, but the network data alone do not allow us to observe whether the choices of these structural positions are intentional or are the unintentional outcome of structural possibilities and constraints. Scientists may decide to change the composition of groups because of the unavailability of previous collaborators or because previous collaborations were not satisfactory. They may also switch because they receive more interesting offers or because they want to invest in new topics. In fact, there are many possible reasons for switching, which would be better explored via qualitative methods.

Despite these limits, we believe that our analytical approach successfully models the total amount of funding scientists received for research collaboration in Italian academia. We managed to explain a good amount of variance across all the disciplinary areas, and we think that the strategy of manipulating network data to obtain variables that describe the macro-levels of university and sub-disciplinary affiliations is promising. By deriving the university-by-university and the sub-discipline-by-sub-discipline networks, we were able to account for the nested properties of individual collaborations without having to deal with the problem of the high number of group affiliations. Other ways of measuring such structural properties and more sophisticated analysis of nested dependencies developed could be adopted. We leave these possibilities for future research.

References

Anselin, L., & Hudak, S. (1992). Spatial econometrics in practice: A review of software options. *Regional Science and Urban Economics,* Elsevier, *22*(3), 509–536.
Bellotti, E. (2012). Getting funded. Multi-level network of physicists in Italy. *Social Networks, 34*, 215–229.
Bellotti, E. (2014). *Qualitative networks. Mixed methods in sociological research.* London: Routledge.
Beltrame, L. (2008). La struttura del campo scientifico: una geografia delle traiettorie dei fisici delle particelle. In E. Bellotti, L. Beltrame, & P. Volontè (Eds.), *Il campo sociale della fisica particellare in Italia. uno studio sociologico.* Bolzano: Bolzano University Press.

Borgatti, S. P., Everett, M. G., & Freeman, L. C. (2002). *Ucinet 6 for Windows: Software for social network analysis*. Harvard: Analytic Technologies.
Breiger, R. (1974). The duality of persons and groups. *Social Forces, 53*, 181–190.
Browne, W. J., Goldstein, H., & Rasbash, J. (2001). Multiple membership multiple classification (MMMC) models. *Statistical Modelling, 1*, 103–124.
Burt, R. S. (2005). *Brokerage and closure. An introduction to social capital*. Oxford: Oxford University Press.
Butts, C. (2007). *sna: Tools for social network analysis*. Statnet Project http://statnetproject.org/, Seattle, WA. R package version 1.5, http://cran.r-project.org/package=sna
Cliff, A. D., & Ord, J. K. (1975). *Spatial autocorrelation*. London: Pion.
Daraganova, G., & Robins, G. (2013). Autologistic actor attribute models. In D. Lusher, J. Koskinen, & G. Robins (Eds.), *Exponential random graph models for social networks*. New York: Cambridge University Press.
Doreian, P. D. (1992). Models of network effects on social actors. In L. C. Freeman, D. R. White, & A. K. Kimball Romney (Eds.), *Research methods in social network analysis*. New Brunswick: Transaction Pub.
Dow, M. M., White, D. R., & Burton, M. L. (1983). Multivariate modeling with interdependent network data. *Behavior Science Research, 17*, 216–245.
Dow, M. M., Burton, M. L., White, D. R., & Reitz, K. P. (1984). Galton's problem as network autocorrelation. *American Ethnologist, 11*, 754–770.
Erosheva, E. A., & Fienberg, S. E. (2011). Mixed membership models. In M. Lovric (Ed.), *International encyclopedia of statistical science* (pp. 824–826). Berlin: Springer.
Fararo, T. J., & Doreian, P. (1984). Tripartite structural analysis: Generalizing the Breiger–Wilson formalism. *Social Networks, 6*, 141–175.
Freeman, L. C. (1979). Centrality in social networks: Conceptual clarification. *Social Networks, 1*(3), 215–239.
Freeman, L. C., Borgatti, S. P., & White, D. R. (1991). Centrality in valued graphs: A measure of betweenness based on network flow. *Social Networks, 13*(2), 141–154.
Lazega, E., Jourda, M. T., Mounier, L., & Stofer, R. (2008). Catching up with big fish in the big pond? Multi-level network analysis through linked design. *Social Networks, 30*, 157–176.
Leenders, R. T. A. J. (2002). Modeling social influence through network autocorrelation: Constructing the weight matrix. *Social Networks, 24*, 21–47.
Naroll, R. (1961). Two solutions to Galton's problem. *Philosophy of Science, 28*, 15–39.
Naroll, R. (1965). Galton's problem: The logic of cross-cultural analysis. *Social Research, 32*, 428–451.
Ord, K. (1975). Estimation methods for models of spatial interaction. *Journal of the American Statistical Association, 70*, 120–126.
Schaefer, J. (Ed.). (1974). *Studies in cultural diffusion: Galton's problem*. New Haven: HRAFlex Books.
Snijders, T. A. B., & Bosker, R. J. (2012). *Multilevel analysis: An introduction to basic and advanced multilevel modelling* (2nd ed.). London: Sage.
Steglich, C. E. G., Snijders, T. A. B., & Pearson, M. (2010). Dynamic networks and behavior: Separating selection from influence. *Sociological Methodology, 40*(1), 329–393.
Tranmer, M., Steel, D., & Browne, W. J. (2014). Multiple-membership multiple-classification models for social network and group dependences. *Journal of the Royal Statistical Society: Series A (Statistics in Society), 177*(Part 2), 439–455.
Wang, P., Robins, G., Pattison, P., & Lazega, E. (2013). Exponential random graph models for multilevel networks. *Social Networks, 35*(1), 96–115.
Wang, W., Neuman, E. J., & Newman, D. A. (2014). Statistical power of the social network autocorrelation model. *Social Networks, 38*, 88–99.
White, D. R., Burton, M. L., & Dow, M. M. (1981). Sexual division of labor in African agriculture: A network autocorrelation analysis. *American Anthropologist, 83*, 824–849.

Chapter 10
Market as a Multilevel System

Julien Brailly, Guillaume Favre, Josiane Chatellet, and Emmanuel Lazega

Globalized markets require long distance partnerships between companies, "global pipelines" as Bathelt and Schuldt (2008) call them. But what kind of relationships do these partnerships represent? Behind each partnership between companies there are always inter-individual ties (Gulati 1995). If a partnership between two organizations necessitates inter-individual collaboration at the beginning of a contracting process between companies, the more a partnership is repeated between two companies, the more it breaks away from the inter-individual relationship to become an inter-organizational tie that does not need specific acquaintances between its members (Lorenz 1999). In order to understand how international ties are created between companies one should study the coordination and the complex interdependencies between these two kinds of actors and these two levels of actions: individuals and organizations.

Granovetter's (1985) article on embeddedness is famous for asserting at a high level of generality that economic phenomena take place in social structures and are shaped by social networks. Individuals do not act as atoms socially, their behaviour is not entirely defined by macro-structures, and their actions depend on a relational context. In the area of economic sociology, research has exposed the importance of social networks in markets, indicating the relevance of relational

---

J. Brailly (✉)
Swinburne University of Technology, Center for Transformative Innovation, Melbourne, Australia
e-mail: jbrailly@swin.edu.au

G. Favre
University of Toulouse Jean-Jaurès, LISST-Cers CNRS, Toulouse, France
e-mail: guillaume.favre@univ-tlse2.fr

J. Chatellet
Université Paris-Dauphine, IRISSO-CNRS, PSL, Paris, France

E. Lazega
Institut d'Etudes Politiques de Paris, SPC, CSO-CNRS, 19 rue Amélie, 75007 Paris, France

structures for the emergence of economic activities (for syntheses of the state of the art, see for example Granovetter and Swedberg 1992; Brass et al. 2004). Many have also questioned the value of such a general notion of embeddedness of economic activities in social structures (for example Burt 1992; Swedberg 1997; Lazega 1996, 2001) in order to go beyond a mechanistic interaction between these kinds of relationships. Depending on the level of analysis, two approaches can be distinguished. One focuses on inter-organizational networks, showing, for example, that companies are embedded in a web of commercial relationships but also of alliances and business partnerships that affect their performances, successes, or chances of survival (Powell 1996; Powell et al. 2005; Uzzi 1996, 1997). Another approach studies informal relationships such as friendship, advice, information exchange or collaboration between entrepreneurs at the inter-individual level (Krackhardt 1994; Ingram and Roberts 2000; Lazega and Mounier 2002). Such approaches aim to reveal informal social structures in order to underline the role of social resources and social capital in economic activities. In most handbooks in economic sociology or social network analysis (for example, Smelser and Swedberg 2010; Knoke 2013; Scott and Carrington 2011), inter-organizational and inter-individual networks are treated separately as if they were different topics. This separation is due to the fact that much of existing research in this area focuses only on one level of analysis at a time.

Both approaches start with the same question: how do markets and economic activities work in practice? But by separating the two levels of analysis, particularly in a context of globalized markets in which ties are long-distance relationships, they miss the global process of emergence of economic activities and tie formation at each level (deal-making, for example). From our perspective economic activities and markets are influenced by both levels. A deal between two companies, which is an inter-organizational tie, depends on inter-individual relationships and *vice versa*. Economic relationships such as deals between two organizations and informal relationships between their members are interdependent. To explore this dual dimension, a multilevel social networks framework has been developed by Lazega and his co-authors (2007, 2008). This approach is based on the study of multi-level networks observing two superposed and partially nested, interdependent levels of agency, an inter-organizational system of action and an inter-individual one.

Supposing that these levels are nested does not imply that they evolve symmetrically and in sync. As emphasized by Lazega (2012, 2013, 2014), the co-evolution of the two levels is complex, dynamic, and can be partially disconnected if not asynchronous –raising the issue of the costs of synchronization (Lazega and Penalva 2011). This is a problem of agency, both individual and collective. Different levels may not evolve and change simultaneously. Structural organization of each level as well as the attributes or context explaining tie formation at each level can be different. We argue that this is why a multilevel approach is of interest: in order to reframe the issue of embeddedness. The challenge is to understand how social systems at both levels co-evolve and how actors at both levels coordinate to generate the socio-economic structure of the market. What specific multilevel social processes construct and explain the structure of an economic milieu?

Building upon this framework we study network formation at each level of a specific market. We show that inter-individual and inter-organizational networks are partly interdependent but also that different processes emerge at each level. Our empirical case is a trade fair for television programs in Eastern Europe. In this trade fair sellers and buyers of TV programs (distributors and TV channels) meet once a year to discuss contracts, make deals, keep informed about new films, series, and game shows, and observe market evolution. We study the informal exchange of information between trade-fair attendees and formal deal ties between their companies by examining network formation at each level. We find that these networks are heavily interdependent but that each level has its own specific processes. We emphasize that the process of tie formation between two organizations has a different contexts than that between two individuals in terms of temporality. We conclude by showing that, in spite of different temporalities, the two levels coevolve.

Reframing Embeddedness as a Multilevel Issue

From Embeddedness to Multilevel Hypotheses

Asserting that economic action is embedded in relational structure leads to an explanation of how this embeddedness works. According to what can be labeled a "contractualist" approach (Powell 1996; Powell et al. 2005; Uzzi 1996, 1997) it is possible to reconstruct a deal network between a set of organizations to reveal the economic social structure of an industry or a market. Ethnographies of social interactions between market participants emphasize, for example, the need for trust to sign a contract (Uzzi 1997). Such an approach only focuses on one kind of relationship. But, embeddedness assumes the existence of at least two kinds of relationships: economic and social. Following the work of Granovetter (1973, 1985) some researchers have developed multiplex models that include both kinds of relationships (for example: Mizruchi and Stearns 2001). From this perspective, only one kind of actor is examined, either individual or organizational, or in our terminology one level of action. From our perspective, it can be helpful to consider two categories of actors: individuals (with social relationships) and organizations (with economic relationships).

In our proposed reframed embeddedness approach, the organizational level is more than an organizational contextualization of inter-individual action, as in traditional multilevel statistical approaches (Bryk and Raudenbush 1992; Goldstein 1995; Snijders and Bosker 1999) or in the social network multilevel analysis of Snijders and Baeverldt (2003). It is populated by actors who act and create a context for their actions and interactions at the individual level. This conceptual position is helpful in exploring the emergence and functioning of a market. Indeed, an organization should not be conceived as a unified and homogenous social object, but as a social system built collectively by a heterogeneous set of individuals (Crozier and Friedberg 1977; Friedberg 1997). A deal between two companies can be looked at as a set of relationships between individuals. Let us imagine two organizations of significant size in a market, represented respectively by a sales manager and an acquisition manager. These two individuals have the opportunity to meet and agree on the object of a transaction, the main aspects of the contract, and possibly the price. The contract will then be submitted to the higher-level management of their respective companies for approval. The legal department will define the details of the contract; the technical department will manage the dispatching of the product; the finance department will bill and track the payment; and so on. It will obviously be the same on the buyer's side. In short, once an agreement is reached between a buyer and a seller, organizational machinery is set in motion, and we are no longer able to assign this relationship to the sales and acquisitions managers. The personal relationship between the buyer and the seller does not disappear. These individuals will keep in touch. They initiated the contract and it is often likely that, if it were to be renewed, it would be at the initiative of one of them. However this relationship moves on to a different level and becomes inter-organizational because it involves other actors and their hierarchical organizations. In the meantime, this inter-organizational relationship could become a context for other members of both organizations to create inter-personal relationships – as described by concepts such as extended relational capital and embedded brokerage (Lazega et al. 2013). Therefore, it is necessary to examine this duality between inter-individual and inter-organizational relationships in order to understand these transactions, to look at both levels in the same socio-economic space, without conflating them.

An organizational network cannot be reduced to the basic concatenation of the inter-individual network of its employees, especially when looking at international corporations. Indeed, in such organizations, decision-making processes and information circulation are very long and involve a multiplicity of persons. In addition, it is often difficult to identify who represents the organization for a specific task. One of the contributions of intra-organizational network analysis is precisely the attempt to reveal the informal structure behind the formal organizational chart and to specify the social processes characterizing this organization as a social milieu (Lazega 2001). Such processes streamline individual action and show that the inter-organizational milieu represents a specific level of collective action (Lazega 2009; Lazega and Penalva 2011).

By taking into account together or separately different levels of analysis and different kinds of relationships, we can define different levels of complexity of what could be called the "embeddedness hypothesis," that represent each level with its elementary structural unit. Figure 10.1 summarizes these different hypotheses. In this contribution, we will explore the higher levels of complexity of this "multilevel network hypothesis" as previously defined. As a consequence, we consider the market as a social *meta-system* constituted by two levels of agency. It is created by the superimposition of at least two networks of different levels which are partially nested. That implies two different hypotheses (Brailly and Lazega 2012). First, as in traditional social network analysis, a *horizontal structural dependency hypothesis*

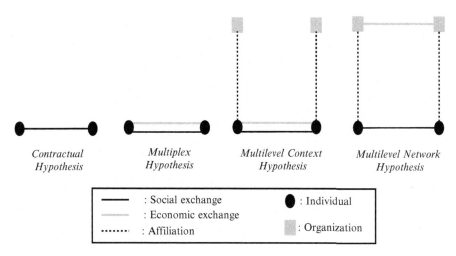

Fig. 10.1 Increasing complexity of the reframed embeddedness hypothesis

within both levels: actors at each level act in a social context and can meet. Second, a *vertical structural dependency hypothesis* between the levels: the individual network partly depends on the network of his/her company and *vice versa*. These levels of actions are partially nested. Therefore, for each level, specific structural processes emerge and explain the network morphology. But in the meantime, levels are interdependent and influence each other. We can translate these ideas into the following general and descriptive hypotheses to be tested empirically:

Hypothesis 1 Network morphologies are different at each level (Structural Morphology).

Hypothesis 2 The structures of different levels influence each other (Multilevel Embeddedness).

In order to test these first hypotheses, we use complete networks as defined by Wasserman and Faust (1994). The *horizontal complexity* of a social space requires considering that the social context is not only an exogenous factor influencing actors' behaviour, but an outcome emerging through social processes produced by these actors (Pattison and Robins 2004). Rather than decompose the network into a set of dyads, *Exponential Random Graph Models* (ERGM) contextualize these links in their neighborhood, for example centrality, dyadic, or triadic effects (Wasserman and Pattison 1996; Robins et al. 2005; Snijders et al. 2006; Lusher et al. 2013). For the *vertical complexity*, we need to take into account a feedback between these two levels, for which Breiger's "dual" approach (1974) is usually considered to be the starting point. Using two-mode networks, it is possible to construct two one-mode networks by derivation from the affiliations links: groups are linked together if they share at least one individual and individuals are linked if they belong together in at least one group. Whereas the dual approach focuses on link between levels, Lazega et al. (2007, 2008) proposed a method that articulates both kinds of complexity. This approach analyzes simultaneously two levels of agency synthesized in partly nested complete networks articulated with affiliation links. This method helps to preserve the vertical complexity of social systems. As a consequence, this work aims to contribute to this Multilevel Network Analysis (MNA) research program (Lazega and Mounier 2002), rather than to the Multilevel Analysis of Networks (MAN).

This framework is useful for analyzing markets and economic activities. Following Lazega et al. (2013), it is possible to explore the impact of multilevel relationships on the performance of actors. These multilevel relationships are an opportunity to expand an individual's personal network with the relations of his/her company (it is easier for an individual to contact another who works in a different company if their companies have a relationship). In markets, individuals can take advantage of the reputation of their organization. Conversely, an organization can take advantage of the popularity of its employees, which could help to explain hiring and firing strategies. This "multilevel" reputation effect can maintain, exacerbate or reduce status inequalities between actors at both levels. It also makes it possible to reveal forms of hidden costs introduced by other levels. As emphasized by Archer (2000) or Lazega (2013, 2014), the co-evolution of two levels is complex, dynamic, and partially disconnected.

The Multilevel Embeddedness Hypotheses in the Context of a Trade Fair

To formulate further hypotheses and illustrate this approach, we use the case of a trade fair for the distribution of television programs in Eastern Europe. Fairs can be considered as small market arenas in which sellers and buyers can meet through face-to-face contact. These events are temporary organizations where knowledge about the market emerges and circulates among attendees and enables a collective learning process between firms (Bathelt and Schuldt 2008). These events also play a crucial role in the construction of markets by fostering the emergence of a social environment and the production of specific norms and values (Aspers and Darr 2011).

From "Same time next year"...

Many authors in geographic economics and management have studied these events Bathelt et al. (2004); Bathelt and Schuldt (2008, 2010), (Schuldt and Bathelt 2011), which help companies in the globalized economy to identify new partners, suppliers, or clients from different parts of the world. The main argument is that these international ties – or *global pipelines* – do not require a permanent co-localisation, but only a temporary and recurrent co-localisation that concerns only a few steps in the deal-making process. According to these authors, these *global pipelines* are created during international trade fairs that bring together in the same place, for a few days, the *microcosm* of an industry. They emphasize that this is the only way for them to have a global, quick and precise vision of the whole market, and to compare themselves to their competitors. From the attendees' point of view, attending these events is relatively costly, but it is a good way to meet new and key people (Seringhaus and Rosson 1998). Moreover, the more companies attend these events, the more their upstream preparation costs (prospection, communication, logistics...) will decrease (Power and Jansson 2008). If the main goals of the companies during these trade fairs are to sell and buy or to create new partnerships, these events are also symbolic places where reputation is constructed (Seringhaus and Rosson 1998, 2001). Indeed, if a firm attends a trade fair regularly, it could be considered as a signal that the firm is thriving. The goal can also be simply "*to be there*" and to be seen (Power and Jansson 2008).

This literature considers that the main advantage of these events is that information circulates and is built through this circulation within the global network, which generates knowledge pools. It produces a *global buzz*[1] that provides learning opportunities during and after the event, and thus supports the maintenance of long-distance business relationship (Maskell et al. 2006; Power and Jansson 2008). In parallel, these authors give a structural content to the global buzz concept: "*During a fair, information is constantly transmitted from one agent to another. This process is repeatedly interpreted, evaluated and enriched with additional relevant information and knowledge. The decisive point is that while acquiring new knowledge, participants act simultaneously as both recipients and broadcasters of global buzz. The potential advantages and benefits of applying this knowledge become clearer as the trade fair evolves and interpretations are drawn from the variety of meetings*" (Bathelt and Schuldt 2010, p. 1962).

Above all, many authors agree that trade fairs are spaces for individual and organizational network construction. During these events, attendees increase the size of their personal network with new prospects and refresh, develop or simply maintain existing contacts: "*Relationships need to be built over time and nurtured through repeated contact at different events and that they met the same people again and again at the fairs*" (Power and Jansson 2008, p. 432). This dyadic experience implies personalization of the relationships between buyers and sellers – especially because the actors already know one part of mutual expectations – and allows for establishing trust ties between organizations (Power and Jansson 2008; Maskell

---

[1] Parallel to the *local buzz* of permanent clusters (Storper and Venables 2004), temporary clusters generate *global buzz* if the event combines the following conditions: explicit co-participation to maximize face-to-face interactions; possibilities for observation; existence of practice and epistemic communities from different parts of the world; dense and multiplex socio-economic relationships (Bathelt and Schuldt 2010).

et al. 2006). The fact that this event exists is proof that a deal-making process that requires long-distance coordination also requires occasional, but regular, face-to-face meetings. As a result a high frequency of co-participation of two actors in the same event increases their chances of creating social and economic relationships (Maskell et al. 2006).

Because inter-organizational partnerships need trust, information, and mutual knowledge, the recurrence of co-participation reduces risks and facilitates inter-organizational links: Maskell et al. (2006) coin this recurrent event *Same time next year*. This leads to the next multilevel hypothesis:

Hypothesis 3 The more actors co-participate in an event over a long time period, the higher the probability of having a relationship (Same time next year co-participation)

... To "Next time this year"

However, one could consider that the previous approaches decontextualize the event and separate it from all the other trade fairs bringing together the members of the same industry. Indeed, as underlined by Power and Jansson (2008) many trade fairs are organized in the same industry during a single year, and often organizations and individuals attend several such events. This repetition of events gives influence to the work of individual actors. They have to prepare the logistics, communications, and prospection; travel and invest several days in attending the fair; follow-up with contacts after the event; and then prepare for the next trade fair (Power and Jansson 2008). The different events are not isolated from each other; actors take into account this diversity of events and prepare their work by anticipating each of these international meetings. Moreover actors meet with each other and create relationships at each event. But many of these meetings can overlap. As a result, all the trade fairs of an industry are connected through the work of the actors but also through their social and economic relationships. Trade fairs are part of an annual global circuit and *"are less temporary clusters than they are cyclical clusters; they are complexes of overlapping spaces that are scheduled and arranged in such a way that spaces can be reproduced, reenacted, and renewed over time"* (Power and Jansson 2008, p. 423). Social and economic relationships and reputation during the cycle of the temporary clusters connect these events. Therefore, to the *Same time next year* hypothesis, we must add a *Next time this year hypothesis*:

Hypothesis 4 The more actors co-participate in different events during a short period of time, the higher the probability of having a relationship (Next time this year co-participation)

One could detect a tension between Hypotheses 3 and 4. Power and Jansson consider that the greater the instability of consumer tastes in an industry, the more knowledge is contingent and specific to an event (because the fashion cycle is shorter). Therefore, because trust among actors and the construction of reputation are long-term processes while the acquisition of relevant information is a short-term process, there may be a tension between them. The current literature does not separate explicitly the impact of co-participation at each level. This is why we aim to answer the following questions: what temporality is more important in explaining a deal between two companies or a relationship between two individuals? *Same time next year* or *Next time this year*? Above all, with respect to our multilevel embeddedness hypotheses, is it the same for both levels?

A Trade Fair for TV Programs in Eastern and Central Europe

Multilevel Network Data Collection During a Trade Fair . . .

The trade fair that we study focuses on the distribution of TV programs. Sellers are the sales managers of TV program distributors and producers who come from diverse parts of the world (especially from Western Europe, Asia, Northern and Southern America). They attend the event to sell copyrights for broadcasting of TV programs to acquisition or programming managers from regional and local TV channels (Central and Eastern European). Concretely, the event is organized once a year in a prestigious hotel in Budapest (Hungary). Sellers sit in booths with television sets to present their catalogues of films, series and shows. The buyers' goal is to select programs that will match their audience and perhaps bring new viewers. They walk around the location to visit sellers and choose in which programs to invest. Some companies are represented by several sellers or buyers who each specialize in a particular type of programs (for example: animation, series, or documentaries) and/or specialize in a specific geographic area (for example Balkan countries, central Europe, central Asia). Such companies are international media groups or the most important TV channels in specific countries. Generally only one employee interacts with each commercial partner.

The work of these sales and acquisitions representatives is clearly relational. Relationships between buyers and sellers are very personalized; they know and meet with each other regularly (or at least try to). Once a contract is signed, the relationship is often reactivated in order to renegotiate the rights, or prepare for a new transaction. These partnerships are often repeated until a distributor becomes an official supplier of a channel. Their job consists also in being aware of international and local trends in audiovisual markets: which are the successful programs? What are the latest deals? What is broadcast in which country? and so forth.

For sellers (but also for buyers), obtaining informal information is strategic because it is a good way to target potential clients and to understand their needs, their resources, their reliability, and their purchasing and bargaining power. For buyers, trade fairs are an opportunity to obtain information about market trends, new programs and new technologies. Generally, informal information is a good way to identify new commercial opportunities. As a consequence, to explore the construction of partnerships and deals between organizations it is necessary to take into consideration relationships between individuals and especially informal information exchanges.

The data that we present here were collected during the 2011 trade fair. Officially, 911 individuals were present – 451 buyers and 337 sellers – affiliated to 510 companies. Because it was impossible for us to collect the responses of 911 individuals with questionnaires during the 3 days of the trade fairs, we chose to focus on the animation segment of this market (buyers and sellers of animated programs). Animation is one of the three categories of audio-visual products (the other two are fiction and documentaries) and can be defined as a sequence of pictures giving the illusion of movement.

This choice follows both nominalist and realist strategies developed by Laumann et al. (1989). A *realist strategy* is based on the actor's perceptions of the boundaries of their milieu. Concerning the audiovisual field, people are aware of these boundaries. As emphasized by Havens (2003), buzz and information concerning a specific segment in this field are not relevant for another (for example business information in the adult program segment of the market is not relevant in the children's programming segment). The animation segment is a distinct action system. Indeed, buying the famous format[2] *Who wants to be a millionaire?* is different from buying products such as *The Lion King* or a Miyazaki film. For example, one interviewee declared that "in animation, you must have a child's soul". As a result, the definition of the boundaries based on this animation segment is relevant for a realist strategy.

The *nominalist strategy* is based on a researcher's theoretical choices. Firstly, we want to study a stable segment in terms of volume of exchanges. As long as there are children, there will be a demand for animation contents. In addition, this segment is characterized by a strong heterogeneity of business models. Companies could be commercial or public television stations, independent buyers, small producers, distributors, or huge companies such as Disney.

To select individuals and organizations interested in this segment, before the trade fair in 2011, we visited the websites of all the attendees. We selected all the sites that had at least one animation program in their catalogue (if they are distributors) or in their program schedule (if they are television channels). With these criteria we selected a list of 261 individuals affiliated to 184 organizations and obtained responses from 128 individuals (49 %) affiliated to 109 companies (60 %).[3] As we can see in Tables 10.1 and 10.2, Central European buyers and English-speaking media groups are underrepresented. Two reasons explain that: firstly, they had

---

[2] A TV program that is written on paper but has not yet been actually produced.

[3] A team of eight persons (four sociologists and four hostesses) collected for each individual their information exchange network and the contract network of their organization through face-to-face interviews (20 min on average) during the trade fair. In order to improve the response rate after the event, we also tried to reach attendees by fax, phone, mail, email and internet.

many meetings during the fair, so they were busy; secondly, some of them have specific clauses in their employment contract prohibiting answering this kind of questionnaire.

We designed a multilevel study of this event. In our perspective, the first level of analysis is composed of individual buyers and sellers and the second level is the companies. We asked the following sociometric questions and asked the respondents to check, in the list of the studied population, with whom they had each kind of relationship:

Question 1 Trade fairs such as MIPTV[4] or [studied event] are good ways to get access to informal information concerning competitors, suppliers, clients, successful programs or trends in the market. Among the persons in the following list, from whom did you obtain this kind of advice or information during or before [studied event]? *(Could you please check their names in the "ADVICE" column)*

Question 2 Among the people in the following list, with whom did you make a deal since the last [studied event], 12 months ago? *(Could you please check their names in the "DEAL" column?)*

Question 1 corresponds to the informal inter-individual network. The average degree for the studied population is 5.55; the median is 5 for indegree and 4 for outdegree. This network contains 85 mutual links (24 % reciprocity rate). Among the 261 persons selected, the response rate of the 10 % most quoted individuals is 60 %, and 55 % for the 25 % most quoted individuals. Compared to the global response rate (49 %), we can say that the "élite" of the inter-individual network is somewhat better represented in our dataset.

Question 2 corresponds to the inter-organizational network, which represents the economic structure of the milieu. Because they are sales and acquisitions representatives, these individuals are aware the deals closed by their company. Although the answers are provided by individuals, this network of contracts can be considered an inter-organizational network. Indeed, approximately 45 % of individuals quoted organization names and not individuals' names. During interviews, they justify this with several reasons: several individuals and divisions (accounting, legal, sales) could be involved during the deal-making process; the deal could be signed with other colleagues, previously in charge of this area, during negotiations initiated years ago. As a consequence, we described this network by organizations. It contains 347 deals (average degree $=$ 6.34 and median $=$ 5). Among the 184 organizations selected, the response rate of the 10 % most quoted is 95 %, and 83 % for the 25 % most quoted companies. Compared to the general response rate (60 %), we can say that the "élite" of the inter-organizational network is better represented.

---

[4]MIPTV is the most important TV program trade fair in the world. It will be described more precisely in the next section.

As Lazega et al. (2008) did, we articulate these levels with affiliation links between individuals and organizations. The following (Fig. 10.2) represents the "meta-system" of the three networks: information exchange between individuals; deals between companies; and affiliations. We can easily observe two dimensions of structural dependencies: horizontally, within each level, and vertically between the two levels.

...Included in a Global Series of Similar Events

This trade fair is one of many taking place in the world. The TV programs distribution sector is characterized by the importance of fairs, festivals, and conferences that bring stakeholders of the profession together in the same place during a few days (Havens 2003, 2007). Especially for sellers, the TV programs market is globalized and these events are organized frequently all around the world.

In order to study the impact of temporary co-localization at both levels, we must take into consideration the plurality of these events. To begin with, festivals and trade fairs can be distinguished. Festivals constitute cooperation and quality evaluation settings, whereas trade fairs are more competitive and commercial places. This distinction is theoretical. For example, the *Cannes Festival* organizes the film market, and the most important trade fair, the *Marché International des Programmes de Télévision* (International Market of TV Programs – MIPTV) reserves a market space for coproduction. Two other dimensions must be introduced: the types of products that are exchanged (films, animation, documentaries) and the geographical origin of one side of the market (e.g.: buyers from Asia or sellers from France).

Because our study focuses on Central and Eastern Europe and the animation segment, we can be more thorough for all the events related to these categories globally. We selected 19 other events for which – when possible – we collected the list of attendees at each level. Based on these data, we created three different co-participation networks at both levels. First, we selected the MIPTV and MIPCOM participation data, which are the world most important generalist and non-specialized trade fairs in the TV program distribution market. They gather on average 12,000 participants. We treat the co-participation to these events separately (MIP variable). Second, we added up the participation data of 17 other events that took place at the most 1 year before "our" trade fair at each level to test the *Next time same year* hypothesis. Third, we added up co-participation data for the five previous events of "our" trade fair at each level to test the *Same time next year* hypothesis. In the next two sections we test our hypotheses at both levels separately with an ERGM estimation.[5] The question is how co-participation can shed light on multilevel embeddedness. What multilevel social process is implied?

---

[5] ERGM models presented here are estimated with PNet (Wang et al. 2006).

10 Market as a Multilevel System

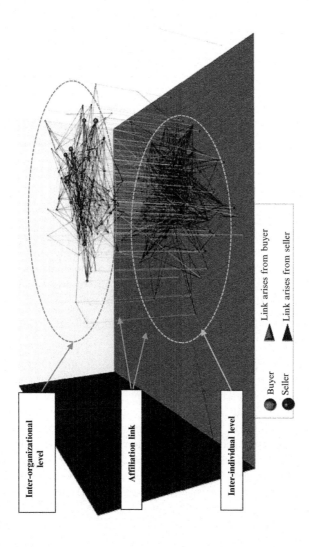

Fig. 10.2 Visualization of the multilevel social network of the trade fair

Different Temporalities Between Levels

Inter-organizational Level: Same Time Next Year in an Oligopoly with Fringes

We consider here the inter-organizational deals network composed of 109 companies (symmetric network). As previously mentioned, we suppose that specific social mechanisms occur at each level (hypothesis 1). Concerning the inter-organizational level, we follow Benhamou (2004) and her definition of the audiovisual field as an oligopoly with fringes. This means that a limited number of very large companies dominate the market: in network terminology, they are very "popular," and this explains the highly skewed degree distribution in this network. At the global scale, this "hyper core" is made up of the major companies. This kind of oligopoly is characterized by a high density within the core: popular actors exchange intensively together.

In order to investigate this, we ran the core/periphery algorithm of Borgatti and Everett (2000), available in UCINET, and obtained a core composed of 34 organizations. The mean centrality of the organizations in this core is 12.2 against 3.7 for the periphery. Moreover, the density within this core is 23.2 % as opposed to 2.2 % within the periphery. Organizations in this core are quite heterogeneous in terms of business models and geographical origins. Anglophile media groups and commercial TV stations are overrepresented in the fair. Some small companies, such as independent buyers or distribution specialists, are also in this core. We can thus reformulate hypothesis H1 for the inter-organizational level:

H1.1: Structural Morphology The inter-organizational network represents an oligopoly market

In order to test our hypotheses, we included in the estimation the following data as dyadic covariates. At the inter-organizational level, multilevel embeddedness (H2) can be captured by the effect of the shrunk advice network by organization (equal to 1 if the affiliate individuals exchange advice during or before the event, regardless of the orientation of the link). The *Same time next year* co-participation hypothesis (H3) can be approached through the number of co-participations between companies in the five previous events (max = 5). In a similar way, *Next time this year* co-participation (H4) is approximated by the number of co-participations between companies at the 17 other events as dyadic covariates (max = 5). We test these hypotheses by controlling the effect of the economic category of the actors (in the deal network, the majority of relationships are naturally between buyers and sellers), of geography (because of the existence of quotas of national production, deals between companies from the same geographical areas are more frequent), and of co-participation in the two generalist events (MIP).

Table 10.1 represents dyadic and Markov high-order models for this symmetric network. The first column reports the results of the baseline model, including only exogenous control effects. Because it is a contract network, most of the links are

Table 10.1 ERG model estimates of structural and actor-relation effects of inter-organizational deal network

	Model 1	Model 2	Model 3
Structural dependencies			
Density	−3.0979 (0.159)*	−4.445 (0.206)*	−7.542 (0.553)*
Alternating k-star (lambda = 2)	–	–	0.7309 (0.152)*
Alternating k-two-paths (lambda = 4)	–	–	0.0597 (0.009)*
Baseline effects			
Economic category (Interaction)	−1.6566 (0.25)*	−1.1507 (0.268)*	−1.189 (0.269)*
Economic category (Activity)	0.6481 (0.169)*	0.3557 (0.19)	0.583 (0.184)*
Geographical origin (Matching)	0.6734 (0.166)*	0.3092 (0.19)	0.3494 (0.181)
Co-participation effects			
MIP (Interaction)	–	0.286 (0.074)*	0.1496 (0.059)*
17 other events in 2011 (Dyad Covar.)	–	0.1759 (0.101)	0.0867 (0.101)
5 previous events (Dyad Covar.)	–	0.2418 (0.037)*	0.1203 (0.031)*
Multilevel embeddedness effect			
Advice link between affiliate individuals (Dyad Covar)	–	2.0851 (0.116)*	1.9103 (0.116)*

Note: Effects with a star are significant with a t-ratio less than 0.05 (approached Wald test (Koskinen and Daraganova 2013)). For structural effects visualization, see Appendix 1

between the two sides of the market: buyers and sellers. Organizations coming from the same geographic area closed more deals together, but this effect disappears when we introduce the structural dependencies (model M3).

The second column reports the results of the dyadic model with baseline effects and the embeddedness and co-participation covariates (hypotheses 2, 3 and 4). This model shows that regular co-participation in the same event over the long term has a positive and significant effect on deal making (*Same time next year*). Co-participation in the biggest world trade fairs has a significant impact in this dyadic model. Above all, co-participation in 20 other events during the year before "our" event does not have a significant impact. We can conclude that it is the historical and long-term frequency of contacts that explains deals between companies, and not short-term frequency regardless of the context: *Same time next year* rather than *Next time this year*. The last dyadic covariate shows that the multilevel embeddedness hypothesis is the strongest exogenous effect in this model. An information exchange link between individuals facilitates deal making between their respective companies.

The last column reports the results of the general ERG model with structural high-order effects and the effects corresponding to the previous hypotheses. We notice that except for geographic homophily, which disappears, all of the previous observations are validated. Concerning the endogenous effects, the *alternating k-star* parameter shows a skewed degree distribution. Some organizations are very active in this deal network. The fact that the triadic effect has a positive parameter shows a concentration of ties in some specific parts of the graph (Pattison and Robins 2004; Snijders et al. 2006). But here, triadic closure is rarer because this is a deal network which implies few ties among sellers or among buyers. However the concentration of the tetradic configurations indicates the existence of some dense parts of the graph. Here, *alternating k-two-path* is significant and above all sufficient (with the star parameter) to fit the other network statistic, especially the triadic configuration (see goodness of fit for this model in Appendix 2). In addition, the weighting coefficient for this effect shows a highly skewed two-path distribution, and then a concentration of the links in a few sub regions of the graph, which creates a core/periphery structure. We can say that some companies are very active and have many deals with each other; in other words, the same popular sellers close many deals with the same popular buyers. This is an oligopolistic structure.

To sum up, the inter-organizational network corresponds to an oligopolistic market that is embedded in the inter-individual relations and in which the deal is explained by the previous co-localisations in the same context.

Inter-individual Level: Next Time This Year in a Coopetition Milieu

We consider here the inter-individual information exchange network composed of 128 individuals (oriented network). As mentioned above, we suppose that each level has a specific structural organization (hypothesis 1). Following Ingram and Roberts (2000), we can observe collaboration within the sellers' side. Because we study a business-to-business market, we think the buyers' side is more structured than in a business-to-consumer market. Buyers can also exchange information. Even if two actors are competitors, they can collaborate. This is why we think that the whole system is characterized by *coopetition* (Brandenburger and Nalebuff 2011). This neologism composed of competition and cooperation refers to the fact that actors who could be considered to be competitors actually collaborate (Ingram and Roberts 2000; Lazega 2001; Éloire 2010). We can illustrate this phenomenon in our data with the fact that among sellers the density of information exchange is 2.6 %, while 2.3 % among buyers. We can thus reformulate hypothesis H1 for the inter-individual level:

H1.2: Structural Morphology The inter-individual network represents a coopetitive social milieu

If the structure is different, the impact of the exogenous effects can be also different. In order to test hypotheses H1, H2, H3 and H4, we include the following data as dyadic covariates in the estimation of the models. At the inter-individual level, multilevel embeddedness (H2) can be captured by the expanded deals network by individuals (equal to 1 if the affiliate organizations make a deal during or before the event) or by official meeting between the two affiliate organizations during the trade fair[6] (equal to 1 if they had at least one meeting scheduled). *Same time next year* co-participation hypothesis (H3) can be tested by the number of co-participations between each individual at the five previous events (max = 5). In a similar way, *Next time this year* co-participation (H4) by the number of co-participation between individuals at 12 other events as dyadic covariates (max = 4). We test these hypotheses by controlling the effect of the economic category of the actors (seller or buyer) and the geographic homophily effect (as previously defined).

Table 10.2 corresponds to dyadic and Markov high-order ERG models for this network. The first column reports the results of the baseline model. At first, the geographic homophily effect is positive: individuals who come from the same region exchange information with each other. Second, the individual economic category on the trade fair is certainly the strongest effect. As in the inter-organizational level, the social structure of this market cuts across the boundary between sellers and buyers. Information exchange is greater between individuals of different categories than within categories (note that odds-ratios for this effect show that interaction between sellers is higher than between buyers).

The second column reports the results of the dyadic model with baseline effects and the embeddedness and co-participation covariates (hypotheses 2, 3, and 4). Here, every covariate regarding co-participation is positive and significant. The last two dyadic covariates underline an inter-organizational contextualization of the inter-individual link. We could say here that a deal between the organizations of two individuals constitutes a specific context for inter-individual interaction. The covariate concerning the inter-organizational meeting during the event has a positive influence (and significant) on the inter-individual link. Therefore, a part of the social relationships are nested in economic relationships, and more generally in inter-organizational relationships. These effects are very strong and positive. Social relationships are indeed embedded in economic relationships.

The last column reports the results of the general ERG model with structural high-order effects. The parameter concerning the co-participation in five previous events is now close to zero. In parallel we tried to introduce only the number of participations to the last five events and the results are the same: neither are significant and always close to zero. So when we add structural parameters, it is not the historical and long-term frequency that best explains the relationship between

---

[6]The meeting network was extracted from the trade fair organizer's meeting platform.

Table 10.2 ERG model estimates of structural and actor-relation effects on the presence of inter-individual information exchange network ties

	Model 4	Model 5	Model 6
Structural dependencies			
Density	−4.171 (0.1273)*	−4.616 (0.150)*	−8.518 (0.320)*
Reciprocity	2.0839 (0.1535)*	1.5613 (0.159)*	1.8240 (0.177)*
Alternating k-in-star (2)	–	–	0.9704 (0.110)*
Alternating k-out-star (2)	–	–	1.1653 (0.106)*
Alternating transitive k-triangles (2)	–	–	0.6255 (0.150)*
Alternating down and up k-triangles (2)	–	–	−0.439 (0.175)*
Alternating transitive k-two-paths (2)	–	–	−0.077 (0.010)*
Alternating down and up k-two-paths (2)	–	–	0.1200 (0.027)*
Baseline effects			
Economic category (Interaction)	−2.0004 (0.1720)	−1.755 (0.199)*	−2.031 (0.223)*
Economic category (Sender)	0.9727 (0.1434)	0.8539 (0.164)*	1.2501 (0.163)*
Economic category (Receiver)	1.2916 (0.1435)*	1.1641 (0.161)*	1.2467 (0.163)*
Geographical origin (Matching)	0.7788 (0.1050)*	0.7818 (0.107)*	0.7149 (0.103)*
Co-participation			
5 previous events (Dyad Covar.)	–	0.1043 (0.026)*	0.0343 (0.019)
12 other events in 2011 (Dyad Covar.)	–	0.6971 (0.108)*	0.5573 (0.091)*
MIP presence (Interaction)	–	0.3842 (0.088)*	0.2081 (0.070)*
Multilevel and contextual embeddedness			
Interorganizational official meeting during the event	–	1.0232 (0.098)*	0.8429 (0.094)*
Deal between affiliate organizations	–	1.0928 (0.088)*	0.9308 (0.088)*

Note: Effects with a star are significant with a t-ratio less than 0.05 (approached Wald test (Koskinen and Daraganova 2013)). For structural effects visualization see Appendix 3

two individuals, but short-term frequency regardless of the context: *Next time this year* rather than *Same time next year*.

In an ERGM the structural parameters represent the self-organized part of the network. Regardless of the attributes parameter, the social milieu generates some specific forces that explain the existence of a link between actors. Star parameters show that some actors are very popular (*Alternating k in-star* positive) and some actors are very active on the network (*Alternating k out-star* positive). It could also show a tendency towards hierarchy in the network. Beyond these degree effects, we could say that three specific social mechanisms explain the structure: exchange, collaboration and competition.

First, the tendency to *reciprocity* between actors is the strongest effect. The social exchange is more mutual than in a "random" distribution and this tendency builds up the network. We can think that both actors in a relationship are interested in obtaining some information. For example, in a buyer/seller relationship, the seller can obtain information about the local market trends and, on the other side, the buyer can seek information about successful programs and what is broadcast in other countries.

Second, the articulation of the *alternating transitive k-triangle* (positive) and the *alternating transitive k-two-paths* (negative) could be interpreted as a collaboration mechanism. Generally individuals have a shorter access to informants. We do not have a broker effect: when individual A gives some information to B and B to C, generally, C also has access to A. Social pressure closes the transitive two-paths. We could say that this milieu is characterized by a social *collaboration* mechanism between potential competitors.

Third, in the whole network there are more structurally equivalent actors than expected: *alternating two-paths down and up* parameter is positive and significant. But, when two individuals give or obtain information to or from the same actors (they are structurally equivalent) they have a lower chance of exchanging information with each other: *alternating down and up triangle* parameter is negative. Thus this network is characterized by many structurally equivalent individuals who do not exchange with each other. We may conclude that the third socio-economic mechanism in this milieu is *competition*.

The articulation of the last four parameters (and thus the two last socio-economic processes) shows a multi-core global structure in which the majority of the cores are connected to each other by some in- or out-2-stars. This milieu seems to cover economic and social processes and to be characterized by a coopetition phenomenon.

To sum up, the inter-individual network represents a *coopetition* milieu, evolving in other contexts during the short term, and embedded in economic.

Discussion and Conclusion

Different levels do not evolve simultaneously following the same path. How can we interpret this?

Firstly, these differences indicate that multilevel temporalities should be considered in terms of embeddedness: how do actors at each level manage these different temporalities? These show the complexity of economic performance in such multilevel settings. In the market for TV programs, our ethnographic study suggests that tacit knowledge and private information are crucial for individuals to identify commercial opportunities. The best way to access these is to attend many events during a short time period. But in parallel, their organizations have to be perceived as reliable by participating over a long time period in successive events at the same place. If deals are initiated by specific employees in an interorganizational context, an organizational network is more than the basic sum or concatenation of employee relationships. During interviews, several experienced individuals explained to us that they are free to prepare the trade fair, but that they have a lot to do afterwards: updating several databases, follow-up meetings, writing reports, etc. This helps to understand (and complexify) our results. We can observe different temporalities in the system: inter-individual relationships change faster and inter-organizational relations change more slowly. Organizational relationships have a different timeframe than interpersonal links. This is why some organizations developed specific mechanisms to cope with these different temporalities. Our results capture in part experience effects but in a dyadic way (when we add these effects as actor effects the results are the same). Whereas the morphologies at each level are different (because they are about different actors and relationships), this underlines that the efficiency of the meta-unity individual/organization is a complex articulation between these two sets of actors, forever on the razor's edge.

Secondly, a traditional ERGM at each level shows some differences between the two levels. To further investigate this meta-system, it could be interesting to use the formalization of Wang et al. (2013) concerning Multilevel ERGMs. Unlike previous work, our dataset is composed of oriented (level one) and non-oriented (level two) networks. Furthermore, the embeddedness hypothesis aims to study two kinds of actors, the two sides of the market: buyers and sellers. In this sense, as in a multilevel network, we can distinguish three sub-networks: between sellers, between buyers, and between buyers and sellers (Iacobucci and Wasserman 1990). This multi-sided specification is fundamental because relationships between and within buyers and sellers are different, as relationships between and within individuals and organizations. A basic specification of the coparticipation effects by this proposition shows that the embeddedness hypothesis on a market is more complex (see Table 10.3 in Appendix 4). This different temporality is above all the result of the fact that the relation at each level is constructed in a specific context. At the inter-individual level, a triadic closure is often permitted by an intra-milieu relationship. This relationship is constructed most of the time in the *Next time this year*, short-term framework. Yet this relation between competitors allows them to obtain some strategic information, for example about prices (Ingram and Roberts 2000) or suppliers (White 2002; Eloire 2010).

These results show that embeddedness is not only a dyadic process or a tetradic multilevel configuration but a six-order sub-structure including individuals and organizations, and also buyers and sellers. To sum up, embeddedness can be redefined as a multilevel problem in a multi-sided system.

Creating international ties in the context of a globalized market requires a complex multilevel process that involves companies and their employees. In the case of television program distribution in Eastern Europe, the networks reveal different structures and involve different mechanisms of tie formation. On the one hand, network morphologies are clearly different. Our analyses show that structural and co-participation effects are different between the two levels. We observe a *Same time next year* process for deal-making between organizations, a *Next time this year* process for information exchanges between individuals, and a multilevel structural dependency. Some data characteristics can explain this result: the content of the link, temporality, and the characteristics of the actors (buyers or sellers). While we can easily observe triadic mechanisms of cooperation and information exchanges between individuals, triadic mechanisms are less likely to occur in a competitive deal network between companies.

But on the other hand the structures of different levels strongly influence each other and are interdependent. The long-term deal network between companies influences cooperation ties between individuals, which in return can bring new business opportunities and constraints to their companies.

Thus reframing the embeddedness paradigm with a multilevel network analysis (MNA) perspective seems to be a fruitful approach to understand globalization of markets. Trade fairs such as the event under study seem to be arenas for creating long-distance relationships paving the way for long-term interorganizational partnerships. If we take into account that individual actors can move from one company to another or that a company could be represented by several employees, we have to study these two levels separately to understand the complex dynamic process of the creation of international ties between companies.

Appendixes

Appendix 1: Configuration Visualization for the Interorganizational Network

PNet name	Configuration visualisation
Arc	●—●
Alternating k-star	(k-star diagram)
Alternating two-path	(two-path diagram)

Appendix 2: Goodness of Fit for the Interorganizational Level

PNet name	Observed	Mean	Standard deviation	t-ratio
Edge	347	348.91	34.89	−0.06
2-star	3307	3195.09	566.36	0.20
3-star	13,590	12,677.50	3892.20	0.23
4-star	48,435	48,923.55	29,084.34	−0.02
5-star	146,009	190,931.50	208,698.59	−0.22
triangles	118	118.08	30.11	0.00
4-clique	8	5.98	4.54	0.44
5-clique	0	0.06	0.27	−0.20
6-clique	0	0.00	0.01	−0.01
7-clique	0	0.00	0.00	NA
Isolates	10	9.11	3.34	0.27
Triangle2	291	249.56	118.68	0.35
Bow_tie	1151	1317.59	803.30	−0.21
3Path	30,582	28,220.36	7156.81	0.33
4Cycle	**1202**	**794.43**	**255.31**	**1.60**
AS(2.00)	1021.602	1028.65	126.43	−0.06
AS(2.00)	1021.602	1028.65	126.43	−0.06
AT(2.00)	252.262	259.55	53.80	−0.14
AT(2.00)	252.262	259.55	53.80	−0.14
A2P(4.00)	2808.958	2841.31	463.98	−0.07
AC(2.00)	8	5.96	4.49	0.46
AET(2.00)	688	690.82	179.33	−0.02
Std Dev degree dist	5.172	4.87	0.39	0.77
Skew degree dist	1.243	1.22	0.49	0.05
Global Clustering	0.107	0.11	0.01	−0.21
Mean Local Clustering	0.108	0.10	0.02	0.21
Variance Local Clustering	0.02	0.02	0.01	0.17

Appendix 3: Configuration Visualization for the Interindividual Network

PNet name	Configuration visualisation
Edge	
Reciprocity	
Alternating k-in-star	
Alternating k-out-star	
Alternating transitive k-triangles	
Alternating transitive k-two-paths	
Alternating down and up k-triangles	
Alternating down and up k-two-paths	

Appendix 4

Table 10.3 ERGM model for the inter-individual network with coparticipation effects specified by economic category

	Model 7
Structural dependencies	
Density	−8.401 (0.360)*
Reciprocity	1.8173 (0.192)*
Alternating in-star (2)	0.9665 (0.112)*
Alternating out-star (2)	1.1568 (0.112)*
Alternating transitive k-triangles (2)	0.6317 (0.152)*
Alternating down and up k-triangles (2)	−0.432 (0.170)*

(continued)

Table 10.3 (continued)

	Model 7
Alternating transitive k-two-paths (2)	−0.075 (0.009)*
Alternating down and up k-two-paths (2)	0.1214 (0.027)*
Baseline effects	
Economic category (Interaction)	−1.642 (0.308)*
Economic category (Sender)	1.0553 (0.253)*
Economic category (Receiver)	1.0687 (0.242)*
Geographical origin (Matching)	0.7027 (0.115)*
Multilevel and contextual embeddedness	
Interorganizational official meeting during the event	0.8338 (0.099)*
Contract link between affiliate organizations	0.9208 (0.084)*
Co-participation	
MIP presence (Interaction)	0.2040 (0.074)*
5 previous events SELLER (*Dyad Covar.*)	**−0.166 (0.050)***
5 previous events BUYER (*Dyad Covar.*)	**−0.061 (0.083)**
5 previous events SB (*Dyad Covar.*)	**0.1740 (0.041)***
5 previous events BS (*Dyad Covar.*)	**0.0554 (0.024)***
12 other events in 2011 − SELLER (*Dyad Covar.*)	0.4881 (0.188)*
12 other events in 2011 − BUYER (*Dyad Covar.*)	0.7970 (0.331)*
12 other events in 2011 − SB (*Dyad Covar.*)	**−0.273 (0.257)**
12 other events in 2011 − BS (*Dyad Covar.*)	1.1178 (0.275)*

Note: Effects with a star are significant with a t-ratio less than 0.05 (approached Wald test (Koskinen and Daraganova 2013)). For structural effects visualization, see Appendix 1

References

Archer, M. S. (2000). *Being human: The problem of agency* (pp. 83, 84, 132). Cambridge University Press.
Aspers, P., & Darr, A. (2011). Trade shows and the creation of market and industry. *The Sociological Review, 59*, 758–778.
Bathelt, H., & Schuldt, N. (2008). Temporary face-to-face contact and the ecologies of global and virtual buzz. *SPACES Online, 6*, 1–23.
Bathelt, H., & Schuldt, N. (2010). International trade fairs and global buzz, Part I: Ecology of global buzz. *European Planning Studies, 18*, 1957–1974.
Bathelt, H., Malmberg, A., & Maskell, P. (2004). Clusters and knowledge: Local buzz, global pipelines and the process of knowledge creation. *Progress in Human Geography, 28*, 31–56.
Benhamou, F. (2004). *L'économie de la culture*. Paris: La découverte.
Borgatti, S. P., & Everett, M. G. (2000). Models of core/periphery structures. *Social Networks, 21*, 375–395.
Brailly, J., & Lazega, E. (2012). Diversité des approches de la modélisation multiniveaux en analyses de réseaux sociaux et organisationnels. *Mathématiques et Sciences Sociales, 198*, 5–32.
Brandenburger, A. M., & Nalebuff, B. J. (2011). *Co-opetition*. New York: Random House LLC.

Brass, D., Galaskiewicz, J., Greve, H., & Tsai, W. (2004). Taking stock of networks and organizations: A multilevel perspective. *Academy of Management Journal, 47*, 795–819.
Breiger, R. L. (1974). The duality of persons and groups. *Social Forces, 53*, 181–190.
Bryk, A. S., & Raudenbush, S. (1992). *Hierarchical linear models*. Newbury Park: Sage.
Burt, R. S. (1992). *Structural holes: The social structure of competition*. Cambridge, MA: Harvard University Press.
Crozier, M., & Friedberg, E. (1977). *L'acteur et le système*. Paris: Seuil.
Éloire, F. (2010). Une approche sociologique de la concurrence sur un marché le cas. *Revue Française de Sociologie, 51*, 481–517.
Friedberg, E. (1997). *Le pouvoir et la règle. Dynamiques de l'action organisée*. Paris: Seuil.
Goldstein, H. (1995). *Multilevel statistical models*. London: Edward Arnold.
Granovetter, M. S. (1973). The strength of weak ties. *American Journal of Sociology, 78*, 1360–1380.
Granovetter, M. S. (1985). Economic action and social structure: The problem of embeddedness? *American Journal of Sociology, 91*, 481–510.
Granovetter, M. S., & Swedberg, R. (Eds.). (1992). *The sociology of economic life*. Boulder: Westview press.
Gulati, R. (1995). Does familiarity breed trust? The implications of repeated ties for contractual choices in alliances. *Academy of Management Journal, 38*(1), 85–112.
Havens, T. J. (2003). On exhibiting global television: The business and cultural functions of global television fairs. *Journal of Broadcasting and Electronic Media, 47*, 18–35.
Havens, T. J. (2007). The hybrid grid: Globalization, cultural power and Hungarian television schedules. *Media, Culture and Society, 29*, 219–239.
Iacobucci, D., & Wasserman, S. (1990). Social networks with two sets of actors. *Psychometrika, 55*, 707–720.
Ingram, P., & Roberts, P. W. (2000). Friendships among competitors in the Sydney hotel industry. *American Journal of Sociology, 106*, 387–423.
Knoke, D. (2013). *Economic networks*. Cambridge: Polity Press.
Koskinen, J., & Daraganova, G. (2013). Dependence graphs and sufficient statistics. In D. Lusher, J. Koskinen, & G. Robins (Eds.), *Exponential random graph models for social networks: Theory, methods and applications* (pp. 77–90). New York: Cambridge University Press.
Krackhardt, D. (1994). Graph theoretic dimensions of informal organizations. In K. Carley & M. Prietula (Eds.), *Computational organizational theory* (pp. 89–111). Hillside: Lawrence Erlbaum.
Laumann, E. O., Marsden, P. V., & Prensky, D. (1989). The boundary specification problem in network analysis. In R. Burt & M. Minor (Eds.), *Research methods in social network analysis* (Vol. 61, pp. 87–115). Fairfax: George Mason University Press.
Lazega, E. (1996). Arrangements contractuels et structures relationnelles. *Revue Française de Sociologie, 37*, 439–456.
Lazega, E. (2001). *The Collegial phenomenon*. Oxford: Oxford University Press.
Lazega, E., & Mounier, L. (2002). Interdependent entrepreneurs and the social discipline of their cooperation: A research program for structural economic sociology in a society of organizations. In O. Favereau & E. Lazega (Eds.), *Conventions and structures in economic organization* (pp. 147–199). Cheltenham: Edward Elgar.
Lazega, E. (2009). Théorie de la coopération entre concurrents: Organisation, marché et analyse de réseaux. In P. Steiner & F. Vatin (Eds.), *Traité de sociologie économique* (pp. 547–585). Paris: Presse Universitaires de France.
Lazega, E. (2012). Sociologie néo-structurale. In R. Keucheyan & G. Bronner (Eds.), *Introduction à la théorie sociale contemporaine*. Paris: Presses Universitaires de France.
Lazega, E. (2013). Network analysis in the 'Morphogenetic Society' project: A neo-structural exploration and illustration. In M. S. Archer (Ed.), *Social morphogenesis* (pp. 167–186). New York: Springer.

Lazega, E. (2014). Morphogenesis unbound from the dynamics of multilevel networks: A neo-structural perspective. In M. S. Archer (Ed.), *Late modernity: Trajectories towards morphogenic society*. New York: Springer.

Lazega, E., & Penalva-Icher, E. (2011). Réseaux sociaux numériques et coopération entre concurrents:"I don't want to belong to any club that will accept people like me as a member". *Hermes, 59*, 43–49.

Lazega, E., Jourda, M.-T., Mounier, L., & Stofer, R. (2007). Des poissons et des mares: l'analyse de réseaux multiniveaux. *Revue Française de Sociologie, 48*, 93–131.

Lazega, E., Jourda, M.-T., Mounier, L., & Stofer, R. (2008). Catching up with big fish in the big pond? Multi-level network analysis through linked design. *Social Networks, 30*, 159–176.

Lazega, E., Jourda, M.-T., & Mounier, L. (2013). Network lift from dual alters: Extended opportunity structures from a multilevel and structural perspective. *European Sociological Review, 29*, 1226–1238.

Lorenz, E. (1999). Trust, contract and economic cooperation. *Cambridge Journal of Economics, 23*(3), 301–315.

Lusher, D., Koskinen, J., & Robins, G. (Eds.). (2013). *Exponential random graph models for social networks: Theory, methods, and applications* (Structural Analysis in the Social Sciences Series). New York: Cambridge University Press.

Maskell, P., Bathelt, H., & Malmberg, A. (2006). Building global knowledge pipelines: The role of temporary clusters. *European Planning Studies, 14*, 997–1013.

Mizruchi, M., & Stearns, L. (2001). Getting deals done: The use of social networks in bank decision-making. *American Sociological Review, 66*, 647–671.

Pattison, P. E., & Robins, G. L. (2004). Building models for social space: Neighbourhood-based models for social networks and affiliation structures. *Mathematics and Social Sciences, 168*, 11–29.

Powell, W. W. (1996). Inter-organizational collaboration in the biotechnology industry. *Journal of Institutional and Theoretical Economics (JITE)/Zeitschrift für die gesamte Staatswissenschaft, 152*(1), 129–159.

Powell, W. W., White, D. R., Koput, K. W., & Owen-Smith, J. (2005). Network dynamics and field evolution: The growth of interorganizational collaboration in the life sciences1. *American Journal of Sociology, 110*(4), 1132–1205.

Power, D., & Jansson, J. (2008). Cyclical clusters in global circuits: Overlapping spaces and furniture industry trade fairs. *Economic Geography, 84*, 423–448.

Robins, G. L., Pattison, P. E., & Woolcock, J. (2005). Social networks and small worlds. *American Journal of Sociology, 110*, 894–936.

Schuldt, N., & Bathelt, H. (2011). International trade fairs and global buzz. Part II: Practices of global buzz. *European Planning Studies, 19*, 1–22.

Scott, J., & Carrington, P. J. (Eds.). (2011). *The SAGE handbook of social network analysis*. London: SAGE Publications.

Seringhaus, R., & Rosson, P. (1998). Management and performance of international trade fair exhibitors: Government stands vs. independent stands. *International Marketing Review, 15*, 398–412.

Seringhaus, R., & Rosson, P. (2001). Firm experience and international trade fairs. *Journal of Marketing Management, 17*, 877–901.

Smelser, N. J., & Swedberg, R. (Eds.). (2010). *The handbook of economic sociology*. Princeton: Princeton University Press.

Snijders, T. A. B., & Baerveldt, C. (2003). A multilevel network study of the effects of delinquent behaviour on friendship evolution. *Journal of Mathematical Sociology, 27*, 123–151.

Snijders, T. A. B., & Bosker, R. J. (1999). *Multilevel analysis: An introduction to basic and advanced multilevel modeling*. London: Sage Publications.

Snijders, T. A. B., Pattison, P. E., Robins, G. L., & Handcock, M. (2006). New specifications for exponential random graph models. *Sociological Methodology, 36*, 99–153.

Storper, M., & Venables, A. J. (2004). Buzz: Face-to-face contact and the urban economy. *Journal of Economic Geography, 4*, 351–370.

Swedberg, R. (1997). New economic sociology: What has been accomplished, what is ahead? *Acta Sociologica, 40*, 161–182.

Uzzi, B. (1996). The sources and consequences of embeddedness for the economic performance of organizations: The network effect. *American Sociological Review, 61*, 674–698.

Uzzi, B. (1997). Social structure and competition in interfirm networks: The paradox of embeddedness. *Administrative Science Quarterly, 42*, 35–67.

Wang, P., Robins, G. L., & Pattison P. E. (2006). *Pnet: A program for the simulation and estimation of exponential random graph models*. Available at: http://sna.unimelb.edu.au/PNet

Wang, P., Robins, G. L., Pattison, P. E., & Lazega, E. (2013). Exponential random graph models for multilevel networks. *Social Networks, 35*, 96–115.

Wasserman, S., & Faust, K. (1994). *Social network analysis: Methods and applications*. Cambridge: Cambridge University Press.

Wasserman, S., & Pattison, P. E. (1996). Logit models and logistic regressions for social networks. I. An introduction to Markov graphs and p*. *Psychometrika, 61*, 401–425.

White, H. C. (2002). *Markets from networks: Socioeconomic models of production*. Princeton: Princeton University Press.

Chapter 11
Knowledge Networks in High-Tech Clusters: A Multilevel Perspective on Interpersonal and Inter-organizational Collaboration

Julia Brennecke and Olaf N. Rank

Introduction

In today's fast-changing and complex high-tech industries, neither individuals nor organizations comprise all the material or immaterial resources relevant for sustained competitive advantage. Collaboration among knowledge workers and among the organizations they are nested in is of foremost importance for corporate success (e.g., Alexiev et al. 2010; Baum et al. 2000). Knowledge networks are created at the level of the individual knowledge worker or the level of their organizations, enabling and constraining the efforts of individuals and organizations to acquire, transfer, and create knowledge (Phelps et al. 2012). Existing research has investigated knowledge networks created in high-tech contexts focusing either on individuals and their engagement in interpersonal exchange (e.g., Bouty 2000; Pina-Stranger and Lazega 2011) or on organizations' embeddedness in networks of mainly formal collaborations (e.g., Ahuja 2000; Owen-Smith and Powell 2004). With some notable exceptions (Berends et al. 2011; Lazega et al. 2008) few studies have jointly examined knowledge networks of managers or researchers and of the organizations they are nested in. Consequently, we still lack an understanding on how individual-level and organizational-level knowledge networks differ with respect to their underlying structural logic (Rank et al. 2010) and, more importantly, we know little about how network structure emerging at one level impacts structure emerging at the other level. Our aim is to fill this void by investigating the processes

---

J. Brennecke (✉)
Swinburne University of Technology, Centre for Transformative Innovation, Melbourne, Australia
e-mail: jbrennecke@swin.edu.au

O.N. Rank
Universität Freiburg, Freiburg im Breisgau, Germany

driving knowledge sharing and cooperation among individuals and organizations belonging to regional high-tech clusters from a multilevel network perspective.

Clusters are concentrations of organizations in a particular field and region. They enable individuals and organizations in knowledge-intensive industries to get in contact with each other and collaborate (e.g., Porter 2000). At the individual level, firm managers and members of research institutes (subsequently referred to as researchers) that are part of clusters exchange information and knowledge. At the organizational level, cluster organizations formally collaborate, for instance conducting joint research and development (R&D) projects. Since managers and researchers exchanging knowledge at the micro-level are nested within organizations collaborating at the macro-level complex multilevel networks emerge in these regional clusters. Building on existing research on single-level knowledge networks (for a review see Phelps et al. 2012) as well as on the few existing studies on multilevel networks (Berends et al. 2011; Lazega et al. 2008), we seek to find out which cross-level processes determine the creation of individual-level and organizational-level ties in these clusters and draw conclusions on how structure at one organizational level is related to structure at the other level. Specifically, we examine whether managers and researchers attune their interpersonal knowledge ties to the formal collaboration activities of organizations and vice versa. We reason that bottom-up and top-down processes might mutually affect the structure of multilevel networks (Berends et al. 2011; Rosenkopf and Schleicher 2008; Shipilov 2012). On the one hand, informal interpersonal ties between managers and researchers are supposed to impact the creation of formal R&D collaborations. On the other hand, R&D collaborations might influence the interpersonal exchange of knowledge. We hypothesize that different cross-level processes are likely to give rise to distinct patterns of ties that characterize the overall structure of multilevel knowledge networks. To examine which patterns characterize networks in regional high-tech clusters, we apply exponential random graph models for multilevel networks to relational data collected in two clusters in Germany. The results of our model estimations enable us to draw conclusions about the structure-generating processes determining multilevel knowledge exchange in the cluster context.

Our study contributes to research on knowledge networks in high-tech clusters by adding a multilevel perspective. We show that while informal individual-level and formal organizational-level knowledge networks created by nested actors partly follow their own structural logic, they are at the same time logically intertwined. Interpersonal knowledge ties influence the maintenance of formal R&D collaborations and vice versa. To fully understand knowledge exchange in high-tech clusters it is therefore necessary to take a multilevel network perspective.

Considering cross-level interdependencies between network levels we also add to the understanding of the determinants of interpersonal exchange and formal collaboration in the cluster context. We demonstrate how firms' embeddedness in formal knowledge networks influences the networking activities of managers and researchers. Based on that, we are able to draw conclusions about whether individuals acquire knowledge independent of the opportunity structures provided by their organizations and thus fully exploit the possibilities provided by clusters.

Concerning formal R&D collaborations our research highlights how managers' and researchers' informal knowledge ties might help or hinder firms' efforts to find collaboration partners. Thus, our study highlights the extent to which informal knowledge ties are beneficial for organizations beyond learning and knowledge transfer (e.g., McDonald et al. 2008).

Theory and Hypotheses

We investigate multilevel knowledge networks in regional high-tech clusters, i.e., networks among individuals and organizations that compete in a particular field and cooperate at the same time (Porter 2000). Due to their geographical co-location, cluster organizations benefit from agglomeration economies such as knowledge spillovers and an increased probability of getting in contact with each other (Alcácer and Chung 2013; Owen-Smith and Powell 2004). In addition, aiming to promote regional economic development (Maurer and Ebers 2006) policy-making initiatives often foster the institutionalization of clusters in particular regions and industries (Alecke et al. 2006; Zeller 2001). They support the foundation of formal cluster administrators that further promote cooperation and knowledge exchange by organizing events for member organizations. These factors make network ties among co-located organizations and among their managers and researchers especially likely.

Cross-level interdependencies among organizational-level and individual-level knowledge networks exist when the presence or absence of ties at one organizational level influences the existence of ties at the other level. In regards to knowledge networks in high-tech clusters, we hypothesize that these interdependencies give rise to local network patterns generated by tendencies towards cross-level assortativity on the one hand. On the other hand, we assume cross-level closure to be a crucial structuring principle of knowledge networks. Cross-level assortativity is assumed to indicate interactions between the positions of managers and researchers in the micro-level knowledge network and the positions of the organizations they are nested in the macro-level collaboration network. In other words, managers and researchers centrally embedded in the informal network might be nested in organizations with many formal R&D collaborations. Cross-level closure is the alignment of ties among dyads of individuals and the organizations they are nested in and exists if ties are present at the individual as well as the organizational level. We first discuss cross-level assortativity before turning to cross-level closure as processes generating multilevel knowledge networks in high-tech clusters.

Cross-Level Assortativity in Multilevel Knowledge Networks

Assortativity describes the tendency for actors with a similar number of (incoming or outgoing) ties to be connected (Newman 2002; Snijders et al. 2010). For the investigation of multilevel networks, assortativity can be extended from its application to single-level networks to describe the networking behavior of nested actors. In our study, it depicts the relationship between the number of interpersonal knowledge ties that managers and researchers maintain and the number of R&D projects that their organizations are involved in. With respect to interpersonal ties we differentiate between whether managers and researchers provide knowledge to others, or seek knowledge from them. In the following section, we first discuss assortativity effects for managers and researchers providing knowledge to their peers and subsequently focus on those seeking knowledge from others in connection with the organizational-level maintenance of R&D projects.

From a bottom-up perspective, we argue that organizations may become sought-after partners for joint R&D because managers or researchers who are popular sources for knowledge at the individual-level attract partners for formal organizational-level collaborations. As individuals provide informal knowledge to others they might signal competence, status, and a general openness towards knowledge sharing (Spence 1974) which might lead to other organizations becoming interested in working on joint R&D projects. In other words, the individuals' reputation might spill over to the organizational level (Eisenhardt and Schoonhoven 1996) and allow their organizations to establish formal collaboration ties. The cluster context might reinforce this effect. Individuals get in contact with each other due to the regional agglomeration in general, or specifically at organized events. Thus, the popularity of managers or researchers can directly be observed by other cluster members and attention is drawn to their organizations.

Cross-level reputation spillovers may similarly occur top-down and lead to managers and researchers becoming popular sources for knowledge because their organizations engage in many R&D projects. High levels of organizational engagement in R&D collaboration are likely to create the impression that the managers of these active organizations have access to broad knowledge bases and innovation. This impression, in turn, could lead to other managers and researchers asking them for knowledge and information on an interpersonal level.

Hypothesis 1a: There is a positive relationship between individuals' popularity as providers of knowledge and their organizations' tendency to maintain formal R&D collaborations.

Cross-level assortativity in multilevel knowledge networks can equally apply to the interaction between individuals seeking a lot of knowledge and information from others and their organizations' centrality in the formal collaboration network. From a bottom-up point of view, it might simply be that managers' centrality resulting from their efforts to search for knowledge using interpersonal ties leads to a high visibility within the cluster and attracts attention to their organizations. This, in turn, might help these organizations to find collaboration partners. Alternatively, informally seeking a lot of knowledge might be interpreted negatively within the cluster context. Individuals could leave the impression of being unable to come up with innovative ideas themselves or trying to cobble together as much external knowledge as possible. Since knowledge is largely seen as the single most valuable resource of high tech firms and research institutes (e.g., DeCarolis and Deeds 1999), which organizations typically try to protect (e.g., Oliver 2004), such behavior could be evaluated negatively by other cluster members. Managers and researchers who are central in the informal network because they seek a lot of knowledge might hence create a negative image of themselves which could negatively affect their firm's ability to attract partners for R&D collaborations.

From a top-down perspective, individuals nested in central organizations might become active seekers of knowledge in order to match their organizations' involvement in R&D collaborations. A high number of formal R&D collaborations might lead to an increased need to gather external knowledge via interpersonal ties. In addition, individuals might try to benefit from the opportunity structures provided by their organization and use its visibility to improve their own position in the interpersonal network. Again, a negative relationship between organizations' centrality in the formal knowledge network and individuals' knowledge-seeking activities seems possible to the extent that individuals might try to compensate a lack of formal collaborations by establishing interpersonal knowledge ties. Doing so, they might also try to pave the way for future collaborations. In this case, the absence of organizational-level ties would exert a positive top-down impact on the individuals' knowledge-seeking activities. As in this specific case our arguments do not allow drawing an unambiguous conclusion concerning the direction of the relationship (i.e., positive or negative), we leave it open to empirical investigation and state in a general form:

Hypothesis 1b: There is a relationship between individuals' knowledge-seeking activities and their organizations' tendency to maintain formal R&D collaborations.

Cross-Level Closure in Multilevel Knowledge Networks

Network closure can generally be defined as a high level of interconnectedness among actors in a network (Burt 2001). The tendency for closure in social networks can be explained by balance theory (Heider 1958) arguing that actors strive towards consistency in their social relations. Just like assortativity, closure is a concept commonly applied to single-level networks and can be extended to a multilevel setting. With respect to the multilevel knowledge networks we study, closure occurs when a tie is present between two individuals at the micro level while simultaneously a macro-level tie connects the organizations they are nested in.

From a bottom-up perspective, closure in multilevel networks can emerge as an interpersonal tie might lead to the formalization of a joint R&D project at the organizational level. The informal exchange of knowledge might enable managers and researchers to discover the potential for their organizations to collaborate. Moreover, interpersonal contacts allow managers and researchers to collect information on the trustworthiness and reliability of a potential collaboration partner before formalizing a tie (e.g., Barden and Mitchell 2007; Berends et al. 2011; Rosenkopf and Schleicher 2008). The latter point is of foremost importance with respect to knowledge networks because R&D collaborations with external parties include the risk of losing intellectual capital to a competitor (Norman 2002). In this connection, the regional cluster provides a context allowing managers and researchers to get to know each other and their organizations and thereby evaluate whether a potential collaboration partner matches their organizations' needs and expectations. Providing empirical evidence for the impact of individual-level on organizational-level ties in different contexts, studies have shown that director interlocks (Gulati and Westphal 1999; Rosenkopf and Schleicher 2008), individuals' joint memberships in technical committees (Rosenkopf et al. 2001; Rosenkopf and Schleicher 2008), as well as interpersonal exchange (Berends et al. 2011) are related to formal collaborations between dyads of firms.

From a top down point of view, formal R&D collaborations between two organizations might equally lead to an informal knowledge tie between their managers and researchers. Berends and colleagues (2011) provide empirical evidence for this direction of causality. Individuals might simply get to know each other through the formal R&D collaboration and consequently start exchanging interpersonal knowledge. They might even perceive the informal exchange of knowledge at the micro-level and the formal collaboration at the macro-level as complementary efforts having a joint impact on the success of the collaboration. Alternatively, they might perceive informal and formal knowledge ties as substitutes and deliberately try not to mirror their organizations' ties to avoid accessing redundant knowledge. Lazega and colleagues (2008) call this the "independent" strategy used by individuals to manage resource flows. Despite the latter point, the sum of bottom-up and top-down arguments suggests that informal and knowledge ties are likely to overlap. Therefore we state:

Hypothesis 2: There is a positive relationship between two individuals being connected by a knowledge tie and their organizations collaborating on an R&D project.

Data, Measures, and Analyses

Research Sites and Respondents

Our empirical analysis is based on a comparative case study of managers and researchers belonging to organizations in two high-tech clusters. The cases include clusters in the metrology industry and the photonics industry located in different regions of Germany. In the following, we will refer to them as "MetroNet" and "PhotoNet." Both clusters are organized by an institutional framework and include an administration that fosters cooperation and knowledge exchange by organizing events for its members. One of the major targets of both clusters is to provide an information and communications platform for participating organizations and their managers and researchers. They explicitly aim to initiate and support collaboration efforts by the co-located organizations. Membership in both clusters is voluntary and requires a yearly fee. Member organizations include mostly small to medium-sized high-tech firms and research institutes but also service intermediaries such as consultants, venture capital providers, and regional associations. Since joint R&D projects typically emerge among firms and research institutes, we limit our analysis to these member organizations and their managers and researchers.

We conducted online surveys in each cluster, including all member organizations as well as the firms' CEOs and members of research institutes in our sample. Moreover, we asked the CEOs and researchers as well as the administrative managers of each cluster to identify additional persons within the member organizations who participated actively in the activities of their cluster. In particularly small firms comprising only a limited number of employees, the CEO was the single most active network member. In many cases, however, additional managers and researchers were identified and included in our sample. Our final sample includes information on 26 organizations and 51 individuals in the MetroNet cluster and 54 organizations and 71 individuals in the PhotoNet cluster.

Network Data and Actor-Level Attributes

The managers and researchers completed the questionnaire first, answering questions concerning their individual-level knowledge ties with the other identified individuals within their cluster. Secondly, they provided information on their organizations' joint R&D projects with the other member organizations of their cluster. To collect data on both networks we used rosters containing all the identified managers and researchers of the respective organizations and all the member organizations of the clusters in an alphabetical order. Respondents were asked to mark as many of the individuals and organizations as relational partners as they deemed appropriate.

To capture the individual-level knowledge network, we asked the respondents to "Please mark all contacts you regularly turn to for work-related information and knowledge" (for a similar approach see for instance Borgatti and Cross 2003; Rank et al. 2010). To collect data on R&D collaborations, we asked the respondents, "Please mark all organizations with whom your organization conducts a joint project in research and development." All network data were recorded dichotomously thereby distinguishing only between the presence and absence of ties. For each cluster, data were arranged in three matrices that together capture the multilevel network. Two binary adjacency matrices capture the individual-level and the organizational-level knowledge networks. To consider the nested structure of mangers within their firms and research institutes we constructed affiliation matrices for both clusters. The individual-level network includes information on knowledge ties among managers and researchers belonging to the same organization as well as among managers and researchers belonging to different organizations. Both single-level networks were included in the analysis as directed networks.

In addition to the relational data, we include different actor-level control variables for individuals and organizations. For managers and researchers we collected demographic information on their educational level, organizational tenure, professional background, and occupational status. Concerning the educational level we differentiated between managers and researchers holding a doctoral degree (1) and those without (0). We did so because holding a doctoral degree has important career implications not only in academia but also in knowledge-intensive industries in Germany. We included professional background and occupational status categorical variables. Based on the job description of the respondents, we distinguished between general management (1), manufacturing, research, and development (2), marketing and sales (3), and others (e.g., procurement) (4). Occupational status is defined a respondent's position within the organization's hierarchy distinguishing between lower (1), middle (2), and upper (3) level positions. Finally, we accounted for the fact that organizational tenure may influence interpersonal collaboration. Organizational tenure was measured in decades. In addition to these demographic variables, we account for individuals' organizational background distinguishing between managers (1) and researchers (0). Concerning organizations we control for organizational type as a binary actor-attribute distinguishing between firms (1) and research institutes (0). Doing this, we are able to tell whether profit-oriented and scientific actors differ with respect to their knowledge-related tie-creation activities. In addition, we control for organizational size measured by the number of employees of firms and research institutes in hundreds. Because of its skewed distribution, organizational size was log-transformed.

Exponential Random Graph Models for Multilevel Networks

We analyze our data applying exponential random graph models (ERGMs) for multilevel networks (see Chap. 5 in this volume). In the models for each cluster, we include single-level parameters capturing the structure of the micro- and the macro-level knowledge networks. We select parameters commonly used in research on the structuring principles of single-level networks (e.g., Lazega and Pattison 1999; Lomi and Pattison 2006) and use them to compare the structuring principles of informal individual-level and formal organizational-level knowledge networks. To identify interdependencies between knowledge networks at the micro-level and the macro-level we include different cross-level parameters proposed by Wang and colleagues (2013). A first group of parameters, cross-level three-paths, captures tendencies towards cross-level assortativity measuring interactions between the centrality of organizations in the collaboration network and the centrality of their managers and researchers in the informal knowledge network. Second, a cross-level four-cycle parameter captures the relationship between formal collaboration ties connecting two organizations and informal knowledge ties established between these two

Table 11.1 Cross-level patterns characterizing multilevel networks

Parameter	Visualization	Interpretation[a]
Cross-level assortativity (three-paths)		
Assortativity based on popularity		Tendency for popular organizations named as project partners by many other organizations also to have popular managers/researchers from whom many others seek knowledge
Mixed assortativity A		Interaction between popularity at one level and expansiveness at the other level: expansive organizations have popular managers/researchers
Assortativity based on activity		Tendency for outgoing organizations naming many project partners to have outgoing managers/researchers seeking a lot of knowledge from others
Mixed assortativity B		Interaction between popularity at one level and expansiveness at the other level: popular organizations have outgoing managers/researchers
Cross-level closure (four-cycle)		
Cross-level entrainment		Individuals seek knowledge from others belonging to organizations which their organization named as project partner
Manager knowledge and affiliation network		
Affiliation-based arc		Managers/researchers from the same organization seek knowledge from each other
Affiliation-based reciprocity		Managers/researchers from the same organization reciprocally exchange knowledge

Notes. □ = organization; ○ = manager/researcher
[a]The provided interpretations refer to the parameters as if they resulted in positive significant effects

organizations' managers. Finally, a third group of affiliation-based parameters captures knowledge ties between managers belonging to the same organization and we include them as control variables. All multilevel parameters included in the models are summarized in Table 11.1.

By including single-level as well as cross-level structural parameters we are able to estimate their relative contribution as drivers of local structural patterns while conditioning their occurrence on the likelihood of observing the overall network (Robins et al. 2007). To obtain model convergence, the graph density had to be fixed for model estimation for the multilevel network emerging within the PhotoNet cluster (for further information on this procedure see Snijders et al. 2006).

Results

Figure 11.1 visualizes the individual-level, organizational-level, and affiliation networks as components of the multilevel network for MetroNet and PhotoNet. The visualizations of the individual-level and organizational-level networks show that in each network some actors are more centrally embedded forming a core of connected entities while other actors are more peripheral. In addition, in each network there is a small number of isolated actors not having any knowledge ties to other cluster members. The visualization of the affiliation networks highlights how many individuals per organization were surveyed in each cluster.

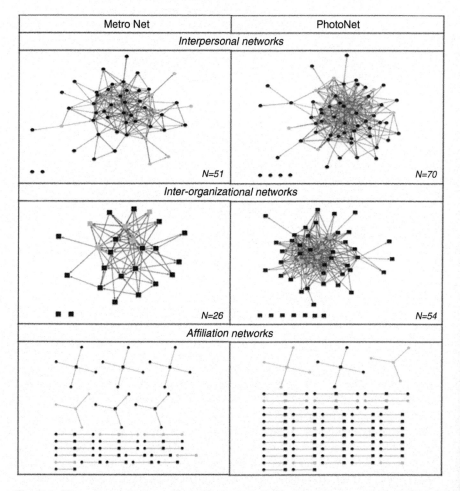

Fig. 11.1 Network visualizations. *Notes. Circles* = individuals; *squares* = organizations; *light grey* = researchers/research institutes; *dark grey* = managers/firms; created with Visone 2.7

Table 11.2 summarizes the descriptive statistics capturing the most important features of the micro- and macro-level networks in each cluster. Table 11.3 presents results of model estimations for the two clusters. The results in the table are arranged in sections, with the first section representing parameters for the micro-level knowledge networks and individual attributes, and the second section comprising parameters for the macro-level R&D collaboration networks and organizational attributes respectively. The third section displays all cross-level effects included in our models. Testing the models for their goodness-of-fit by following the recommendations of Robins and colleagues (2009) and Wang and colleagues (2013), we find that they yield good fit suggesting that the observed networks can be reproduced adequately based on the model.

Single-Level Network Structure

Focusing on the effects capturing the structure of the individual-level knowledge networks, we find tendencies towards reciprocity and transitivity as well as tendencies against cyclic closure in both clusters. Likewise, we find tendencies towards centralization. In the MetroNet cluster, the Out2-star is positive indicating that some individuals are more active seekers of knowledge than others. However, as indicated by the insignificant alternating expansiveness parameter there is a ceiling effect to this. The PhotoNet cluster is even more centralized. The positive In2-star and Out2-star effects as well as the positive alternating expansiveness effect indicate that there is high variation with respect to the individuals' in- and out-degrees. Thus, some managers and researchers are more active seekers and providers of knowledge than others. The attribute-based effects highlight that in the MetroNet cluster, managers of for-profit firms engage less in the informal exchange of knowledge than expected in a random network. Moreover, they exhibit a tendency towards homophily based on their organizational background and occupational status meaning that firm managers tend to establish knowledge ties to other managers while researchers tend to create ties to other researchers and individuals with the same status establish ties to each other. In the MetroNet and PhotoNet clusters individuals with a higher organizational tenure get asked for knowledge more often than expected by chance. In addition, in the PhotoNet cluster, we find tendencies toward homophily based on individuals' tenure and their professional background.

The organizational-level networks are equally characterized by a strong tendency towards reciprocity which – given the operationalization of the R&D collaboration network – is not surprising. Reciprocity in this case simply indicates a high level of agreement among managers and researchers concerning R&D collaborations between their organizations. Both macro-level networks are characterized by a tendency towards centralization, as some organizations are significantly more active in establishing joint R&D projects with other members. We also find tendencies for transitivity within the PhotoNet cluster. Interestingly, while in the MetroNet cluster the most active member organizations are research institutes, in the PhotoNet

Table 11.2 Descriptive statistics for the clusters

	MetroNet	PhotoNet
Firms and research institutes in cluster	31	82
Participating member organizations	26	54
(1) Firms	21 (80.8 %)	46 (85.2 %)
(0) Research institutes	5 (19.2 %)	8 (14.8 %)
Density organizational-level network	14.9 %	10.3 %
Mean degree organizational-level network	3.73	5.44
Stddev(in-degree) organizational-level network	3.09	5.98
Stddev(out-degree) organizational-level network	3.42	6.31
Organizational size (no. of employees in hundreds)		
Mean	3.03	5.80
Standard deviation	8.42	20.17
Minimum	0.02	0.01
Maximum	42.80	130.00
Participating individuals	51	70
(1) Managers	42 (82.4 %)	54 (77.1 %)
(0) Researchers	9 (17.6 %)	16 (22.9 %)
Density individual-level network	10.5 %	7.9 %
Mean degree individual-level network	5.24	5.46
Stddev(in-degree) individual-level network	4.56	5.67
Stddev(out-degree) individual-level network	5.00	5.95
Level of education		
(1) Individuals with doctoral degree	13 (35.5 %)	43 (61.4 %)
(0) Individuals without doctoral degree	38 (74.5 %)	27 (38.6 %)
Organizational tenure (in decades)		
Mean	1.36	1.16
Standard deviation	0.86	0.84
Minimum	0.10	0.10
Maximum	3.60	4.00
Professional background		
(1) General management	7 (13.7 %)	30 (42.9 %)
(2) Manufacturing, research and development	29 (56.9 %)	30 (42.9 %)
(3) Marketing and sales	12 (23.5 %)	7 (10.0 %)
(4) Others	3 (5.9 %)	3 (4.3 %)
Occupational status		
(1) Upper	13 (25.5 %)	39 (55.7 %)
(2) Middle	22 (43.1 %)	26 (37.1 %)
(3) Lower	16 (31.4 %)	5 (7.1 %)

11 Knowledge Networks in High-Tech Clusters

Table 11.3 Results of the exponential random graph models

Network level	Parameter	MetroNet: Estimate (S.E.)	PhotoNet: Estimate (S.E.)
Individual-level network	Arc	−3.586* (0.462)	−
	Reciprocity	2.573* (0.320)	2.762* (0.268)
	In2-Star	−	0.044* (0.012)
	Alternating popularity	−0.176 (0.236)	0.301 (0.195)
	Out2-Star	0.034* (0.014)	0.065* (0.008)
	Alternating expansiveness	−0.259 (0.245)	0.471* (0.189)
	Alternating transitivity	1.158* (0.155)	0.617* (0.116)
	Alternating cyclic closure	−0.248* (0.103)	−0.406* (0.066)
	Educational level sender	0.072 (0.178)	−0.025 (0.234)
	Educational level receiver	−0.224 (0.208)	−0.126 (0.245)
	Educational level homophily	−0.143 (0.439)	0.244 (0.294)
	Organizational background sender	−0.872* (0.334)	0.057 (0.198)
	Organizational background receiver	−0.690* (0.323)	0.317 (0.216)
	Organizational background homophily	1.075* (0.335)	−0.050 (0.247)
	Organizational tenure sender	−0.006 (0.030)	0.005 (0.001)
	Organizational tenure receiver	0.067* (0.030)	0.016* (0.001)
	Organizational tenure homophily	−0.037 (0.030)	−0.013* (0.001)
	Professional background homophily	0.172 (0.093)	0.281* (0.087)
	Occupational status homophily	0.231* (0.114)	0.040 (0.079)
Organizational-level network	Arc	−3.651* (0.923)	−
	Reciprocity	1.769* (0.456)	0.712* (0.304)
	Alternating popularity	0.178 (0.423)	0.853* (0.260)
	Out2-Star	−	0.097* (0.013)
	Alternating expansiveness	0.925* (0.373)	0.738* (0.240)
	Alternating transitivity	0.063 (0.225)	0.530* (0.183)
	Alternating cyclic closure	0.058 (0.156)	−0.003 (0.062)
	Type of organization sender	−1.321* (0.538)	0.713* (0.338)
	Type of organization receiver	−0.302 (0.527)	−0.189 (0.396)
	Type of organization homophily	0.516 (0.571)	−0.875 (0.441)
	Size sender	0.100 (0.100)	0.030 (0.100)
	Size receiver	0.250* (0.100)	0.060 (0.100)
	Size homophily	−0.110 (0.100)	−0.060* (0.010)
Multilevel network	Assortativity based on popularity	0.044* (0.018)	0.016* (0.008)
	Mixed assortativity A	0.002 (0.023)	−0.003 (0.006)
	Assortativity based on activity	−0.002 (0.023)	−0.020* (0.007)
	Mixed assortativity B	−0.064* (0.019)	−0.023* (0.009)
	Cross-level entrainment	0.178* (0.062)	0.584* (0.066)
	Affiliation-based density	4.670* (0.797)	3.199* (0.523)
	Affiliation-based reciprocity	−4.238* (0.926)	−3.600* (0.943)

Notes. Unstandardized estimates are reported; *statistically significant effect at or beyond the 0.05 level; $\lambda = 2$

cluster the most active organizations are for-profit firms, which can be seen from the significant sender effects for "type of organization." With respect to organizational size, we find that while in MetroNet, larger organizations are named more often as formal collaboration partners, in PhotoNet similar-sized organizations tend to collaborate on joint R&D projects.

Multilevel Network Structure

To test our Hypothesis 1a, we focus on the "assortativity based on popularity" and the "mixed assortativity A" parameters. While the "mixed assortativity A" parameters are insignificant in each model, we find that both multilevel networks are characterized by a tendency towards cross-level assortativity based on individuals' and their organizations' popularity. In other words, managers and researchers asked for their knowledge by many other individuals belong to organizations named as formal collaboration partners a lot. We take these findings as partial support for our Hypothesis 1a. Concerning Hypothesis 1b, we find that the "assortativity based on activity" parameter is negative and significant only within the PhotoNet cluster. The "mixed assortativity B" parameters are negative in both clusters. These results indicate that there is a negative interaction between organizations' centrality in the formal collaboration networks at the macro-level and their managers' and researchers' expansiveness in both clusters. Hence, the less organizations were nominated as formal collaboration partners, the more their managers and researchers sought knowledge via informal ties and vice versa. We take this finding as support for Hypothesis 1b, stating that there is a negative relationship between individuals' knowledge-seeking activities and their organizations' tendency to maintain formal R&D collaborations.

Focusing on the "cross-level entrainment" effects included in the models to test our Hypothesis 2, we find a positive tendency towards cross-level cyclic closure within both clusters. There is a higher than expected by chance tendency for individuals to be connected by an informal knowledge tie if their organizations formally collaborate. These findings clearly support our Hypotheses 2. Finally, the affiliation-based arc and reciprocity effects included as controls in both models show that, not surprisingly, managers and researchers belonging to the same organization seek knowledge from each other more often than expected by chance. However, the reciprocity effect for intra-organizational transfer of knowledge is negative. Thus while in general the informal knowledge networks are characterized by reciprocated exchange among individuals, controlling for context we see that in our case this seems to apply to boundary-spanning ties only. Managers or researchers belonging to the same organizations refrain from exchanging knowledge reciprocally.

Discussion

In this study, we investigated the processes driving knowledge sharing and cooperation among individuals and among organizations in regional high-tech clusters. Our findings suggest that knowledge networks in high-tech clusters are characterized by complex structural patterns. Only to a certain degree do individuals' informal knowledge networks and their organizations' formal R&D collaborations follow their own structural logic. Taking a multilevel perspective it becomes evident that individual-level and organizational-level networks in high-tech clusters are highly intertwined. Bottom-up and top-down processes lead to specific forms of cross-level assortativity and cross-level closure characterizing multilevel knowledge exchange.

Before turning to the cross-level processes determining network generation, a brief comparison of the structural features of the micro- and the macro-level networks sheds light on the processes driving the creation of informal as compared to formal knowledge ties in high-tech clusters. We find that social preferences towards reciprocity and transitivity drive the informal exchange of knowledge among managers and researchers. In conjunction with the tendency against cyclic closure, this tendency towards transitive exchange indicates that informal knowledge seeking takes place in clusters which seem to be locally hierarchical. In other words, not all individuals within the clusters are similarly involved in seeking and providing knowledge; instead there are differences in status among individuals. Moreover, tendencies towards homophily based on different individual-level attributes characterize interpersonal exchange in both clusters. Taken together, these findings highlight the important role that individuals' social preferences play in the structure of the micro-level knowledge network. While this is largely in line with existing research (e.g., Agneessens and Wittek 2012; Rank et al. 2010) it does not necessarily correspond to the purpose of regional clusters, which aim to connect individuals based on their rational-economic needs for complementary knowledge. In comparison, the structure of the organizational-level R&D networks seems to be more consistent with the idea of forming connections based on rational-economic considerations. Specifically, in the MetroNet cluster, we find that the organizational-level collaboration network is neither driven by transitive nor by cyclic clustering. A tendency towards heterophily based on the type of organization represents another indicator for rational-economic motives driving formal R&D collaborations at PhotoNet, whereas neither a tendency towards homophily nor towards heterophily can be identified in the MetroNet cluster. We conclude that efforts to find complementary partners have priority at the organizational level. In sum, comparing and contrasting the structuring principles of the micro- and macro-level knowledge networks highlights that distinct processes drive collaboration at either level within knowledge-intensive clusters.

To further extend our understanding of knowledge sharing and cooperation in high-tech clusters we focus on the cross-level processes determining the structure of multilevel knowledge networks. First, we discuss bottom-up processes taking place across network levels demonstrating that informal knowledge networks of individuals influence their organizations' embeddedness in the formal R&D collaboration network. We find that managers and researchers who are popular sources for informal knowledge and information are nested in the organizations which are attractive partners for joint R&D projects. Thus, within multilevel knowledge networks, individuals' reputations as providers of knowledge spills over to the organizational level. However, there is an "anti-degree" assortativity effect (Wang et al. 2013) based on managers' and researchers' activity as knowledge seekers and their organizations' tendency to engage in R&D projects. In other words, the more active their managers or researchers are seeking knowledge in the interpersonal network the less their organizations formally collaborate and vice versa. In terms of the bottom-up influence of individual-level on organizational-level knowledge ties, this finding indicates that managers and researchers who seek a lot of knowledge – in contrast to those who provide a lot of knowledge – diminish their organizations' ability to find collaboration partners in the cluster context. They might create the impression of trying to free ride by informally tapping the knowledge bases of other individuals and their organizations. This behavior seems to be sanctioned at the organizational level by fewer formal collaboration opportunities. Finally, our cross-level closure finding highlights that interpersonal ties between two individuals increase the probability of a R&D collaboration between their organizations. Managers and researchers seem to use interpersonal exchange to find out about collaboration opportunities and estimate the trustworthiness of potential partners. Informal knowledge ties are thus important not only for gathering information and learning (e.g., McDonald et al. 2008; Oliver and Liebeskind 1997), they seem to function equally as instruments for entering formal knowledge collaborations.

As to the top-down influence of formal R&D collaborations on interpersonal knowledge networks the results of our study are similarly revealing. First, cross-level reputation spillovers lead to managers and researchers becoming popular sources for knowledge because their organizations engage in many projects with other firms. The organizations' activity thus seems to impact the visibility of their managers or researchers within the cluster context. Other managers and researchers seek knowledge from individuals belonging to central organizations as they seem to have access to broad knowledge resources and to be experienced and successful as initiators of formal collaborations. Alternatively, others might perceive them more generally as valuable network acquaintances to be associated with in order to benefit from their reputation (Kilduff and Krackhardt 1994). Second, individuals' activity as knowledge seekers is affected by their organizations' R&D collaborations. The negative interaction between managers' and researchers' activity in the informal network and their organizations' centrality in the formal collaboration network indicates that managers and researchers try to compensate for the lack of collaboration opportunities at the organizational level. In this sense, individuals calibrate their interpersonal knowledge seeking activities according to the (lack of) formal collaboration activities in their organizations. Finally, the cross-level closure findings highlight that individuals establish knowledge ties to managers or researchers belonging to formal collaboration partners more often than expected by chance. This practice might be perceived to create synergy effects as complementary knowledge can be gained at the micro- and the macro-levels.

In addition to our research question, our results highlight that different social processes seem to determine intra-organizational as compared to inter-organizational knowledge seeking by managers and researchers. Taking into account joint organizational memberships it becomes clear that individuals belonging to different organizations exchange knowledge reciprocally. This finding is in line with theoretical and empirical arguments provided by Pina-Stranger and Lazega (2010). The authors show that managers of biotech firms in an inter-organizational context share status with other managers as a relational strategy by taking the dual role of seeker and provider of advice. In contrast, intra-organizational knowledge seeking displays the characteristics of mentoring relationships where a junior manager seeks knowledge from a senior but not the other way around. As an alternative explanation, there might not be a need for direct reciprocation among individuals belonging to the same organization as the risk of being exploited opportunistically is lower within than between organizations. The finding further highlights how we can gain a more detailed understanding of the processes leading to the generation of structure by taking a multilevel perspective. As a delimiting factor, we have to point out that the result needs to be interpreted with caution as we did not survey all managers and researchers within the organizations under study. Hence, future research is needed for confirmation.

Our study not only contributes to research on knowledge sharing and cooperation in high-tech clusters, it adds generally to the emerging stream of multilevel network research (e.g., Berends et al. 2011; Brass et al. 2004; Lazega et al. 2008; Moliterno and Mahony 2011; Wang et al. 2013). We highlight that concepts used to analyze single-level networks, such as assortativity and closure, can be extended by a multilevel perspective. In their extended form these concepts help to understand relational processes spanning multiple organizational levels. In addition, we demonstrate that multilevel knowledge networks might be a part of social reality where bottom-up and top-down processes co-exist and give rise to the same cross-level patterns characterizing the overall network. While – analyzing cross-sectional data – we are not actually able to disentangle bottom-up and top-down processes, this mutuality would be in line with findings from Berends and colleagues (2011) and Rosenkopf and Schleicher (2008).

Our modeling approach enables us to leave the dyad level of stochastic estimations and derive conclusions about the occurrence of single-level and cross-level patterns while controlling for the overall structure of the multilevel network. In contrast to existing qualitative findings (e.g., Berends et al. 2011) our approach allows for the statement that cross-level interdependencies actually occur within our multilevel networks more often than expected by chance. Finally, in contrast to work by Gulati and Westphal (1999), Rosenkopf and colleagues (2001), and Rosenkopf and Schleicher (2008) we do not conflate levels of analysis by aggregating ties established by individuals to the organizational level and investigating tie multiplexity. Instead, we theoretically and empirically acknowledge the separate agency of individuals and organizations by building on a nested multilevel arrangement.

Our findings are practically meaningful as they help managers and researchers to understand how their interpersonal networking activities interact with their organizations' formal knowledge cooperation. As formal R&D collaborations are of foremost importance for high-tech firms to remain competitive (e.g., Powell et al. 1996) a good knowledge of how to attract and repel formal collaboration partners by informally providing and seeking knowledge is especially important for firm managers. Our research also helps individuals become aware of how their knowledge-seeking behavior is influenced by social preferences and contextual factors. If managers and researchers seek knowledge from others based on interpersonal similarity or because of an existing firm-level tie, this can lead to them not contacting the most knowledgeable advisors on a topic. Assuming that they joined the institutionalized cluster to get in contact with new people and organizations that offer complementary knowledge within their region and industry they are hence not capitalizing fully on the opportunities provided by the cluster.

There are some limitations that should be addressed by future research. In our study we do not disentangle bottom-up and top-down processes. Building on earlier findings that they mutually impact network emergence (e.g., Berends et al. 2011; Rosenkopf and Schleicher 2008), we show that bottom-up and top-down processes give rise to the same structural patterns characterizing multilevel networks. Disentangling the bottom-up and top-down processes empirically would require extensive longitudinal data to take into account different phases of network development as well as different time horizons in which actors at the two levels of agency establish and change their relations. Future research should take on the challenge of investigating such complex processes in order to examine the question of causality. In addition, it was not within the scope of our study to investigate the impact of multilevel network patterns on any micro- or macro-level success factors. It would be of highest interest to find out whether the alignment of formal and informal ties actually leads to the acquisition of complementary knowledge at both levels that positively impacts the success of collaborations. Likewise, future research should try to unravel in how far individual-level knowledge ties benefit organizational performance and the other way around.

Conclusion

In today's corporate environment, the exchange of knowledge across organizational boundaries is of critical importance, especially for high-tech firms wishing to remain competitive. As a consequence, formal knowledge networks at the level of organizations and informal individual-level knowledge networks among managers and researchers characterize high-tech industries. Our study shows how these organizational-level and individual-level knowledge networks are mutually influential. Focusing on knowledge networks emerging in the context of regional clusters, we highlight how R&D collaborations among organizations impact the interpersonal exchange of knowledge among managers and researchers and vice versa. Taking a multilevel network perspective, we extend the existing understanding of knowledge networks by demonstrating that individuals who are willing to share their knowledge with colleagues belong to organizations involved in many R&D collaborations. These managers and their organizations thus benefit from each others' central positions in the networks by having access to extensive sources of external knowledge. However, the opposite holds true when managers and researchers informally ask for knowledge from many of their colleagues. Our results show that extensive knowledge-seekers belong to organizations with fewer formal R&D collaborations. This can either be a sign of them trying to compensate for the lack of organizational-level collaborations or that they are harming their organizations' chances to find collaboration partners. Finally, if two organizations collaborate on a joint R&D project there is a good chance that their managers and researchers also informally exchange knowledge with each other. Formal and informal knowledge networks thus overlap and open up the potential to realize synergies.

References

Agneessens, F., & Wittek, R. (2012). Where do intra-organizational advice relations come from? The role of informal status and social capital in social exchange. *Social Networks, 34*(3), 333–345.
Ahuja, G. (2000). Collaboration networks, structural holes, and innovation: A longitudinal study. *Administrative Science Quarterly, 45*(3), 425–455.
Alcácer, J., & Chung, W. (2013). Location strategies for agglomeration economies. *Strategic Management Journal*: Online first.
Alecke, B., Alsleben, C., Scharr, F., & Untiedt, G. (2006). Are there really high-tech clusters? The geographic concentration of German manufacturing industries and its determinants. *Annals of Regional Science, 40*(1), 19–42.
Alexiev, A. S., Jansen, J. J. P., van den Bosch, F. A. J., & Volberda, H. W. (2010). Top management team advice seeking and exploratory innovation: The moderating role of TMT heterogeneity. *Journal of Management Studies, 47*(7), 1343–1364.
Barden, J. Q., & Mitchell, W. (2007). Disentangling the influences of leaders' relational embeddedness on interorganizational exchange. *Academy of Management Journal, 50*(6), 1440–1461.
Baum, J. A. C., Calabrese, T., & Silverman, B. S. (2000). Don't go it alone: Alliance network composition and startups' performance in Canadian biotechnology. *Strategic Management Journal, 21*(3), 267–294.
Berends, H., van Burg, E., & van Raaij, E. M. (2011). Contacts and contracts: Cross-level network dynamics in the development of an aircraft material. *Organization Science, 22*(4), 940–960.
Borgatti, S. P., & Cross, R. (2003). A relational view of information seeking and learning in social networks. *Management Science, 49*(4), 432–445.
Bouty, I. (2000). Interpersonal and interaction influences on informal resource exchanges between R&D researchers across organizational boundaries. *Academy of Management Journal, 43*(1), 50–65.
Brass, D. J., Galaskiewicz, J., Greve, H. R., & Tsai, W. (2004). Taking stock of networks and organizations: A multilevel perspective. *Academy of Management Journal, 47*(6), 795–817.
Burt, R. S. (2001). Structural holes versus network closure as social capital. In N. Lin, K. S. Cook, & R. S. Burt (Eds.), *Social capital. Theory and research* (pp. 31–56). New York: Aldine de Gruyter.

DeCarolis, D. M., & Deeds, D. L. (1999). The impact of stocks and flows of organizational knowledge on firm performance: An empirical investigation of the biotechnology industry. *Strategic Management Journal, 20*(10), 953–968.

Eisenhardt, K. M., & Schoonhoven, C. B. (1996). Resource-based view of strategic alliance formation: Strategic and social effects in entrepreneurial firms. *Organization Science, 7*(2), 136–150.

Gulati, R., & Westphal, J. D. (1999). Cooperative or controlling? The effects of CEO-board relations and the content of interlocks on the formation of joint ventures. *Administrative Science Quarterly, 44*(3), 473–506.

Heider, F. (1958). *The psychology of interpersonal relations*. London: Wiley.

Kilduff, M., & Krackhardt, D. (1994). Bringing the individual back in: A structural analysis of the internal market for reputation in organizations. *Academy of Management Journal, 37*(1), 87–108.

Lazega, E., & Pattison, P. E. (1999). Multiplexity, generalized exchange and cooperation in organizations: A case study. *Social Networks, 21*(1), 67–90.

Lazega, E., Jourda, M.-T., Mounier, L., & Stofer, R. (2008). Catching up with big fish in the big pond? Multi-level network analysis through linked design. *Social Networks, 30*(2), 159–176.

Lomi, A., & Pattison, P. E. (2006). Manufacturing relations: An empirical study of the organization of production across multiple networks. *Organization Science, 17*(3), 313–332.

Maurer, I., & Ebers, M. (2006). Dynamics of social capital and their performance implications: Lessons from biotechnology start-ups. *Administrative Science Quarterly, 51*(2), 262–292.

McDonald, M. L., Khanna, P., & Westphal, J. D. (2008). Getting them to think outside the circle: Corporate governance, CEOs' external advice networks, and firm performance. *Academy of Management Journal, 51*(3), 453–475.

Moliterno, T. P., & Mahony, D. M. (2011). Network theory of organization: A multilevel approach. *Journal of Management, 37*(2), 443–467.

Newman, M. E. J. (2002). Assortative mixing in networks. *Physical Review Letters, 89*(20), 208701.

Norman, P. M. (2002). Protecting knowledge in strategic alliances: Resource and relational characteristics. *The Journal of High Technology Management Research, 13*(2), 177–202.

Oliver, A. L. (2004). On the duality of competition and collaboration: Network-based knowledge relations in the biotechnology industry. *Scandinavian Journal of Management, 20*(1–2), 151–171.

Oliver, A. L., & Liebeskind, J. P. (1997). Three levels of networking for sourcing intellectual capital in biotechnology: Implications for studying interorganizational networks. *International Studies of Management & Organization, 27*(4), 76–103.

Owen-Smith, J., & Powell, W. W. (2004). Knowledge networks as channels and conduits: The effects of spillovers in the Boston biotechnology community. *Organization Science, 15*(1), 5–21.

Phelps, C., Heidl, R., & Wadhwa, A. (2012). Knowledge, networks, and knowledge networks: A review and research agenda. *Journal of Management, 38*(4), 1115–1166.

Pina-Stranger, A., & Lazega, E. (2010). Inter-organisational collective learning: The case of biotechnology in France. *European Journal of International Management, 4*(6), 602–620.

Pina-Stranger, A., & Lazega, E. (2011). Bringing personalized ties back in: Their added value for biotech entrepreneurs and venture capitalists interorganizational networks. *Sociological Quarterly, 52*(2), 268–292.

Porter, M. E. (2000). Location, competition, and economic development: Local clusters in a global economy. *Economic Development Quarterly, 14*(1), 15–34.

Powell, W. W., Koput, K. W., & Smith-Doerr, L. (1996). Interorganizational collaboration and the locus of innovation: Networks of learning in biotechnology. *Administrative Science Quarterly, 41*(1), 116–145.

Rank, O. N., Robins, G. L., & Pattison, P. E. (2010). Structural logic of intraorganizational networks. *Organization Science, 21*(3), 745–764.

Robins, G. L., Pattison, P. E., Kalish, Y., & Lusher, D. (2007). An introduction to exponential random graph (p*) models for social networks. *Social Networks, 29*(2), 173–191.

Robins, G. L., Pattison, P. E., & Wang, P. (2009). Closure, connectivity and degree distributions: Exponential random graph (p*) models for directed social networks. *Social Networks, 31*(2), 105–117.

Rosenkopf, L., & Schleicher, T. (2008). Below the tip of the iceberg: The co-evolution of formal and informal interorganizational relations in the wireless telecommunications industry. *Managerial and Decision Economics, 29*(5), 425–441.

Rosenkopf, L., Metiu, A., & George, V. P. (2001). From the bottom up? Technical committee activity and alliance formation. *Administrative Science Quarterly, 46*(4), 748–772.

Shipilov, A. V. (2012). Strategic multiplexity. *Strategic Organization, 10*(3), 215–222.

Snijders, T. A. B., Pattison, P. E., Robins, G. L., & Handcock, M. S. (2006). New specifications for exponential random graph models. *Sociological Methodology, 36*(1), 99–153.

Snijders, T. A. B., van de Bunt, G. G., & Steglich, C. E. G. (2010). Introduction to stochastic actor-based models for network dynamics. *Social Networks, 32*(1), 44–60.

Spence, A. M. (1974). *Market signaling*. Cambridge, MA: Harvard University Press.

Wang, P., Robins, G., Pattison, P., & Lazega, E. (2013). Exponential random graph models for multilevel networks. *Social Networks, 35*(1), 96–115.

Zeller, C. (2001). Clustering biotech: A recipe for success? Spatial patterns of growth of biotechnology in Munich, Rhineland and Hamburg. *Small Business Economics, 17*(1–2), 123–141.

Chapter 12
Inter-organizational Network Influence on Long-Term and Short-Term Inter-individual Relationships: The Case of a Trade Fair for TV Programs Distribution in Sub-Saharan Africa

Guillaume Favre, Julien Brailly, Josiane Chatellet, and Emmanuel Lazega

In this chapter we study the influence of inter-organizational relationships on the formation of inter-individual relationships in a context of a trade fair. From a multilevel network analysis perspective (MNA), research has examined the influence of the network at one level on the network at another level (for example Lazega et al. 2007, 2008, 2013; Favre et al. 2012; Brailly et al. 2016 forthcoming; Hollway and Koskinen 2015). This research often shows that inter-organizational ties have a strong influence on inter-individual relationship formation and viceversa. This mutual influence can be seen as a process of adjustment between levels of action that Lazega (2015, and forthcoming) calls "synchronization." In the organizational society, most of the time, the evolution of inter-organizational networks is the force that drives the evolution of inter-individual networks. From this perspective, individuals have to incur 'costs of synchronization' to adjust their behavior over time to the organizational context and demands, especially when they wish to reshape their opportunity structure. Our argument is that temporary organizations in the global economy such as trade fairs are a way to break free, or to some extent "emancipate" (Lazega 2015), from organizational structure by providing new opportunities for individuals to create long distance ties.

G. Favre (✉)
University of Toulouse Jean-Jaurès, LISST-Cers CNRS, Toulouse, France
e-mail: guillaume.favre@univ-tlse2.fr

J. Brailly
Swinburne University of Technology, Center for Transformative Innovation, Melbourne, Australia
e-mail: jbrailly@swin.edu.au

J. Chatellet
Université Paris-Dauphine, IRISSO-CNRS, PSL, Paris, France

E. Lazega
Institut d'Etudes Politiques de Paris, SPC, CSO-CNRS, 19 rue Amélie, 75007 Paris, France

Through the study of a trade fair for TV program distribution in sub-Saharan Africa, we study the influence of inter-organizational ties (deals and partnerships) on short-term-inter-individual relationships created during the event and on long-term relationships created outside the trade fair but reactivated during the event. We try to understand how this event participates in the formation of a social milieu around the distribution of TV programs in Africa.

Indeed, during this kind of event, company representatives have an important relational activity. They try to create new ties with other companies in order to find new commercial opportunities. But if actors can create new ties during this kind of events, lots of relationships preexist and are only reactivated and renewed. Representatives may know each other from other contexts: they may have met during other events in which they both participated; they may have worked for the same company; or their company may already have closed partnerships which create the context for inter-individual tie formation. In order to study how this event influences the emergence of a social milieu in an industry, it is necessary to distinguish long-term relationships which preexist and the new relationships created during the event that Bathelt and Schuldt (2008) call 'global pipelines,' namely transnational relationships that companies create in a global economy in order to initiate international partnerships. The temporality of ties is now an important question in social network analysis. Different network temporalities involve different social mechanisms (Quintane 2012; Quintane et al. 2013). More precisely, we argue that the multilevel influences are different for short-term and long-term inter-individual ties. We assume that inter-organizational networks are more stable than inter-individual networks, since individuals can easily create and destroy ties. Through our case study, we show that while the inter-organizational contract network influences the long-term inter-individual network, it has a weak influence on the short-term relationships, which supports the idea that synchronization of levels is an important social problem, and that trade fairs are a way either to escape from the constraints that come attached in markets, or a way to manage it.

In order to explore the dual dimension of markets, we use a multilevel social networks framework, developed by Lazega and his co-authors (2007, 2008). This approach is based on the study of multilevel networks observing two superposed and partially nested, interdependent levels of agency, an inter-organizational system of action and an inter-individual one.

Relationship Creation During Trade Fairs

Despite of the development of communication technologies and the digital economy, actors in global markets still rely on physical meeting places such as professional trade fairs, exhibitions or conventions. In many industries, these trade fairs are important: during a few days they group the main actors of a profession in a microcosm where participants can have a fast and accurate vision of market structures.

Trade Fairs, Long-Term and Short-Term Relationships

Trade fairs have drawn the attention of the researchers for a number of reasons. Indeed, during the communication technologies age, it is surprising that trade fairs still exist, given that companies can communicate and create long distance relationships without face-to-face contacts. Research shows that trade fairs are more than simple marketplaces to exchange goods: they are places to organize markets. There are many kinds of professional events in a range of different sectors. Music or film festivals, book or wine fairs, art biennials, etc. – countless events are organized in many parts of the world and for many sectors and industries (Bathelt and Schuldt 2008; Lampel and Meyer 2008; Maskell et al. 2006; Moeran and Pedersen 2011). Trade fairs are often studied by the management sciences to describe how companies rely on these events to do business or to obtain information about the industry and its evolution (see for example Hansen 2004; Sanchez-Maranon et al. 1996; Seringhaus and Rosson 2001). From sociological and organizational studies point of view, several studies have been conducted on trade fairs as places for organizing industries. They create relationships between members from several companies and influence the construction of a social milieu. These places play an important role for emerging industries (Aspers and Darr 2011). Bringing together all the actors of an industry in one place, they concretize the existence of this milieu and its boundaries. They also participate in the definition of status hierarchies within industries. These hierarchies can be observed through the various types of limited access in trade fairs such as VIP access to different areas of television program trade fairs (Havens 2006) or in *fashion weeks* (Entwistle and Rocamora 2006; Skov 2006), but also through the booths, their sizes and their levels of sophistication.

These events help to build a collective identity in an industry and even forms of collective action. Garcia-Parpet (2005) shows for example how the Loire wine fair (*Salon des vins de Loire*) has participated in the construction of an identity for these wines and has promoted the creation of common resources for international exportation. In many industries, social norms and rules are shared and diffused during fairs. As Smith (2011) shows through an analysis of auction rooms, social norms may be simple, like dress codes, or less visible elements, such as appropriate behaviors during auctions. This phenomenon is reinforced by the fact that fairs play an important role in labor markets where members often move from one company to another (Power and Jansson 2008). But from our social network perspective, the important point is that trade fairs are intermediation devices between supply and demand. They allow face-to-face meetings and embed the market with personal relationships (in the sense of Granovetter 1985). Some authors underline the learning opportunities of these events. Attendees can observe their competitors (Skov 2006; White 1981); get information about products, pricing scripts (Velthuis 2003) or market trends in an industry (Bathelt et al. 2004). Trade fairs help companies in the globalized economy to identify new partners, suppliers or clients from different parts of the world. The main argument is that these international ties – or 'global pipelines' (Bathelt and Schuldt 2008) – do not require permanent co-localization, but a temporary and recurrent co-localization that concerns only a few steps in the deal-making process. According to these authors, these global pipelines are created during international trade fairs.

Although all these studies underline the relational dimension of these events, few study this dimension concretely using social network analysis. If we focus more precisely on this dimension, we have to distinguish the relationships that are exclusively created during one trade fair from relationships that preexist the event. Indeed if trade fairs are an important place to create new inter-individual and inter-organizational relationships we have to take into account that other contexts of interactions can exist. On the first hand, as underlined by Power and Jansson (2008) many trade fairs are organized in the same industry during a single year and organizations and individuals often attend several events. On the other hand, many relationships or partnerships already exist between companies and are simply reactivated during a trade fair. As a result, in order to understand how a trade fair concretely influences the creation of the social milieu of an industry, we have to distinguish these two kinds of relationships: long-term and short-term.

The Influence of Trade Fairs and Inter-organizational Partnerships on Inter-individual Relationships

The relationships which are created during this kind of event are inter-individual relationships. Companies are officially participating to these events but they are always represented by sales, commercial or acquisition representatives. Inter-individual ties are created in order to initiate commercial partnerships – inter-organizational ties – between organizations. Inter-organizational partnership networks are stable structures that evolve slower than inter-individual ties (Brailly et al. 2016 forthcoming). Individuals can quickly create and destroy ties but inter-organizational partnerships are fixed once they have been closed. When the employees of a company attend a trade fair, the inter-organizational structure already exists and they must take it into account while creating the basis of new partnerships. The perception of this inter-organizational structure influences the relational strategies of these individuals.

Inter-organizational networks are frequently studied by researchers. But while generally inter-organizational network structures and inter-individual networks are analyzed separately, we believe that inter-organizational structures strongly influence the relationship creation process at the inter-individual level. Following Brailly et al. (2015), we propose to study them jointly and to try to reframe our perspective on how this embeddedness impacts social and economic ties. This multilevel analysis of networks has been developed recently and we can start to understand how multilevel positions influence individual performance (Bellotti 2012; Lazega et al. 2008). Other studies also show how individuals can use inter-organizational ties to extend their relational capital (Lazega et al. 2013). But we have less knowledge of how inter-organizational structures influence inter-individual relationships. In this volume, Lazega (2015) proposes a theoretical framework to analyze the evolution of multilevel networks. Following Snijders' perspective on networks dynamics (Snijders 1996) and White's analysis of chains of opportunities (White 1970), Lazega argues that the evolution of the network of one level can be seen as the energy which drives the evolution of networks of a second level: what he calls 'synchronization' is the set of efforts invested by actors at both levels to coordinate their evolutions In this perspective each level needs to adjust to the other, and actors (individuals or their organizations) face 'synchronization costs' in adapting or aligning their behavior to adjust to the other level. As an example, a researcher whose research center creates a relationship with another research center could be forced to collaborate with other people, at the risk of giving up other partnerships that have already been initiated. In Lazega's perspective, these costs are incurred in unequal and often invisible ways, by individuals who need to adapt to such organizational movements, while other individuals are more successful at managing the inter-organizational level by creating meso-level organizations and using them as "tools with a life of their own" to mitigate the constraints of synchronization.

From an economic sociology perspective, our argument is that in markets, inter-organizational and inter-individual networks are also strongly related. The dealings or partnerships structures between companies strongly influence their employees' behavior. But in our view trade fairs are a way to escape from these inter-organizational constraints. Individuals can break free of organizational ties, initiate new partnerships, and obtain new business and job opportunities. Beyond that, trade fairs could be considered as the meso-level intermediary or temporary organizations that Lazega describes, and controlling them is a way to control inter-organizational structure and synchronization costs. Indeed, Bathelt and Schuldt (2008) describe trade fairs as places where the market structure is produced and reproduced. Attending trade fairs is a way to initiate long distance inter-organizational relationships and influence inter-organizational structure.

We consider here two multilevel configurations that can influence inter-individual tie creation: *embeddedness* and *structural equivalence*. What we call *embeddedness* is a multilevel structural configuration in which a linkage is created between two individuals when there is an inter-organizational tie between their companies (see Fig. 12.1). If a partnership already exists between two organizations, it can provide a context for the creation of a new relationship between two individuals. This phenomenon has been shown by Lazega et al. (2013) with the concept of 'extended relational capital.' In the field of cancer research, they show that researchers can extend their relationships by targeting individuals who are affiliated to a research center with which their laboratory has a partnership. The inter-organizational tie provides a context for inter-individual relationship creation. In addition, this *embeddedness* configuration can also occur when the inter-individual relationship is the basis of the inter-organizational relationship. Indeed, behind each partnership between companies there are always inter-individual ties (Gulati and Sytch 2008; Gulati 1995). If a partnership between two organizations necessitates

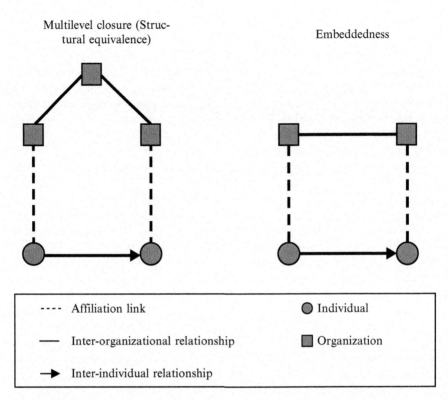

Fig. 12.1 Two kind of influence of inter-organizational relationships on inter-individual relationships

inter-individual collaboration at the beginning of a contracting process between companies, the more a partnership is repeated between two companies, the more it breaks away from the inter-individual relationship to become an inter-organizational tie that does not need specific acquaintances between its members (Lorenz 1999).

The other multilevel configuration which can influence inter-individual configuration is *structural equivalence* at the organizational level (Fig. 12.1). We can also call this configuration a *multilevel closure*: two individuals whose companies have the same commercial partners have a tendency to create a relationship. Structural equivalence in a commercial network could be interpreted as a situation of competition between two companies. In a market two actors are competitors because they depend on the same types of resources and the same sources of resources (Burt and Carlton 1989; Burt and Talmud 1993; Burt 1988). For example, through the analysis of transactions between audit firms and their clients, Han (1994) shows that firms tend to influence each other within sub-markets corresponding to different levels of quality which boundaries are drawn by sets of structurally equivalent companies. Similarly, Burt (1988) deconstructs the American industries by identifying structurally equivalent sub-markets and demonstrates that they cover very stable sectors of the US economy. When we study the influence of this configuration of inter-organizational relationships on inter-individual ties, we observe the effect of competition between companies on individual relational behavior. Indeed some studies have shown that individuals tend to have informal relationships with their direct competitors, including being friends (Ingram and Roberts 2000) or exchanges social resources with them (Éloire 2010; Pina-Stranger and Lazega 2010). In our case study, these informal relationships are a way to get access to information about market trends, commercial opportunities or information about reliability of potential clients or providers. Our hypothesis is that sellers and buyers perceive these competitive dimensions at the inter-organizational level and turn to members of companies with which they are in competition to access social resources and useful information about the market.

We know that both of these multilevel configurations can influence relationship formation at the inter-individual level. But as we said earlier, in a context of a trade fair we can observe two kinds of relationships: short-term and long-term. We propose to study how the stable inter-organizational partnership network structures influence long-term and short-term relationships in the case of a trade fair. In our view these inter-organizational configurations will influence in different ways the relationships that are created during the trade fair and long-term relationships. If trade fairs are, as we said previously, a way for individuals to break free from the inter-organizational structure, these configurations will have less influence on the short-term network than on the long-term.

A Study of a Trade Fair for TV Programs in Sub-Saharan Africa

Our case study is a trade fair for TV program exchanges in sub-Saharan Africa. Between the producers of programs and the final consumers there are many intermediaries with different roles: producers, distributors, broadcasters, satellite manufacturers, cable operators, channel packagers, etc. In simple terms, it is possible to divide this value chain into three key stages: program production, distribution and broadcasting. The trade fair under study is about the second stage: distribution and acquisition of TV programs copyrights. This event groups sellers of programs, i.e. all holders of TV program copyrights (audiovisual production companies, media groups and distribution intermediaries), and purchasers of TV programs (TV channels, video on demand platforms or intermediaries). When a transaction takes place, the copyrights for a given geographic area are transmitted to the buyer who can then broadcast the program. The TV program distribution industry is characterized by the importance of fairs, festivals and conferences during which industry actors can meet (Bielby 2008; Havens 2006). The specific event under consideration is organized once a year in a convention center in Johannesburg. Sellers sit in booths with television sets to present their catalogues of films, series and shows. The buyers' goal is to select programs which will fit their audience and perhaps bring new viewers. They walk around the place to visit sellers and choose programs in which to invest. For sellers (but also for buyers), obtaining informal information is strategic because it is a good way to target potential clients, their needs, their resources, their reliability and their purchasing and bargaining power. For buyers trade fairs are an opportunity to obtain information about market trends, new programs and new technologies. Generally, informal information is a good way to identify new commercial opportunities. As a consequence, to explore the construction of partnerships between organizations, it is necessary to take into consideration relationships between individuals and especially informal information exchanges.

A Multilevel Social Network Study

We ran a survey during the 2012 edition of the trade fair. We first conducted interviews with 62 attendees of the fair. These interviews were designed to study the concrete tasks actors have to carry out to sell or buy programs; to identify different forms of interdependencies between actors; and to understand the issues and debates of this industry. This survey provided the basis for developing a questionnaire. We designed a multilevel study of this event. In our perspective, the first level of analysis is composed of individual buyers and sellers and the second level is their companies. The questionnaire was designed to collect data about the companies and the participants, and about their relationships. It included sociometric questions, such as who at the fair had provided the attendees with useful information for their work (the question listed five examples of information: about a competitor, about market trends, about programs trends, about the reliability of partners and business opportunities exchanges). Respondents were asked to check the names of people with whom they had exchanged informal information before or during the show in the list of attendees.

A second question was designed to further refine the previous one. Among the participants from whom the respondent declared s/he had obtained information, s/he had to check the name of the persons s/he had met outside the trade fair. This question was designed to differentiate two kinds of relationships: the short-term relationships created during the trade fair and long-term relationships renewed or simply reactivated during the fair.

Another question asked about the companies with which their company had closed a deal during the fair or during the previous year. This question corresponds to the inter-organizational network, which represents the economic structure of the milieu. Although the answers are provided by individuals, this network of contracts can be considered an inter-organizational network. Indeed, approximately 45 % of individuals quoted organization names and not individuals' names. During interviews, they justify this with several reasons: several individuals and divisions (accounting, legal, sales) could be involved during the deal-making process; the

Table 12.1 Basic statistics of the three collected networks

	Short-term (individuals)	Long-term (individuals)	Deal (companies)
Number of nodes	118	118	109
Number of arcs	639	480	779
Density	.046	.035	.066
Average degree	10.831	8.136	14.294
Reciprocity rate (dyad based)	.099	.146	na

deal could be signed with other colleagues, previously in charge of this area, during negotiations initiated years ago. As a consequence, we analyzed this network by organizations (Table 12.1).

The trade fair under study included 450 companies and 916 individuals. With so many participants it seemed impossible to collect survey results from each participant. We had to make boundary choices following a nominalist strategy (Laumann et al. 1989). Since our objective was to study the formation of a social milieu of the TV programs distribution in Africa, we limited our survey to individuals whose company had participated at least twice in the previous editions of the fair. Our assumption was that these people were already integrated in this milieu and had established several relationships during the previous editions of the fair. Our hypothesis was that individuals whose company had participated in the fair were generally more central than others in the network.[1] By targeting these actors, the goal was to address the dense regions of the global network. This boundary definition leads us to select 338 individuals for the population of the study. Most of the questionnaires were completed by respondents during face-to-face interviews. After the event we called each participant who did not answer during the event and asked them to complete an electronic version of the questionnaire. Finally, we managed to collect 126 responses among 338 participants which represent 37 % of responses for the inter-individual network and 59 % for the inter-organizational network.

We are thus able to reconstruct three social networks: two individual networks, one of informal information exchange relationships created during the trade fair and one of informal information exchange relationships existing before the trade fair; and, on the second level, a network of transactions between their companies. In this chapter, we consider these inter-individual networks as dependent variables. We try to understand the role of multilevel effects on the creation of long-term and short-term inter-individual relationships.

---

[1] This assumption was based on previous studies of this trade fair, which show a strong correlation between centrality and experience in the trade fair.

Independent Variables

We focus in this chapter on the influence of inter-organizational relationships on inter-individual relationships. In this perspective, our independent variables are based on the inter-organizational network. As we said earlier, we study two multilevel configurations which can influence tie formation between individuals: embeddedness and structural equivalence. We create three dyadic variables to explain inter-individual relationship formation based on the inter-organizational network.

The variable *Deal between companies* represents the embeddedness hypothesis. It is a dyadic binary variable that indicates whether a deal has been closed between to individuals' companies.

A second set of variables are used to test the structural equivalence hypothesis. The *Same providers*, and *Same clients* variables are dyadic continuous variables which measure the number of two-paths between two individuals' companies in the deal network. It measures the number of clients or providers that these companies have in common. The goal is to test the effect of competition, measured by structural equivalence between companies, on inter-individual relationships. This measure is divided in two variables: the number of common partners for selling companies is indicated by the *same clients* variable, while the *same providers* variable is used for buying companies.

Control Variables

We also use a set of control variables in order to control various effects or contexts which can influence inter-individual relationship formation during or outside the trade fair (Table 12.2).

We study a trade fair which is a market context for relationship formation. Sellers try to meet buyers who are looking for the type of TV programs that they are selling and *vice versa*. In order to control this effect on relationship formation, we create a *Matching supply and demand* variable which measure the likeness between the catalogue of a seller and the kind of programs a buyer is looking for. This variable is based on data extracted from the trade fair database. When participants register for the event, they have to declare the kind of programs they sell or look for during the trade fair, selecting among 27 categories of programs (e.g. TV series, feature films, sporting events, game shows, etc.). This variable is based on this dataset using a Jaccard index to measure the level of matching. The more a seller's programs match what a buyer is looking for, the closer the index will be to one.

Participants may also exchange information because they met during other industry trade fairs. As we said earlier, there are many trade fairs in this industry. The most important are *MipTV, MipCom, NATPE* and *Los Angeles Screenings* (Bielby 2008). We collected the list of attendees to 19 global events of TV program

Table 12.2 Basic statistics for the networks analysis

		Mean	SD	Min	Max	2	3	4	5	6	7	8	9	10
1	Matching supply and demand	.09	.13	0	1	−.71	−.09	.00	−.12	.17	.06	−.07	.15	.08
2	Same category	.55	.50	0	1		.16	.03	.16	−.17	−.02	.16	−.14	−.06
3	Co-participation	.93	1.61	0	19			.00	.04	.02	−.03	.18	.03	.10
4	Same company	.00	.05	0	1				.16	−.02	.21	.20	−.01	.06
5	Same region	.11	.31	0	1					−.01	.12	.10	−.01	.07
6	Deal between companies	.08	.27	0	1						.11	.08	.19	.29
7	Same providers	.40	1.46	0	32							−.13	.00	.06
8	Same clients	.71	1.55	0	32								.01	.09
9	Short term relationships	.05	.21	0	1									−.04
10	Long term relationships	.03	.19	0	1									

distribution since 2009 from the websites of these trade fairs. We constructed a *Co-participation* variable based on these data. This is a dyadic continuous variable which indicates the number of trade fairs in which two individuals participate in common since 2009.

Finally, we construct three binary control variables. The *Same region* variable control a homophily effect of the region of the company's headquarters. (Six regions: French-speaking Africa, English-speaking Africa, Europe, Northern America, Asia and Southern America). The *Same category* variable indicates if two individuals have the same category during the trade fair (buyer or seller). The *Same company* variable indicate if two individuals are employed by the same company.

Analysis of the Structures of Long-Term and Short-Term Relationships

Method

In order to study inter-individual relationship creation, we used quadratic-assignment procedure (QAP) for logistic regressions using network data. It begins with a standard logistic regression across the corresponding cells of the dependent and independent matrices. QAP procedure has a second step where additional regressions (in our case 5000) are estimated by randomly permuting the rows and columns of the dependent matrix. The significance of the coefficient of a variable is determined by comparing its magnitude in the initial regression to the magnitudes of the coefficients for that variable in the random regressions. If a positive coefficient is of a magnitude that is greater than 95 % of the randomly generated coefficients, it is considered to be significant.

Results

First, we ran QAP logit model on the short-term relationships, i.e. new relationships created during the context of the trade fair (Table 12.3). As we can see in model 2, this network is mainly a commercial network. Matching between supply and demand have a strong effect on network formation, meaning that sellers and buyers are likely to exchange information if they sell and buy the same categories of products. We can also see that the same category effect is negative and significant which mean that relationships between buyers and sellers are more likely to occur than relationships between buyers or between sellers. On the other side, being from the same region does not have a strong effect (it is barely significant) on the ties that are created during the trade fair, which indicates that the relationships that are created during the trade fairs have a tendency to be transnational.

Table 12.3 QAP Logit model for short term relationships

		Model 1	Model 2	Exp(b)
Control variables	Intercept	−3.286***	−3.180***	.042
	Matching supply and demand		1.493**	4.450
	Same category		−1.068***	.344
	Co-participation		.126**	1.134
	Same company		−12.115***	.000
	Same region		.284 .	1.328
Multilevel effects	Deal between companies	1.899***	1.488***	4.429
	Same providers	.075	−.074	.929
	Same clients	−.045	.016	1.016
Pseudo R^2		.51	.51	

Note: Data are based on 15,750 observations, QAP Logit model (Double Dekker semi-partialling test, 5000 permutations), Pseudo $R^2 = .51$
. $P<.1$; * $P<.05$; ** $P<.01$; *** $P<.001$

We can also see that the control variable "being in the same company" has a strong negative effect on the creation of short-term relationships (since members already know each other) and that there is a positive effect of co-participation to other events (confirming the dynamics brought to light by Brailly et al. 2015).

Concerning the effects of the inter-organizational network, we can see in the model 1 that the hypothesis of *embeddedness* is confirmed. When companies have already closed a deal, or when a deal was closed during the fair, the individuals have a tendency to create inter-individual relationships. Because our dataset is not dynamic it is difficult to interpret precisely this result. As we said earlier, the inter-individual relationship can preexist and generate trust in order to create an inter-organizational partnership. But the inter-organizational relationship can also preexist, providing a context for the creation of inter-individual ties. However, there is globally a weak effect of the inter-organizational network: there is not any effect of multilevel closure (or structural equivalence). Two individuals whose companies have deal ties to the same companies will not have a short-term tie. The ties created during the trade fair are not influenced by the structural equivalence effect. This result is confirmed by model 2, in which we control these multilevel effects using the different control variables. However, the embeddedness effect is still significant although it is less strong.

The results are quite different for the long-term network (Table 12.4). On the one hand, as we can see in model 4, the network seems to be also guided by commercial relationships. The same category parameter is still negative and significant which means that relationships between sellers and buyers are more likely to occur than relationships between sellers or between buyers. But on the other hand, the matching supply and demand effect is not significant anymore which means that these relationships do not only follow a commercial dimension. This long-term network seems to be more a network of relationships between competitors than the short-term version. The same region parameter is strong and significant. Individual

Table 12.4 Model for long term relationships

		Model 3	Model 4	Exp(b)
Control variables	Intercept	−4.125***	−4.502***	.011
	Matching supply and demand		.969	2.635
	Same category		−.362*	.696
	Co-participation		.247***	1.280
	Same company		.979	2.662
	Same region		1.079***	2.940
Multilevel effects	Deal between companies	2.533***	2.525***	12.491
	Same providers	.093 .	.053	1.055
	Same clients	.155**	.117*	1.124
Pseudo R^2		.53	.53	

Note: Data are based on 15,750 observations, QAP Logit model (Double Dekker semi-partialling test, 5000 permutations), Pseudo $R^2 = .53$
. $P < .1$; * $P < .05$; ** $P < .01$; *** $P < .001$

actors whose companies' headquarters are in the same region are more likely to have long-term relationships. Companies based in the same region are often in a situation of competition because, if they are sellers, they sell the same kind of programs (programs are in the same language, with the same standard of production and likely cultural similarities) and, if they are buyers, they broadcast in the same region. We can also observe a strong co-participation to other events effect. This parameter is even stronger than in the model for the short-term relationships. Indeed the other global events of the industry offer a context for creating relationships which can be reactivated during the trade fair under study.

But the most important point is that the multilevel configurations have much more influence than in the short-term network. First, in model 3, the embeddedness hypothesis is confirmed. As in the short-term network, individual actors tend to create long-term relationships when their companies have a partnership, but the parameter is much stronger than in the short-term network, even in the model in which we take into account the control variables. Deals between companies are clearly embedded in inter-individual long-term relationships. Moreover, the structural equivalence effect in the deal network is confirmed for sellers. We can observe for sellers a tendency towards multilevel closure: sellers whose companies have common clients have a tendency to create long-term relationships. This effect shows that for long-term relationships individual sellers tend to cross competition boundaries to get information from people working in other companies. This seller that we interviewed during the trade fair explains this phenomenon.

> « We always have to speak with the other persons, to know eventually who is doing what in which country, or if a new client is contacting us, to see if we know people who has already worked with them. To know if they are serious, if it is interesting to develop commercial relationships with them. We always... investigate a little bit we could say... [inside your company?] No no! It depends but we often speak with competitors with whom we have good relationships, who are on the same offer. »
>
> A seller at the trade fair

	Long term relationships	Short term relationships
Matching supply and demand		++
Same category	-	--
Co-participation	+	+
Same company		---
Same region	++	
Deal between companies	+++	++
Same providers		
Same clients	+	

Fig. 12.2 Simplified results for long-term and short-term relationships models. Note: +: $b>0$; ++: $b>1$; +++: $b>2$

This seller explains that he obtained information during negotiations with buyers from direct competitors, i.e. with sellers who had already closed a deal with the same buyer. The information provided by this competitor is much more precise than any other information: he knows the buyer directly and can evaluate the reliability and the trustworthiness of the buyer. We then understand why these sellers prefer to look for information with their direct competitors rather than other sellers: the information they get is more useful. But in order to get such information, sellers need to share long-term relationships. On the other hand, even if the structural equivalence effect for buyers is lightly significant in model 3 it is not significant anymore when we take into account the control variables in model 4. Only long-term relationships between sellers are influenced by this multilevel closure.

Through these two multilevel mechanisms, the inter-organizational deal network has more influence on long-term relationships between individuals than on short-term relationships (Fig. 12.2).

Conclusion and Discussion

In this chapter we tried to contribute to the multilevel network analysis perspective (MAN). We studied the influence of inter-organizational deal networks on inter-individual information exchanges during a trade fair. The main contribution of this chapter is to show that inter-organizational networks can strongly influence some inter-individual relationships but not every type of relationship. We study two kinds of multilevel configurations which can affect relationship creation at the inter-individual level: embeddedness and inter-organizational structural equivalence. While long-term ties in the industry, i.e. ties not created during the trade fair, are strongly influenced by the inter-organizational network, short-term relationships created during the trade fair are less influenced by this second level.

We can read this result as what Lazega (Chap. 2 in this volume) describes as one possible process of multilevel synchronization between superposed dynamics. The long-term relationships are more adjusted to the stable inter-organizational structure than the short-term relationships. This result also shows that during trade fairs, individuals are able to break free from the inter-organizational structure and create new relationships without taking into account their companies' positions. They can adopt a cosmopolitan behavior and construct global pipelines as described by Bathelt and Schuldt (2008). From this perspective, trade fairs can be considered as meso-level organizations that can be used or created by individuals in order to control the organizational level.

But this result can be also read in another way and this is another contribution of this chapter: through this multilevel framework we are able to redefine competition as mainly an organizational phenomenon. Indeed, individual sellers and buyers can move from a company to another. They can be employed in a company and move to another during their career. As a result, they are able to share information with their direct competitors (actors whose companies are structurally equivalent in a deal network). Conversely, competition barriers seem to be obstacles during the trade fair. Individuals are in a situation of competition during the event but not outside.

Through the study of this trade fair for television program exchange, we have tried to show how this type of event facilitates the emergence of a social milieu. In the globalization of trade, these fairs give way to social processes among the participants: observation between competitors, definition of a social milieu and its borders, collective learning and integration into that milieu. Creating international ties in the context of a globalized market requires a complex multilevel process that involves companies and their employees. Using a social network analysis of information exchanges among the attendees helps to understand how these international ties are created, but one limitation of the study that we have presented here is that it does not take into account simultaneously relationship formation at each level. The future developments of multilevel ERGM (Wang et al. 2013) could be a solution to take into account networks of different levels and with three kinds of relationships.

Another limitation of this dataset is a problem of dynamics. We know that this process of relationship creation necessitates dynamic data to study precisely the influence of each level. Measuring long-term and short-term relationships was a solution to identify the temporality of these social mechanisms, but using two different cross-sectional network measurements, could be an avenue future research to understand the complex interactions between organizations and individuals for the emergence of this social milieu.

Appendices

Appendix 1: Visualization of Long-Term Information Exchange Network Between Individuals

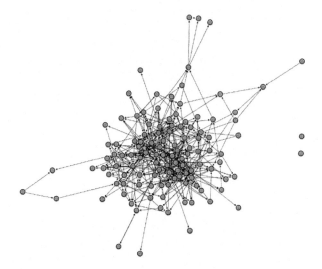

Appendix 2: Visualization of Short-Term Information Exchange Network Between Individuals

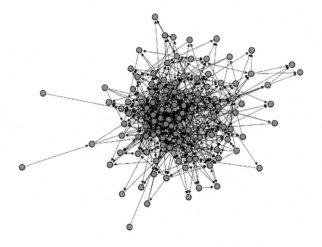

Appendix 3: Visualization of Deal Network Between Companies

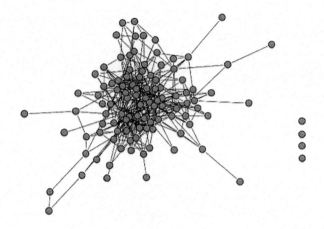

References

Aspers, P., & Darr, A. (2011). Trade shows and the creation of market and industry. *The Sociological Review, 59*(4), 758–778.
Bathelt, H., & Schuldt, N. (2008). Between luminaires and meat grinders: International trade fairs as temporary clusters. *Regional Studies, 42*(6), 853–868.
Bathelt, H., Malmberg, A., & Maskell, P. (2004). Clusters and knowledge: Local buzz, global pipelines and the process of knowledge creation. *Progress in Human Geography, 28*(1), 31–56.
Bellotti, E. (2012). Getting funded. Multi-level network of physicists in Italy. *Social Networks, 34*(2), 215–229.
Bielby, D. D. (2008). *Global TV: Exporting television and culture in the world market*. New York: New York University Press.
Brailly, J., Favre, G., Chatellet, J., & Lazega, E. (2015). Exponential random graph models for a multilevel network – A case study of the audiovisual market in Eastern Europe. In E. Lazega & T. A. B. Snijders (Eds.), *Multi-level network analysis for the social sciences: Theory, methods and applications*. Cham: Springer.
Brailly, J., Favre, G., Lazega, E., & Chatellet, J. (2016 forthcoming). Embeddedness as a multilevel problem: A case study in economic sociology. *Social Networks*.
Burt, R. S. (1988). The stability of American markets. *American Journal of Sociology, 94*(2), 356–395.
Burt, R. S., & Carlton, D. S. (1989). Another look at the network boundaries of American markets. *American Journal of Sociology, 95*(3), 723–753.
Burt, R. S., & Talmud, I. (1993). Market niche. *Social Networks, 15*(2), 133–149.
Éloire, F. (2010). Une approche sociologique de la concurrence sur un marché Le cas. *Revue Française de Sociologie, 51*(3), 481–517.
Entwistle, J., & Rocamora, A. (2006). The field of fashion materialized: A study of London Fashion Week. *Sociology, 40*(4), 735–751.
Favre, G., Brailly, J., Chatellet, J., & Lazega, E. (2012). De la relación inter-individual a la relación inter-organizacional: Un análisis de redes multinivel de un mercado de programas de televisión en África subsahariana. *REDES-Revista hispana para el Análisis de redes sociales, 23*, 113–145.

Garcia-Parpet, M.-F. (2005). Le Salon des vins de Loire: convivialité et vocation internationale. *Ethnologie Française, 35*(1), 63–72.
Granovetter, M. (1985). Economic action and social structure: The problem of embeddedness. *American Journal of Sociology, 91*(3), 481–510.
Gulati, R. (1995). Does familiarity breed trust? The implications of repeated ties for contractual choice in alliances. *Academy of Management Journal, 38*(1), 85–112.
Gulati, R., & Sytch, M. (2008). Does familiarity breed trust? Revisiting the antecedents of trust. *Managerial and Decision Economics, 29*(2–3), 165–190.
Han, S.-K. (1994). Mimetic isomorphism and its effect on the audit services market. *Social Forces, 73*(2), 637.
Hansen, K. (2004). Measuring performance at trade shows: Scale development and validation. *Journal of Business Research, 57*(1), 1–13.
Havens, T. (2006). *Global television marketplace*. London: BFI.
Hollway, J., & Koskinen, J. (2015). Multilevel bilateralism and multilateralism. In E. Lazega & T. A. B. Snijders (Eds.), *Multi-level network analysis for the social sciences: Theory, methods and applications*. Cham: Springer.
Ingram, P., & Roberts, P. W. (2000). Friendships among competitors in the Sydney hotel industry. *American Journal of Sociology, 106*(2), 387–423.
Lampel, J., & Meyer, A. D. (2008). Guest editors' introduction: Field-configuring events as structuring mechanisms: How conferences, ceremonies, and trade shows constitute new technologies, industries, and markets. *Journal of Management Studies, 45*(6), 1025–1035.
Laumann, E. O., Marsden, P. V., & Prensky, D. (1989). The boundary specification problem in network analysis. In *Research methods in social network analysis* (Vol. 61–87). New Brunswick: Transaction Publishers.
Lazega, E. (2015). 'Morphogenesis unbound' from the dynamics of multilevel networks: A neo-structural perspective. In M. S. Archer (Ed.), *Late modernity: Trajectories towards morphogenic society* (pp. 173–191). Switzerland: Springer International Publishing.
Lazega, E. (2015, forthcoming). Mobilités, turnover relationnel et coûts de synchronisation: L'action collective au prisme de la dynamique des réseaux multiniveaux. *L'Année Sociologique*.
Lazega, E. (2015). The multiple flavours of multilevel issues for networks. In E. Lazega & T. A. B. Snijders (Eds.), *Multi-level network analysis for the social sciences: Theory, methods and applications*. Cham: Springer.
Lazega, E., Jourda, M.-T., Mounier, L., & Stofer, R. (2007). Des poissons et des mares: l'analyse de réseaux multi-niveaux. *Revue Française de Sociologie, 48*(1), 93–131.
Lazega, E., Jourda, M.-T., Mounier, L., & Stofer, R. (2008). Catching up with big fish in the big pond? Multi-level network analysis through linked design. *Social Networks, 30*(2), 159–176.
Lazega, E., Jourda, M.-T., & Mounier, L. (2013). Network lift from dual alters: Extended opportunity structures from a multilevel and structural perspective. *European Sociological Review, 29*(6), 1226–1238.
Lorenz, E. (1999). Trust, contract and economic cooperation. *Cambridge Journal of Economics, 23*(3), 301–315.
Maskell, P., Bathelt, H., & Malmberg, A. (2006). Building global knowledge pipelines: The role of temporary clusters. *European Planning Studies, 14*(8), 997–1013.
Moeran, B., & Pedersen, J. S. (2011). Introduction. In *Negotiating values in the creative industries: Fairs, festivals and competitive events* (pp. 1–35). New York: Cambridge University Press.
Pina-Stranger, A., & Lazega, E. (2010). Inter-organisational collective learning: The case of biotechnology in France. *European Journal of International Management, 4*(6), 602–620.
Power, D., & Jansson, J. (2008). Cyclical clusters in global circuits: Overlapping spaces in furniture trade fairs. *Economic Geography, 84*(4), 423–448.
Quintane, E. (2012). How do brokers broker? An investigation of the temporality of structural holes. *Academy of Management Proceedings, 2012*(1), 1–1.

Quintane, E., Pattison, P. E., Robins, G. L., & Mol, J. M. (2013). Short- and long-term stability in organizational networks: Temporal structures of project teams. *Social Networks, 35*(4), 528–540.

Sanchez-Maranon, M., Delgado, R., Parraga, J., Delgado, G., Sharland, A., & Balogh, P. (1996). The value of nonselling activities at international trade shows. *Industrial Marketing Management, 25*(1), 59–66.

Seringhaus, F. H. R., & Rosson, P. J. (2001). Firm experience and international trade fairs. *Journal of Marketing Management, 17*(7–8), 877–901.

Skov, L. (2006). The role of trade fairs in the global fashion business. *Current Sociology, 54*(5), 764–783.

Smith, C. W. (2011). Staging auctions: Enabling exchange values to be contested and established. In *Negotiating values in the creative industries: Fairs, festivals and competitive events* (pp. 94–118). New York: Cambridge University Press.

Snijders, T. A. B. (1996). Stochastic actor-oriented models for network change. *The Journal of Mathematical Sociology, 21*(1–2), 149–172.

Velthuis, O. (2003). Symbolic meanings of prices: Constructing the value of contemporary art in Amsterdam and New York galleries. *Theory and Society, 32*(2), 181–215.

Wang, P., Robins, G., Pattison, P., & Lazega, E. (2013). Exponential random graph models for multilevel networks. *Social Networks, 35*(1), 96–115.

White, H. C. (1970). *Chains of opportunity: System models of mobility in organizations* (1st ed.). Cambridge, MA: Harvard University Press.

White, H. C. (1981). Where do markets come from? *American Journal of Sociology, 87*(3), 517–547.

Chapter 13
Multilevel Bilateralism and Multilateralism: States' Bilateral and Multilateral Fisheries Treaties and Their Secretariats

James Hollway and Johan Koskinen

Introduction

Actors have many needs and face many challenges that require them to establish relationships with other actors. Take for example the tragedy of the commons, in which an optimal outcome can only be reached through collective management among all users of a resource (see Barkin and DeSombre 2000, 344).

Such relationships can take different forms. Many such relationships are bilateral, existing exclusively between a dyad. Other relationships are more diffuse, taking place as part of multilateral groups. Both bilateralism and multilateralism are regular features of many areas of international politics including security (Hafner-Burton and Montgomery 2006), trade (Ingram et al. 2005), and the environment (Ward 2006). Within these literatures, bilateralism and multilateralism are typically treated as analytically separate: bilateral alliances and collective security arrangements (Snyder and Kick 1979); bilateral investment treaties (BITs) and the WTO (Shaw 2003; Tobin and Rose-Ackerman 2010, 747); and, the environmental example explored here, bilateral and multilateral fisheries agreements (see Kinne 2013, where only bilateral fisheries agreements are included). Yet, despite this analytic division, the relationship between bilateralism and multilateralism has rarely been explored empirically (for an exception in a security context see Cha 2010).

J. Hollway (✉)
Department of International Relations/Political Science, Graduate Institute, Geneva, Switzerland
e-mail: james.hollway@graduateinstitute.ch

J. Koskinen
Social Statistics Discipline Area, University of Manchester, Manchester, UK

This chapter asks "how different dimensions of cooperative arrangements are linked to each other [and] whether changes across dimensions move in tandem or if they are driven by different factors" (Volgy et al. 2009, 7). In other words, when do actors establish bilateral relationships and when do they join multilateral groups? This is a step towards addressing questions such as when cooperation between individual actors results in new, collective actors.

In this chapter, we take as an example the global fisheries governance complex. Shared fish stocks are important to many countries' economies, but "rarely managed well" (Barkin and DeSombre 2000, 342). Nonetheless, they represent a type of resource that legally and practically cannot be managed unilaterally. Recognizing this, states have long attempted to address issues surrounding shared fisheries by international treaty (Daggett 1934), both bilateral and multilateral. It is thus an excellent example of our case, but one that is focused enough to provide some degree of comparability.

Of this data we ask two sets of questions. First, we are interested in when states choose bilateral fisheries agreements (BFAs) and/or multilateral fisheries agreements (MFAs). Here, as we will explain, we are particularly interested in centralization within each network, and across the two networks. Second, we are interested in what makes some multilateral fisheries agreements more popular than others. In particular, we are interested in the contribution of the "managed" status of some multilateral fisheries agreements—that is, that the agreement is related to a secretariat with the purpose of managing the implementation of the agreement. We also explore the role of similarities between these multilateral fisheries agreements.

We argue here that the interaction between bilateralism and multilateralism can be fruitfully analyzed using a multilevel network paradigm. Actors operate across multiple levels, and some leverage on issues of how actors relate can be gained through multilevel network research. More speculatively, a multilevel network perspective on such issues also raises the potential for investigating the interaction between individual and collective agency (Breiger 1974).

To pursue these issues, we employ recent multilevel exponential random graph modeling techniques to explore the structural patterns of countries' bilateralism and multilateralism in global fisheries governance. We find that there is significant centralization of this behavior, but that there is not necessarily a correspondence in this centralized activity between bilateral and multilateral networks. Moreover, it appears that both design (secretariat), a property of the MFAs, and content (similarity), the relation of the MFAs, are important for the structure of the complex. In particular MFAs with a greater potential for action tend to be more strongly tied to other MFAs. This chapter argues that we need more theory and research exploring and explaining when actors act bilaterally and when they act multilaterally, and particularly research that takes into account how they interconnect in multilevel ways.

Bilateralism and Multilateralism

In this section, we argue that states choose treaties based on efficiency considerations. Efficiency can manifest itself in many ways. First, we consider how states choose either bilateral or multilateral treaties. Second, we consider how countries make choices among multilateral treaties.

Bilateralism or Multilateralism

States pursue international relations through institutions because they cannot achieve their goals unilaterally (Barkin and DeSombre 2000, 340). These institutions can take the form of bilateral agreements or multilateral mechanisms such as treaties and international organisations.[1] These two institutional forms differ in important ways.

Bilateralism is structurally and conceptually the simpler of the two. A bilateral relationship involves the establishment of a private agreement between two parties. This privity compartmentalizes dyadic relationships, enabling the terms of each relation to be differentiated "case-by-case [...] on a priori particularistic grounds or situational exigencies" (Ruggie 1992, 571). Such specificity can be employed to deal with matters concerning only the two parties exclusively, such as maritime delimitation, or for establishing preferential terms, such as special access to fisheries resources straddling maritime borders.

Multilateralism is quite different. Ruggie (1992, 571) defines multilateralism in contradistinction to bilateralism as

> an institutional form which coordinates relations among three or more states on the basis of 'generalized' principles of conduct—that is, principles which specify appropriate conduct for a class of actions, without regard to the particularistic interests of the parties or the strategic exigencies that may exist in any specific occurrence.

That at least three parties are implicated has important implications. First, multilateralism can offer significant efficiency gains over bilateral agreements. Negotiating with several parties at a time can increase transparency, information, and the credibility of commitments, and reduce transaction costs providing economies of scale (Cha 2010, 163). Second, reaching multilateral agreement typically requires more complex compromises than bilateral agreements. However, these compromises can be mutually beneficial. In a tragedy of the commons-style situation, for instance, actors recognize that restraint in exploiting a common-pool resource would be beneficial to their own interests, as long as it is matched by others. Fortunately, it is said that the social or normative pressure imposed by "multilateral structures and rules constitute the most effective way to control a state's power and dampen its

---

[1] This is not a comprehensive list of the ways in which institutions have been defined, but it serves our current purposes. (See Ruggie 1992)

unilateralist inclinations" (Cha 2010, 160). Third, these complex compromises also give rise to generalized organizing principles that "entail a[socially constructed] indivisibility among the members of a collectivity with respect to the range of behavior in question" (Ruggie 1992, 571). This indivisibility is generated by the "diffuse reciprocity" of members' commitment to shared goals (Keohane 1986, 19–24). In this respect, multilateralism "refers to the constitutive rules that order relations in given domains of international life—their architectural dimension, so to speak" (Ruggie 1992, 572). In other words, multilateral agreements constitute an issue area.

Multilateralism, though, "is a highly demanding institutional form" says Ruggie (1992, 572), "and if its relative incidence at any time were to be high, that fact would pose an interesting puzzle to be explained". Yet Barkin and DeSombre (2000, 340) state that, because of its evident advantages, "multilateral mechanisms for international environmental management is thus the norm, both logically and empirically". In the case of global fisheries governance, both bilateralism and multilateralism are employed. But do actors employ them in equal measure?

We argue here that bilateralism and multilateralism are distinct but interconnected foreign policies and that actors typically choose to invest in one policy or the other. To investigate this question, we leverage the network concept of centralization. We would expect those states that have many bilateral agreements to make more (see Fig. 13.1a, BILATERAL CENTRALISATION), and those states that have many multilateral agreements to join more (Fig. 13.1b, MULTILATERAL CENTRALISATION), but that these will not necessarily be the same states. Instead, states may choose to invest further in whichever form of cooperation they have found useful. This effect will result in a negative tendency for balanced behavior across both forms of cooperation (Fig. 13.1c, i.e. negative ACTIVITY CORRESPONDENCE). Where states engage in both bilateral and multilateral forms of cooperation, they will nonetheless display a preference through asymmetric behavior (Fig. 13.1d, ASYMMETRIC CENTRALISATION).

Managed or Unmanaged Multilateralism

When states negotiate multilateral agreements, they face another decision: whether to establish a treaty secretariat or not. Treaty secretariats "assist the parties in the

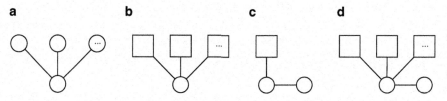

Fig. 13.1 Centralisation effects. (**a**) Bilateral centralisation (AS). (**b**) Multilateral centralisation (ASA). (**c**) Activity correspondence (Star2AX). (**d**) Asymmetric centralisation (StarAX1A)

management and implementation of the treaty" (Sandford 1994, 17). They are the administrative hub, though perhaps not the decision-making authority, of formal international organisations; "palpable entities with headquarters and letterheads, voting procedures, and generous pension plans" (Ruggie 1992, 574). Sometimes they are "large international bureaucracies as in the case of the UN Secretariat", but the secretariats of international environmental treaties tend to be small (Sandford 1994, 19)—just a few professionals and a handful of administrative staff in many cases.

States establish secretariats to fulfill four "managerial" roles. First, they manage informational processes relating to the resource governed and the parties' behavior towards that resource. This role as clearing house for information shared among parties is perhaps secretariats' most important role for, in so doing, they accrue some agenda-setting power, particularly where scientific or behavioral uncertainty is acute (Sandford 1994, 18). Second, they often play a role in monitoring compliance, though this depends in part on the mandate given them by the establishing treaty. Third, they contribute to conflict management by providing formal or informal dispute settlement procedures (Sandford 1994, 28). Lastly, they provide much needed continuity. Governments recognize that they may not be in power in 10 years, and their policies—their legacy—might be undone by their successors. Establishing secretariats can thus help to achieve international objectives across long time horizons (Sandford 1994, 19). Note that none of the above roles necessarily imply that the secretariat has any decision-making authority; we use the term "managed" here to identify that a secretariat has been established and mandated to "manage" the day-to-day practice and strategic continuity of treaty business, not that it necessarily holds a mandate to manage its members independently.

Admittedly, "secretariats are but one small aspect of institutions" (Andresen and Skjærseth 1999, 5). We are also not contending that secretariats are directly influential on activity within their purview (Bauer 2006; Bauer et al. 2009). However, the complex, uncertain, and consequential nature of global environmental politics means that states find themselves increasingly establishing secretariats for the multilateral agreements they negotiate. After all, "there is a long way to go from initial agreement to actual implementation" (Andresen and Skjærseth 1999, 6). Whether or not international environmental treaty secretariats are "significant actors", as Sandford (1994, 17) says, they are part of the process of international environmental treaty implementation and, we argue, also of treaty-making. It is in this later role, as sites for the negotiation of further international environmental treaties, that secretariats become the "organizational glue that holds the actors and parts of a treaty system together" (Sandford 1994, 17).

We explore the impact of secretariats on the dependencies of the multilevel global fisheries governance complex here. First, we investigate the popularity of managed multilateral mechanisms (Fig. 13.2a, MANAGED POPULARITY) compared to unmanaged alternatives (those not relating to any secretariat). Next we consider whether states cluster together around multilateral agreements where at least one is managed (Fig. 13.2b, SHARED MANAGEMENT CHOICES). The results tell us

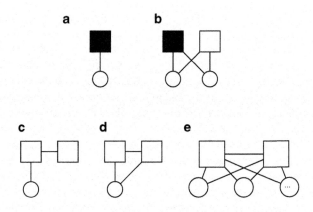

Fig. 13.2 Multilateral Agreement Effects (*Black node* means that binary attribute is 1; *white nodes* may have binary attribute equal to 1 or 0). (**a**) Managed popularity (XEdgeA). (**b**) Shared managed choices (X4CycleB1). (**c**) Choose similar (Star2BX). (**d**) Similar choices (TriangleXBX). (**e**) Shared similar choices (ATXBX)

whether managed multilaterals are associated with more multiple overlaps of multilateral agreements. In a bipartite sense, a prevalence of such four-cycles imply that secretariats want to have strong ties to other MFAs (Robins and Alexander 2004). Such a structure also raises questions about how they are generated. Koskinen and Edling (2012) argue that such four-cycles can be the result of peer referral. Here we can ask whether secretariats act as sites for the exercise of collective agency in negotiating further multilateral agreements, or whether antecedent "unmanaged" treaties blaze a path for later, "managed" versions?[2]

Multilateral agreements do not only differ in how they are instituted (in other words, their design: Koremenos et al. 2001), but also in what they institute. Moreover, multilateral treaties do not exist in a vacuum. Their content is conceived and negotiated in relation to other treaties, and countries select which multilateral agreements to join with reasonable knowledge about how those documents relate (see Jupille et al. 2013). Some multilateral agreements are more similar in content than others. Like any complex document, multilateral treaties are linked in many interesting ways, including their authors, location, and date. However, one of the distinct features of multilateral treaties is that they are more often responsible for the creation or codification of international customary law and its normative evolution as compared to bilateral treaties (Carr and Scott 1999). The normative structures in which such treaties are embedded are important, for it is through their normative interlinkages that multiple agreements complement or come into conflict with one another (see Zelli and van Asselt 2013). Since multilateral agreements constitute the "architecture" of international life (Ruggie 1992, 572), it is important to note where these agreements complement or come into conflict with one another.

To this end, we include two effects here. First, we consider the popularity of multilateral agreements that are similar to other multilateral agreements (Fig. 13.2c, CHOOSE SIMILAR). Such similarity could be defined in many ways. In the data

---

[2] Note that the colored node in Fig. 13.2c indicates that the MFA is a secretariat but the uncolored node is unspecified; that is, it may be either a secretariat or not.

section below, we propose the textual similarity between two treaty documents as a useful general purpose measure of similarity. Since there is no necessary relation to state preferences, we expect this to be non-significant, or possibly negative in sign. Second, we take into account whether states join multilateral agreements that are similar to other multilateral agreements that they have joined (Fig. 13.2d, SIMILAR CHOICES). This is a matter of state preferences, but does not reference the complementarity or conflict inherent in the larger architectural structure. States may view similar choices as 'free' in the sense that they have already committed themselves to similar provisions elsewhere, or they may see a treaty that is similar an unnecessary cost unless it provides some further advantage. This further advantage may come about through MFAs undergoing amendment, which would result in similar treaties and attract the same parties. For this, we also take into account states' clustering around similar multilateral agreements (Fig. 13.2e, SHARED SIMILAR CHOICES). Here we would expect it to be positive.

Data

Following Wasserman and Iacobucci (1991), Lazega et al. (2008), and Wang et al. (2013), we define a multilevel model for the totality of ties between two node sets. We denote a set of countries by $A = \{1, \ldots, n\}$ and multilateral fisheries agreements (MFAs) by $B = \{1, \ldots, m\}$. We conceive of these node sets as representing different levels in the global fisheries governance complex.

Countries are tied dyadically through bilateral treaties giving us an undirected one-mode network represented by the adjacency matrix $X_{A \times A}$. MFAs are connected pairwise amongst themselves by similarities in their text represented by the square, symmetric adjacency matrix $X_{B \times B}$. What connects the two levels are the ties created when a country has an affiliation with an MFA. This is represented by a bipartite network of states and MFAs with an affiliation matrix $X_{A \times B}$. In the following we provide a description of how these ties were measured and what nodal attributes are relevant to our model. The multilevel network on all nodes is represented by a binary adjacency matrix X, that is blocked into the ties in AA, AB, and BB.

Bilateral Fisheries Agreements

The primary actors in global fisheries governance are states. While a statal perspective hardly tells the whole story about global order, the state and its relevance to global governance are unlikely to disappear any time soon (Hurrell 2007, 6). We thus take countries as our nodes A. We include all 195 sovereign states, including landlocked states, because articles 124–125 of the United Nations Convention on the Law of the Sea (UNCLOS) state that all countries have the sovereign right to access and fish the high seas. Moreover, some landlocked states still join fisheries

Country bilateral network

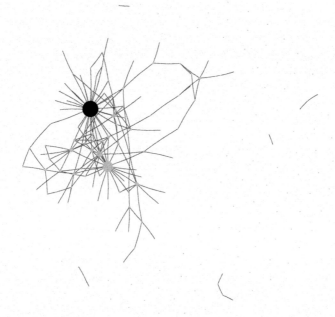

Fig. 13.3 Bilateral fisheries treaty: one-mode network of bilateral fisheries agreements between countries. Node size represents degree and ties associated with *black* node has been treated as exogenous in subsequent analysis

treaties with respect to inland lakes or rivers or to support multilateral norms, which means that there is structural information where there is a lack of participation.

The ties in *AA* consist of states' bilateral fisheries agreements (BFAs) and the network is illustrated in Fig. 13.3. BFAs tend to represent one of two main themes. For countries with abutting maritime borders, BFAs often clarify the nature and extent of these borders, or determine the allocation of fish stocks that straddle these maritime borders, such as between China and Vietnam (Xue 2005). For countries without adjoining maritime borders, bilateral fisheries agreements tend to involve rich, distant water fishing nations, such as Japan or the EU, trading aid for cheap access to fisheries in less-developed coastal or island countries (Petersen 2003; Witbooi 2008).

The data for this and all other networks was retrieved from the two most comprehensive sources for international environmental agreements, ECOLEX (2011) and the IEA database of Mitchell (2013), and complemented by archival research.

We consider four covariates as potentially relevant to explaining the *AA* network. First, we use the amount of fish landed by each country to indicate a country's involvement in the exploitation of global fish stocks. This FISHING data was drawn from the Food and Agriculture Organisation's (FAO) data aggregated in the program FishStatJ (FAO 2011). We expect that the more a state's fishing fleet fishes, the more engaged it will be in negotiating bilateral fisheries agreements.

Second, we include the number of THREATENED SPECIES a state has in its marine area (data from the World Bank: Froese and Pauly 2008). We might expect countries that have threatened species at home to want to protect these fish stocks from further exploitation (and perhaps secure access to more robust fish stocks elsewhere). In either case, we expect it to have a positive influence on treaty-making behavior.

Third, we include GDP (logged thousands) to explore how states' fiscal capacity enables them to enter into and maintain many different bilateral relationships. We also investigate whether there is any systematic homophily or heterophily in capacity across dyads. After all, developed states often trade aid for access to fisheries resources or other advantages. This data was recovered from the UN and the World Bank.

Lastly, as countries are embedded in space, we also include a dyadic covariate to control for distance between two countries. We follow the approach of Daraganova et al. (2012) for incorporating distance into ERGMs, namely using logged Euclidean distance as a dyadic covariate, a functional form that has also been used to mimic gravity-dependence in networks of countries (Koskinen and Lomi 2013).

Multilateral Fisheries Agreements

The second nodeset, B, consists of a "web of [multilateral fishing] treaties covering the preservation of the marine environment" (Shaw 2003, 554). We follow both Mitchell (2013) and ECOLEX (2011) in including all (multilateral) agreements, treaties, conventions, amendments, protocols and exchanges of letters, allowing for structural importance to operate independently of agreement type (Shaw 2003, 88).[3]

Ties are considered present when a country, a has signed, ratified, acceded or succeeded to, or been approved in a multilateral fisheries treaty, b (see Shaw 2003, 817–821). This study does not distinguish between signature and ratification nor does it consider the longitudinal aspects of the data here. It also treats as exogenous the major instruments of the law of the sea such as the United Nations Convention on the Law of the Sea (UNCLOS) and what is informally known as the United Nations Fish Stocks Agreement (UNFSA). These were included in the network, for the structure matters, but since they are special cases they are fixed and not modeled. The fixed ties are represented by grey lines in the network graph of Fig. 13.4.

---

[3] A subset of 200 out of 225 MFAs were finalized after we dropped those for which we had no structural data – occasionally the case for very old or very new MFAs – or for which we could not collect texts, since the treaties' texts are important for the construction of the BB network.

Multilateral Network

Fig. 13.4 Multilateral fisheries agreements: bipartite network of countries (*round, grey*) and MFAs (*squares*). MFAs with secretariats in *black*, others *white*. Ties that have been treated as exogenous in subsequent analysis in *grey*

As with *AA*, we include several salient covariates. On the state-side of the network (*A*), we consider GDP as providing the capacity to enable states' participation in this network. We also investigate whether states' experience of THREATENED SPECIES in their exclusive economic zone motivates their participation in this network.

We also include a covariate on the MFA-side (*B*). Some MFAs provide for the establishment of a secretariat to assist states in the management and implementation of the treaty. This data was also drawn from Mitchell (2013).

Ties Between MFAs

While some recent work has investigated how multilateral environmental agreements relate through citations (Kim 2013), treaty documents are related in varied and subtle ways. Treaties may address similar or quite different subject matter independently of whether it occurs in the same lineage of treaties or refers to the same geographic area. To get at these more subtle similarities, we look at similarity in treaty text.

To construct a network of similarities between treaties' texts it was first necessary to collect the documents of all MFAs. 98 % of all treaty texts in the original dataset were found. These texts underwent some cleaning, and then the `textcat` package in R was used to construct a matrix of Jensen-Shannon divergences between the n-gram frequency distributions of each pair of MFA texts (see Hornik et al. 2013). A tie was deemed to exist if the distance $d(i,j) < 0.01$; a threshold chosen to balance density and detail. In this way, the *BB* network represents the degree to which two treaties' texts call similar vocabulary resources in the pursuit of their aims, thereby arguably accumulating to content. The network is represented in Fig. 13.5.

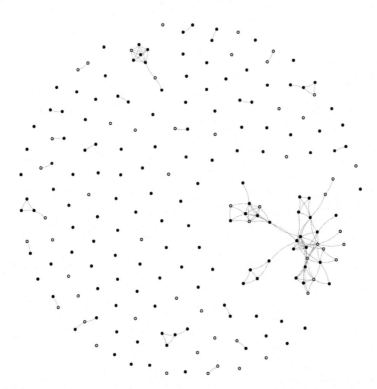

Fig. 13.5 Multilateral fisheries agreements issues: one-mode network of MFAs tied by issue overlap. MFAs with secretariats in *black*, others *grey*

One Multilevel Network

Each of these three networks, *AA*, *AB*, and *BB*, is valid and interesting in its own right: *AA* consists of countries' establishing bilateral fisheries treaties with one another; *AB* comprises countries signing or acceding to multilateral fisheries treaties; and *BB* corresponds to content similarity between the texts of the multilateral fisheries treaties in *AB*. Together these three networks are modeled here as a single, multilevel network of three interdependent parts, *X*. The joint modeling of all the ties using Multilevel ERGM (Wang et al. 2013) allows us to explore the interdependencies specified in section "Bilateralism and Multilateralism". In particular it enables us to interpret the ties of one network by how they are embedded in the others.

Results

To find evidence for the processes discussed in section "Bilateralism and Multilateralism", we specify a Multilevel Exponential Random Graph Model (MERGM) for the multilevel network of countries and MFAs. We specify the model with a focus on the main research questions expressed as effects in Figs. 13.1 and 13.2 above, but include a number of additional effects as controls. In choosing relevant configurations we follow the procedures of Wang et al. (2013). These controls have been motivated both substantially as well as to achieve a reasonable goodness-of-fit. We include as control effects a set of configurations consisting of various combinations of attributes and structure. Many structural controls take the form of clustering effects, such as those cross-network clustering effects presented in Fig. 13.6. Though these effects are interesting in their own right, here we only use them as controls, and explore their meaning further elsewhere. There are also a number of covariate-based controls, outlined in the data description above. Detailed explanations of configurations may be found in Wang et al. (2014). Convergence of the estimation process has been assessed by the standard criterion (Lusher et al. 2013).[4]

Fig. 13.6 Cross-network effects. (**a**) AA-AB closure (TriangleXAX). (**b**) 3-Path (L3XAX). (**c**) Multilevel alignment (C4AXB)

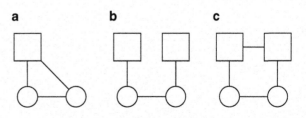

---

[4]Convergence statistics were less than 0.1 in absolute value and there were adequate sample autocorrelations for the statistics.

Table 13.1 Multilevel ERGM parameter estimates for a network on Countries and Multilateral Fisheries Agreements. An asterisk (∗) denotes a parameter that is twice the size of its standard error. The model is estimated using MPNet (MPNet names in parenthesis when needed, see Wang et al. 2014)

	Effect	Parameter	(S.E.)
AA	Edge	5.193	1.231*
	Alternating star (AS)	0.368	0.139*
	Alternating triangle (AT)	0.227	0.121
	GDP (log) capacity (activity)	0.412	0.807
	GDP (log) heterophily (difference)	2.722	1.193*
	Threatened species sum (activity)	0.033	0.031
	Threatened species product (product)	−0.002	0.014
	Fishing volume (activity)	0.175	0.027*
	Fishing difference (difference)	0.055	0.038
	Distance (log)	−1.232	0.107*
AB	Edge	−2.008	0.950*
	Alternating star (A-degree ASA)	2.608	0.322*
	Alternating star (B-degree ASB)	−3.346	0.457*
	GW shared A-nodes (ACA)	−0.448	0.036*
	GDP (log) capacity (activity)	−0.867	0.445
	Threatened species sum (activity)	0.127	0.019*
	Secretariat (XEdgeA)	0.817	0.129*
	Shared Managed (Sec) Choices (X4CycleB1)	0.004	0.001*
BB	Edge	Fixed	
	2-star	−0.130	0.098
	Isolate	−0.955	0.796
	Alternating star (AS)	0.310	0.521
	Alternating triangle ($\lambda = 4$) (AT)	2.459	0.251*
	Alternating independent 2-path (A2P)	0.111	0.114
	Alternating edge-triangle (AET)	−0.214	0.091*
x	Activity correspondence (Star2AX)	−0.943	0.304*
	Asymmetric activity (StarAX1A)	0.464	0.152*
	3-Path (L3XAX)	1.178	0.334*
	Cross-level closure (TriangleXAX)	0.086	0.019*
	Activity correspondence (Star2BX)	0.001	0.003
	Cross-level closure (TriangleXBX)	−0.210	0.091*
	Alt. closure (ATXBX)	0.001	0.000*
	Multilevel alignment (C4AXB)	−0.004	0.014

Results are presented in Table 13.1. For effect names we have mostly adhered to standard terminology as used in Lusher et al. (2013) and Wang et al. (2013), except for those effects that we defined in section "Bilateralism and Multilateralism" above.

In terms of our main research question, we find that there is a centralization of treaty-making around particular countries but that it does not necessarily correspond across networks. Within both the *AA* and *AB* networks, some states appear more active than others. Indeed, the alternating form of the AA and AB star effects shows that this centralization is quite strong. In the case of the *AA* network, the alternating star parameter has a coefficient of 0.37; in the case of the *AB* network, it is 2.61. Interestingly, we do not find that this centralization is driven by capacity (logged GDP) in either network. We do see a pattern of rich countries engaging bilaterally with poor countries however. Countries that fish a lot are drawn by this activity to engage in BFAs, though the fishing activity of their partner appears irrelevant. The status of domestic fish resources spurs countries' involvement in MFAs. This means that while a crisis of conservation does not necessarily motivate bilateral activity, it does seem to motivate multilateral activity, perhaps because this arena has typically attracted more normative goals.

But does bilateral and multilateral activity coincide? In principle, no: the ACTIVITY CORRESPONDENCE (Star2AX: Fig. 13.1c) effect is negative. This means that countries generally carry out a policy of employing either bilateral or multilateral fisheries agreements. However, there are several important caveats to this statement. There is some evidence that there is correspondence where the focal state demonstrates that they have the resources to carry out treaty-making in both contexts (ASYMMETRIC ACTIVITY: StarAX1A, Fig. 13.1d). Nonetheless, this effect does suggest that the activity is asymmetric and states' bilateral and multilateral activity does not appear to be balanced. Countries are generally strategic about where they deploy their resources.

In terms of our secondary research question, it appears that MFA secretariats do affect the structure of this multilevel network. MFAs establishing secretariats are more popular than those that do not (the coefficient of (a) in Fig. 13.2 is 0.82 with standard error of 0.13). There is also evidence that countries appear to cluster around "managed" MFAs, as can be seen with the positive SHARED MANAGED CHOICES parameter (Fig. 13.2b). The introduction of this effect does improve model fit, particularly with respect to bipartite clustering, which suggests this is an important effect worth investigating further.

There is a strong tendency *against* countries being multiply tied to MFAs (ACA). Thus countries do not 'cluster' around MFAs. One exception to this is however when the MFAs share content as evidenced by the alternating closure ATXBX (Fig. 13.2e). Against this background, it is informative that the parameter for SHARED MANAGED CHOICES is positive and statistically significant. This suggests that states only cluster around MFAs with at least one established secretariat (unless the MFAs share content). Possible explanations include that this effect may be driven by secretariats operating as sites for collective agency, leading to the generation of more multilateral agreements. Alternatives could be that the secretariats encourage countries to engage in further MFAs, or that unmanaged treaties pave the way for later secretariats.

Next, we find that countries do not necessarily sign or accede to MFAs because of their similarity to other MFAs (TriangleXBX), and indeed tend to prefer agreements that are dissimilar to MFAs they have already signed. Note that the ties between the MFAs themselves are highly clustered (the alternating triangle statistic AT for *BB* is large). Together with the negative GW shared A-nodes parameter mentioned above, it seems that the MFAs modeled here do not enjoy any popularity or clustering from being similar to other treaties and indeed only have minimal overlap in signatories, *but* MFAs that are similar and already share some signatories *are* more likely to share further signatories (the positive alternating closure parameter). What the combination of these two closure effects may mean is that there are some particularly hot issues for countries that drive signatory overlap.[5] Lastly, there is no evidence that bilaterally connected countries prefer similar MFAs (C4AXB). Coupled with the closure effect described in the last paragraph, it seems that countries prefer *the same* MFAs instead. We found no significant tendency for or against multilevel alignment, though future research will reveal whether this is simply a feature of the content network chosen for the *BB* network.

This model captured most structural features of the multilevel network well, and sufficiently for our purposes (Robins and Lusher 2013, 184–185). Only for the bipartite network (*AB*) degree distributions and some higher-order clustering (XACB) could the model fit be improved. These are nested and accounting for them by including them in the model leads to marked model-instabilities and accounting for all the other statistics seems remarkable considering the complexity of the data.

Discussion

This chapter has demonstrated the value of a multilevel network perspective for studying actors' bilateral and multilateral cooperation. In the example considered here of the global fisheries governance complex, the one-mode bilateral network consists of states' bilateral fisheries agreements with one another and the two-mode multilateral network consists of states' membership in multilateral fisheries agreements. Since the multilateral fisheries agreements are complex, normative instruments, we also distinguish them on the basis of whether they are "managed" or not (whether they relate to an established secretariat) and add a further one-mode network representing their similarity in content.

Together this represents a new, genuinely multilevel relational dataset that concentrates on two interlocking architectures of bilateral fisheries agreements between countries (*AA*) and their overlapping membership in multilateral fisheries agreements (*AB*) and a third connectionist network of content similarity between multilateral fisheries treaty texts (*BB*).

A multilevel network perspective on this data considers the small and big ponds of actors' interactions jointly as interconnected subsystems, and indeed they do appear to be connected in interesting and important ways. While all three networks are valid and interesting in their own right, treating them as one multilevel network

---

[5]Note that we have fixed the most popular treaties here, so this interpretation references other treaties than, say, UNCLOS or UNFSA.

structure reveals additional interdependencies and suggests further mechanisms to explore in future research. We have proposed three statements about this interaction: states prefer to establish either bilateral or multilateral relations; states prefer similar multilateral treaties to those they have already joined; and states prefer "managed" multilateral treaties. All of these statements have been related to states' concerns about efficiency and all have been demonstrated to have some empirical justification.

First, we find that there is a tendency away from any general correspondence of activity, which suggests that states do choose to invest in either bilateralism or multilateralism, rather than balancing these two policies. These policies do not appear to be exclusive, but even where they are mixed there is an asymmetry in their employment.

Additionally, we also found a number of interesting attribute-based explanations. We find that states bilateral treaty activity is driven by how much they fish, but that experience of domestic marine species coming under threat motivates their multilateral treaty activity. This suggests that our thesis that different mechanisms drive the structure of bilateral and multilateral fisheries agreements is well founded. Moreover, it seems that for bilateral agreements, countries prefer partners that are proximate (probably for BFAs establishing maritime borders or regimes governing straddling fish stocks) and more and less developed countries tend to partner (probably for BFAs trading fisheries access for development aid).

Second, we find that states prefer what we call "managed" multilateralism. That is, they prefer multilateral fisheries agreements that either establish or relate to an established treaty secretariat. Such secretariats provide much needed continuity and consistency for actors struggling with complex and consequential issue areas such as that of global fisheries governance. The local dependencies of multilateral fisheries agreements related to secretariats appear to differ from those unrelated to secretariats. The secretariats are more embedded in the multilevel complex, having more signatories and being more strongly connected to other MFAs through multiple overlaps. We cannot tell merely from the binary multilevel network what type of nodes drives what ties, but the contrast between the structural profiles of MFAs endowed with more (secretariats) and less (non-secretariats) agency is telling.

Third, while there is a tendency away from signatory overlap in MFAs, even where their content is related, once related MFAs share several signatories they are likely to share further signatories. We suggest that this indicates that there are some particularly 'hot topics' that proliferate similar multilateral agreements with similar sets of members. In other words, there is a cumulative effect of co-signatories only when they are identified with a specific issue. From the perspective of MFA's content overlap, fewer parties in common entail more content diversity whereas MFAs with many shared signatories see greater content similarity. We cannot tell if either type of tie has precedence from the cross-sectional model employed here, but the systemic nature of the multilevel approach does open up an interesting perspective on the structural features of 'hot topics'.

These are important insights, and suggests plenty of ways to extend the model further. One particularly promising suggestion from the results presented here is to elaborate theories of multilevel structure and agency. Evidently, we need new, multilevel theories of governance complexity to adequately theorize the kinds of multilevel interdependencies identified here for international relations, which is replete with such examples, but also, through the generalization of the mechanisms of bilateralism and multilateralism, to other social contexts.

References

Andresen, S., & Skjaerseth, J. (1999, July 14–16). *Can international secretariats promote effective co-operation?* A background paper written for the United Nations University conference on Synergies and co-ordination between multilateral environmental agreements, Tokyo, Japan.

Barkin, J. S., & DeSombre, E. R. (2000). Unilateralism and multilateralism in international fisheries management. *Global Governance, 6*, 339–360.

Bauer, S. (2006). Does bureaucracy really matter? The authority of intergovernmental treaty secretariats in global environmental politics. *Global Environmental Politics, 6*(1), 23–49.

Bauer, S., Busch, P. O., Siebenhüner, B. (2009). Treaty secretariats in global environmental governance. In F. Biermann, B. Siebenhüner, & A. Schreyögg (Eds.), *International organizations in global environmental governance* (pp. 174–192). Abingdon: Routledge.

Breiger, R. L. (1974). The duality of persons and groups. *Social Forces, 53*, 181–190.

Carr, C. L., & Scott, G. L. (1999). Multilateral treaties and the environment: A case study in the formation of customary international law. *Denver Journal of International Law and Policy, 27*(2), 313–335.

Cha, V. D. (2010). Powerplay: Origins of the US alliance system in Asia. *International Security, 34*(3), 158–196.

Daggett, A. P. (1934). The regulation of maritime fisheries by treaty. *The American Journal of International Law, 28*(4), 693–717.

Daraganova, G., Pattison, P. E., Koskinen, J. H., Mitchell, B., Bill, A., Watts, M., & Baum, S. (2012). Networks and geography: Modelling community network structures as the outcome of both spatial and network processes. *Social Networks, 34*(1), 6–17.

ECOLEX. (2011). The gateway to environmental law. http://www.ecolex.org/start.php.

FAO. (2011) FishStatJ – Software for fishery statistical time series.

Froese, R., & Pauly, D. (2008). Fishbase Database. www.fishbase.org.

Hafner-Burton, E. M., & Montgomery, A. H. (2006). Power positions: International organizations, social networks, and conflict. *Journal of Conflict Resolution, 50*(1), 3–27.

Hornik, K., Mair, P., Rauch, J., Geiger, W., Buchta, C., & Feinerer, I. (2013). The textcat package for n-Gram based text categorization in R. *Journal of Statistical Software, 52*(6), 1–17.

Hurrell, A. (2007). One world? Many worlds? The place of regions in the study of international society. *International Affairs (Royal Institute of International Affairs 1944-), 83*(1), 127–146.

Ingram, P., Robinson, J., & Busch, M. L. (2005). The intergovernmental network of world trade: IGO connectedness, governance, and embeddedness. *The American Journal of Sociology, 111*(3), 824–858.

Jupille, J., Mattli, W., & Snidal, D. (2013). *Institutional choice and global commerce*. Cambridge, UK: Cambridge University Press.

Keohane, R. O. (1986). Reciprocity in international relations. *International Organization, 40*(1), 1–27.

Kim, R. E. (2013). The emergent network structure of the multilateral environmental agreement system. *Global Environmental Change, 23*(5), 980–991.

Kinne, B. J. (2013). Network dynamics and the evolution of international cooperation. *The American Political Science Review, 107*(4), 766–785.

Koremenos, B., Lipson, C., & Snidal, D. (2001). The rational design of international institutions. *International Organization, 55*(4), 761–799.

Koskinen, J. H., & Edling, C. (2012). Modelling the evolution of a bipartite network—Peer referral in interlocking directorates. *Social Networks, 34*(3), 309–322.

Koskinen, J. H., & Lomi, A. (2013). The local structure of globalization. *Journal of Statistical Physics 151*(3–4), 523–548.

Lazega, E., Jourda, M. T., Mounier, L., & Stofer, R. (2008). Catching up with big fish in the big pond? Multi-level network analysis through linked design. *Social Networks, 30*(2), 159–176.

Lusher, D., Koskinen, J. H., & Robins, G. L. (Eds.), (2013). *Exponential random graph models for social networks: Theory, methods and applications.* Cambridge, UK: Cambridge University Press.

Mitchell, R. B. (2013). International environmental agreements database project (version 2013.2). University of Oregon.

Petersen, E. (2003). The catch in trading fishing access for foreign aid. *Marine Policy, 27*(3), 219–228.

Robins, G. L., & Alexander, M. (2004). Small worlds among interlocking directors: Network structure and distance in bipartite graphs. *Computational & Mathematical Organization Theory, 10*(1), 69–94.

Robins, G. L., & Lusher, D. (2013). Illustrations: Simulation, estimation, and goodness of fit. In D. Lusher, J. Koskinen, & G. Robins (Eds.), *Exponential random graph models for social networks: Theory, methods, and applications* (pp. 167–185). Cambridge, UK: Cambridge University Press.

Ruggie, J. G. (1992). Multilateralism: The anatomy of an institution. *International Organization, 46*(3), 561–598.

Sandford, R. (1994). International environmental treaty secretariats: Stage-hands or actors? In H. Ole Bergesen & G. Parmann (Eds.), *Green globe yearbook of international co-operation on environment and development 1994* (pp. 17–29). Oxford, UK: Oxford University Press.

Shaw, M. N. (2003). *International law.* Cambridge, UK: Cambridge University Press.

Snyder, D., & Kick, E. L. (1979). Structural position in the world system and economic growth, 1955–1970: A multiple-network analysis of transnational interactions. *The American Journal of Sociology, 84*(5), 1096–1126.

Tobin, J. L., Rose-Ackerman, S. (2010). When BITs have some bite: The political-economic environment for bilateral investment treaties. *The Review of International Organizations, 6*(1), 1–32.

Volgy, T. J., Sabic, Z., Roter, P., Fausett, E., & Rodgers, S. (2009). In search of the post-cold war world order: Questions, issues, and perspectives. In T.J. Volgy, Z. Šabič, P. Roter, & A. Gerlak (Eds.), *Mapping the new world order* (pp. 1–28). Chichester: Wiley-Blackwell.

Wang, P., Robins, G. L., Pattison, P. E., & Lazega, E. (2013). Exponential random graph models for multilevel networks. *Social Networks, 35*(1), 96–115.

Wang, P., Robins, G. L., Pattison, P. E., & Koskinen, J. H. (2014). *MPNet: Program for the simulation and estimation of (p*) exponential random graph models for multilevel networks*, Melbourne.

Ward, H. (2006). International linkages and environmental sustainability: The effectiveness of the regime network. *Journal of Peace Research, 43*(2), 149–166.

Wasserman, S., & Iacobucci, D. (1991). Statistical modelling of one mode and two mode networks: Simultaneous analysis of graphs and bipartite graphs. *British Journal of Mathematical and Statistical Psychology, 44*(1), 13–43.

Witbooi, E. (2008). The infusion of sustainability into bilateral fisheries agreements with developing countries: The European Union example. *Marine Policy, 32*, 669–679.

Xue, G. (2005). Bilateral fisheries agreements for the cooperative management of the shared resources of the China seas: A note. *Ocean Development and International Law, 36*(4), 363–374.

Zelli, F., & van Asselt, H. (2013). Introduction: The institutional fragmentation of global environmental governance: Causes, consequences, and responses. *Global Environmental Politics, 13*(3), 1–13.

Chapter 14
Knowledge Sharing in Organizations: A Multilevel Network Analysis

Paola Zappa and Alessandro Lomi

Introduction

Social networks and the multiple roles that they play in organizations have received increasing attention over the last decades (Borgatti and Foster 2003; Brass et al. 2004). The general argument is that social networks represent both conduits through which material and symbolic resources flow within organizations, as well as signals of the underlying hard-to-observe qualities of organizational members connected by social relations (Podolny 2001). The presence and absence of ties between organizational members has been systematically associated to important interpersonal differences in outcomes like productivity (Reagans and Zuckerman 2001), resources (Podolny and Baron 1997), reputation (Kilduff and Krackhardt 1994), status (Lomi and Torló 2014), power (Brass and Burkhardt 1993), and autonomy (Burt 1992).

The extensive literature on organizational social networks builds on the conviction that organizations are meaningful settings for studying social relations. But considering organizations as settings for studying social networks has far-reaching implications that have not received sufficient attention until recently (McEvily et al. 2014). Organizations are first and foremost hierarchical social systems with multiple and partially nested levels of action (March and Simon 1958; Simon 1996). Perhaps the most obvious implication of adopting organizations as settings for studying social networks is that hierarchical elements shape the interaction among organizational members within, but also across structural layers.

Organizations typically consist of individuals nested within a variety of social aggregates such as, for example, teams, functions, departments or subsidiaries.

P. Zappa (✉) • A. Lomi
Social Network Analysis Research Center, Faculty of Economics, University of Italian Switzerland, Via G. Buffi, 13, 6904 Lugano, Switzerland
e-mail: paola.zappa@usi.ch

© Springer International Publishing Switzerland 2016
E. Lazega, T.A.B. Snijders (eds.), *Multilevel Network Analysis for the Social Sciences*, Methodos Series 12, DOI 10.1007/978-3-319-24520-1_14

Organizational members are connected to one another within and across the boundaries of these aggregates by a variety of mandated (or "formal") and emergent (or "informal") relations. Such relations are rarely independent of one another. For this reason, it is important to assess the influence that the structure of relations at one level exerts on the structure of relations at another level (Moliterno and Mahony 2011).

Obvious as this statement may be, virtually no study of intra-organizational networks is available that takes into account the multilevel formal structures providing the foci for the development of social relations in organizations (McEvily et al. 2014). This is surprising because one of the main promises of network approaches to organizations is to capture connections across multiple structural levels.

As Contractor, Wasserman, and Faust aptly observe (2006: 684):

> [O]ne of the key advantages of a network perspective is the ability to collect, collate, and study data at various levels of analysis (...). However, for the purposes of analyses most network data are either transformed to a single level of analysis (...) which necessarily loses some of the richness in the data, or are analyzed separately at different levels of analysis thus precluding direct comparisons of theoretical influences at different levels.

The network perspective that Contractor et al. (2006) advocate involves direct modeling of tie variables and explicit development of hypotheses about how such variables may be affected by multilevel network dependences. Contractor et al. (2006) suggest adoption of the Exponential Random Graph (ERGM) class of models (a.k.a. p-star – or $p*$ models) as a potential solution to the problem of modeling multilevel networks. This modeling approach has since been developed into a comprehensive analytical framework for the analysis of multilevel networks (Wang et al. 2013). In this paper we show how recently derived ERGMs for multilevel networks (Multilevel ERGMs or MERGMs) may be adopted for analyzing networks in organizational settings. We think that the flexibility of this framework provides the basis for the development of novel insights on social networks in organizations.

The objective of this paper is to illustrate some of the benefits of understanding formal organizations as multilevel network systems by examining the interdependence between formal and social interaction in organizations. We show how such an approach supports a more informative and contextually richer representation of the interdependences between formal and informal relations in organizations.

We document the existence, complexity, and context-dependence of the relationships linking informal networks between lower-level actors (individuals in the case that we will be presenting) to formal networks between higher-level actors (subsidiary units in our case) in organizations. We argue that ignoring the formal relations existing between higher-level units may lead to overestimating the autonomy of social networks from the formal authority structure existing within organizations. Because authority relations cross-cut organizational levels, this issue cannot be fully addressed in studies of social networks within organizations conducted at a single level.

We argue that the unique value of the most recent generation of MERGMs is to turn this problem into empirically testable hypotheses. Hence, adopting this methodological approach allows us to learn more about how both social as well as structural conditions affect the likelihood that network ties cross-cut formal organizational boundaries. This is important because research on social networks conducted at a single level is incapable of establishing the autonomy of network ties with respect to formal organizational structure. This is a particularly notable weakness in current organizational research on the role that boundary-spanning ties play in a variety of important organizational outcomes such as, for example, knowledge transfer (Hansen 2002), innovation (Hargadon and Sutton 1997), generation of new ideas (Burt 2004), and organizational performance (Argote and Ingram 2000).

Using field data that we have collected on communication and advice relations among the 47 members of a top management team within an international multiunit industrial group we show how this weakness may be addressed. We reconstruct the complete network of hierarchical reporting relations defined among managers within and across the subsidiary companies of the corporate group. The resulting structure defines a multilevel network in which the lower-level units (individual managers) are linked by interpersonal communication and advice relationships, and the higher-level units (subsidiary units) are linked by formal reporting relations. The two levels are linked by a bipartite relationship that affiliates individual managers to subsidiary units. We exploit the natural multilevel structure of social networks within organizations to specify and estimate MERGMs for different intra-organizational networks (advice and communication). We show that the effects of the formal structure on social networks are contingent upon the specific kind of network that is being considered.

After this general introduction, we organize the chapter as follows. In the next section we discuss the general background of our work and introduce the problem of knowledge transfer and sharing in organizations. We state the main questions that our study addresses. In section "Models for Multilevel Networks" we briefly summarize our analytical strategy based on MERGMs. Section "Empirical Illustration" describes data and model specifications. Section "Results" contains the empirical results. Section "Discussion and Conclusions" concludes the paper by framing the results in the context of current research on organizational networks.

General Background and Questions

Organizations as Multilevel Network Systems

One of the main motivations for analyzing social networks has been to provide a theoretical framework for examining relations at various structural levels of action (White et al. 1976). Among the many substantive contexts for the analysis of social networks, organizations provide perhaps the clearest illustration of the need to consider how action may – or may not – be connected across structural levels. Because organizations are multilevel hierarchical objects (Simon 1962), questions about how social networks link action across levels are central to our understanding of how organizations actually work. In organizations, for example, network relations may link individuals across departments, teams, functions or subsidiaries (Borgatti and Foster 2003).

Building explicitly on Breiger's classic insight (1974), Brass et al. (2004: 801) clearly recognize multilevel networks in organizations as an unavoidable consequence of interpersonal relations cross-cutting the formal boundaries because:

> Ties between people in different units [...] create ties between organizational units, illustrating the "duality" of groups and individuals (Breiger 1974). When two individuals interact, they not only represent an interpersonal tie, but they also represent the groups of which they are members. Thus, interunit ties are often a function of interpersonal ties.

Less commonly recognized is that "interpersonal ties" may be just as easily the consequence of interunit ties – thus inducing a multilevel network structure. Interunit ties may be determined by technology through the workflow (Thompson 1967), or by formal relations that define the organizational hierarchy in terms of dependence between individuals within and across subunits (Perrow 1970; Pfeffer 1981). Most available studies have analyzed networks observed at different levels separately, typically ignoring the possible existence of dependences across levels. The combination between the affiliation of organizational members (lower-level actors) to departments, teams, functions or subsidiaries (higher-level actors), and the existence of social relations among organizational members as well as of a formal structure among aggregate units, implies that organizations are hierarchical systems of nested relations – i.e., multilevel network systems – almost by construction. This claim has far-reaching consequences because the autonomy of social networks between organizational members cannot be established without accounting for the powerful effects of ties between organizational subunits defined at a higher level of analysis. Because in organizations lower-level actors are hierarchically nested within higher-level actors, lower-level (interpersonal) ties may be embedded in higher-level (interunit) ties. If this is the case, the structure of relations observed at one level is likely to affect the structure of relations observed at another (typically lower) level (Moliterno and Mahony 2011). In this perspective, interpersonal ties derive from the exercise of "discretion with constraints" (Kleinbaum et al. 2013) – i.e. they are affected by the multiple social foci that organizations offer to their members (Lomi et al. 2014).

Organizational research has only recently started recognizing the multilevel network nature of organizations that these considerations imply (Baum and Ingram 2002; Brass 2000; Brass et al. 2004; Oh et al. 2006). Interest in multilevel networks arises from the promise of a more realistic representation of important organizational outcomes, such as, for example, coordination, identity construction, and learning (Kogut and Zander 1996). Accounting for dependences across levels would provide a better assessment of the actual autonomy and differential value of social networks in organizations. It would be possible, in particular, to detect whether and how interpersonal relations in organizations are shaped by (I) the joint membership of participants in aggregate units, and (II) the presence of relations between units.

Until relatively recent times, the implications of dependences across network levels have not been explicitly articulated. This is partly due to the lack of suitable methods for dealing with the complex multilevel network structures that are involved. Most of the available empirical studies have treated organizational structure as an attribute of individuals rather than as a distinct level of action. As a consequence, fundamental questions about the relations between network ties connecting units defined at different levels could not even be asked. As we discuss in the next section, our relatively primitive understanding of these multilevel issues severely limits our current understanding of how social networks in organizations actually work. Equally important is the fact that our limited ability to represent and analyze multilevel networks in organizations casts doubt on some of the most influential results produced by decades of organizational research on knowledge-sharing and knowledge-transfer processes.

Social Networks and Organizational Structure

Understanding multilevel network mechanisms is of direct relevance to the conspicuous and influential body of research on learning, knowledge sharing and knowledge transfer within organizations accumulated during the last quarter of century (Argote et al. 1990; Argote and Ingram 2000; Hansen 2002; Tortoriello et al. 2012).

This literature has argued – and repeatedly shown – that networks of informal interaction represent the main conduits through which knowledge flows within organizations (Krackhardt and Hanson 1993). Informal relations based on communication and advice seeking can allow organizational members to sample the experience of distant others, and bring new solutions, practices, and ideas to bear on local problems. These knowledge transfer relations, embedded in informal social networks that cross-cut formal organizational boundaries, promote organizational learning – i.e., processes through which organizations create, disseminate and exploit knowledge (Kogut and Zander 1996; March and Simon 1958; Simon 1991).

More specifically, informal relationships focused on advice and communication allow organizational participants to access sets of distant others, and hence reach heterogeneous knowledge resources that are not locally available (Reagan and McEvily 2003) – and that may be otherwise difficult to mobilize, understand and integrate across formal boundaries (Nonaka 1994).

The connection that social networks create between different knowledge pools separated by formal subunits seems to be the main mechanism behind the recurrent observation that diversity of information sources is systematically linked to organizational innovation (Beckman et al. 2004; Burt 2004). To the best of our knowledge, however, no study is available that has established the autonomy of emergent social ties of interpersonal knowledge exchange from the mandated hierarchical relations defining a formal organizational structure.

For the reasons that we have identified in the prior section, the multilevel nature of social networks in organizations suggests that the independence between emergent social ties and formal structure would be more usefully framed as a hypothesis to be tested, rather than as an assumption to be maintained. What is at stake in such a test would be the value, interpretation, and ultimate meaning of social networks in organizations as they have been studied so far. If informal social relations connecting individuals across intra-organizational boundaries depend on the presence of formally mandated relations existing between the subunits in which individuals are contained, then the knowledge-transfer properties that current research assigns to organizational networks could turn out to be spurious in specific settings or contextual conditions. Once formal hierarchical relations among organizational subunits are accounted for, the extent to which social networks between individuals across subunits can still be observed becomes an open question that begs empirical investigation.

Social relations among organizational members may be affected by formal hierarchical relations existing among organizational subunits in at least two ways. The first involves a generalization of the transactive memory argument (Ren et al. 2006). By virtue of being in subunits that are more central, prominent or critical, organizational members may be both more visible, as well as more aware of the overall distribution of knowledge resources in the organization (Ren and Argote 2011). More generally, members in subunits with differential standing may more easily attract deference relations across boundaries (such as, for example, requests for advice), and generate additional opportunities for establishing crosscutting communication relations. The joint effect of visibility and awareness provided by "being in the right place" (Brass 1984) is a higher level of "popularity" and "activity" of organizational participants located in prominent subunits. These multilevel network effects are likely to be a sort of "basking in the reflected glory" effect determined by affiliation to prominent subunits or groups within organizations (Cialdini et al. 1976).

The second way in which formal relations may affect social relations involves an extensive interpretation of the social foci argument (Feld 1981). Social relations between individuals are likely to be affected by the presence of formal hierarchical relations between organizational subunits to the extent that hierarchical relations provide a social focus for the development of interpersonal network ties where: "A social focus is defined as a social, psychological, legal or physical entity around which joint activities are organized" (Feld 1981: 1016). Formal hierarchical relations existing between subunits possess all the defining features of a social focus present in Feld's definition. Because "individuals whose activities are organized around the same focus will tend to become interpersonally tied and form a cluster" (Feld 1981: 1016), relations of hierarchical subordination existing among subunits will tend to generate connection between participants across subunits (Lomi et al. 2014). As in the first case discussed, relations between subunits affect relations between participants across subunits via clearly identifiable multilevel network mechanisms.

The argument we have developed so far may be summarized in terms of a basic multilevel question: How, exactly, does the presence of mandated hierarchical relations between organizational subunits affect the presence of network ties connecting organizational members across subunits? To the extent that hierarchical relations among subunits provide the focus for the development of social relations among individuals, then a default expectation would be that informal interaction among individuals aligns to prescribed hierarchical relations among organizational subunits. If this is the case, we should expect to see cross-cutting network ties connecting organizational members who belong to subunits that are themselves connected by relations of hierarchical subordination. Does this expectation hold independently of the kind of network relation that connects individuals across subunits? This question is important because the effect of the formal structure may be contingent on the kind of relation that organizational members develop. This would suggest that the autonomy of informal social relations from mandated hierarchical relations varies across network settings.

Motivated by these basic questions, in the next section we outline Multilevel Exponential Random Graph Models as one possible analytical strategy that may assist in addressing these questions.

Models for Multilevel Networks

The specific forms of interdependences between levels that we have discussed may be assessed by directly specifying Multilevel Exponential Random Graph Models (Wang et al. 2013, 2015) (MERGMs henceforth). MERGMs are a new class of ERGMs specifically designed for modeling multilevel network data. MERGMs are currently the only method that allows for explicit assessments of specific forms of network interdependences across levels.

Let $M = [A, X, B]$ denote the network variable for a two-level network, and $m = [a, x, b]$ the corresponding realizations. M includes a network $A = [A_{hl}]$ of size u representing a relation among a set U of higher-level actors $h = 1, \ldots, l, \ldots u$ nodes in U; a network $B = [B_{ij}]$ which represents a relation among a set V of lower level actors with $i = 1, \ldots, j, \ldots v$ nodes in V; and a two-mode network $X = [X_{ih}]$ representing the affiliation of i to h. Let, finally, $Y = [Y^A, Y^B]$ denote the set of attributes for actors of levels A and B, and $y = [y^A, y^B]$ their realizations.

MERGMs are specified as follows:

$$\Pr(M = m | Y = y) = \frac{1}{\kappa} \exp \sum_Q \{a_Q Z_Q^T(m) + \theta_Q Z_Q^T(m, y)\} \quad (12.1)$$

- M is the set of all possible multilevel networks of size $(u \times v)$ and m is the observed network.
- Y is a set of vectors of individual- and subunit-specific characteristics and y is the observed set.

- Q represents a potential network configuration. The summation Σ is over all different configurations included in the model.
- $Z_Q(m) = \sum_m \prod_{M_{ij} \in Q} m_{ij}$ are structural network statistics corresponding to configuration Q. These statistics involve network tie variables only and count, for each actor in the network, the number of configurations or effects of each type in which the actor is involved.
- a_Q is the vector of parameters corresponding to the structural effects $Z_Q(m)$.
- $Z_Q(m, y) = \sum_m \prod_{M_{ij} \in Q} m_{ij} y_i$ is the vector of attribute configurations or effects – i.e., statistics which account for the interaction between network tie variables and nodal attribute covariates.
- θ_Q is the vector of parameters corresponding to the attribute effects $Z_Q(m,y)$.
- κ is a normalizing constant included to ensure that (12.1) is a proper probability distribution.

Equation (12.1) describes a general probability distribution of networks and assumes that the probability of observing the empirical multilevel network structure depends on a small set of configurations. MERGMs parameterize a number of configurations. A first class involves the standard ERGM effects that model each network separately (Robins et al. 2009; Snijders et al. 2006). A second class consists of the effects that account for the interdependence between two or three networks (Wang et al. 2013, 2015). We introduce these classes of configurations below, situating them within our empirical exercise.

Empirical Illustration

Data

The data used in the empirical part of the paper contain information on knowledge-sharing relations among members of the top management team in an international multiunit industrial group active in the design, manufacturing and sale of leisure motor yachts (Lomi et al. 2014). The group consists of five subsidiary units and a small team of consultants. For the sake of clarity, in the remainder of the paper we refer to subsidiary units and to the team of consultants as "subunits." The subunits act as quasi-independent companies. Each subunit has its own product line, target market segment, customer base, dealer network, management, and organizational and brand identities. Hence, each occupies an almost completely distinct market niche. This context makes subunits unlikely to compete with one another and promotes collaboration and communication among them. In particular, coordination within the group and collaboration across the boundaries of subsidiaries are crucial. Boundary-spanning interaction allows organizational members to share information on technical solutions, and on potential customers or competitors collected through the global dealers' network. Likewise, innovative technological and management solutions developed in one subunit may have implications for others. For these reasons, organizational members – especially those working in the same functional areas, but in different subsidiaries – are highly encouraged to cooperate and coordinate their actions.

We examined interaction in the context of communication and advice relations among the 47 members of the group's top management team as identified by the group CEO. We also included in the list a team of five consultants, because of their direct and personal relations with the president-founder of the group and because of their crucial role in boat design. Each member was unambiguously and uniquely assigned to one subunit.

We administered a questionnaire individually and personally to each member of the top-management team. The questionnaire was used to collect relational information as well as individual characteristics of the organizational members. A member of the research team was always present to offer assistance and to ensure that the data collected were as accurate and complete as possible. This allowed us to obtain a 100 % response rate.

We examined relations of task advice and work-related communication because these contents are directly relevant for intra-organizational knowledge transfer. The advice relation captures problem-driven interaction. We selected advice relations because extensive evidence indicates that they support meaningful knowledge sharing within organizations (Cross et al. 2001; Lazega 2001). Professional and work-related communication relations better represent routine interaction among the managers. We included communication relations because we also wanted to capture channels for intra-organizational knowledge flow that are activated less episodically.

Interpersonal interaction was reconstructed by presenting each manager with the list containing the names of the other 46 managers in the team. To convert answers into a multilevel network structure, we assumed for both relationships that the generic cell $b_{ij} = 1$ if manager i nominates j as a partner respectively for advice seeking (network B_1) and communication (network B_2) on work related matters. B_1 and B_2 are both lower-level networks and are sized (47×47). Table 14.1 reports the main descriptive statistics for the two interpersonal networks.

Hierarchical relations between subsidiaries were reconstructed by using information on the formal reporting relations among members of the top management

Table 14.1 Network descriptive for interpersonal networks

Variable	Advice network	Communication network
Density	0.229	0.076
Average degree	10.553	3.489
Degree standard deviation	7.015 (in); 8.395 (out)	1.852 (in); 2.653 (out)
Degree skewness	1.113 (in); 1.736 (out)	−0.195 (in); 0.689 (out)
Reciprocity	0.341	0.505
GCC transitive closure	0.469	0.494
GCC cyclic closure	0.357	0.420

team. We interviewed the corporate CEO and asked him to indicate "who reports to whom." We provided him with the names of the 47 participants arranged in the rows and in the columns of a square matrix. We asked him to indicate whenever the column person reported to the row person. For example, we assumed that the generic cell $a_{ij} = 1$ if the "Chief engineer" (column) j in subsidiary k reported to the "Chief Corporate Engineer" (row) i in subsidiary l. In this case i would be hierarchically superior to i (ij). We used the information on systematic reporting relations between managers to generate matrix A – the matrix of formal relations between the subsidiaries. The higher-level (reporting) network between the subsidiaries will be network A, sized *(6 × 6)*: the generic cell $a_{lk} = 1$ if subsidiary l is hierarchically superior to subsidiary k, i.e., if there is at least one manager j in k reporting to a manager i in l.

Finally, an affiliation network represents top-managers' affiliation to companies. The generic cell $x_{il} = 1$ if manager i belongs to subsidiary l. According to the notation that we have introduced this is network X, sized *(47 × 6)*. Figure 14.1 displays symbolically the complete multilevel network structure.

We also collected actor-specific attributes and used them to construct the control variables incorporated in our empirical model specifications. These variables account for interpersonal differences that may affect the likelihood of observing network ties. We collected socio-demographic (nationality) and work-related (organizational function and job grade) attributes for managers and organizational characteristics (size) for subunits.

Figure 14.2 displays the empirical multilevel network for communication relations. The figure clearly points to the coexistence of communication ties between managers who are affiliated to the same subunits and ties between managers who

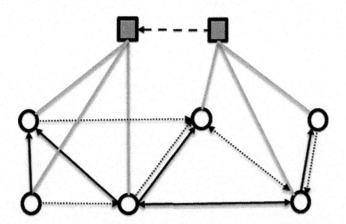

Fig. 14.1 Multilevel network. *Circles* are managers and *squares* are subunits. *Dashed black links* are (hierarchical) subordination ties between pairs of subunits (network A). *Grey links* are affiliation ties of managers to subunits (network X). *Dotted black links* are advice ties (network B_1) and *black links* are communication ties (network B_2) between managers

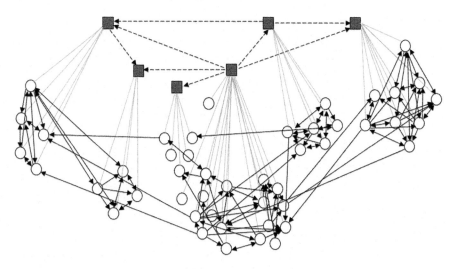

Fig. 14.2 Multilevel network for communication relations. *Circles* are managers and *squares* are subunits. *Dashed black links* are (hierarchical) subordination ties between pairs of subunits (network A). *Grey links* are affiliation ties of managers to subunits (network X). *Black links* are communication ties (network B_2) between managers

are members in different subunits. The average manager degree is 3.02 for within subunit ties, and 0.47 for between unit ties for the communication relation, and 4.87 and 5.68 for the advice relationships.

In the analysis that follows, we compare the effects of hierarchical relations between subunits on advice seeking and on communication relations between managers separately.

Model Specification and Estimation

In formal organizations, neither the affiliations nor the organizational structure depend on individual or subunit choices, at least in the short-term. Change in organization structure is likely to occur at a much slower rate than change in informal interpersonal ties. Consequently, we considered the networks defined by formal relations (A and X) as exogenous and kept them fixed during the estimation process. Our analysis focuses on interpersonal network ties.

To make the two multilevel networks (and the interpersonal relations) comparable, we specified the same set of effects for them both. We modeled the multilevel networks as a combination of two kinds of configurations: (1) ERGM effects which account for interpersonal interaction (B); (2) MERGM effects which account for the affiliation of individuals to a subunit (interaction between B and X) and for interdependences between the interpersonal and interunit networks through

Table 14.2 ERGMs lower-level configurations

Effect	Configuration	Qualitative interpretation
Density		Tendency of managers to build ties with colleagues
Reciprocity		Tendency of managers to build ties with reciprocating colleagues
Activity spread		Tendency of managers to be active – i.e., to send ties to many colleagues
Popularity spread		Tendency of managers to be popular – i.e., to receive ties from many colleagues
2-paths		Basic tendency of managers to send ties to and to receive ties from colleagues
Transitive closure		Tendency of managers to build ties with colleagues of colleagues
Cyclic closure		Tendency of managers to build ties with colleagues in small groups without any expectation of being reciprocated
Multiple two-paths		Tendency of managers against interaction within small groups of colleagues
Covariate match		Tendency of managers to build ties with colleagues with same covariate value

Circles are managers and black links are informal (communication or advice) ties between pairs of individuals. Black is a manager with a relevant attribute

affiliation (interaction among *A*, *B* and *X*). We distinguished between structural and attribute effects for both kinds of configurations.

We start our discussion commenting on the ERGM effects used to model the interpersonal network (Table 14.2). We included *Density* to account for the baseline tendency of managers toward interacting with others. Since maintaining several ties is costly, the *Density* parameter usually carries a negative sign. We specified *Reciprocity* to verify the likelihood that interpersonal ties are reciprocated. With *Popularity* and *Activity spread* we modeled the degree distributions and captured the tendency toward the existence of "hubs".

Closure configurations verify the propensity toward network clustering. In the context of intra-organizational relations of knowledge transfer, closure also captures embeddedness and redundancy of information. We tested closure specifying two effects, *Transitive closure* and *Cyclic closure*, the most common closure configurations. The former models the likelihood that managers interact with one another if they share several partners. The latter accounts for generalized exchange of knowledge – i.e., for knowledge exchange without bounds of reciprocity (Breiger and Ennis 1997; Lazega and Pattison 1999). As a control, we added *Multiple two-*

paths configuration, accounting for the correlation between in- and out-degree and suggesting whether the same people are senders and receivers of ties. *Multiple two-paths* captures also tendency against closure.

Finally, the *Covariate match* effect accounts for the likelihood that managers interact informally with similar others. We controlled for homophily in respect to nationality, job grade, and organizational function.

The second class of effects consists of MERGM configurations modeling interdependencies between the lower- and higher-level network structures linked through affiliation (Wang et al. 2013, 2015) (see Table 14.3). These configurations account for progressively more complex effects of the formal organizational structure on interpersonal interaction. *Affiliation based closure arc* tests homophily based on a shared affiliation (Contractor et al. 2006; Monge and Contractor 2001). Showing that managers are more likely to interact with colleagues who are members of the same subunit, this effect indicates that knowledge transfer tends to occur more within subunit boundaries. Also, *Affiliation based closure arc* suggests that interaction is shaped by a local hierarchical ordering, with interpersonal ties in one direction only.

Cross-level in-degree and *out-degree assortativity* effects test the association between centrality across levels. These effects represent the tendency for popular/active people to be affiliated to popular/active subunits and can be interpreted as the MERGM formalization of the structural linked design (Lazega et al. 2008). A positive parameter of these effects would suggest that the centrality of managers in interpersonal interaction is mainly due to the position of their subunit in the hierarchical interunit structure. Hence, these effects would point to a "sidestepped" role of the individual.

Cross-level alignment effects account for cross-level mirroring or overlap such that members of connected groups are themselves connected. In the context of knowledge sharing, a positive parameter of these effects would indicate that interpersonal knowledge transfer is sustained by interunit formal ties. We specified three effects that account for a different kind of dependence of interpersonal ties on interunit ties. *Cross-level alignment entrainment* assumes that interunit and interpersonal ties have the same direction. The qualitative interpretation of such an effect is that interpersonal interaction is shaped by a hierarchical ordering due to interunit ties – i.e., managers are likely to seek information from colleagues who are members in hierarchically subordinate subunits. *Cross-level alignment exchange* accounts for the opposite effect. It assumes that interpersonal and interunit ties have opposite directionality, so that managers seek information from colleagues who are members in hierarchically superior subunits. *Cross-level alignment exchange reciprocal B*, finally, indicates that managers are likely to build reciprocal ties with colleagues who are members in other subsidiaries, connected to theirs by hierarchical dependence. Interpersonal interaction, then, enables a reduction in the hierarchical distance between managers due to the formal interunit structure.

Finally, we included the association between interunit and interpersonal ties due to control subunit and manager covariates. Similar to the baseline *Covariate match* effect specified for the interpersonal network, *Cross-level alignment Covari-*

Table 14.3 MERGMs higher-level configurations

Effect	Configuration	Qualitative interpretation
Affiliation based closure		Tendency of managers to build ties with colleagues based on common membership in subunits
Cross-level in-degree assortativity		Tendency of popular managers in interpersonal network to be affiliated to popular (i.e., hierarchically subordinate) subunits in interunit network
Cross-level out-degree assortativity		Tendency of active managers in the interpersonal network to be members in active (i.e., hierarchically superordinate) subunits in interunit network
Cross-level alignment entrainment		Tendency of managers to build ties with colleagues members in subunits hierarchically subordinate to their subunit
Cross-level alignment Exchange		Tendency of managers to build ties with colleagues members in subunits hierarchically superordinate to their subunit
Cross-level alignment exchange reciprocal B		Tendency of managers to build ties with reciprocating colleagues members in hierarchically linked subunits
Cross-level a.entr. unit covariate match		Tendency of managers members in subunits with a given covariate value to build ties with colleagues members in hierarchically sub-ordinate subunits with same covariate value
Cross-level a. exch. unit covariate match		Tendency of managers members in subunits with a given covariate value to build ties with colleagues members in hierarchically super-ordinate subunits with same covariate value
Cross-level a.entr. individual covariate match		Tendency of managers with a given covariate value to build ties with colleagues with the same covariate value and members in hierarchically subordinate subunits
Cross-level a. exch. individual covariate match		Tendency of managers with a given covariate value to build ties with colleagues with same covariate value and members in hierarchically superordinate subunits
Cross-level a. exch. reciprocal B individual covariate match		Tendency of managers with a covariate value to build ties with reciprocating colleagues with same covariate value and members in hierarchically linked subunits

Squares are subunits. Dashed black links are (hierarchical) subordination relationship ties between pairs of subunits. Grey links are affiliation ties of managers to subunits. Black are managers/subunits with a relevant attribute

ate match tests whether managers' propensity toward seeking information from colleagues affiliated to connected subunits increases when managers or subunits have similar characteristics. Specifying *Cross-level alignment entrainment* and *exchange Covariate match* for subunit size, we assessed manager propensity toward building ties with colleagues affiliated to hierarchically dependent subunits, when the subunits employ around the same number of managers – a fairly obvious effect.

Cross-level alignment entrainment, exchange and *exchange reciprocal B Covariate match* for managers' job grades and organizational functions verify whether the same tendency is higher when managers have similar work-related characteristics.

Results

We organize the discussion of our results around Table 14.4, which reports the estimates of a MERGM for the interdependence between interpersonal (advice, communication), and interunit relations. The comparison of the configuration parameters between the two multilevel networks reveals similar tendencies. The *Arc* parameter carries a negative sign, as it is typically the case in empirical networks, thus outlining the existence of a ceiling effect to establishing interpersonal ties. Also, the tendencies toward reciprocating ties (significantly positive *Reciprocity* effect) and interacting in small hierarchical groups – as indicated by the combination of a positive *Transitive* and a negative *Cyclic closure* – are the main relational behaviors that characterize both advice and communication networks. The tendency toward closure is enforced by the negative *Multiple two-paths*, suggesting that triangles are unlikely to remain open. Also, both networks are shaped by a propensity toward seeking information from managers with the same nationality (significantly positive *Nationality match*). By contrast, the degree-related effects indicate the convergence of ties toward few managers in the advice network only. In particular, the significantly positive *Activity spread* (the tendency of the out-degree distribution to be skewed) points to the presence of a few managers who rely on many colleagues as sources of advice, thus diversifying their range of available knowledge.

The parameters of several higher-level configurations are significant, suggesting an association between information sharing among managers and the formal interunit structure. The *Affiliation based closure arc* is significantly positive for both relations, showing that they are affected by a positive tendency toward interacting with colleagues within the same subunit. This result captures the well-known tendency of organizational subunits to retain both ties and information within their boundaries (Reagans and McEvily 2003).

Cross-level in-degree assortativity is significantly positive for the communication network only. This configuration captures the first class of theoretical mechanisms – i.e., association between subunit and manager centrality in their own network. The positive parameter value indicates that managers who are more popular and sought after by colleagues in day-to-day communications are members of subunits which are more popular and, have to report to many others in the formal network – i.e., hierarchically subordinate subunits. The qualitative implication of this effect is that information is likely to flow from members of subordinate to members of superior subunits.

Table 14.4 MERGM estimations for interdependences between interpersonal and interunit networks

	Advice Network estimate (st.err.)	Communication Network estimate (st.err.)
Interpersonal communication		
Arc	−7.14 (0.64)*	−7.08 (1.12)*
Reciprocity	0.90 (0.28)*	2.59 (0.46)*
Popularity spread	0.02 (0.09)	−0.49 (0.36)
Activity spread	0.40 (0.09)*	0.35 (0.18)
Transitive closure	1.38 (0.19)*	0.87 (0.21)*
Cyclic closure	−0.26 (0.06)*	−0.36 (0.16)*
Multiple two-paths	−0.08 (0.02)*	−0.09 (0.06)*
Grade match	0.04 (0.17)	−0.01 (0.21)
Function match	−0.25 (0.22)	0.30 (0.22)
Nationality match	0.58 (0.12)*	0.85 (0.30)*
Cross-level interdependences		
Affiliation based closure	1.90 (0.28)*	2.80 (0.65)*
Cross-level in-degree assortativity	−0.07 (0.13)	1.08 (0.38)*
Cross-level out-degree assortativity	−0.14 (0.05)*	0.15 (0.14)
Cross-level alignment, entrainment	−0.68 (0.48)	−0.08 (0.78)
Cross-level alignment, exchange	−0.59 (0.32)	−1.00 (0.95)
Cross-level alignment, reciprocal B	0.08 (0.20)	2.02 (0.84)*
Cross-level alignment, entrainment subunit size match	0.08 (0.04)*	−0.04 (0.06)
Cross-level alignment, exchange subunit size match	0.06 (0.03)*	0.07 (0.07)
Cross-level alignment, entrainment manager grade match	−0.89 (0.47)	−1.14 (1.15)
Cross-level alignment, exchange manager grade match	0.98 (0.30)*	1.10 (1.23)
Cross-level alignment, reciprocal B manager grade match	0.37 (0.59)	0.28 (1.92)
Cross-level alignment, entrainment manager function match	−0.08 (0.53)	2.21 (0.86)*
Cross-level alignment, exchange manager function match	0.49 (0.40)	2.05 (1.30)
Cross-level alignment, reciprocal B manager function match	1.45 (0.61)*	−4.30 (1.92)*

*indicates that the ratio of statistic to standard error is greater than 2 (standard errors in parentheses)

The *Cross-level alignment* effects refer to the second class of theoretical mechanisms – i.e., association between interunit and interpersonal ties. The positive *Cross-level alignment reciprocal B* for the communication network indicates that interunit ties are likely to be matched by reciprocal interpersonal ties between managers affiliated to the connected subunits. That is to say, managers are likely to establish mutual communication relationships with colleagues who are members of subunits with which a hierarchical link already exists. *Cross-level alignment reciprocal B* emphasizes that interpersonal ties cross-cutting subunit boundaries are more likely when they are sustained by formal interunit ties. They provide managers with opportunity to meet and share information (Kleinbaum et al. 2013). *Cross-level alignment reciprocal B*, finally, underlines the importance of reciprocity as driver of boundary spanning.

By contrast, the not significant *Cross-level alignment* effects for the advice network suggest that the tendency for advice ties between managers to span subunit boundaries is not affected by the presence of hierarchical formal ties between the subunits in which managers are members.

The qualitative implication of the different parameter values of most *Cross-level* configurations (i.e., both *degree assortativity* and *alignment*) between the two networks is that the association of interunit and interpersonal ties – and, therefore, boundary spanning – takes place in different ways for advice and communication relationships. Advice relationships develop almost independently from the formal organizational structure, while communication relations align (weakly) with it.

More precisely, in the case of advice relationships the formal organizational structure seems to operate mostly through a matching process which involves subunit and manager covariates. In detail, the significantly positive *Cross-level alignment entrainment* and *exchange subunit size match* suggest that managers are likely to seek advice from colleagues affiliated to connected subunits (thus, crossing subunit boundaries) which have a size – and, therefore possibly a relevance within the formal organizational structure – similar to theirs. Managers are likely to build ties that both maintain (*Cross-level alignment entrainment subunit size match*) and reverse (*Cross-level alignment exchange subunit size match*) the direction of inter-unit formal ties, seeking advice from colleagues who are members respectively in hierarchically subordinate or superior subunits.

The significantly positive *Cross-level alignment exchange manager job grade match* for advice relations suggests that managers in the same job grade are more likely to build boundary-spanning ties with colleagues affiliated to superior subunits, thus reversing the ordering induced by the formal structure. The significantly positive *Cross-level alignment reciprocal B manager function match* points to the likelihood that managers in the same organizational function build mutual boundary-spanning ties with colleagues affiliated to connected subunits. In doing so, mutual ties reduce the formal hierarchical ordering.

The communication network is shaped by the opposite tendency. The combination between the significantly positive *Cross-level alignment entrainment* and the significantly negative *Cross-level alignment reciprocal B manager function match* indicates that managers in the same organizational function are more likely to build cross-cutting communication ties that preserve the formal hierarchical ordering. The (weak) alignment between communication ties and formal inter-unit ties, suggested by the positive *Cross-level alignment reciprocal B* is reversed by managers' homophily in the organizational function.

Discussion and Conclusions

Interest in multilevel theories is not new in the analysis of social networks. The recent call for multilevel network *models*, however, has the merit of stimulating convergence between recent theoretical and methodological developments in the analysis of multilevel networks. In organizational studies, a multilevel understanding of social networks seems to be long overdue, because organizations are multilevel network systems almost by construction. Organizations are formal hierarchical systems, where individual action is embedded in aggregate entities whose interconnections are likely to affect the structure of interpersonal networks within and across the formal boundaries that are drawn around organizational subunits. To the best of our knowledge, no empirical study has yet derived the full consequence of this multilevel view on organizational networks. Surprisingly, most of the available research on networks within organizations has ignored their multilevel structure. We have argued that this is precisely what makes organizations interesting and instructive contexts for studying social networks.

We have offered an integrated analytical framework for assessing multilevel network dependences explicitly, suggesting that organizations would be better conceived as a two-level system, consisting in the combination of informal ties between individuals, formal ties between subunits, and affiliation ties between individuals and subunits. We have brought new Multilevel Exponential Random Graph Models (MERGMs) to bear on the problem of understanding cross-cutting ties within organizations. The empirical value of the analytic strategy proposed has been documented in the context of intra-organizational knowledge-sharing and knowledge-transfer networks, examining how knowledge-sharing relations among individuals may cross formal boundaries defined around organizational subunits. In particular, the paper has focused on the extent to which boundary spanning is affected by the presence of interunit ties. Using data that we have collected on different knowledge-sharing relationships within a multiunit organization where subunits are linked to each other by hierarchical ties, we have drawn attention to various multilevel mechanisms that could indicate different types of subordination of informal interpersonal ties to formal interunit ties.

The main finding concerns the influence of the interunit formal structure on interpersonal interaction. We have replicated the well-established result that subunits are generally likely to retain interpersonal ties within their boundaries. In our sample, information sharing is more likely to take place between participants who are members of the same subunit. Boundary spanning is a relatively infrequent event. When it does take place, boundary spanning is likely to be affected by hierarchical interunit ties, consistent with our assumptions. We have tested and verified two different ways in which the formal organizational structure can affect presence and direction of interpersonal boundary spanning ties.

First, in line with transactive memory arguments, managers affiliated to more central subunits – i.e., subunits which have to report to many others in the formal network – are more likely to be selected as partners for interpersonal relations. In our sample, we have found this is a significant tendency for communication relations.

Second, in line with social foci arguments, formal hierarchical ties are likely to sustain boundary-spanning ties. Hence, managers working in subunits that are themselves already connected by mandated hierarchical relations display a higher propensity toward seeking information from each other. Our results indicate that, within the patterns of interaction offered by interunit ties, managers are also likely to exert some autonomy. The dependence of interpersonal communication relations on mandated hierarchical relations is partly weakened by the capability of interpersonal interaction to reduce the hierarchical ordering.

As an additional finding, boundary spanning between members of connected subunits can be activated also by homophily between subunits or individuals. In our sample, we have observed this tendency for advice relations.

Finally, differences in communication and advice-seeking ties highlight the context-dependent influence of the interunit formal structure on interpersonal interaction. The effect of formal interunit ties is contingent on the specific relationship examined – a conclusion that will need to be carefully scrutinized in future research.

Our general conclusion is that no social network in organizations should be studied in isolation from the formal structure that shapes social relations between individuals. The unique contribution of the multilevel perspective that we have articulated in this paper is a rich contextual assessment of the incremental value of social networks for our understanding of how formal organizations actually work. In this sense, this paper may be interpreted as a preliminary step toward the development of a more general multilevel network theory of organizations.

Acknowledgement We gratefully acknowledge financial support from the Fonds National Suisse de la Recherche Scientifique (Swiss National Science Foundation. SNSF Grant 615 number CRSII1_147666/1).

References

Argote, L., & Ingram, P. (2000). Knowledge transfer: A basis for competitive advantage in firms. *Organizational Behavior and Human Decision Processes, 82*(1), 150–169.

Argote, L., Beckman, S. L., & Epple, D. (1990). The persistence and transfer of learning in industrial settings. *Management Science, 36*, 140–154.

Baum, J. A., & Ingram, P. (2002). Interorganizational learning and network organization: Toward a behavioral theory of the interfirm. In M. Augier & J.G. March (Eds.), The Economics of Choice, Change, and Organization: Essays in Memory of Richard M. Cyert (pp. 191–218). Cheltenham, MA: Edward Elgar.

Beckman, C. M., Haunschild, P. R., & Phillips, D. J. (2004). Friends or strangers? Firm-specific uncertainty, market uncertainty, and network partner selection. *Organization Science, 15*(3), 259–275.

Borgatti, S. P., & Foster, P. C. (2003). The network paradigm in organizational research: A review and typology. *Journal of Management, 29*(6), 991–1013.

Brass, D. J. (1984). Being in the right place: A structural analysis of individual influence in an organization. *Administrative Science Quarterly, 29*(4), 518–539.

Brass, D. J. (2000). Networks and frog ponds: Trends in multilevel research. In K. J. Klein & W. J. Kozlowski (Eds.), *Multilevel theory, research, and methods in organizations: Foundations, extensions, and new directions* (pp. 557–571). San Francisco: Jossey-Bass.
Brass, D. J., & Burkhardt, M. E. (1993). Potential power and power use: An investigation of structure and behavior. *Academy of Management Journal, 36*(3), 441–470.
Brass, D. J., Galaskiewicz, J., Greve, H. R., & Tsai, W. (2004). Taking stock of networks and organizations: A multilevel perspective. *Academy of Management Journal, 47*(6), 795–817.
Breiger, R. L. (1974). The duality of persons and groups. *Social Forces, 53*(2), 181–190.
Breiger, R., & Ennis, J. (1997). Generalized exchange in social networks: Statistics and structure. *L'Année Sociologique (1940/1948), 47*(1), 73–88.
Burt, R. S. (1992). The social structure of competition. In N. Nohria & R. Eccles (Eds.), *Networks and organizations: Structure, form, and action* (pp. 57–91). Boston: Harvard Business School Press.
Burt, R. S. (2004). Structural holes and good ideas1. *American Journal of Sociology, 110*(2), 349–399.
Cialdini, R. B., Borden, R. J., Thorne, A., Walker, M. R., Freeman, S., & Sloan, L. R. (1976). Basking in the reflected glory: Three (football) field studies. *Journal of Personality and Social Psychology, 34*(3), 366–375.
Contractor, N., Wasserman, S., & Faust, K. (2006). Testing multi-theoretical multilevel hypotheses about organizational networks: An analytic framework and empirical example. *Academy of Management Review, 31*(3), 681–703.
Cross, R., Borgatti, S. P., & Parker, A. (2001). Beyond answers: Dimensions of the advice network. *Social Networks, 23*(3), 215–235.
Feld, S. L. (1981). The focused organization of social ties. *American Journal of Sociology, 86*(5), 1015–1035.
Hansen, M. T. (2002). Knowledge networks: Explaining effective knowledge sharing in multiunit companies. *Organization Science, 13*, 232–248.
Hargadon, A., & Sutton, R. I. (1997). Technology brokering and innovation in a product development firm. *Administrative Science Quarterly, 42*(4), 716–749.
Kilduff, M., & Krackhardt, D. (1994). Bringing the individual back in: A structural analysis of the internal market for reputation in organizations. *Academy of Management Journal, 37*(1), 87–108.
Kleinbaum, A. M., Stuart, T. E., & Tushman, M. L. (2013). Discretion within constraint: Homophily and structure in a formal organization. *Organization Science, 24*(5), 1316–1336.
Kogut, B., & Zander, U. (1996). What firms do? Coordination, identity, and learning. *Organization Science, 7*(5), 502–518.
Krackhardt, D., & Hanson, J. R. (1993). Informal networks. *Harvard Business Review, 71*, 104–111.
Lazega, E. (2001). *The collegial phenomenon: The social mechanisms of cooperation among peers in a corporate law partnership*. Oxford: Oxford University Press.
Lazega, E., & Pattison, P. E. (1999). Multiplexity, generalized exchange and cooperation in organizations: A case study. *Social Networks, 21*(1), 67–90.
Lazega, E., Jourda, M. T., Mounier, L., & Stofer, R. (2008). Catching up with big fish in the big pond? Multi-level network analysis through linked design. *Social Networks, 30*(2), 159–176.
Lomi, A., & Torló, V. J. (2014). The network dynamics of social status: Problems and possibilities. In S. P. Borgatti, D. J. Brass, D. S. Halgin, J. Labianca, & A. Mehra (Eds.), *Contemporary perspectives on organizational social network analysis* (Research in the Sociology of Organizations, pp. 399–416). Sydney: Emerald Press.
Lomi, A., Lusher, D., Pattison, P. E., & Robins, G. (2014). The focused organization of advice relations: A study in boundary crossing. *Organization Science, 25*, 438–457.
March, J. G., & Simon, H. A. (1958). *Organizations*. Oxford: Wiley.
McEvily, B., Soda, G., & Tortoriello, M. (2014). More formally: Rediscovering the missing link between formal organization and informal social structure1. *The Academy of Management Annals, 8*(1), 299–345.

Moliterno, T. P., & Mahony, D. M. (2011). Network theory of organization: A multilevel approach. *Journal of Management, 37*(2), 443–467.

Monge, P. R., & Contractor, N. S. (2001). Emergence of communication networks. In *The new handbook of organizational communication: Advances in theory, research, and methods* (pp. 440–502) Thousand Oaks, CA: Sage.

Nonaka, I. (1994). A dynamic theory of organizational knowledge creation. *Organization Science, 5*(1), 14–37.

Oh, H., Labianca, G., & Chung, M. H. (2006). A multilevel model of group social capital. *Academy of Management Review, 31*, 569–582.

Perrow, C. B. (1970). *Organizational analysis: A sociological view*. London: Tavistock Publications.

Pfeffer, J. (1981). *Power in organizations*. Marshfield: Pitman.

Podolny, J. M. (2001). Networks as the pipes and prisms of the market 1. *American Journal of Sociology, 107*(1), 33–60.

Podolny, J. M., & Baron, J. N. (1997). Resources and relationships: Social networks and mobility in the workplace. *American Sociological Review, 62*(5), 673–693.

Reagans, R., & McEvily, B. (2003). Network structure and knowledge transfer: The effects of cohesion and range. *Administrative Science Quarterly, 48*(2), 240–267.

Reagans, R., & Zuckerman, E. W. (2001). Networks, diversity, and productivity: The social capital of corporate R&D teams. *Organization Science, 12*(4), 502–517.

Ren, Y., & Argote, L. (2011). Transactive memory systems 1985–2010: An integrative framework of key dimensions, antecedents, and consequences. *Academy of Management Annals, 5*, 189–229.

Ren, Y., Carley, K. M., & Argote, L. (2006). The contingent effects of transactive memory: When is it more beneficial to know what others know? *Management Science, 52*(5), 671–682.

Robins, G. L., Pattison, P. E., & Wang, P. (2009). Closure, connectivity and degree distributions: Exponential random graph ($p*$) models for social networks. *Social Networks, 31*(2), 105–117.

Simon, H. A. (1962). The architecture of complexity. *Proceedings of the American Philosophical Society, 106*, 467–482.

Simon, H. A. (1991). Bounded rationality and organizational learning. *Organization Science, 2*(1), 125–134.

Simon, H. A. (1996). *The sciences of the artificial* (3rd ed.). Cambridge, MA: MIT Press.

Snijders, T. A. B., Pattison, P. E., Robins, G. L., & Handcock, M. S. (2006). New specifications for exponential random graph models. *Sociological Methodology, 36*(1), 99–153.

Thompson, J. (1967). *Organizations in action: Social science bases of administrative theory*. New York: McGraw-Hill.

Tortoriello, M., Reagans, R., & McEvily, W. (2012). Bridging the knowledge gap: The influence of strong ties, network cohesion, and network range on the transfer of knowledge between organizational units. *Organization Science, 23*(4), 1024–1039.

Wang, P., Robins, G. L., Pattison, P. E., & Lazega, E. (2013). Exponential random graph models for multilevel networks. *Social Networks, 35*(1), 96–115.

Wang, P., Robins, G.L., Pattison, P.E. & Lazega, E. (2015). Social selection models for multilevel networks. Social Networks, doi: 10.1016/j.socnet.2014.12.003 (in press).

White, H. C., Boorman, S. A., & Breiger, R. L. (1976). Social structure from multiple networks. I. Blockmodels of roles and positions. *American Journal of Sociology, 81*(4), 730–780.

Chapter 15
General Conclusion

Emmanuel Lazega and Tom A.B. Snijders

Multilevel statistical models that combine both individual and contextual effects in order to calculate the probability of an individual to adopt a certain behavior or to achieve a given level of performance have been developed, with multilevel analysis, over the past two generations (Raudenbush and Bryk 1992, 2002; Goldstein 1987, 2011; Snijders and Bosker 1999, 2012; Courgeau 2003, 2007). These models provide a statistical approach in which – once the effects of the most obvious determining factors are recognized – the remaining factors that reveal less obvious properties of behavior and performance at the individual level, are represented by random effects specified for the individual level but also for one or more contextual levels; some of these are interactions between individual characteristics and contextual levels. However, these models have shown their limits, particularly when the behavior and achievements of individuals within groups take into account group membership without taking into account links between groups or links between members within groups. For "standard" (although useful) multilevel approaches, horizontal interdependencies among members derive only from common group membership.

The fundamental question of the influence of social structure on the behavior and achievements of actors has been reexamined in recent decades thanks to the development of structural sociology and the analysis of social networks. Structural approaches, which examine elements of social structure in order to contextualize

---

E. Lazega (✉)
Institut d'Etudes Politiques de Paris, SPC, CSO-CNRS, 19 rue Amélie, 75007 Paris, France
e-mail: emmanuel.lazega@sciencespo.fr

T.A.B. Snijders
Department of Sociology, University of Groningen, Grote Rozenstraat 31, 9712 TG Groningen, The Netherlands

Nuffield College, University of Oxford, Oxford, UK
e-mail: tom.snijders@nuffield.ox.ac.uk

© Springer International Publishing Switzerland 2016
E. Lazega, T.A.B. Snijders (eds.), *Multilevel Network Analysis for the Social Sciences*, Methodos Series 12, DOI 10.1007/978-3-319-24520-1_15

human action, help with detailed readings of systems of interdependencies between actors. Structural models, inspired by those proposed by White et al. (1976), remain close to actors, to their interdependent relationships, to their positions, and to the interdependent relationships between these positions. Adding a network dimension to this modeling helps to account for horizontal dependencies by assuming that these groups have an internal structure as well as links to each other, thus providing a more realistic contextualization of behavior and achievements. As shown in this volume, this provides a basis for systematic meso-sociological analysis and for enrichment of standard multilevel analyses, and there is a large range of fruitful work currently being done along these lines.

Individual actors' relational work is often part of complex relational settings. Actors' personal and collective networks include both individuals and groups or organizations. Breiger (1974) pioneered basic ways to express these dependencies by two-mode networks. In this book, we presented a bouquet of approaches to this issue of multilevel network analysis. This book is among a series of first steps in the contemporary elaboration of a general multilevel network analytical framework using a variety of multilevel network analytical approaches. In his chapter, Tom Snijders summarizes what is essential for a 'multilevel' point of view in network analysis: units of different natures; that have their own type of influence on variables; with random/unexplained variability associated with each 'level.' The first principles of this are present already in traditional network analysis, as is shown by the joint presence of relational and actor-bound variables in models for network analysis, e.g., in network autocorrelation models (Multilevel Network Modeling Group 2012; see Chap. 4 by Agneessens and Koskinen and Chap. 9 by Bellotti, Guadalupi, and Conaldi). Multiple membership models for actor-level data (as in Chap. 5 by Tranmer and Lazega) are another way to represent the effects of networks and subgroups on actor-level dependent variables.

Most of the research presented in this book, however, focuses on the explanation of network structure more than on the use of network structure to explain actor-level variables. Recent modeling developments have led to three important extensions of existing models representing social structure, with networks as the dependent variable, enabling these models to incorporate more complex structures in which networks themselves are embedded. The first is by embedding statistical models for social networks as a random effects model in a contextual model. The model is for data structures of multiple networks, postulating that the networks are not connected mutually, each having the same within-network model, and with parameters that differ between networks according to a probability distribution such as a multivariate normal or a discrete latent class model. This general approach is called a hierarchical network model by Sweet et al. (2013), who give an elaboration for latent space models. An earlier example is the multilevel p_2 model (Zijlstra et al. 2006). The Bayesian multi-group stochastic actor-oriented model proposed by Koskinen and Snijders (2016) is an example in preparation.

The second extension is the multilevel exponential random graph model pioneered by Wang et al. (2013). Data structures here are multilevel networks, defined as networks with multiple actor sets and multiple types of ties, generalizing two-mode networks. This model represents connections between the contexts, and more generally enables the joint representation of the interdependent structures of networks defined at diverse levels. This volume contains examples of multilevel exponential random graph models in many chapters – those by Wang, Robins, and Matous (Chap. 6); by Zappa and Lomi (Chap. 14); by Hollway and Koskinen (Chap. 13); and the study by Brennecke and Rank (Chap. 11). For longitudinal data this can be modeled by actor-oriented models as in Snijders et al. (2013), and Chap. 2 by Snijders gives a sketch of further multilevel extensions.

The third extension is the multilevel blockmodel of Žiberna (2014). This approach represents the superposed interdependent structures of networks defined at diverse levels by blockmodels that partition the units at each level separately according to a suitable joint criterion function. The chapter by Žiberna and Lazega (Chap. 8) in this volume gives an introduction and an elaborate example.

Why is it important for the social sciences to further develop and apply such methods of multilevel network analysis? A double trend of individualization (created by introducing increasingly open competition as one goes down the socio-economic stratification) and Weberian rationalization (stemming from the search for control and efficiency through the rise of bureaucracy) has constructed a society that Charles Perrow (1991) calls "organizational" and Ronald Breiger (1974) "dual." Rationalization in turn imposes strong interdependencies and simultaneously requires unprecedented amounts of coordination among actors. Actors try to manage exceptionally complex interdependencies (functional, epistemic, normative, emotional, etc.) in increasingly sophisticated ways at different levels simultaneously (Brailly and Lazega 2012). In this organizational society, these management practices can marginalize or exclude, make or break careers, determine in part the distribution of power and status, influence the social processes that lead to change.

Thus, a social fact must be observed at analytically different levels of collective action, which makes the analysis of individual relations inseparable from that of the organizational relations. To take into account this vertical complexity of a social world contained in the cohabitation of several levels, it is necessary to articulate these levels and their dynamics. There are many theories on the importance of social relations for the action capabilities of individuals in this context. From a perspective focused exclusively on the individual, relational capital is defined as a set of resources to which individuals have access based on their relationships or position in a relational structure. There are fewer theories on the importance of socio-economic relations (that is, relatively stable relational structures made up of social relations) for the joint action capabilities of both individuals and groups/organizations. This multilevel approach explores a complex meso-social reality of accumulation, of appropriation, and of the sharing of multiple resources mobilized at different levels of collective agency. This reality, still poorly known, is difficult to observe without a network approach.

If it is true that contemporary society is an "organizational society" (Coleman 1982; Perrow 1991), in the sense that action and performance measured at the individual level strongly depend on the capacity of the actor to construct and to use organizations as "tools with a life of their own" (Selznick 1949), and thus to manage his/her interdependencies at different levels in a strategic manner, then the study of interdependencies jointly at the inter-individual and the inter-organizational level is important for numerous types of problems. We should not overlook the potential applications of this approach in many domains of the social sciences; for example, for the study of relationships between organizations, careers, social stratification, inequalities, and political action. The organizational society is a class society in which control of organizations as such "tools with a life of their own" has become increasingly important for any kind of collective action (Tilly 1998).

Empirically, developing contemporary knowledge of the meso-social level is based on a research program focused on the co-evolution of interdependent systems of individuals and organizations at the different "floors" of social reality. This co-evolution is not well known: what are the effects of evolution of one level on the evolution of another? What constraints of synchronization of these evolutions exist in economic and social reality? If different forms of synchronization exist, how are they selected, and who pays the cost? Synchronization of evolutions at different levels of social reality takes place, for example, in relational adjustments required by mobility in professional careers. We can hypothesize that this synchronization takes place in part in contemporary flexible labor markets, the many costs of which (financial, relational, health, etc.) are easily dumped on the weakest. These adaptations and their invisible costs, almost always considered to be the responsibility of individuals and rarely that of the organization, are still not measured.

With an increasing number of scholars (from Breiger 1974 to Brass et al. 2004, to the contributors of this volume), social scientists believe that these methodological strategies will help in exploring this meso-level of society. The term meso-social refers to all the organizational forms of collective self-assertion at the "intermediate" level between the state and individuals in civil society, from business corporations to citizen and professional associations and the other collective interests (including kinship) constitutive of the real social world. Indeed the analysis of multilevel networks is appropriate for questions related to the difference between individual relational capital (Burt 1992) and organizational (or corporate) social capital, a general topic of research in previous decades (Coleman 1990; Leenders and Gabbay 1999). In a work environment, individual relational capital is a set of resources that actors as individuals bring to the performance of their tasks through their own personal contacts. Organizational social capital can be defined as resources that actors receive from the organization to which they belong, and that helps them with their work, but also as social processes that help the organization to manage the dilemmas of its collective action. Organizational resources can be capitalized by this collective entity, sometimes over several generations, so as to make these processes work for cooperation instead of against it (Lazega 2001).

This difference between these two forms of capital raises in new ways the question of their combination, of multi-level interdependencies, and of the manner in which actors manage these interdependencies. It adds an underestimated importance for multilevel network reasoning in the social sciences, on the issues of relationship between positions in multilevel relational structures, individual and collective action, and achievements (measured at both the individual and collective levels). For example, using this knowledge for dual positioning in systems of superposed interdependencies allows us, especially when this positioning is articulated to actors' relational strategies, to fine-tune hypotheses about these issues.

This approach will reach its full potential when longitudinal observations at multiple levels of analyses are available. The articulation of both multilevel and dynamic structural analyses remains to be explored, as in the directions pioneered by Snijders and Baerveldt (2003) and Snijders et al. (2013). Collective action in an organizational society requires synchronization of temporalities between the inter-individual level and the inter-organizational one. The relational infrastructure of each level has to be taken into account by and at the other level, and the mutual timing of these interdependencies seems to be of crucial importance. This approach will open up research on institutional change and the evolution and redesign of inter-organizational systems. Looking at collective action from a multilevel perspective explores the cumulative effect of inequalities that take place at two levels of agency without imprisoning the individual in a monadic iron cage that precludes room to maneuver. There is no absolute determinism between position and action precisely because each level has its own temporality and actors can sometimes reshape their opportunity structure by using asynchronies and by creating social forms based on relational infrastructures that illustrate or reveal inequalities, but that are also actors' responses to these inequalities.

This makes cooperation at each level of agency contingent on what happens at the other levels of collective agency, not only at the micro- or macro-levels. For an actor at any level, dealing with what happens at the other levels by contextualizing their choices and behavior is a precondition for building relational social forms and intermediary infrastructures so as to be able to use organizations as tools with a life of their own and benefit from their social processes, such as solidarity, collective learning (see Brailly et al., Chap. 10; Favre et al., Chap. 12) and regulation. It is often the case that actors are aware of this, especially when they see that inequalities among players prevent their own investments from being productive: synchronization costs incurred by actors are lost for some, productive for others; stabilized and predictable for some, unstable and unpredictable for others.

Organizations are structured by their environment, but also structure their environment. They participate in a permanent construction or reproduction of a macro-level of society. They affect the distribution of resources, the hierarchy of their members' allegiances, and the constitution of dispositions and attitudes. Organizations both participate in and reflect these changes: public institutions, companies, communities, and non-profit associations affect and change the wider institutional context. Attention focused on the role of organizations in the construction of the macro-level is not only theoretically interesting; it is especially important today in a period of significant economic restructuring as well as institutional changes in which giant private actors of governance wield as much power as States.

Large public and private organizations are the key institutions of contemporary organizational society. Academic social sciences must not leave to businesses, police, and the military the responsibility for providing sketchy knowledge of interdependencies, social processes, and social capital in this organizational society (Lazega 2015). The only way to rise up to this responsibility is to take on the task of using complex methods such as that presented in this book to systematically study the meso-social level. Improving the public intelligibility of the organizational society is a way to use sophisticated knowledge of economic and social interdependencies among individual and/or organizational actors in the definition of general interest – a definition that is, as always, a conflictual construction.

This program for multilevel network research on the organizational society raises many challenges. Such methods identify different levels of agency, but also intermediary levels and social forms (such as systems of social niches and systems of heterogeneous dimensions of status), and relational infrastructures that help members in constructing new organizations at higher levels of agency and in managing intertwined dilemmas of collective action. Specific challenges are taken up by these methodological contributions: among the most difficult, we find combining network dynamics and multilevel analysis by providing statistical approaches to how changes at each level of collective agency drive the evolution of changes at other levels of collective agency. In all these domains, much remains to be done.

References

Brailly, J., & Lazega, E. (2012). Diversité des approches de la modélisation multiniveaux en analyses de réseaux sociaux et organisationnels. *Mathématiques et Sciences Sociales, 198*, 5–32.
Brass, D. J., Galaskiewicz, J., Greve, H. R., & Tsui, W. (2004). Taking stock of networks and organizations: A multilevel perspective. *Academy of Management Journal, 47*, 795–819.
Breiger, R. L. (1974). The duality of persons and groups. *Social Forces, 53*, 181–190.
Burt, R. S. (1992). *Structural holes: A study of the social structure of competition.* Cambridge: Harvard University Press.
Coleman, J. S. (1982). *The asymmetric society.* Syracuse: Syracuse University Press.
Coleman, J. S. (1990). *Foundations of social theory.* Cambridge, MA: Harvard University Press.
Courgeau, D. (Ed.). (2003). *Methodology and epistemology of multilevel analysis* (Collection methods). Dordrecht: Kluwer Academic Publishers.
Courgeau, D. (2007). *Multilevel synthesis: From the group to the individual.* Dordrecht: Springer.
Goldstein, H. (2011, first edition 1987). *Multilevel statistical models* (4th ed.). Chichester: Wiley.
Koskinen, J. H., & Snijders, T. A. B. (2016). Multilevel longitudinal analysis of social networks (In preparation).
Lazega, E. (2001). *The collegial phenomenon: The social mechanisms of cooperation among peers in a corporate law partnership.* Oxford: Oxford University Press.
Lazega, E. (2015). Body captors and network profiles: A neo-structural note on digitalized social control and morphogenesis. In M. S. Archer (Ed.), *Generative mechanisms transforming the social order* (pp. 113–133). Dordrecht: Springer.
Leenders, R., & Gabbay, S. (Eds.). (1999). *Corporate social capital and liabilities.* Boston: Kluwer.
Multilevel Network Modeling Group. (2012). *What are multilevel networks.* University of Manchester. Available at: http://mnmg.co.uk/Multilevel%20Networks.pdf
Perrow, C. (1991). A society of organizations. *Theory and Society, 20*, 725–762.

Raudenbush, W., & Bryk, A. S. (2002; first edition 1992). *Hierarchical linear models* (2nd ed.). Newbury Park: Sage.

Selznick, P. (1949). *TVA and the grass roots: A study of politics and organization*. Berkeley: University of California Press.

Snijders, T. A. B., & Baerveldt, C. (2003). A multilevel network study of the effects of delinquent behavior on friendship evolution. *Journal of Mathematical Sociology, 27*, 123–151.

Snijders, T. A. B., & Bosker R. J. (2012, first edition 1999). *Multilevel analysis: An introduction to basic and advanced multilevel modeling* (2nd ed.). London: Sage.

Snijders, T. A. B., Lomi, A., & Torlò, V. J. (2013). A model for the multiplex dynamics of two-mode and one-mode networks, with an application to employment preference, friendship, and advice. *Social Networks, 35*, 265–276.

Sweet, T. M., Thomas, A. C., & Junker, B. W. (2013). Hierarchical network models for education research: Hierarchical latent space models. *Journal of Educational and Behavioral Statistics, 38*, 295–318.

Tilly, C. (1998). *Durable inequality*. Berkeley: University of California Press.

Wang, P., Robins, G. L., Pattison, P. E., & Lazega, E. (2013). Exponential random graph models for multilevel networks. *Social Networks, 35*, 96–115.

White, H. C., Boorman, S. A., & Breiger, R. L. (1976). Social structure from multiple networks. I. Blockmodels of roles and positions. *American Journal of Sociology, 81*, 730–780.

Žiberna, A. (2014). Blockmodeling of multilevel networks. *Social Networks, 39*, 46–61.

Zijlstra, B. J. H., van Duijn, M. A. J., & Snijders, T. A. B. (2006). The multilevel p_2 model. *Methodology: European Journal of Research Methods for the Behavioral and Social Sciences, 2*, 42–47.

Author Index

A
Achen, C.H., 32
Adler, P.S., 81, 83, 85
Agneessens, F., 5, 24, 81–101, 127, 131, 287, 356
Ahuja, G., 273
Airoldi, E.M., 35
Aitkin, M., 17
Alcácer, J., 275
Alecke, B., 275
Alexander, M., 140, 320
Alexiev, A.S., 273
Alker, H.R., 17
Alsleben, C., 275
Amati, V., 35
Anand, J., 146
Anderson, C.J., 175
Andresen, S., 319
Anselin, L., 216
Arabie, P., 178, 179, 191
Archer, M.S., 56, 72, 250
Argote, L., 66, 335, 337, 338
Armbrüster, T., 75
Asparouhov, T., 23
Aspers, P., 250, 297
Audrey, S., 33
Autry, C.W., 146

B
Baba, Y., 207
Baccaïni, B., 2
Bacharach, S.B., 84
Baerveldt, C., 2, 32, 34, 359
Baldwin, T.T., 90
Balogh, P., 297
Bamberger, P.A., 84
Bantel, K., 84
Barbillon, P., 56, 74
Barden, J.Q., 278
Bar-Hen, A., 47, 74
Barkin, J.S., 315–318
Baron, J.N., 85, 91, 333
Batagelj, V., 175, 177, 181
Bathelt, H., 8, 73, 245, 250, 251, 296, 297, 299, 310
Bauer, S., 319
Baum, J.A., 273, 336
Baum, S., 323
Bearman, P.S., 114
Becker, M.P., 45
Beckman, C.M., 337
Beckman, S.L., 337
Bedell, M.D., 90
Bellotti, E., 7, 24, 175, 213–243, 298
Beltrame, L., 221
Benhamou, F., 258
Bennink, M., 23
Berends, H., 50, 146, 273, 274, 278, 289, 290
Berkowitz, L., 104
Berkowitz, S.D., 12, 103, 172
Bielby, D.D., 301, 304
Bill, A., 323
Blalock, H.M., 17
Blau, P.M., 84, 155
Blei, D.M., 35
Bloor, M., 33
Bock, H.H., 207
Boda, Z., 28, 30, 35, 39
Bodin, Ö., 127

Bolin, J.E., 111
Boorman, S.A., 175
Borden, R.J., 338
Borgatti, S.P., 81, 84, 145–147, 150, 154, 175, 179, 214, 258, 279, 333, 336
Börner, K., 208
Bosker, R.J., 2, 3, 18, 32, 33, 82, 86, 93, 111, 214, 215, 247, 355
Boudon, R., 44
Bouty, I., 273
Boyd, D., 147
Brailly, J., 8, 9, 39, 47, 48, 50, 52, 53, 61, 74, 245–268, 295–312, 357, 359
Brandenburger, A.M., 260
Brandes, U., 47
Brass, D.J., 2, 36, 83, 88, 175, 246, 289, 333, 336, 338, 358
Breiger, R.L., 2, 10, 47, 55, 73, 173, 175, 179, 214–216, 249, 316, 336, 344, 356–358
Brennecke, J., 9, 38, 48, 273–291, 357
Bressoux, P., 2
Bronner, G., 12, 76, 269
Browne, W.J., 20, 24, 112, 119, 214, 215, 217
Brusco, M., 181
Bryk, A.S., 2, 17, 18, 20, 32, 33, 247, 355
Brynildsen, W.D., 33
Brynjolfsson, E., 147
Buchta, C., 325
Bulder, B., 81, 83
Burkhardt, M.E., 83, 333
Burstein, L., 17
Burt, R.S., 81, 83, 84, 131, 175, 231, 235, 246, 277, 300, 333, 335, 337, 358
Burton, M.L., 214, 215
Busch, M.L., 315
Busch, P.O., 319
Butts, C., 109, 214

C

Calabrese, T., 273
Campbell, K.E., 84
Campbell, R., 33
Cantor, N., 90
Carley, K.M., 338
Carlin, J., 96
Carr, C.L., 320
Carrington, P.J., 24, 246
Cha, V.D., 315, 317, 318
Charlton, C.M., 118
Chatellet, J., 8, 9, 245–268, 295–312
Chavalarias, D., 47, 51
Checkley, M., 61
Chen, M.D., 90

Cheong, Y.F., 34
Chung, M.-H., 85, 336
Chung, W., 275
Cialdini, R.B., 338
Cliff, A.D., 216
Cochran, W.G., 34
Coleman, J.S., 2, 15, 16, 33, 42, 85, 357, 358
Comet, C., 50
Conaldi, G., 213–243, 356
Congdon, R.T., 34
Contractor, N.S., 345
Cook, J.M., 84
Cook, K., 46, 75, 102
Courgeau, D., 1, 2, 17, 47, 53, 355
Coustère, P., 2
Cox, D.R., 19, 21, 33
Crawford, K., 147
Croon, M.A., 23
Cross, R., 83–85, 279, 341
Crozier, M., 49, 248
Cummings, J.N., 83–85

D

Daggett, A.P., 316
Daraganova, G., 31, 217, 323
Darr, A., 250, 297
Darrell Bock, R., 43
De Klepper, M., 81
De Leeuw, J., 17
De Stefano, D., 151
DeCarolis, D.M., 277
Deeds, D.L., 277
Dehning, W., 75
Dekker, D., 24
Del Vecchio, N., 146
Delarre, S., 50
Delbecq, A.L., 85
Delgado, G., 297
Delgado, M.R., 297
Denton, H.G., 146
DeSombre, E.R., 315–318
D'Esposito, M.R., 146, 151
Dirks, K.T., 91
Dogan, M., 42
Donnet, S., 74
Doreian, P., 24, 55, 93, 108, 146, 175, 176, 179, 180, 216, 217
Dow, M.M., 214, 215
Draper, D., 20
Du Toit, M., 34
Dubois, S., v
Duke, J.B., 93

Dunson, D., 96
Duran, P., 47

E
Ebers, M., 275
Eccles, R.G., 102, 352
Edling, C., 39, 320
Eisenhardt, K.M., 276
Elliott, P., 131, 132, 137
Eloire, F., 50, 260, 264, 301
Ennis, J., 344
Ensel, W.M., 84
Entwisle, B., 32
Entwistle, J., 297
Epple, D., 337
Erbring, L., 93
Erdös, P., 125
Erickson, B.H., 81
Erosheva, E.A., 214
Everett, M.G., 145, 146, 150, 175, 179, 258

F
Fararo, T.J., 55, 216
Fausett, E., 316
Faust, K., 24, 127, 145, 147–152, 249, 334
Favereau, O., 76, 208, 269
Favre, G., 8, 9, 47, 48, 50, 52, 61, 74, 245–268, 295–312
Feinberg, M.E., 33
Feinerer, I., 325
Feld, S.L., 338
Ferligoj, A., 146, 175–177, 179–181, 186, 202, 205
Fienberg, S.E., 214
Finch, W.H., 111
Flap, H.D., 81, 83, 90
Florey, F., 114
Foster, P.C., 333, 336
Frank, K.A., 24
Frank, O., 5, 26, 125, 127, 169
Frank, R.H., 67
Freeman, L.C., 225, 233
Freeman, S., 338
Friedberg, E., 248
Friedkin, N.E., 24, 81
Froese, R., 323

G
Gabbay, S.M., 81, 358
Galaskiewicz, J., 2, 36, 150, 152, 175, 246, 289, 333, 336

Garcia-Parpet, M.-F., 297
Gatmaytan, D.B., 62
Geiger, W., 325
Gelfand, M., 166
Gelman, A., 20, 96
George, V.P., 278
Gest, S., 33
Ghoshal, S., 81, 83, 90
Glückler, J., 74
Goldstein, H., 2, 17, 18, 23, 93, 111, 112, 247
Granovetter, M.S., 8, 83, 84, 245–247
Greenacre, M., 148, 150, 152, 156, 163, 166
Greenan, C.C., 33
Greenland, S., 20
Greve, H.R., 2, 36, 175, 246, 289, 333, 336
Griffis, S.E., 146
Grosser, T., 90
Grund, T., 62
Guadalupi, L., 213–243
Gulati, R., 8, 245, 278, 289, 299

H
Hafner-Burton, E.M., 315, 331
Halgin, D.S., 81, 147
Hammer, I., 74
Han, S.-K., 300
Handcock, M.S., 26, 128
Hansen, K., 297
Hansen, M.T., 85, 335, 337
Hanson, J.R., 337
Hargadon, A., 335
Harlow, R.E., 90
Harris, K.M., 114
Hastie, T., 163
Haunschild, P.R., 337
Havens, T.J., 254, 256
Hayashi, C., 207
Heck, R.H., 111
Hedges, L.V., 32
Heider, F., 277
Heidl, R., 146, 273, 274
Hill, P.W., 112
Hinds, P., 166
Hoff, P.D., 24, 25
Holland, P.W., 148, 175
Holliday, J., 33, 34
Hollway, J., 10, 39, 48, 295, 315–331
Hopkins, K., 90
Hopkins, M.S., 147
Hornik, K., 325
House, J.S., 90
Hubert, L., 178, 191
Hudak, S., 216

Hughes, R., 33
Huitsing, G., 34
Hurlbert, J.S., 84, 90
Hurrell, A., 321

I
Iacobucci, D., 4, 37, 55, 127, 175, 264, 321
Ibarra, H., 84
Ingram, P., 246, 260, 264, 301, 315, 335–337
Inkpen, A.C., 81, 83
Ishikawa, T., 135

J
Jackson, S., 84
Janneck, M., 75
Jansen, J.J.P., 273
Jansson, J., 251, 252, 297, 298
Jehn, K.A., 91
Johnson, J.C., 146
Johnson, J.L., 90
Jones, J., 114
Jourda, M.-T., 5, 8, 9, 36, 47, 72, 73, 88, 115–117, 127, 173–177, 181, 182, 184, 185, 193, 206, 214, 226, 246, 248–250, 256, 273, 274, 278, 289, 295, 296, 298, 299, 321, 344
Junker, B.W., 34, 35
Jupille, J., 320

K
Kalish, Y., 125, 164, 281
Kandel, D.B., 84
Kane, A., 66
Kaneda, T., 32
Kashy, D.A., 25
Katz, J.S., 85
Kauffeld, S., 146
Kelley, K., 111
Kempthorne, O., 17
Kenny, D.A., 2, 25
Keohane, R.O., 318
Keucheyan, R., 12, 76, 269
Khanna, P., 275, 288
Kick, E.L., 315
Kidwell, V., 81
Kilduff, M., 288, 333
Kim, R.E., 325
Kinne, B.J., 315
Klein, K.J., 146
Kleinbaum, A.M., 336, 348
Knoke, D., 246

Koenig, R., 85
Kogut, B., 336, 337
Koput, K.W., 246, 247, 290
Koremenos, B., 320
Koskinen, J.H., 5, 10, 24, 26, 30, 35, 38, 39, 48, 81–101, 295, 315–330
Kozlowski, S.W., 146, 323, 326, 329
Kozlowski, W.J., 351
Krackhardt, D., 49, 84, 85, 246, 288, 333, 337
Kraimer, M.L., 83, 85
Kramer, R.M., 90
Kreft, I.G.G., 17
Krishnan, R., 94
Krivitsky, P.N., 26
Kronegger, L., 186, 202, 205
Kruschwitz, N., 147
Kuskova, V., 6, 145–170
Kwon, S.W., 81, 83, 85

L
La Voie, L., 25
Labianca, G. (Joe), 85, 90, 336
Lampel, J., 297
Langfred, C.W., 91
Laskey, K.B., 175
Latapy, M., 146
Laumann, E.O., 254, 303
LaValle, S., 147
Lazarsfeld, P.F., 16, 17, 19, 21
Lazega, E., 1–11, 24, 36, 47–74, 83, 88, 107–123, 127, 173–207, 214, 226, 245–268, 273, 274, 278, 280, 289, 295–312, 321, 341, 344, 345, 355–360
Leavitt, H.J., 85
Leenders, R.Th.A.J., 24, 81, 94, 109, 215, 234, 358
Leinhardt, S., 148
Lemercier, C., 64, 66, 70
Leroy-Audouin, C., 2
Lesser, E., 147
Levine, J., 66
Levitt, P.R., 179
Liden, R.C., 83, 85
Liebeskind, J.P., 288
Lievens, J., 90, 92
Light, J.M., 33
Lin, N., 81, 83, 84
Lipson, C., 320
Liu, L., 166
Lomi, A., 10, 38, 280, 323, 333–351
Longford, N., 17
Lorenz, E., 245, 300
Lorrain, F., 131

Lovas, B., 85
Lovric, M., 244
Lubbers, M.J., 34
Lüdtke, O., 23
Lusher, D., 5, 24, 26, 27, 30, 38, 125, 249, 326, 329
Lyon, J., 166

M

Mader, M., 47, 69
Magnien, C., 146
Mahony, D.M., 289, 334, 336
Mair, P., 325
Mali, F., 186
Malmberg, A., 250–252, 297
March, J.G., 333, 337
Marsden, P.V., 84, 93
Marsh, H.W., 23
Martin, B.R., 85
Maskell, P., 251, 252, 297
Mason, W.M., 17
Matous, P., 5, 125–141, 357
Mattli, W., 320
Maurer, I., 275
McAfee, A., 147
McDonald, M.L., 275, 288
McEvily, B., 84, 333, 334, 337, 347
McEvily, W., 337
McPherson, M., 84
Mehra, A., 76, 352
Meijer, E., 43, 44
Melançon, G., 2
Menzel, H., 16, 17, 19, 21
Mercken, L., 34
Merton, R.K., 49
Metiu, A., 278, 289
Meyer, A.D., 297
Minor, M.J., 102, 269
Mitchell, B., 323
Mitchell, R.B., 322–324
Mitchell, W., 278
Mizruchi, M., 247
Moeran, B., 297
Mojo, D., 134
Mol, J.M., 296
Moliterno, T.P., 289, 334, 336
Molm, L.D., 85
Monge, P.R., 345
Montes-Lihn, J., 50, 74
Montgomery, A.H., 315
Moody, J., 33
Moore, C.B., 146
Moore, L., 33, 34

Morris, C.N., 32
Mors, M.L., 85
Mounier, L., 5, 8–10, 36, 47–51, 55, 56, 60, 64, 66, 69, 72–74, 127, 173–177, 181, 182, 184, 185, 193, 206, 214, 226, 246, 248, 250, 256, 273, 274, 278, 295, 296, 298, 299, 321, 345
Mrvar, A., 181

N

Nahapiet, J., 81, 83
Nalebuff, B.J., 260
Naroll, R., 216
Nenadic, O., 152, 156, 166
Neuman, E.J., 216
Newman, D.A., 216
Newman, M.E.J., 275
Nies, K.M., 33
Nohria, N., 102, 352
Nonaka, I., 337
Norman, P.M., 278
Nowicki, K., 24, 175

O

Oh, H., 85, 336
Ohsumi, N., 207
Older, M., v
Ole Bergesen, H., 332
Oliver, A.L., 277, 288
Olkin, I., 32
Olson, M., 49
Ord, J.K., 216
O'Reilly III, C.A., 90
Ortega, J., 66
Osgood, D.W., 33
Ottenwelter, C., v
Oubenal, M., 50
Owen-Smith, J., 246, 247, 273, 275

P

Parker, A., 341
Parker, R., 118
Parkhe, A., 146
Parmann, G., 332
Parraga, J., 297
Parry-Langdon, N., 33
Pattison, P.E., 26, 49, 163, 164, 169, 249, 260, 280, 345
Pauly, D., 323
Payne, G.T., 146
Pearson, M., 216

Pedersen, J.S., 297
Pelled, L.H., 84
Penalva-Icher, E., 50, 51, 246, 248
Perrow, C., 2, 47, 48, 72, 336
Petersen, E., 322
Pfeffer, J., 336
Phelps, C., 146, 273, 274
Phillips, D.J., 337
Pina-Stranger, A., 50, 273, 289, 301
Podolny, J.M., 85, 91, 333
Porter, M.E., 274, 275
Portes, A., 81, 83
Powell, W.W., 246, 247, 273, 275, 290
Power, D., 251, 252, 297, 298
Preciado, P., 28, 30, 35, 39
Prensky, D., 303
Price, C.D., 34
Prieur, Ch., 47

Q
Quintane, E., 296

R
Rabe-Hesketh, S., 111
Raftery, A.E., 24–26
Ragozini, G., 170
Rand, W.M., 178
Rank, O.N., 38, 273–291
Rasbash, J., 20, 23, 34, 111, 118
Rauch, J., 325
Raudenbush, S.W., 2, 17, 18, 20, 32–34, 111
Reagans, R.E., 84, 333, 347
Reitz, K.P., 214, 215
Ren, Y., 338
Rényi, A., 125
Requena, F., 90
Rinaldo, A., 128
Rindfuss, R.R., 32
Ripley, R.M., 28, 30, 35, 39
Rivellini, G., 35
Roberts, J.M., 146, 151, 163
Roberts, K.H., 90
Roberts, P.W., 246, 260, 264, 301
Robins, G., 5, 31, 125–141, 148, 163, 164, 169, 217
Robinson, W.S., 1, 17
Robitzsch, A., 23
Rocamora, A., 297
Rodgers, S., 316
Rokkan, S., 42

Romney, A.K., 244
Rosenkopf, L., 274, 278, 289, 290
Rosson, P., 251, 297
Roter, P., 316
Rousseau, D.M., 10, 12
Rozenblat, C., 2
Rubin, D., 20, 96
Ruggie, J.G., 317–320
Rusby, J.C., 33

S
Sabic, Z., 316
Sanchez-Maranon, M., 297
Sandford, R., 319
Sapulete, S., 64, 66, 69, 173–207
Sasson, L., 102
Satornino, C.B., 181
Schaefer, D.R., 34
Schaefer, J., 216
Scharnhorst, A., 208
Scharr, F., 275
Scheffé, H., 17
Schleicher, T., 274, 278, 289, 290
Schoonhoven, C.B., 276
Schreyogg, A., 331
Schuldt, N., 8, 245, 250, 251, 296, 297, 299, 310
Scott, G.L., 320
Scott, J., 246
Selznick, P., 4, 47, 49
Seringhaus, R., 251
Shah, P.P., 91
Sharland, A., 297
Shaw, M.E., 85
Shaw, M.N., 315, 323
Shockley, R., 147
Siebenhuner, B., 319
Silverman, B.S., 273
Simon, H.A., 333, 336, 337
Simpkins, S.D., 34
Sinclair, P., 33, 34
Skjærseth, J.B., 319
Skov, L., 297
Skrondal, A., 111
Skvoretz, J., 127, 147
Slaten, E., 90
Sleebos, E., 81
Sloan, L.R., 338
Smelser, N., 246
Smith, C.W., 297
Smith-Doerr, L., 290

Smith-Lovin, L., 84
Snidal, D., 320
Snijders, T.A.B., 1–11, 15–42, 47, 54, 62, 65, 69, 72, 81, 82, 86, 93, 175, 214, 215, 247, 249, 260, 275, 281, 299
Snyder, D., 315
Sobel, M.E., 45
Soda, G., 333, 334
Sparrowe, R.T., 83, 85
Spence, A.M., 276
Starkey, F., 33
Stearns, L., 247
Steel, D., 5, 24, 114, 215, 217, 218, 223, 224
Steele, F., 23, 34, 111, 118
Steglich, C.E.G., 27, 31, 33, 61, 216
Steinley, D., 181, 202
Stenberg, S.-Å., 93
Sterba, S.K., 19, 21, 33
Stern, H., 96
Stern, R.N., 84
Stofer, R., 5, 9, 10, 36, 49, 55, 56, 88, 115–117, 127, 173, 175, 182, 187, 202, 214, 226, 249, 256, 273, 274, 289, 295, 298, 321, 345
Storper, M., 251
Strauss, D., 5, 125, 127, 169
Stuart, T.E., 336, 349
Sutton, R.I., 335
Swedberg, R., 246
Sweet, T.M., 34, 35
Sytch, M., 299

T
Tabata, L.N., 111
Tabor, J., 114
Talmud, I., 300
Tanaka, Y., 207
Tanner, J.M., 43
Tantrum, J.M., 26
Tengö, M., 127
Terzera, L., 35
Thoits, P.A., 90
Thomas, A.C., 34, 35, 94
Thomas, S.L., 111
Thompson, J., 336
Thorne, A., 338
Tilly, C., 48, 72, 73
Tobin, J.L., 315
Todo, Y., 135
Torló, V.J., 333
Tortoriello, M., 337

Tranmer, M., 5, 24, 107–123, 215, 217, 218, 223, 224
Trautwein, U., 23
Tripier, A., 56, 175, 182, 187, 202
Tsai, W., 90
Tsang, E.W.K., 81, 83
Tsui, W., 2
Tubaro, P., 64
Tushman, M.L., 336, 349

U
Udry, J.R., 114
Umberson, D., 90, 91
Untiedt, G., 275
Uzzi, B., 90, 246, 247

V
van Asselt, H., 320
van Burg, E., 50, 146, 273, 274, 278, 289, 290
van Busschbach, J.T., 24
van de Bunt, G.G., 81, 275
Van de Ven, A.H., 85
van den Bosch, F.A.J., 273
van Duijn, M.A.J., 24, 25
van Raaij, E.M., 50, 146, 273, 274, 278, 289, 290
van Veldhoven, M.J.P.M., 23
Varanda, M., 50
Vashdi, D., 84
Vaughn, J.C., 84
Veenstra, R., 34
Vehtari, A., 20, 96
Velthuis, O., 297
Venables, A.J., 251
Venkataramani, V., 90
Vermeij, L., 35
Vermunt, J.K., 23
Vest, A.E., 34
Viechtbauer, W., 34
Volberda, H.W., 273
Volgy, T.J., 316
Völker, B., 90
Volontè, P., 243
Vörös, A., 28, 30, 35, 39

W
Wadhwa, A., 146, 273, 274
Waege, H., 90, 93

Walker, M.R., 338
Wang, P., 4, 6, 8, 10, 36–39, 55, 116, 125–141, 163, 174, 175, 215, 217, 218, 256, 264, 280, 283, 288, 289, 310, 321, 326–327, 334, 339, 340, 345
Wang, W., 216
Ward, H., 315
Wasserman, S., 4, 24, 26, 37, 127, 145–170, 175, 249, 264, 321, 334
Watts, M., 323
Wayne, S.J., 83, 85
Wellman, B., 24, 145
Westphal, J.D., 289
White, D.R., 214, 215
White, H.C., 7, 52, 61, 131, 175, 179, 206, 264, 297, 299, 335
Wickham, H., 156, 166
Wilk, M.B., 17
Witbooi, E., 322
Wittek, R., 81, 90, 287
Wong, G.Y., 17
Woolcock, J., 249

X
Xin, K.R., 84
Xing, E.P., 35
Xue, G., 322

Y
Yajima, K., 207
Yogev, T., 62

Z
Zander, U., 336, 337
Zappa, P., 10, 38, 127, 333–351
Zeller, C., 275
Zelli, F., 320
Zhang, B., 94
Zhang, Z., 118
Zhao, Z.J., 146
Zhou, Y., 128
Zhu, M., 6, 39, 145–170
Žiberna, A., 7, 173–207
Zijlstra, B.H., 2, 35
Zuckerman, E.W., 333

Subject Index

A
Action
   collective, 2, 4, 7, 49–51, 53, 54, 60, 67, 70–73, 206, 248, 297
   individual, 60, 71, 248, 350
Actor (individual, organizational), 8, 24, 49, 56, 61, 63, 64, 146, 225, 252, 265, 308, 316, 334
Advice relationship, 335, 343, 349
Affiliation networks
   bipartite, 8, 126, 128, 129, 139, 147, 148, 151, 153, 156, 157, 214, 218, 221, 223, 324, 329
   one mode, 10, 36–40, 126–128, 131, 132, 139, 145, 147, 149, 150, 152, 157, 161, 173–175, 177, 178, 180, 183, 216, 223, 224, 249, 321, 322, 325, 329
   tripartite, 216, 221
   two modes, 36–40, 55, 126, 145, 146, 149–151, 161, 166, 173–175, 177, 179–184, 198, 200, 216, 249, 339
Agency (individual, collective), 2, 4, 48–56, 61, 64, 171, 173–207, 246, 289, 316, 320, 328
Asynchrony, 60–61
Autologistic actor attribute models (ALAAM), 217, 219

B
Bilateral/bilateralism, 10, 315–331
Bilateral fisheries agreements (BFAs), 315, 316, 321–323, 328–330

Blockmodeling
   conversion approach, 175, 176, 178–179, 193, 206
   generalized, 175, 176, 179–181
   multilevel, 176–181, 206
   separate analysis, 175–178
   true multilevel approach, 176, 180–181, 198–201, 206
Boundary-crossing ties, 10
Bridging cores, 7, 186, 189, 191, 192, 200–202, 204–206
Brokerage, 8, 83, 101, 129, 214, 231, 232, 235, 236, 238, 243, 248

C
Capital, social/relational, 24, 53, 63, 73, 81, 82, 84, 86, 101, 185, 206, 246, 248, 298, 299
Career, 1, 61, 66, 72, 221, 234, 242, 280, 310
Centrality, 52, 57, 63, 66, 70, 83, 86, 88, 91, 101, 117, 185, 226, 243, 249, 258, 276, 277, 280, 286, 288, 303, 345, 347
Centralization, 5, 65–68, 82, 84, 85, 91, 97, 99, 101, 128, 129, 137, 139, 184, 233, 283, 316, 318, 327, 328
Class (social), 2, 23, 34, 47, 57, 58, 86, 111, 155, 177, 317, 334, 339, 340, 345, 348
Closure, 6, 64, 128, 129, 137, 140, 141, 232, 235, 236, 238, 242, 243, 260, 264, 275, 277–278, 281, 283, 285–289, 300, 307–309, 326–328, 341, 344–348

Clustering, 110, 119, 137, 138, 140, 184, 266, 287, 321, 326, 328, 329, 344
Collective agency, 2, 4, 49, 51–55, 71, 173–207, 316, 320, 328
  multiple levels of, 4, 48–50, 75, 76
Collective properties, 17, 19
Commitment, 10, 48, 49, 52, 317, 318
Conflation, 55–56
Context, 1, 2, 4, 5, 8, 9, 21, 24, 27, 34, 40, 48, 52–54, 56, 61, 64, 71, 73, 74, 81–87, 90, 101, 109, 111, 125, 127, 132, 135, 167, 175, 206, 245–253, 259–264, 273, 274, 276, 278, 286, 288–290, 295, 296, 298, 299, 301, 304, 306–308, 310, 315, 328, 331, 334, 335, 340, 341, 344, 345, 350, 351
Contextual analysis, 16, 17
Cooperation, 36, 49, 50, 53, 127, 201, 256, 260, 265, 274, 275, 278, 287, 289, 290, 316, 318, 329
Coopetition, 260–263
Coordination
  across levels, 51, 52, 336
  within level, 48, 50
Core-periphery structure, 69, 182, 202, 205, 206, 225
Corporate entities, 4, 61–64, 72
Correspondence analysis, 6, 145–170
Cost
  opportunity, 71, 73
  synchronization, 4, 47–74, 299

D
Dependencies (cross-level), 38
Disciplines, 8, 59, 203, 214, 219, 221–226, 228–235, 238–241, 243
Division of work, 7, 52, 68, 73, 173–207
Duality (co-constitution), 2, 48
Dynamics, 2, 4, 10, 27–29, 47–74, 206, 242, 246, 250, 265, 299, 307, 310

E
Ecological fallacy, 17, 86, 110
Emancipation, 54, 59–61
Embeddedness, 8, 9, 245–253, 256, 258, 259, 261–265, 268, 273, 274, 288, 298, 299, 304, 307–309, 344
Emergence, 1, 50, 54, 60–61, 68, 70, 73, 246, 247, 250, 290, 296, 310
Expert, 184

Exponential random graph model (ERGM/p*), 3–10, 24, 26–27, 30, 31, 34, 36–42, 125–141, 148, 163–165, 169, 170, 175, 215, 217, 225, 249, 256, 262, 264, 274, 280–281, 323, 334, 339, 340, 343, 344

F
Field-configuring event, 61
Fisheries, 10, 39, 315–331
Fish/pond, 57, 59, 115, 118, 121, 185, 186, 197
Fixed effects, 18, 30, 94–96, 98, 99, 109, 111, 119, 218, 223–226, 236, 243
Flow betweenness, 225, 226, 232, 233, 236, 243
Form (social), 4, 50–54, 60, 61, 63, 71–73

G
Games (multiplayer), 148, 154, 166, 169
Governance (global fisheries), 316, 318, 319, 321, 329, 330

H
Heterophily, 84, 287, 323, 327
Hierarchical linear model, 18–19, 21–25, 32, 35, 215
Homophily, 83, 84, 133, 137, 139, 224, 230, 232, 238, 260, 261, 283, 285, 287, 306, 323, 345, 349, 351

I
Inequalities, social, 4, 71–74
Infrastructure (relational), 4, 47–74
Institution, 48, 64, 68, 70, 127, 174, 175, 214, 220, 225, 226, 232, 235, 238, 241, 317, 319
Interdependence
  functional, 40, 48
  social, 3, 5, 48, 55, 62, 82
  vertical, horizontal, 2, 3
Interdisciplinarity, 230, 235
Intermediary level, 49–53, 70–72
International, 10, 39, 62, 65, 71, 245, 248, 251–253, 256, 264, 265, 296–298, 310, 315–320, 322, 331, 335, 340

K
Knowledge (sharing, transfer), 9, 10, 38, 274–276, 287, 289, 333–351

Subject Index

L

Latent space model/latent Euclidean space model, 24–26, 30, 35, 217
Level
  of analysis, 1, 223, 228, 233, 234, 241, 246, 255, 334, 336
  intermediary, 49–53, 70–72
  macro, 9, 10, 71, 214, 218, 222, 226, 232–235, 241–243, 274, 275, 277, 278, 283, 286, 287, 289, 290
  meso, 4, 6, 10, 47–54, 71, 73, 74, 127–129, 133, 135, 137–141, 213, 214, 218, 224, 226, 232–235, 241, 299, 310
  micro, 9, 10, 214, 218, 226, 228–232, 235, 238, 241, 274, 275, 277, 278, 280, 283, 287
Linear regression, 18, 19, 94, 215

M

MAN. *See* Multilevel analysis of networks (MAN)
Markov chain Monte Carlo (MCMC), 20, 82, 96, 118–120, 134
Matrix algebra, 222
MERGM. *See* Multilevel exponential random graph models (MERGM)
Meta analysis, 32, 33
MFAs. *See* Multilateral fisheries agreements (MFAs)
Mixed membership models, 20, 214, 215, 218
MMMC model. *See* Multiple-membership multiple classification (MMMC) model
MNA. *See* Multilevel network analysis (MNA)
Mobility
  organized, in loops, 61–64
  vacancy chains, relational turnover, 61–64
MRQAP/QAP, 24, 306, 307
Multilateral fisheries agreements (MFAs), 315, 316, 320, 321, 323–330
Multilateral/multilateralism, 10, 39, 315–331
Multilevel
  one-mode network, 38–40, 127, 128, 131, 132, 145, 147, 149, 152, 161, 174, 175, 177, 178, 180, 183, 216, 224, 249, 321, 322, 325
  two-mode network, 36–40, 55, 145, 146, 149, 151, 161, 166, 173–175, 177, 179–184, 198, 200, 216, 249, 339
Multilevel analysis of networks (MAN), 4, 41, 42, 215, 217, 219, 250, 298, 309
Multilevel exponential random graph models (MERGM), 4, 10, 117, 316, 326, 334, 335, 339, 340, 343, 345–348, 350

Multilevel network analysis (MNA), 1–5, 10, 16, 31–36, 55, 101, 125–141, 161, 215, 217, 219, 225, 250, 265, 295, 309, 333–351
Multilevel Network Modeling Group (MNMG), 3, 174
Multilevel network models, 3–10, 23, 31, 36–41, 47–74, 97, 100, 107–123, 125–127, 129, 131, 135, 136, 140, 141, 145–170, 173–177, 181–186, 198–200, 205, 206, 213–243, 248, 253–256, 264, 265, 274, 276, 277, 279–282, 285, 286, 289–291, 296, 299, 316, 321, 326, 328–330, 334–343, 350, 351
Multiple-membership multiple classification (MMMC) model, 5, 107, 108, 112, 114–116, 118, 119, 122–123, 217–219, 223, 224

N

Nested structure/nesting hierarchy, 2, 17, 22, 218, 279
Network autocorrelation model (NAM), 3, 24, 93, 95, 96, 98–100, 107–109, 115, 214, 215, 217, 241
Network dependencies, 5, 24, 30, 95, 101, 108, 109, 117, 216, 217, 334, 350
Network disturbance model, 214, 215, 218, 223–226, 236, 241, 243
Network effects model, 93, 94, 108, 216
Networks (affiliation, multimode, multilevel, multirelational), 1, 3–10, 23, 31, 36–41, 47–74, 97, 99, 107–123, 125–127, 129–131, 135, 136, 140, 141, 145–170, 173–177, 179–186, 198–200, 205, 206, 213–243, 248, 253–256, 264, 265, 274, 276, 277, 279–282, 285, 286, 289–291, 296, 299, 316, 321, 326, 328–330, 334–343, 347, 350, 351
Niche (social), 4, 52, 54, 62, 71
Non-nested data structure, 19–20

O

OMRT model. *See* Organizational mobility and relational turnover (OMRT) model
Opportunity structure
  dual, 56, 60–61, 72, 73
  extended, 72, 193
  reshaping, 4, 71
Optimization, 181
Optimum (global, local), 198

Organizational mobility and relational turnover (OMRT) model, 4, 54, 63, 64, 68, 72–74
Organization/organizational
  inter network, 7, 8, 36, 49, 53, 55, 56, 58, 61, 71, 72, 173–207, 246, 247, 255, 258–260, 295–312
  intra network, 36, 54, 248, 334, 344, 350
  society, 2–4, 47–74
  structure, 9, 54, 65, 146, 206, 295, 335, 337–339, 343, 345, 349, 350
  theory, 351
Overlap (structural), 330

P
Place, 62, 64–71, 108, 111, 338
Position, 5, 8, 29, 47, 55–57, 59, 61, 62, 64–71, 82–84, 86, 88, 91, 96, 101, 231, 235, 247, 280
$p2$ model, 2, 3, 24, 25, 30, 35

R
Random coefficient(s), 17, 115, 123
Random effects, 2, 18, 21, 24–26, 30, 31, 33–35, 82, 93–96, 99, 109–111, 113, 116, 215, 218, 224
Random errors, 94, 192, 195, 198, 215, 217, 218, 224, 226, 236, 239
Relational capital, 53, 63, 73, 185, 206, 248, 298, 299
Relational infrastructure, 4, 47–74
Relational strategies (multilevel), 48, 185, 187–191, 195, 197, 201
Research Projects of National Interests (PRIN), 219–226, 230
Resource (advice), 337
Role set, division of work, 173–207
Role, system, 7, 52, 206
RSiena, or Siena model, 39, 40

S
SAOM. See Stochastic actor-oriented model (SAOM)
Scientific
  collaborations, 214, 215, 218, 242
  communities, 213
  fields, 7, 214
  organizations, 213
Semi-periphery, 69, 188, 189
Siena (model), or RSiena, 39, 40

Similarity, 22, 41, 83, 84, 114, 146, 151, 174, 178, 185, 192, 202, 203, 216, 224, 239, 241, 242, 290, 308, 316, 320, 321, 325, 326, 328–330
Social capital, 24, 63, 73, 81, 82, 84, 86, 101, 246
Social costs (dumping, incurring), 2, 53
Social forms (niche, status), 4, 51, 54, 60
Social networks, 1, 3–5, 7, 10, 16, 23–33, 42, 81, 82, 90, 108, 109, 126, 127, 141, 145, 150, 176, 213–219, 245–248, 257, 277, 296–298, 302–306, 310, 333–339, 350, 351
Social relations model, 2, 25
Sociology of science, 56, 213, 234
Spatial effects model, 216
Specialty, 186, 189, 202, 203, 206
Spinning top model, 64–71
  multilevel, 68, 70
States/countries, 10, 39, 62, 134, 148, 253, 263, 315–331
Status
  fish/pond, 115, 185, 186, 197
  relative, dual, 57, 66, 68, 289
Stochastic actor-oriented model (SAOM), 24, 27–31, 34–37, 39–41, 217, 242
Stochastic block model, 24, 69, 175
Strategy, 56, 59, 60, 68, 71, 118–119, 147, 201, 207, 215, 218, 219, 231, 235, 243, 254, 278, 303, 335, 339, 350
  relational, 186, 189–191, 195, 197, 201, 289
Structural holes, 83, 231, 232
Synchronization
  benefits, 64–71
  costs, 4, 47–74, 299
  stabilization, 51–53

T
Team (overlapping, performance), 146–148, 153, 155–158, 161, 163, 164, 167, 168
Temporality, 4, 9, 51–54, 64, 71, 247, 253, 258–265, 296, 310
Trade fair, 8, 9, 52, 61, 247, 250–257, 259, 261, 264, 265, 295–312
Transitive/transitivity, 27, 29, 30, 262, 263, 267, 268, 283, 285, 287, 341, 344, 347, 348

Treaty/treaties, 10, 39, 315–331
Turnover (relational), 4, 54, 61–65, 70, 73
Two-mode network
    affiliation network, 10, 36, 55, 130, 145, 147–150, 155, 161, 164, 214–216, 218, 281, 282, 342
    bipartite network, 8, 126, 128, 129, 139, 147, 148, 151, 153, 156, 157, 214, 218, 221, 223, 324, 329

U
Unit(s) of analysis, 1–2, 15, 108

V
Vacancy chains, 61
Valued degree, 226

Y
Yule's Q, 230–232, 235, 236, 239